Israel's Prophetic Tradition

Israel's Prophetic Tradition

Essays in Honour of Peter R. Ackroyd

edited by

RICHARD COGGINS,
ANTHONY PHILLIPS
AND
MICHAEL KNIBB

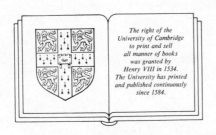

The right of the
University of Cambridge
to print and sell
all manner of books
was granted by
Henry VIII in 1534.
The University has printed
and published continuously
since 1584.

CAMBRIDGE UNIVERSITY PRESS

Cambridge

London   New York   New Rochelle

Melbourne   Sydney

Published by the Press Syndicate of the University of Cambridge
The Pitt Building, Trumpington Street, Cambridge CB2 1RP
32 East 57th Street, New York, NY 10022, USA
10 Stamford Road, Oakleigh, Melbourne 3166, Australia

First published 1982
First paperback edition 1984

Printed in Great Britain at the University Press, Cambridge

Library of Congress catalogue card number: 81-17065

British Library Cataloguing in Publication Data
Israel's prophetic tradition.
1. Ackroyd, Peter R. – Addresses, essays, lectures
2. Prophets   3. Bible. O.T.
I. Coggins, Richard   II. Phillips, Anthony
III. Knibb, Michael   IV. Ackroyd, Peter R.
221.8'2916'3   BS1199.P/
ISBN 0 521 24223 1 hard covers
ISBN 0 521 31886 6 paperback

Contents

Contents

Preface

Scholarly advance in the humanities often depends less upon sensational new discoveries than upon the questioning and re-evaluation of what had become unquestioned assumptions, and it is in this latter area that Peter Ackroyd's especial contribution to Old Testament scholarship will probably be judged to rest. From his doctoral thesis on the proper criteria for Maccabean dating of the Psalms, through his questioning of the accepted view of the exile and restoration and his dominant role in bringing about a fresh evaluation of the achievement of the Chronicler, he has insisted on asking the awkward questions and has perceived that the underlying truth is always liable to be more complex than is allowed for by any neat generalisation. The range of his Old Testament interests is amply demonstrated by the bibliography of his published works included in this volume; the one gap is that he has not yet had opportunity to write a major commentary, and his many friends will hope that his retirement will provide such an opportunity. The Torch commentary on Chronicles–Ezra–Nehemiah and the Cambridge pair on 1 and 2 Samuel give some indication of the riches that might be expected.

The world of Old Testament scholarship at large will make its own assessment of Peter Ackroyd's achievement; the present editors owe him a further debt as teacher and colleague. It is a recurring source of amused satisfaction to observe undergraduate students, at first bewildered by the way in which his lectures make them question their simple certainties, gradually being led to see depths they had not previously imagined. Always an exacting teacher, he has responded warmly and generously to the ideas of his pupils, whether in a student essay or in the shaping of a thesis, and the seminar he has run at King's College has long been a source of stimulation both for close colleagues and for a stream of always warmly welcomed visitors.

His colleagues at King's have rightly valued his contribution to the life of the college. He was the first elected Dean of the Faculty of

Theology in its present form, and he has been a valued counsellor both in the college as a whole and in the University of London, of whose Senate and Academic Council he was a member from 1971 to 1980. A host of other academic and administrative duties have come his way, and these he has always carried out with skill and efficiency, though perhaps not with unalloyed pleasure, for he has never been one of those professors who seem to welcome opportunities to leave the subject they profess to engage in administrative chores.

This note of appreciation would be sadly incomplete without some brief reference to the personal friendship and hospitality that have always characterised him. Students and colleagues alike have enjoyed a series of agreeable occasions formerly at Herne Hill and more recently in Westminster or in the family country retreat in Suffolk, and have admired the closely-knit but always outward-looking family – Evelyn engaged in the thankless tasks of a councillor in the London Borough of Southwark, the five children now all over the country and gaining distinction in the law and medicine and other professions. In wishing Peter a long and happy retirement, we know that he will value the additional leisure to see more of his family and to pursue his many other interests but we know also that his mind will not be idle and that Old Testament scholarship can look forward to many more challenging and thought-provoking contributions.

A brief note on the background of the present volume may be helpful. Too many *Festschriften* illustrate the variety of interests of their honorands without any corresponding unity, and editors and publishers were agreed from the outset that it would be important to produce a volume that related to one recognisable theme. This decision may help to explain the absence from the list of contributors of some whose interests have lain in other fields. Furthermore, it was not feasible to invite any American scholar to contribute and this has been a matter for some regret; Peter Ackroyd's reputation in the United States is very high, as the constant flow of invitations to lecture there which he has received bears testimony. All these omissions still left the editors with an *embarras de richesse* of scholars who might properly have been invited to contribute to the present project, and they are most grateful for the ready co-operation of those who have taken part. The contributions were all completed by April 1980.

Finally, thanks are due to all those who have helped to produce this volume: the contributors, all of whom produced their copy by the date requested, Mrs Lorne Cox and Miss Catherine Chisholm of King's College for secretarial assistance, the Syndics and staff of the Cambridge University Press for the ready way in which they have helped forward the production of what, it is hoped, will prove a worthy tribute to a distinguished scholar.

Biographical Note

PETER RUNHAM ACKROYD

Born: 15 September 1917

B. A. Cambridge, 1938 (Class 1 in Modern Languages)
B. D. London, 1940 (Class 1)
M.Th. London, 1942
Ph.D. Cambridge, 1945
D.D. London, 1970

Lecturer in Old Testament Studies, University of Leeds, 1948–52
Lecturer in Divinity, University of Cambridge, 1952–61
Samuel Davidson Professor of Old Testament Studies, University of London, 1961–82

Fellow of King's College London, 1969
Hon. D.D. St Andrews, 1970
President of the Society for Old Testament Study, 1972

Editor, Society for Old Testament Study *Book-List*, 1967–73
Editor, *Palestine Exploration Quarterly*, 1971–
General Editor, Cambridge Bible Commentary on the New English Bible

Publications

1942   'A Note on the Hebrew Roots *bāʾaš* and *bôš*', *JTS* 43, 160f.
'The Continuity of Pentecost', *Theology* 45, 46f.

1947   Articles for *Chambers' Encyclopaedia* (revised, 1962).
'Beyond Fundamentalism', *The Christian World* 4697.

1951   'The Hebrew Root *bāʾaš*', *JTS* n.s. 2, 31–6.
Freedom in Action: Studies in the Acts of the Apostles (Independent Press).
'Teraphim', *ET* 62, 378–80.
'Studies in the Book of Haggai', *JJS* 2, 163–76 (continued, *JJS* 3 (1952), 1–13).

1952   'The Composition of the Song of Deborah', *VT* 2, 160–2.
'The Book of Haggai and Zechariah i–viii', *JJS* 3, 151–6.
'Between the Testaments', *The Norwich Syllabus*, 21–34.

1953 'Criteria for the Maccabean Dating of the Old Testament Literature',
     VT 3, 113–32.
     'Harvest and Rededication', *Christian World Pulpit* 164, 127f.

1955 'Studying the Scriptures' (University Sermon abbreviated),
     Cambridge Review 76, 286.
     'Jesus the Interpreter' (University Sermon in full), *Christian World
     Pulpit* 167, 33–5.

1956 'Some Interpretative Glosses in the Book of Haggai', *JJS* 7, 163–7.
     'Amos vii, 14', *ET* 68, 94.
     Hebrew Man (SCM, rev. ed. 1973), translated from L. Köhler,
     Der Hebräische Mensch.

1957 *The Text of the Old Testament* (Blackwell), translated from
     E. Würthwein, *Der Text des Alten Testaments*.

1958 'Two Old Testament Historical Problems of the Early Persian Period',
     JNES 17, 13–27.

1959 *The People of the Old Testament* (Christophers, rev. ed. Chatto and
     Windus, 1964); Hindi translation, 1971; rev. English ed. Christian
     Literature Society (Madras, 1981).
     'The 153 Fishes in John xxi, 11 – a further note', *JTS* n.s. 10, 94.
     'Commentaries on Ezekiel', *Theology* 62, 97–100.

1960 Revision of translation of M. Noth, *History of Israel* (A. and C. Black).

1961–5 Editor of Bible Key Words (A. and C. Black).
     Faith, 1961.
     Law, 1962.
     Hope, 1963.
     Wrath, 1964.
     Life and Death, 1965.

1962–4 'Survey of Old Testament Literature', *Theology* 65 (1962), 321–4;
     66 (1963), 410–13; 67 (1964), 546–9.

1962 *Continuity: A Contribution to the Study of the Old Testament Religious
     Tradition* (Blackwell).
     'Hosea'; 'Haggai'; 'Zechariah' in *The New Peake Commentary*
     (Nelson), pp. 603–13; 643–55.
     'The Vitality of the Word of God in the Old Testament', *ASTI* 1,
     7–23.
     'Recent Biblical Theologies, vii: G. A. F. Knight's "A Christian
     Theology of the Old Testament"', *ET* 73, 164–8.
     'Understanding Amos', *Learning for Living* 2, 6–9.
     'Israel', *Handbook for History Teachers* (University of London
     Institute of Education), pp. 430–1.

1963 *The Old Testament Tradition*, Problems in Christian Education
     (National Society, London).

'The Old Testament in the Christian Church', *Theology* 66, 46–52.
'The Place of the Old Testament in the Church's Teaching and Worship', *ET* 74, 164–7.
Articles in *Hastings' Dictionary of the Bible*, ed. by Grant and Rowley (T. and T. Clark).
'Hosea and Jacob', *VT* 13, 245–59.
'Jeremiah x, 1–16', *JTS* n.s. 14, 385–90.

1963   'The Fourth Congress of the International Organisation for the Study of the Old Testament, Bonn, 1962', *ET* 75, 19–20.
'A Note on Isaiah ii, 1', *ZAW* 75, 320–1.
'Revising the Psalter', *The Kingsman* 6, 13–20.
'The History of Israel', *A Companion to the Bible*, ed. by H. H. Rowley (T. and T. Clark), pp. 281–332.

1964   'Threefoldness in the Teaching of Jesus', *ET* 75, 316.

1965   'The Revision and Use of the Psalms', *English Church Music*, 13–18.
The Old Testament: An Introduction (Blackwell). Translation of 3rd ed. of O. Eissfeldt, *Einleitung in das Alte Testament*.
'Bacteriology in the Bible', *ET* 76, 230.

1966   *The Dead Sea Scrolls and Christian Faith* (Church Information Office).
'Translating the Psalms', *The Bible Translator* 17, 1 (January), 1–11 with Dr M. A. Knibb.
'Some Notes on the Psalms', *JTS* n.s. 17, 392–9.

1967   'History and Theology in the Writings of the Chronicler', *CTM* 38, 501–15.
'Samaria', *Archaeology and Old Testament Study*, ed. by D. W. Thomas (Oxford), pp. 343–54.

1967   'What kind of belief about Jesus?', *Anglican Theological Review*, 1–15.
'Two Hebrew Notes', *ASTI* 5, 82–6.

1968   'The Interpretation of the Exile and Restoration', *Canadian Journal of Theology* 14, 3–12.
'Job the Agnostic', *Context. Journal of the Lutheran School of Theology* 1, 15–26 (reprinted *The Kingsman* 11 (1969), 10–19).
'The Meaning of Hebrew דּוֹר Considered', *JSS* 13, 3–10.
Exile and Restoration (SCM, London; Westminster Press, Philadelphia).
'Meaning and Exegesis', *Words and Meanings. Essays Presented to D. W. Thomas*, ed. P. R. Ackroyd and B. Lindars (Cambridge), pp. 1–14.
'Historians and Prophets', *Svensk Exegetisk Årsbok* 33, 18–54.

1969   'נסח – εἰς τέλος', *ET* 80, 126.

1970   *Israel under Babylon and Persia*, New Clarendon Bible, vol. iv

(Oxford). *I and II Chronicles, Ezra, Nehemiah, Ruth, Jonah, I and II Maccabees*, Mowbrays Mini-Commentary 7.
'The Old Testament in the Making', *Cambridge History of the Bible*, vol. I, ed. P. R. Ackroyd and C. F. Evans.
'The Open Canon', *Colloquium: Australian and New Zealand Theological Review* 3, 279–91.

1970   *The Age of the Chronicler* (Selwyn Lectures), supplement to *Colloquium*.

1970–9 'Foreign Theological Literature Survey: Old Testament', *ET* 82 (1970), 40–4; 83 (1971), 36-40; 84 (1972), 68–72; 85 (1973), 40–5; 86 (1974), 72–7; 87 (1975), 68–71; 88 (1977), 103-7; 89 (1978), 139–43; 91 (1979), 8–13.

1971   *First Book of Samuel*, Cambridge Bible Commentary.
'The Old Testament', *Preface to Christian Studies*, ed. F. G. Healey (Lutterworth), pp. 59–81.
'Theology and Education', *Colloquium* 4, 77–91 (reprinted in *Scripture Bulletin* 4 (1973), 81–8).
'Aspects of the Jeremiah Tradition', *Indian Journal of Theology* 20, 1–2, 1–12.
'The Theology of Tradition – An Approach to Old Testament Theological Problems', *Bangalore Theological Forum* 3, 2, 49–64.
'Isaiah', *The Interpreter's One-Volume Commentary on the Bible*, ed. M. Laymon (Abingdon, Nashville; Collins, London), pp. 329–71.
'Comment I', *View–Review* 23, 2 (July).

1971   'In Divers Manners', *The Kingsman* 14, 13–18.

1972   'The Temple Vessels – A Continuity Theme', *VTS* 23, 166–81.

1973   *I and II Chronicles, Ezra, Nehemiah*, Torch Commentary.
'The Theology of the Chronicler', *Lexington Theological Quarterly* 8, 101–16 (reprinted in *The Kingsman* 17 (1974), 29–38).
'An Authoritative Version of the Bible?', *ET* 85, 374–7.

1974   'An Interpretation of the Babylonian Exile: A Study of II Kings 20, Isaiah 38–9', *SJTh* 27, 329–52.
Editor of *Bible Bibliography 1967–1973 Old Testament* (Blackwell).
'International Old Testament Studies', *ET* 86, 150f.

1975   'A Footnote on *'āhēb* in the David–Jonathan Narratives', *VT* 25, 213f.
Cambridge History of the Bible, vol. I, ed. P. R. Ackroyd and C. F. Evans (corrected and supplemented paperback ed.).

1976   'God and People in the Chronicler's Presentation of Ezra', in J. Coppens (ed.), *La Notion biblique de Dieu*, BEThL 41 (Duculot, Gembloux), pp. 145–62.

1976   'Chronicles, I and II', 'Kings, I and II', *Interpreter's Dictionary of the Bible*, supplement (Abingdon Press), pp. 156–8; 516–9.

1977   'The Chronicler as Exegete', *JSOT* 1–2, 2–32.
'Continuity and Discontinuity', in *Tradition and Theology in the Old Testament*, ed. D. A. Knight (Fortress Press), pp. 215–34.
The Second Book of Samuel, Cambridge Bible Commentary.
'Original Text and Canonical Text', *USQR* 32, 3, 4, 166–73.

1978   *Doors of Perception: A Guide to Reading the Psalms* (Faith Press);
Dutch translation, 1979.
'Biblical Classics I. John Skinner: Prophecy and Religion', *ET* 89, 356–9.
'Isaiah i–xii: Presentation of a Prophet', *Congress Volume, Göttingen 1977*, SVT 29, pp. 16–48.

1979   'Note to Parzon "Iron" in the Song of Deborah', *JSS* 24, 19–20.
'History of Israel in the Exilic and Post-Exilic Periods', *Tradition and Interpretation*, ed. G. W. Anderson (Oxford), pp. 320–50.
'Faith and its Reformulation in the Post-Exilic Period: Sources' and 'Faith and its Reformulation in the Post-Exilic Period: Prophetic Material', *Theology Digest* 27–4, 323–34, 335–46.
'יָד, etc.', *TWAT* 3, 421–55.

1981   'The Succession Narrative (so-called)', *Interpretation* 35, 4, pp. 383–86.

1982   'The Death of Hezekiah – A Pointer to the Future?', in *De la loi au Messie: Le développement d'une espérance. Etudes d'histoire et de théologie offertes à Henri Cazelles*, ed. J. Doré, M. Carrez, P. Grelot (Desclée, Paris).
'Theological Reflections on the Book of Isaiah. Three interrelated studies. I. Theology of a Book', *King's Theological Review* IV, 2 (Studies II and III to appear in v, 1, 2).
Cambridge History of Judaism vol. I: 'Judah in the Persian Period' (forthcoming).
Reviews of Old Testament Books in:
JTS, Theology, ET, Heythrop Journal, Interpretation, BSOAS, Methodist Recorder, Kingsman, Congregational Quarterly, Book List of the Society for Old Testament Study etc.

Forth-   'Isaiah 36–39: Structure and Function', in W. C. Delsman,
coming   J. T. Nelis, J. R. T. M. Peters, W. H. Ph. Römer, A. S. van der Woude (eds.) *Von Kanaan bis Kerala, Festschrift für Prof. Mag. Dr. Dr. J. P. M. van der Ploeg O.P. zur Vollendung des siebzigsten Lebensjahres am 4. Juli 1979*, AOAT 211 (Butzon and Berker, Kevelaer; Neukirchener-Verlag, 1981).

Abbreviations

AfK	*Archiv für Kulturgeschichte*
AOAT	Alter Orient und Altes Testament
ASTI	*Annual of the Swedish Theological Institute in Jerusalem*
ATD	Das Alte Testament Deutsch
AThANT	Abhandlungen zur Theologie des Alten und Neuen Testaments
BA	*The Biblical Archaeologist*
BASOR	*Bulletin of the American Schools of Oriental Research*
BBB	Bonner Biblische Beiträge
BDB	F. Brown, S. R. Driver and C. A. Briggs, *A Hebrew and English Lexicon of the Old Testament* (Oxford, 1907)
BEThL	Bibliotheca Ephemeridum Theologicarum Lovaniensium
BFChrTh	Beiträge zur Förderung christlicher Theologie
BhTh	Beiträge zur historischen Theologie
BJRL	*Bulletin of the John Rylands Library*
BKAT	Biblischer Kommentar, Altes Testament
BSOAS	*Bulletin of the School of Oriental and African Studies*
BSt	Biblische Studien
BWA(N)T	Beiträge zur Wissenschaft vom Alten (und Neuen) Testament
BZ	*Biblische Zeitschrift*
BZAW	Beihefte zur Zeitschrift für die Alttestamentliche Wissenschaft
CBQ	*Catholic Biblical Quarterly*
CHJ	Cambridge History of Judaism
CTM	*Concordia Theological Monthly*
ET	*Expository Times*
EvTh	*Evangelische Theologie*
FRLANT	Forschungen zur Religion und Literatur des Alten und Neuen Testaments
GK	E. Kautzsch (ed.), *Gesenius' Hebrew Grammar*, translated by A. E. Cowley, 2nd ed. (Oxford, 1910)

Abbreviations

HAT	Handbuch zum Alten Testament
HistRel	*History of Religions*
HK	Handkommentar zum Alten Testament
HTR	*Harvard Theological Review*
HUCA	*Hebrew Union College Annual*
ICC	International Critical Commentary
IDB	*The Interpreter's Dictionary of the Bible* (4 vols and supplementary vol., Nashville and New York, 1962, 1976)
IEJ	*Israel Exploration Journal*
JBL	*Journal of Biblical Literature*
JJS	*Journal of Jewish Studies*
JNES	*Journal of Near Eastern Studies*
JSJ	*Journal for the Study of Judaism*
JSOT	*Journal for the Study of the Old Testament*
JSS	*Journal of Semitic Studies*
JTC	*Journal for Theology and the Church*
JTS	*Journal of Theological Studies*
KAT	Kommentar zum Alten Testament
KBL	L. Koehler and W. Baumgartner, *Hebräisches und Aramäisches Lexicon zum Alten Testament* (Leiden, 1953; 3rd ed. 1967–)
KHC	Kurzer Hand-Commentar zum Alten Testament
NedThT	*Nederlands Theologisch Tijdschrift*
NICOT	The New International Commentary on the Old Testament
NKZ	*Neue Kirchliche Zeitschrift*
n.s.	new series
OrAnt	*Oriens Antiquus*
OTS	Oudtestamentische Studiën
RB	*Revue biblique*
RE	*Review and Expositor*
RHPhR	*Revue d'histoire et de philosophie religieuses*
RThPh	*Revue de théologie et de philosophie*
SAT	Die Schriften des Alten Testaments
SBL	The Society of Biblical Literature
SBT	Studies in Biblical Theology
SEA	*Svensk Exegetisk Årsbok*
SJLA	Studies in Judaism in Late Antiquity
SJTh	*Scottish Journal of Theology*
StANT	Studien zum Alten und Neuen Testament
SVT	Supplements to *Vetus Testamentum*
TDNT	*Theological Dictionary of the New Testament*

xviii

TDOT	*Theological Dictionary of the Old Testament* ed. Botterweck and Ringgren
TGUOS	*Transactions of the Glasgow University Oriental Society*
THAT	*Theologisches Handwörterbuch zum Alten Testament*
ThB	Theologische Bücherei
TheolEx	Theologische Existenz heute
ThLZ	*Theologische Literaturzeitung*
ThSt(B)	Theologische Studien, Zürich
ThR	*Theologische Rundschau*
ThZ	*Theologische Zeitschrift*
TRE	*Theologische Realenzyklopädie*
TTS	Trierer Theologische Studien
TWAT	*Theologisches Wörterbuch zum Alten Testament*
USQR	*Union Seminary Quarterly Review*
VT	*Vetus Testamentum*
WMANT	Wissenschaftliche Monographien zum Alten und Neuen Testament
WuD	*Wort und Dienst*
WUNT	Wissenschaftliche Untersuchungen zum Neuen Testament
ZAW	*Zeitschrift für die Alttestamentliche Wissenschaft*
ZDPV	*Zeitschrift der Deutschen Palästina-Vereins*
ZS	*Zeitschrift für Semitistik und verwandte Gebiete*
ZThK	*Zeitschrift für Theologie und Kirche*

Note

Each essay contains its own bibliography, to which reference is made in what should be a self-explanatory way by in-text citation, and several of these bibliographies include works not specifically referred to in the text. Biblical references are to the English chapter and verse, with the Hebrew added where it differs; the text used is either RSV or the individual author's translation.

Prophecy in the ancient Near East

HELMER RINGGREN

An investigation of prophecy in the ancient Near East must start with a definition of the term. What is prophecy? On the basis of the Old Testament evidence prophecy may tentatively be defined as the proclamation of divine messages in a state of inspiration. The Old Testament prophets proclaim messages from Yahweh speaking in his name and using the messenger formula *kō'āmar YHWH,* 'Thus says Yahweh.' In these messages, that is to say, Yahweh speaks in the first person. The character of the inspiration varies: the term *ḥāzāh* indicates some kind of vision, other passages refer to auditions, as e.g. Isa. 5: 9.

Egypt offers very little that is comparable to Old Testament prophecy. Inspired persons are not mentioned, oracles proclaimed by the aid of the statues of the gods hardly deserve to be called prophecy. The fact that the Greeks rendered the priestly title *ḥm-nṯr* by *prophētēs* can hardly substantiate the identification of these priests with the Hebrew prophets. It rather seems that they were oracle priests who reported the answers of the gods to questions put to them by the worshippers. There is an expanded form of the title, *ḥm-nṯr wḥmw,* which probably means 'reporting servant of the god', and it is likely that this refers to their duty of reporting on the answers they received from the god. The term *wḥmw,* 'reporter' or 'herald', is also applied to the bulls Apis and Mnevis as mediators of oracles (Morenz, 1960, p. 109).

Lanczkowski (1960) has tried to interpret the so-called Lament of the Eloquent Peasant as an example of Old Egyptian prophecy. He points to the fact that the peasant utters his 'lament' – partly at least – at the gates of the Temple, just as Jeremiah preaches in the court of the Jerusalem Temple (Jer. 26: 1f) and Amos appears at the sanctuary of Bethel (Amos 7: 10ff).

He also points to the peasant's criticism of social injustice, to his intrepidity and his suffering, comparing this with the Old Testament

1

prophets. But nothing of all this touches upon the essential features of Old Testament prophecy as we have defined it above.

A fact that has remained widely unnoticed is the occurrence of the so-called salvation oracle in Egyptian documents. In the magical texts of the Metternich stela there is a prayer to Re by a woman who has been stung by a scorpion, followed by an oracle: 'Fear not, fear not, my glorious daughter, behold, I am behind you' (Roeder, 1915, p. 84; Ringgren, 1979, p. 45). This, of course, has close resemblance with the oracles of Deutero-Isaiah, but it reflects cultic practice rather than prophetic inspiration.

There are also the prophecy of Neferty (*ANET*, pp. 444f) and the admonitions of Ipuwer (*ANET*, pp. 441f). The former is a *vaticinium ex eventu* foretelling the chaos of the first intermediate period and the restoration brought about by the twelfth dynasty; of the latter only the description of chaos is preserved, but it seems to have been similar to the former. These documents, though they are apparently foretelling the future, should rather be ranked among the forerunners of apocalyptic than as examples of prophecy.

Turning now to ancient Mesopotamia, we first come upon an isolated piece of information from Ebla. According to preliminary reports, there were two classes of prophets at Ebla, *maḫḫû* or 'ecstatic', and *nabi'ūtum*, or 'prophet' (Pettinato, 1976, p. 49). *Maḫḫû* is a common Accadian term, *nabi'ūtum* is the only attestation so far of an equivalent of the Hebrew term *nābī'* outside the Old Testament. Further publication of the Ebla material has to be awaited in order to form an opinion on this early kind of prophecy.

The *maḫḫû* is found again in the Mari letters, here used interchangeably with *āpilum* or 'answerer'. The Mari evidence has been collected and discussed in detail by Ellermeier (1968), and it will not be necessary to repeat the information given in his work. It is sufficient to quote some representative texts and to make some observations concerning details that are especially interesting for a comparative study of Israelite prophecy.

It seems that *āpilum* is the common term for a priest who mediates oracular answers, while *maḫḫû* denotes a specific kind of prophetic inspiration. It is possible that the Ebla evidence will shed new light on the terminological question. The receivers of oracles are both priests and laymen, both men and women. Oracular information may be sought by sleeping in the temple (incubation) and given in the form of dreams. But there are also examples of revelations that were not sought.

Prophetic revelation is referred to as 'seeing', but the terminology does not make it clear whether dreams or other kinds of vision are meant. The revelations were reported to the king, who was often blamed in the message. No particularly literary form can be observed (cf., however, Westermann, 1967, pp. 115ff), though there are examples of the messenger formula and of the god speaking in the first person.

In some cases there are elaborate descriptions of the visionary experience, for instance in the following letter:

> In a dream of mine I was set on going in the company of another man to Mari. On my way (*ina pānīya*) I entered Terqa and right after entering I entered the temple of Dagan and prostrated myself. As I was prostrate, Dagan opened his mouth and spoke to me as follows: 'Did the kings of the Yaminites and their forces make peace with the forces of Zimrilim, who moved up here?' I said, 'No.'
>
> Just before I went out he spoke to me as follows: 'Why are the messengers of Zimrilim not in constant attendance upon me, and why does he not lay his full report before me? Had this been done, I would long ago have delivered the kings of the Yaminites into the power of Zimrilim. Now go, I send you. Thus shall you speak to Zimrilim saying: "Send me your messengers and lay your full report before me, and then I will have the kings of the Yaminites cooked on a fisherman's spit, and I will lay them before you".'
>
> (Ellermeier, pp. 25f; *ANET*, p. 623)

Thus, the god appears to the prophet in a dream, speaks to him and gives him a message to deliver to the king. Special notice should be given to the expression 'Go, I send you' (*alik aštaparka*).

In other cases we are not told how the revelation happened, but the wording of the message is given in full. One prophet writes thus to the king:

> At the (inspection of) the omens (*ina têrēti*) Adad the Lord of Kallassu spoke as follows: 'Am I not Adad the lord of Kallassu who reared him between my thighs and restored him to the throne of his father's house? After restoring him to the throne of his father's house, I again gave him a dwelling-place. Now, since I restored him to the throne of his father's house, I should receive from him an hereditary property. If he does not give it, I am the lord of the throne, territory, and city, and what I gave I will take away. If on the other hand he grants my request, I will give him throne upon throne, house upon house, territory upon territory, city upon city; even the land from east to west will I give him'.
>
> (Ellermeier, pp. 49ff; *ANET*, p. 625)

Here the god through his prophet utters a threat against the king: if he does not comply with the god's will, the god will deprive him of the kingship he has given to him, but if he is obedient, he will get world dominion.

In another letter it is reported that a certain Sheribu, without seeking an oracle in any way, fell into a trance and received the following revelation:

> Thus (spoke) Annunitum: 'O Zimrilim, with a revolt they would put you to the test. Guard yourself. At your side put servants, your controllers whom you love. Station them so they can guard you. Do not go about by yourself. And as for the men who would put you to the test, I shall deliver these men into your hand'.
>
> (Ellermeier, pp. 56f; *ANET*, p. 630)

This oracle contains a warning and a promise of divine protection. It is claimed to be given in the exact wording of the revelation.

In another case we are told that a certain Akhatum went into a trance and spoke as follows:

> O Zimrilim, even though you for your part have spurned me, I for my part shall embrace you. I shall deliver your enemies into your hand.
>
> (Ellermeier, pp. 58f; *ANET*, p. 630)

Here the words of the man who went into a trance are quoted, but the 'I' of the message is obviously the deity. In other words, the prophet delivers verbally the message received.

The prophet's inspiration can be described in terms of dreaming, of seeing or of going into a trance (*maḫû* N from which obviously the title *maḫḫû* is derived).

In addition to the messenger formula, 'Thus says the god', there are other expressions reminiscent of Old Testament language: 'Go, I have sent you' (cf. Isa. 6: 8f), 'Am I not Adad?' (cf. 'Am I not Yahweh?' Isa. 45: 21).

An interesting example of a dialogue between a goddess and a prophet is reported in a text found in the palace of Sin-kashid of Uruk (about 1850 B.C.) (*ANET*, p. 626). The writer of the letter reports that the goddess Nanaya visited him and had him sit down in the doorway of Sin. Then she spoke to him about establishing a faithful shepherd in the land. In his reply the prophet seems to confirm the message: 'Dead Uruk has revived and the faithful shepherd concerning whom a command came from you has been established...' Then the goddess again speaks, obviously bringing her final message, but unfortunately the text is so poorly preserved that most of it is unintelligible. We are not told how the prophet experienced the visit of the goddess; quite possibly it was in a dream. The interesting feature is that he carries on a dialogue with the goddess in a similar way to many Old Testament prophets.

Much later is a report in a letter to King Esarhaddon, in which it is told that a prophetess (*rāgintu*) before the ceremonies of enthronement addressed Iamqi the 'bishop's' son saying: 'You shall bear my kingship' and further, speaking to him in the assembly of the people: 'I have indicated the...of my lord, I have turned you over (to the assembly)' (*ANET*, p. 626). It is obvious that the prophetess does not speak in her own authority but proclaims a message in the name of a god. The term *rāgintu* (from *ragāmu*) does not give any clue to her state of inspiration since it only denotes her as one who 'proclaims' (von Soden, *Akkadisches Handwörterbuch*, pp. 241f).

From the period of the Neo-Assyrian Empire there are two collections of oracles that both have some bearing on our subject (Dietrich, 1973; Jastrow, 1912: II, 1, pp. 158ff). One is concerned with King Esarhaddon, who is promised divine protection and assistance. Several independent oracles are quoted without special introduction; in each case, however, the person – mostly a woman – who delivered the oracle is mentioned. The deity speaks in the first person, beginning or interspersing the oracle with the formula 'Fear not.' Two examples may suffice to illustrate the form and contents of the oracles:

> (Esarhad)don, king of the countries, fear not! (No)tice the wind which blows over you; I speak of it without...Your enemies, like a wild boar in the month of Sivan, from before your feet will flee away. I am the great divine lady, I am the goddess Ishtar of Arbela, who will destroy your enemies from before your feet. What are the words of mine, which I spoke to you, that you did not rely upon? I am Ishtar of Arbela. I shall lie in wait for your enemies, I shall give them to you. I, Ishtar of Arbela, will go before you and behind you: fear not! You are in a state of rebirth: I am in a state of woe, (whether) I stand (or) I sit down.

> (Oracle) from the lips of the woman Ishtar-latashiat of Arbela...

> Fear not, Esarhaddon! I, the god Bel, speak to you. The beams of your heart I strengthen, like your mother, who caused you to exist. Sixty great gods are standing together with me and protect you. The god

Sin is at your right, the god Shamash at your left; sixty great gods stand round about you, ranged for battle. Do not trust men! Turn your eyes to me, look at me! I am Ishtar of Arbela; I have turned Ashur's favour unto you. When you were small, I sustained you. Fear not, praise me! Where is that enemy which blew over you when I did not notice? The future is like the past! I am the god Nabu, lord of the tablet stylus, praise me!

(Oracle) from the lips of the woman Baia of Arbela.

(*ANET*, pp. 449f; Jastrow, pp. 158ff)

Unfortunately no information is given as to the way in which these oracles were revealed. The persons who delivered them are not even called priests or seers. It is interesting that the collection comprises oracles granted by several deities, Ishtar of Arbela, Bel, Ashur. We can infer from this document that the kings of Assyria turned to their gods for oracles at various occasions and we may assume that the oracles were collected either in order to reassure and strengthen the king or to serve as models for later oracle priests (Jastrow, p. 158). The sequence of the oracles does not seem to be chronological; rather oracles delivered by the same person may have been grouped together.

The historical situations of the various oracles are difficult to determine since they contain very few concrete details. In another collection from the time of Esarhaddon (Jastrow, pp. 165ff), the names of the cultic prophets are not given, but there are more hints to the historical situation, names of enemies are given etc.

A third collection concerns Ashurbanipal. It begins as follows:

The goddess Ninlil is highly regarded (as a) sibyl (*rāgintu*). This is the word of Ninlil herself for the king, 'Fear not, Ashurbanipal! Now, as I have spoken, it will come to pass: I shall grant (it) to you. Over the people of the four languages (and) over the armament of the princes you will exercise sovereignty...'

(The kings) of the countries confer together (saying), 'Come, (let us rise) against Ashurbanipal...The fate of our fathers and our grandfathers (the Assyrians) have fixed: (let not his might) cause divisions among us.'

(Nin)lil answered saying, '(The kings) of the lands (I shall over-)throw, place under the yoke, bind their feet in (strong fetters). For the second time I proclaim to you as with the land of Elam and the Cimmerians (I shall proceed). I shall arise, break the thorns, open up widely my way through the briers...'

Ninlil is his mother. Fear not! The mistress of Arbela bore him.

Fear not! As she that bears for her child, (so) I care for you, I have placed you like an amulet on my breast. Fear not, my son, whom I have raised.

(*ANET*, pp. 450f; Jastrow, pp. 171ff)

Incidentally, this oracle provides an astonishing parallel to Ps. 2 in the Old Testament; we notice such motifs as the revolt of the kings, the divine oracle of victory, the king's sonship. A comparison with the annals of the same king shows that the reference is probably to a revolt in Egypt and Ethiopia (Jastrow, p. 172). The fact that the means of revelation is not mentioned creates some doubt whether these oracles can really be called prophecies.

There are other cases where we are told that the revelation was given in a dream. Dreams were often granted to the kings themselves. But they are also mediated by priests. Ashurbanipal, for instance, tells us that during a campaign, a seer (*šabrû*) in the middle of the night read the following oracle in the moon:

Whoever plans evil and exercises hostility against Ashurbanipal, king of Assyria, I will deliver to an evil death etc.

(Jastrow, p. 155)

In another case the same king reports as follows:

The goddess Ishtar heard my anxious sighs and, 'Fear not!' she said, and filled my heart with confidence. 'Inasmuch as you have lifted your hands in prayer (and) your eyes are filled with tears, I have mercy.' During the night in which I appeared before her, a seer reclined and saw a dream. When he awoke Ishtar showed him a night vision. He reported to me as follows: 'Ishtar who dwells in Arbela came in. Right and left quivers were hanging from her. She held the bow in her hand (and) a sharp sword was drawn to do battle. You were standing in front of her and she spoke to you like the mother who bore you. Ishtar called unto you, she who is exalted among the gods, giving you the following instructions: "You will contemplate fulfilling my orders..."'

(*ANET*, p. 451)

Here both dreams and visions in the waking state are referred to. The formula 'Fear not' occurs at the beginning of the report but not in the description of the vision. It is clear anyhow that oracles could be formulated on the basis of dreams and visions, possibly also on the basis of haruspicy, and that in most cases the oracles are placed in the mouth of the deity, who often introduces his/her speech with 'Fear not.'

Jastrow points out that there are also collections of oracular questions, in which the priests try to formulate what they want to know in as exact a manner as possible (Jastrow, pp. 174ff). But there is no immediate connection in phraseology and style between these questions and the oracles preserved. Obviously oracular practice in Mesopotamia included many different methods, and only some of them have any similarity to Old Testament prophecy.

There is another group of Accadian texts that have often been denoted as prophecies (*ANET*, pp. 451f, 606; Grayson, 1975, pp. 24ff; cf. Hallo, 1966). Some of them begin with a mythological introduction in the style of an omen protasis. The main body of the texts contains predictions of good and bad rulers and of events taking place during their reigns. The wording is often obscure or allusive, only a few times are there more exact references:

> A ruler will arise, he will rule for thirteen years. There will be an attack of Elam against Akkad, and the booty of Akkad will be carried off...There will be confusion, disturbance, and unhappy events in the land...; another man whose name is not mentioned will arise, and will seize the throne as king and will put to death his officials... A ruler will arise, he will rule for eight years. The temples of the gods will be restored, at the advice of the king; the rites of the great gods will be restored. There will be rain and high water in the land...But locusts will arise and devour the land, the king will bring hard times upon his land...
>
> (*ANET*, pp. 606f)

The character and function of these texts have been much discussed. It has, however, been possible in certain cases to identify the sequence of historical events alluded to, and, on the basis of such observations, Grayson now describes an Akkadian prophecy as 'a prose composition consisting in the main of a number of "predictions" of past events. It then concludes either with a "prediction" of phenomena in the writer's day or with a genuine attempt to forecast future events. The author uses *vaticinia ex eventu* to establish his credibility and then proceeds to his real purpose' (Grayson, 1975, p. 16). In this respect, as with regard to the general tone, Akkadian 'prophecy' is more akin to Old Testament (and intertestamental) apocalypticism than to real Israelite prophecy (Lambert, 1978, pp. 9–13).

We now turn to an area that is geographically, and perhaps also culturally, closer to ancient Israel, namely, that of the Western Semites.

8

The material is scanty and heterogeneous, but some interesting observations can be made.

The oldest evidence is somewhat shaky since it consists of an oracular pronouncement that is not ascribed to a prophet. In one of the episodes of the Ugaritic Baal epic, the artisan god Kothar wa-Hasis addresses Baal as follows:

> I tell you, O Prince Baal,
> I repeat, Rider of the clouds:
> Behold, your enemy, O Baal,
> Behold, your enemy you shall smite,
> Behold, you shall destroy your foes.
> You shall take your eternal kingdom,
>   your dominion for generation after generation.
>
> (III AB A, 7ff; cf. Haldar, 1945, p. 81)

It is true that this oracle is pronounced by a god and not by a priest or prophet. But it is probable that it reflects the form of other oracles that were normally pronounced by human representatives of the gods.

Somewhat later is the report of an Egyptian official by the name of Wen-Amon about his experiences in Phoenicia. He was sent to claim tribute for his king, but the Phoenician ruler refused to pay. Then suddenly a young man in the city was seized by divine ecstasy and said: 'Take the messenger here. It is Amon who has sent him.' So his mission was successfully carried out (*ANET*, p. 26). No details are given, we do not know the nature of the young man's ecstasy and there is no guarantee that we have the exact wording of the message. But it is important that the words uttered in ecstasy were understood as having divine authority and were consequently obeyed.

A clear statement of prophetic activity is provided by the Aramaic Zakir inscription (*c.* 780 B.C.). King Zakir of Hamath tells us that he was attacked by Hazael, king of Aram, and his allies, who laid siege to the capital. He goes on to say:

> But I lifted up my hands to Baalshamayn, and Baalshamayn answered me, and Baalshamayn spoke to me through seers (*ḥzyn*) and messengers (*'ddn*); and Baalshamayn said to me, Fear not (*'l tzḥl*), because it was I who made you king, and I shall stand with you, and I shall deliver you from all these kings who have forced a siege upon you.
>
> (Gibson, 1975, no. 5, A 11–15)

The situation is clear. The king turns to his god in prayer and asks for help and guidance. The god answers by his prophets, who are called *ḥāzeh*, like the seers (*ḥōzîm*) of ancient Israel, and *'āded*, which corresponds to Ugar. *'dd* 'herald' and perhaps to *'Oded*, as the name of a prophet in 2 Chron. 28: 9. The oracle is introduced by the formula 'Fear not', and it contains a proclamation of the god in the first person.

There is another instance of oracles on the so-called Moabite stone. King Mesha of Moab reports that his god Chemosh said to him: 'Go take Nebo from Israel'; and on another occasion the same god said to him: 'Go down, fight against Horonaim' (Gibson, 1971, no. 16, 11, 14, 32). Unfortunately, no information is given about the way the god spoke to Mesha; it may be that oracular priests or seers interpreted omens or saw dreams or that inspired prophets delivered the message. Since the verbs of the oracles are all in the imperative, there is no way of knowing whether or not the prophet speaks in the name of the god. There is great probability that the situation is similar to that of the Zakir inscription.

A welcome addition to our evidence for West Semitic prophecy came through the discovery of the Deir 'Allā inscription from the Jordan valley (*c.* 700 B.C.) (Hoftijzer–van der Kooij, 1976; cf. Caquot–Lemaire, 1977; Müller, 1978; Ringgren, 1977). Though the text is badly damaged it provides some valuable information about prophecy. We are told that Balaam, son of Beor, was a man who was a seer of the gods. 'And the gods came to him in the night (and addressed him) in the following words; and they said...' (cf. i ll. 1ff). Balaam is thus a *ḥāzeh*, or 'seer', to whom the gods come in a dream or a night vision and speak in words quoted literally. The message itself defies coherent translation, but we learn that Balaam weeps because of what he has seen and that, asked by a certain Eliqa about the reason, he explains his vision and its meaning. Unfortunately, the text is so broken that it is impossible to restore the context. The intelligible phrases suggest chaotic conditions. However, the second part of the inscription strikes a more optimistic note: an *'almāh* (cf. Isa. 7: 14) saturates herself with love (cf. Prov. 7 : 18) and conceives a *nqr*, i.e. *neṣer*, branch (cf. Isa. 11 : 1). The result is peace, friendship and fertility. There may be room for different opinions concerning the meaning of the message, but the reference to Balaam as a seer is perfectly clear; it is also in almost complete agreement with the biblical evidence in this respect. It is obvious, however, as far as the text is legible, that Balaam does not speak in the name of the gods but simply reports on his vision.

The scattered examples of prophecy presented here do not form a coherent pattern. They show that there is similarity in many details between prophecy in the ancient Near East and Old Testament prophecy but also considerable differences. It is the combination of elements that are similar and others that differ that forms the pattern of Biblical prophecy. But it should also be borne in mind that Biblical prophecy, just like its Near Eastern counterpart, is not a homogeneous phenomenon.

Bibliography

A. Caquot and A. Lemaire 'Les Textes araméens de Deir 'Alla', *Syria* 54 (1977), 189ff.

M. Dietrich 'Prophetie in den Keilschrifttexten', in *Jahrbuch für Anthropologie und Religionsgeschichte* 1, (Saarbrücken, 1973), pp. 40ff.

F. Ellermeier *Prophetie in Mari und Israel* (Herzberg, 1968).

J. C. L. Gibson *Textbook of Syrian Semitic Inscriptions I* (Oxford, 1971). *Textbook of Syrian Semitic Inscriptions II* (Oxford, 1975).

A. K. Grayson *Babylonian Historical–Literary Texts* (Toronto, 1975).

A. Haldar *Associations of Cult Prophets among the Ancient Semites* (Uppsala, 1945).

W. Hallo 'Accadian Prophecies', *IEJ* 16 (1966), 31ff.

J. Hoftijzer and G. van der Kooij *Aramaic Texts from Deir ʿAllá* (Leiden, 1976).

M. Jastrow *Die Religion Babyloniens und Assyriens* (Giessen, 1912).

W. G. Lambert *The Background of Jewish Apocalyptic* (London, 1978).

G. Lanczkowski *Altägyptischer Prophetismus*, Ägyptologische Abhandlungen 4 (Wiesbaden, 1960).

S. Morenz *Egyptian Religion* (London, 1973) (English translation of *Ägyptische Religion*) (Stuttgart, 1960).

H. P. Müller 'Einige alttestamentliche Probleme zur aramäischen Inschrift von Dēr 'Allā', *ZDPV* 94 (1978), 56ff.

G. Pettinato 'The Royal Archives of Tell Mardikh-Ebla', *BA* 39 (1976), 44ff.

H. Ringgren *Die Religionen des Alten Orients*, Grundrisse zum Alten Testament, ATD-Ergänzungsreihe, Sonderband (Göttingen, 1979). (The English translation, *Religions of the Ancient Near East* (London, 1973), does not include the section on Egypt to which reference is here made.) 'Bileam och inskriften från Deir 'Alla', *Religion och Bibel* 36 (1977) (English translation forthcoming).

G. Roeder *Urkunden zur Religion des alten Ägypten* (Jena, 1915).

C. Westermann *Basic Forms of Prophetic Speech* (London, 1967). (English translation of *Grundformen prophetischer Rede* (München, 1960)).

The origins of prophecy in Israel

J. R. PORTER

An essay on the origins of Israelite prophecy must necessarily concern itself with at least three distinct, though not wholly unrelated, issues. First, there are the historical problems as to when it is possible to date the emergence of what may be called 'prophecy' in Israel and the factors that led to its appearance there. Secondly, there is the phenomenological question of how far we can recover the characteristics and functions of prophecy before the eighth century, its role in society, its relation to the cultus and similar matters. Thirdly, we have to ask to what extent we can extract authentic and reliable information about the actual careers and activities of the most important 'prophetic' figures who are placed in this period, such as Samuel, Elijah or Elisha, from the material that the Old Testament provides concerning them.

It must be admitted that comparatively little attention has been paid to these issues in the scholarship of the last twenty-five years or so, as is noted in the most recent survey of prophecy, which in fact devotes virtually no attention to the notices of prophecy in the historical books of the Old Testament (McKane, 1979, pp. 163ff). To some extent, investigation in this area has reached a dead end, so that no recent work has superseded the famous essay of H. H. Rowley on the nature of Old Testament prophecy (Rowley, 1952). Perhaps the main reason for this has been the recent dominance of the newer critical approaches, such as the form-critical and the traditio-historical, which has meant that the texts dealing with prophecy in the narrative parts of the Old Testament have been studied largely with a view to determining the different stages of development of the traditions they contain and how these were understood and used by the various tradents or authors. Account has to be taken not only of the ways in which the final editors, the Deuteronomistic school, were concerned to present their own view of prophecy and certain prophetic figures but also of the particular, and not always identical, outlook of the earlier sources that they had at their

12

disposal for this purpose (Bernhardt, 1972). Hence the kind of questions proposed above must seem to many scholars largely unanswerable: we cannot go behind the different pictures of early Israelite prophecy to trace the historical development of a single 'movement'; the available material does not provide us with adequate data to describe prophetic experience, a matter with which the traditions are not concerned and which, perhaps, the circles where they arose would not even have understood; the presence, in the stories about prophetic figures, of legendary and folk-lore elements, of variant traditions of different dates and of episodes with which the protagonists probably originally had nothing to do often make it very difficult to give a trustworthy account of their real personalities and work (von Rad, 1965, pp. 6–32).

Historical questions

Yet, while recognising all these factors, many scholars still attempt to present an overall view of the nature and development of the prophetic phenomenon up to the time of Amos, and the attempt is not without its justification. Our information is contained in writings that purport to be historical narrative and to record historical events, and it is therefore proper to inquire what actual facts may underlie them. Rendtorff's statement is very much to the point: 'above all, the question of the historical beginnings of prophecy must be raised again and again, because until it is answered, everything else must of necessity remain uncertain' (1967, p. 16). One commonly held opinion is that early Israelite prophecy represents a combination of two originally separate strands: a nomadic element that the Israelites brought with them on their entry into Palestine, and a kind of prophecy that was widespread in the settled civilisations of the ancient Near East, which was mediated to Israel through the Canaanites. These two features gradually coalesced from around 1000 B.C. onwards, as evidenced by such 'transitional' figures as Elijah and Elisha, to evolve into 'genuine' Israelite prophecy, which in turn consisted of two groups, the cultic and court prophets on the one hand, and the great individual prophets on the other (Fohrer, 1967, pp. 1–7). Such a schema, which is followed, with more or less significant variations, by a number of scholars, certainly provides a clear and consistent account of the historical origins of prophecy, but it has to be recognised that the whole construction is largely hypothetical and raises a number of problems.

In the first place, this kind of approach has been criticised as resting on unexamined evolutionistic assumptions, which cannot be supported by the evidence of the texts themselves, and it is alleged in particular that the traditions about the so-called 'transitional' figures 'are so particular and varied that they cannot be forced into this sort of developmental pattern' (Engnell, 1970, pp. 125–34). Secondly, there is no agreement as to where the features indicating a nomadic and an ancient Near Eastern, or a more definitely Canaanite, background respectively are to be discerned in the material relating to early Israelite prophecy. The former, as with Fohrer, is often thought to have been associated with the 'seer' type and the latter with the groups of prophets, distinguished primarily by the appearance among them of 'ecstasy', a term that must be investigated later. But, on the one hand, it has been cogently objected that ecstatic prophecy is 'a common human phenomenon' and that there is no reason why it should not have been native to the earliest 'Israel' and known there before the settlement in Canaan (Lindblom, 1958; 1962, pp. 1–46, 95–104). This in turn raises even more fundamental problems, which can hardly be discussed here, as to how far it is really possible, on the basis of the available Old Testament material, to discern clear lineaments of a nomadic stage or strain in Israelite society at all.

On the other hand, in recent scholarship Orlinsky (1965) has suggested that it is the 'seer' type that is most closely related to Israel's environment and that it is the 'prophet' who represents a distinctive and uniquely Israelite factor, although he is forced to argue that bands or sons of prophets and the early individual prophetic figures were really seers and that the term 'prophet' has been applied to them as a result of later developments. So it has been claimed that 'ecstasy' is not merely absent from the canonical prophets, as some earlier scholars had proposed (Jepsen, 1934, pp. 26ff; Mowinckel, 1934), but that it was never an element of genuine and original Israelite prophecy (Parker, 1978). Again, it has been suggested that the origin of the distinctive concept of the $n\bar{a}b\bar{\imath}$' is to be found in the judges, who were Yahweh's institutional spokesmen and to two of whom, Deborah and Samuel, the actual term is applied, so that the genuine Israelite prophet, to be clearly marked off from the ecstatics, can most properly be described as a 'judge–prophet' (Eppstein, 1969, pp. 290ff). A not dissimilar position is taken by Rendtorff in the article already referred to, where the line of true Israelite prophecy is traced backwards from the eighth century to the period of the amphictyony and even beyond to the patriarchal age. Throughout, the prophets represent the charismatic aspect of the amphictyonic leaders, preserved by them at a time when, with the inauguration of kingship, the head of the nation is no longer himself a charismatic, and so charismatic prophecy took its place alongside the monarchy (Noth, 1966, p. 245). The evidence is to be found in the way in which the words and activities of the early prophets often give expression to the concepts of the amphictyonic practice of the holy war (Bach, 1962, pp. 92ff). Particularly important is their supposed 'critical position taken over against a dynastic understanding of the monarchy' (Rendtorff, 1967, p. 21) and the contention that figures such as Samuel, Nathan, Ahijah and Elisha attempt to preserve the element of amphictyonic leadership in the actual royal institution that they had to face. Here attention may also be directed to the important work of de Vries who, on the basis of an exhaustive analysis of the various genres of prophetic legend in the books of Samuel and Kings, concludes that all these stories 'record a dynamic struggle to supervise the kingship' (de Vries, 1978, pp. 149f).

However, it must remain very doubtful whether it is possible either to see so clearly unified a prophetic continuity in the Old Testament evidence or to link it so firmly with traditions and practices of the amphictyony. Quite apart from the increasing recognition that 'Israel' before the monarchy cannot correctly be described as an amphictyony (Mayes, 1974) and the question as to whether the holy-war concept is to be associated originally with the period of the judges (Smend, 1970), Rendtorff's description, as he himself recognises, can hardly find any place for the ecstatic, or perhaps specifically Canaanite, elements that seem to occur in early Israelite prophecy, and the same may be said for the other scholars surveyed in the preceding paragraph, who are forced to assume, as with Orlinsky, that much of what is related of prophets in fact refers to a quite different kind of figure, or as with Eppstein and Parker, that prophecy of the ecstatic type represents a degeneration of the genuine institution, which appeared only as late as the time of the Omri dynasty. Nor is it adequate to consider the prophets as essentially anti-monarchical and to ignore the evidence of the prophet often being 'the helper of the king' (Pedersen, 1940, pp. 124–8). No doubt, as will be seen, there is a link between the judges and the early prophets but the connection does not reside in the common possession of some sort of charismatic office or function, itself a rather dubious and ill-defined idea in the context of ancient Israel (Orlinsky, 1962, p. 377, n. 1). When Rendtorff asks, in relation to the ecstatic groups of 1 Sam. 10 and 19, 'what is the relationship of the ecstatic element, which can be seen here, to the charismatic element?' (p. 52), we must surely reply that the most obvious resemblance between the 'major' judge figures and the prophets is their identical possession by the *rûaḥ yhwh*, which can hardly be considered as other than 'ecstatic'. But this, in fact, is to say no more than that in all early or simple societies spirit possession may occur in the case of many different individuals or groups; it does not of itself provide any direct link, of either a chronological or institutional nature, between the judges and the prophets. In brief, the different attempts we have so far discussed to isolate out what may be called a prophetic 'movement' within ancient Israelite society, with well-defined characteristics and a clear line of development, can only be sustained either by ignoring much of the evidence or by interpreting it in the light of preconceived assumptions as to what must have actually occurred.

Another method that has frequently been employed to fix the beginnings of prophecy in Israel is to start from what is recorded about the *hebel nebî'îm* or the *lahaqat hannebî'îm* in 1 Sam. 10 : 5–6, 10–13; 19 : 18–24, for these passages have commonly been taken as constituting the earliest reliable records of the appearance of Hebrew prophecy in its true sense. On the one side, the prophets described here are often considered as a basically Canaanite phenomenon, which may have emerged not long before this period and which the Israelites took over on the soil of Palestine (Albright, 1968, p. 185). On the other side, Samuel, on the basis of 1 Sam. 19: 20, has been viewed as the head of these groups and as the driving force behind them, in that he both directed them as the spearhead of opposition to the Philistines (Meek, 1950, pp. 156f) and also, more importantly, transformed them into a new kind of prophecy, which was to lead directly to the 'classical' Israelite prophet (Albright, 1961). Again, along the same lines as the reconstruction reviewed above, it has been suggested that as a result of his association with these groups, Samuel 'was probably concerned with transferring the basic functions of the covenant mediator to them and thus insuring that these functions be perpetuated for the people of Yahweh' (Newman, 1962, p. 91).

For much of all this, however, there is very little hard evidence. We do not know whether or not prophetic groups emerged in Israel only in the time of Samuel and Saul, nor is there anything to suggest that they were active in opposition to the Philistines. What can be discovered about the historical character of Samuel himself will be considered later, but it may be questioned whether he should be considered as the founder of authentic Yahwistic prophetism (Engnell, 1970, p. 130 and n. 19), while the idea that the result of his 'call' was that he replaced Eli as the official covenant mediator has to be read into the narrative of 1 Sam. 3, and the descriptions of him as *nābī'* may well be an anachronism (McKenzie, 1974, p. 89). The supposition that the prophetic bands of 1 Sam. 10 and 19, even allowing that Samuel was the leader of the first-mentioned of them, are instances of a widespread movement of which he was the head (McKenzie, 1962) goes beyond what may be legitimately deduced from the texts. Further, in so far as Samuel appears in the Old Testament as the one in whose person the transition from judge to prophet is effected, this is the reflection of the Deuteronomists' particular theory of the course of Israel's development and does not necessarily correspond to historical fact. Most importantly, recent study of the narratives of the prophetic groups in 1 Sam. 10 and 19 has brought out their essentially aetiological character and shown that they do not of themselves provide contemporary evidence for the character of prophecy in the time of Samuel and Saul (Eppstein, 1969; Sturdy, 1970; Lindblom, 1974). No doubt the stories can still be understood as authentic pictures of prophetic phenomena at some period of the nation's life, but we cannot be certain just when that period was and it is precisely the relation of the texts to the actual persons of Samuel and Saul that has to be called in question.

It would seem, then, that we must conclude that, in our present state of knowledge, it is impossible to date with any precision the emergence of 'prophecy' in Israel or to trace a clear development of anything like a prophetic movement, at least before the eighth century. However, there are perhaps one or two useful observations that may still be made about the historical setting of Israelite prophecy.

First, it is usual to isolate various terms such as *nābī'*, *rō'êh*, *ḥōzêh* or *'îš 'elōhîm* as having some sort of relationship to one another, and all needing to be taken into account for any definition of 'prophecy', and to distinguish them from other terms such as *kōhēn*, *šōpēt*, or 'patriarch', which are not considered to have the same relevance. But there is a certain artificiality in such distinctions, and their basis is the conclusions of scholars rather than what is to be found in the pages of the Old Testament. In that society which, in its social structure and historical development, is in many ways very close to ancient Israel, the pre-Islamic Arabs (Porter, 1979, p. 131, n. 35), we find that categories closely corresponding to those we can see in Israel are not sharply distinguished from one another and to some degree overlap (Pedersen,

1950). In the ancient Near East, too, we meet a wide diversity of inspired persons, whose functions cannot always be clearly separated from one another (Haldar, 1945). We should perhaps therefore think, as the root of all these different figures in the Old Testament, of what might be called an undifferentiated holy or inspired man, whose general role in the society was, in Pedersen's illuminating phrase, 'the upholder of holiness', in the various ways that answered to the actual needs of that society. Looked at in this way, we can accept Bernhardt's dictum that 'there is no unequivocal development in the sense that an older form of prophecy is superseded by a younger, but rather a juxtaposition of forms that are often mixed together' (Bernhardt, 1972, p. 42). Hence no one of these 'forms' can be taken as the actual origin of 'prophecy' or confined too closely to a particular period. Space does not allow this point to be illustrated as fully as is desirable, but we may take a single example, that of the 'seer'. It is not correct to view the seer as *the* characteristic form of prophecy in the period before Amos, as many scholars do, nor can his characteristic activity be confined to this period: the fact that five out of the ten occurrences of rō'êh and ten of the sixteen occurrences of ḥōzêh in the Old Testament are found in the Chronicler's work suggests that such persons were for him still a reality and, although he may have assimilated these and other similar figures to the Temple guilds of his day (Johnson, 1962, pp. 69ff), there is no real evidence in his work that he saw their function merely as that of 'an ordinary Temple singer'.

Secondly, however, it is possible, albeit to a limited extent, to trace the background of some of the prophetic forms. To begin with, a number of the terms employed probably originally denoted different techniques for oracular activity: thus the seer used visual means (Guillaume, 1938, pp. 115ff); the nābī', depending on whether the word is considered to have an active or passive sense, was one who announced a message or was called by the deity – perhaps not just at his inauguration as a prophet but regularly – but in any case one who operated through audible means, while the mal'āk used specifically messenger formulae (Westermann, 1967, pp. 98–128). Similarly, possession by the rûaḥ or the manipulation of the Urim and Thummim, to mention only two instances, are examples of different techniques that various holy men might employ. No doubt particular individuals and groups might specialise in one or other of these methods, yet the same person might avail himself of different techniques on different occasions. This would account, in part at any rate, for the fact that more than one term is used for the known early prophetic figures and that their activity displays a variety of prophetic characteristics; thus it is right to speak of a unitary tradition about Samuel, for example, even though, in its existing form, it is built up of sources of various dates and provenance.

But next, different forms of prophetic activity probably arose as a response to historical changes in Israel's life and religion. Prophets would become active at sanctuaries – we avoid for the moment the ambiguous expression 'cultic-prophet' – as the incoming Israelites took over the former Canaanite high-places, and they became established at the royal court to meet the requirements of the new and expanding monarchical system. The prophetic groups evidenced by 1 Sam. 10 and 19 are best understood as a kind of order whose members were specially dedicated to Yahweh and who arose as the religion of Yahweh spread and became dominant in Israel (Fohrer, 1973, p. 228). They were thus similar to, and again not to be sharply distinguished from, groups such as the early Levites (Gunneweg, 1965), the early Nazirites (Eichrodt, 1961, pp. 303–6) and the Rechabites, for whom, on the basis of 2 Kings 10: 15ff, we can posit a development much the same as we have for the Nazirites. Another example is provided by the unit *bene hannebiʾîm*. It is usual to take this expression as a blanket term covering all evidences of prophetic groups in the Old Testament. But all the instances of the term are confined to the two middle decades of the ninth century and to a relatively compact geographical area. 'The sons of the prophets' appears to be a technical expression for the followers of Elisha, under whom a prophetic movement was organised on a national basis (Williams, 1966, pp. 344ff) to resist the religious policy of the Omrides and Jezebel in particular (Rowley, 1963, pp. 39ff). No solid ground exists for identifying them with the prophetic bands of Samuel's day, for the latter are described by different terms, as we have seen, and there is a gap of some 200 years between the two entities (Scott, 1944, p. 47). Recently, an attempt has been made to link them by suggesting that each was organised with a leader called by the title *ʾāb*, whose function was to interpret in intelligible form the incoherent utterances of the ecstatic group (Phillips, 1968, pp. 183–94). Not only is this theory doubtful as an explanation of 1 Sam. 10: 12, since it assumes a historical connection between the saying there and the preceding aetiological narrative, and in any case there is nothing, as will be seen, that makes it necessary for the prophets of the story to have used any kind of speech at all, but also Elisha is never described as *ʾāb* in his relationship to the sons of the prophets, whose members only use the term '*ādôn* or '*îš* '*elōhîm* of him and speak of themselves as his 'servants' not his 'sons'. It may be concluded, then, that 'the sons of the prophets' formed a distinct group, which emerged in response to a specific historical crisis and ceased to exist when its work was done.

Lastly, in this connection, we cannot leave out of account the extent to which modern scholarship has emphasised the diversity, as well as the underlying unity, of early Israel. Israel was made up of a variety of groups, each with its own independent history, it included a number of sanctuaries, each again with its distinctive practices and religious interpretation, and bodies of traditionists who stamped their particular outlook on the material they transmitted. To recognise this situation has both a positive and a negative aspect. On the one hand, it may enable us to discover how different prophetic manifestations or different terms for inspired persons are, in fact, the product of what Orlinsky has called 'chronological–regional factors' (Orlinsky, 1971, p. 343). For example, is '*îš* '*elōhîm* a blanket term for prophetic persons, as it is generally taken, or does a study of its occurrences indicate that it properly refers to a northern prophet and specifically from the area of Ephraim (Hallevy, 1958, p. 243, n. 4)? On the other hand, such considerations once again warn us of the need for caution in generalising about the nature of Old Testament prophecy and for a careful testing of statements about alleged successive eras of development in it. Hence we must ask whether the clear distinction drawn in Deut. 18: 9ff between what is usually called divination and true prophecy reflects a distinctive feature that Israelite prophecy possessed from its very beginning or a theological pattern derived only from Deuteronomic circles; or, again, whether the statement that prophetic forms of divine inquiry largely replaced the priestly ones in the course of the ninth century (Long, 1973, pp. 490f) corresponds to historical fact or is merely deduced from the silence of a literature that has other concerns. In spite of a few hints in recent studies, some of which have been noted above, the kind of approach we have been suggesting to the history of Old Testament prophecy still needs to be worked out and there is here a fruitful field of investigation for scholarship.

Some characteristics of early prophecy

The details of the behaviour and activities of the various prophetic figures, as these are found in the Old Testament, are fully set out, and more or less fully analysed, in the standard works on prophecy (e.g.

Lindblom, 1962, pp. 47–104), so that there is no need to survey them here. There are, however, some aspects of early prophecy that merit a brief discussion, and we may conveniently begin with the concept of 'ecstasy'.

'Ecstasy' is a term that continues to occur in all accounts of Biblical prophecy, and there would be general agreement that it is a phenomenon characteristic of the period under discussion, whatever position is adopted with regard to its presence or otherwise among the later prophets. Unfortunately, the idea is rarely defined with any precision, and much of the long-running debate about the place of ecstasy in Hebrew prophecy has been confused by the different ways different scholars have understood it. Basically the difficulty resides in the inappropriateness of applying a notion stemming from Greek religion and society to the Hebrew milieu (Whitley, 1963, pp. 15ff), so that it is all too easy to make it mean just what one wants when considering the Old Testament evidence. The latter has generally been approached from two points of view. Ecstatic phenomena in Israelite prophecy have been compared with allegedly similar features among a very wide range of different peoples and cultures, although recent studies have tended to interpret them more specifically as part of the structure of the religious system known as 'shamanism' (Kapelrud, 1967; Goldammer, 1972). These phenomena have often been described and explained also according to modern psychological theories (Klein, 1956). Both these approaches are open to criticism. In the hands of most Old Testament scholars, the understanding of the contribution of comparative religion has hardly progressed beyond the old Frazerian position, by which a rag-bag of apparently similar features is collected from cultures widely dispersed in time and space, without any adequate consideration of how far there is likely to be any connection between them or whether they fulfil an identical function in different religious and social contexts. Nor do the texts, in which alone the behaviour patterns in question are available for study, provide the necessary data for the successful application of psychological theories.

If, then, the subject of ecstasy seems to have reached something of an impasse in Old Testament scholarship, yet it may well be that the findings of modern social anthropologists will throw some much-needed light on the Hebrew material that has been thought to evidence this concept. Biblical scholars have in general been slow to acquaint themselves with these findings and they are hardly visible at all in their descriptions of prophecy, but two recent studies (Parker, 1978; Wilson,

1979, the latter of which is particularly significant), at least make a beginning in this direction. Social anthropology is concerned to investigate the importance of religious activity for the particular society in which it occurs, and the social roles of persons who are considered to be in close touch with the divine, and the Old Testament precisely provides us with a picture of a society and evidence for the place of prophetic-type figures within it.

Wilson begins by pointing out that Biblical scholars have generally used the term 'ecstasy' to cover two different ideas that they do not clearly distinguish: ecstasy as indicating the means by which divine communication takes place, the medium of revelation, and ecstasy as meaning particular types of outward behaviour. For the latter, contemporary anthropologists tend to avoid speaking of 'ecstasy' and prefer the expression 'trance', a feature that is found in many different cultures. But there is also found the widespread idea that divine communication comes through a man being possessed by a spirit or god: in the case of early Israelite prophecy, the basic concept is of possession by the 'spirit' or the 'hand' of Yahweh (Roberts, 1971), for it is correct to see such prophecy as essentially Yahwistic. What is important to note is that in other societies where the reality of possession is recognised, this is independent of whatever outward behavioural manifestations may accompany it, although these may be usual and even expected. Trance may or may not accompany the awareness of possession, a point observed independently by Fohrer (1967, p. 8), when he writes of the prophet's 'secret experiences', which may or may not be linked with 'ecstasy'. The trance may take a variety of forms, ranging from uncontrolled physical behaviour to quite normal actions, from the uttering of unintelligible sounds to perfectly rational discourse.

The significance of this for Old Testament 'prophecy' is obvious: it suggests that the older discussions as to whether or not the prophets all manifested trance-like behaviour, whether the earlier did and the later did not or whether the 'seer' communicated with the divine world in a different way from the 'prophet' are wide of the mark and can only be sustained by a selective use of the evidence. As in other cultures, it was not specific types of behaviour that were decisive but the recognition by the group that an individual had been chosen by the deity as his intermediary, as we find in such a passage as I Sam. 3: 20, a fact that could appear in various kinds of recognised activity even by one and the same person on different occasions, as indeed we have previously noted.

Further, anthropological findings underline what was said earlier about the importance of the recognition of the simultaneous existence of different groups and circles in Israel for the understanding of prophecy, for they show that in most societies the behaviour of inspired persons in one religious or social context varies from that of similar persons in other groups. If there is any truth in Wilson's statement that 'ultimately the question of the nature of prophetic possession behaviour must be answered with respect to each individual prophet' – or, we may add, associations of prophets – 'and perhaps even with respect to each social situation in which the prophet worked' (Wilson, 1979, p. 328), the validity, at least for the early period, of the general definitions of 'prophecy' that are provided by so many scholars must be seriously questioned. Again, in a society, one group that has its own characteristic behaviour pattern can easily take a negative attitude to the different pattern of another group, which would account for the often observed fact that in the Old Testament 'ecstatics' are sometimes venerated and sometimes despised. It also enables us to grasp what lies behind the important passage Num. 11: 24–9. First, it can be seen that there is no distinction here between the spirit possession of the elders and that of what is presumably a 'prophetic' group: the difference lies in the accompanying outward behaviour, for the elders exhibit the behaviour characteristic of a *nābī* only on this particular occasion, although there is no reason to assume that they were not considered to be possessed by the spirit thereafter. Secondly, however, the background of the passage is the disapproval by some circle in Israel, represented by the figure of 'Joshua' in the narrative, of the contagious trance state displayed by certain prophets. Such considerations may suggest that the parallel aetiological stories in 1 Sam. 10 and 19 reflect opposed evaluations from different circles of such trance behaviour and that there are no solid grounds for labelling one as 'later' than the other, even if it remains a matter for debate which attitude is represented by which narrative. Opposition between prophets in this period, which has been much discussed (Crenshaw, 1971), is to be understood along the same lines and, once again, we must be chary of explaining all the instances in the same way, whereby, for example, 1 Kings 13 and 22 are closely linked together (de Vries, 1978, pp. 59ff), or the latter chapter is thought to mark the first appearance of a succession of 'false prophets', which can be traced in subsequent periods. So, too, the problem of the usage of the hithpael and niphal forms of the root **nb'* is perhaps best accounted for not as the result of a development by which one in time superseded the other (Rendtorff, 1968, pp. 797–9) but rather as stemming from two circles, in one of which prophetic activity was expressed by 'ecstasy' but in the other by intelligible speech.

Another consideration that requires emphasising, however, is that, although there are different patterns of prophetic behaviour, these are all to some degree stereotyped. A society needs to be able to recognise the divinely possessed person, and hence the Old Testament is aware of the problem of the criteria for 'true' prophecy, although this concern seems to be formulated only at a time later than the one under discussion here. One way in which the society achieves this objective is by comparing the behaviour of people in the past whom it recognises as divinely possessed with what is observed among people in the present. Here we may have the root of the concept of a 'prophetic succession' and we should probably recognise examples of this interest in the emergence of the legend of the succession of Elisha to Elijah (Carroll, 1969; Carlson, 1970) or in the much-discussed verse 1 Sam. 9: 9, the purpose of which seems to be to make clear that a person in the present has the same oracular abilities as his counterpart in the past, whether he was a distinct 'type' or simply had an alternative title. In turn, possessed individuals learn from the society the kind of behaviour that is expected of them and consciously or subconsciously conform to it: modern Old Testament scholarship has rightly observed how regularly the prophets make use of stereotyped speech forms but it has not yet sufficiently investigated the degree to which other prophetic activities also show stereotyped patterns. At least it can be said that a distinction between the individual and the group prophet, in the sense that the latter 'learned his craft' while the former was marked by greater originality and spontaneity, is largely illusory: either would be expected to function in socially acceptable ways and the fact that these may have differed in different circles is not to be explained by any sort of individual–group dichotomy.

What we have suggested is that the most fruitful way of approaching early Hebrew prophecy is from the point of view of its significance for Israelite society and its various manifestations, and to sum up, however inadequately, the function of the prophets, we can hardly do better than revert to Pedersen's description of them as, along with other figures from whom they cannot be sharply differentiated, 'upholders of holiness'. As divine–human intermediaries, they kept the nation in a right relationship with the holiness of Yahweh and by their words and actions increased and strengthened that relationship. On the question of the relationship of the holiness created by the various 'prophetic' figures to the holiness created by the cult, so much ink has been spilt that there is little more to be said (Rowley, 1967, pp. 144–75). Once more, many of the problems seem to be the result of a lack of clarity in defining terms, with the result that scholars often seem to be talking about different things: 'cult' is generally not defined at all or implicitly understood too narrowly in terms of sanctuary and sacrifice. Rather, precise and concrete questions need to be asked: did some or all of the seers and prophets sacrifice, did they take part in liturgical functions, did their function of upholding holiness include the upholding of the holiness of the sanctuary, were they supported from the income received by shrines, how were they related to other figures such as the priests? and so on. From all that has been said earlier, we might expect very varied answers in various cases but hardly any secure grounds for a clear differentiation between the prophets who were 'cultic' and those who were not, at any rate in the early period.

Individual figures

The prophetic figures of whom we have the names, and about whom the Old Testament provides more or less detailed biographical information, seem to have been specially remembered because they were all involved in affairs of state: it was their role in great matters of public concern that marked them off from the mass of other inspired persons, and with this fact we reach an irreducible minimum of historicity with respect to their life and careers. This, of course, is not to say that all the information we have about them is confined to their political activities, still less that it can invariably be regarded as reliable factual history. The basic sources are widely recognised as being prophetic legends, with all the tendency to introduce folk-lore and cultic elements, directed to enhance the personality of the central figure, that this type of literature displays. Further, the legend-cycles themselves have been modified and adapted in the course of their transmission, so that, in their present form, they betray the theological concerns of periods later than those when their heroes actually lived, and here the incorporation of the cycles into the Deuteronomic history work has had specially far-reaching effects. As already noted, most of the discussions during the past few years of the early prophetic figures are primarily traditio-historical studies of the texts, occupied with the isolating-out of individual units and attempting to trace the growth of the tradition as a whole.

The number of such discussions is now considerable: only a selection can be mentioned now, and we shall only attempt to consider them from the standpoint of what they may tell us of the actual life and careers of the individuals who are their subject.

All these considerations apply, for instance, to Balaam, whose place in Israelite prophecy remains difficult to assess. His memory was no doubt preserved because he was associated with an important episode in the relations of Israel with Moab. The most authentic information preserved about him is that he was a Mesopotamian seer, but in Numbers he acts under the direct inspiration of Yahweh. Hence, older works have always used what we are told of Balaam's behaviour as evidence for certain characteristics of Israelite prophecy, but more recent work has tended to shift its interests to the form taken by the tradition about him. Attempts have been made to show that the narrative portion is built up of originally separate units, representing various conventional themes of Israelite prophetic legend (Gross, 1974), while the sayings have been held to reveal a type of 'seer utterance', the *Sitz im Leben* of which was the life of nomadic groups before the occupation of Palestine (Vetter, 1975). The value of such an understanding of the Balaam material, however debatable some of the details may be, is that it opens up a new area of information about the characteristics of early Israelite prophecy, to supplement what we have in the books of Samuel and Kings. Nevertheless, this does not preclude the view that the material reflects a specific historical event or that we must still give full weight to the Mesopotamian features in what we are told of Balaam's activities (Daiches, 1950).

With regard to Samuel, he again is primarily remembered because of his involvement in the establishment of the monarchy, and it is the traditions of the emergence of kingship that have been the focus of most recent work on those chapters of 1 Samuel where Samuel himself appears. As a figure in his own right, little has been added to the conclusions of Weiser's well-known monograph (Weiser, 1962). Although his method can properly be labelled as 'traditio-historical', he is concerned to uncover the lineaments of the historical Samuel and to separate out the purely fictional elements, such as the victory over the Philistines in 1 Sam. 7, which arose from the magnifying of Samuel in northern prophetic circles. In fact, part of the value of Weiser's study is that it shows that the actual historical figure of Samuel cannot be understood in terms of one single category – he did in fact embody 'priestly', 'prophetic' and 'judge' functions in his own person – thus providing sound confirmation for the more general considerations adduced in the second part of this essay.

Nathan and Gad, also, appear in the Old Testament only in connection with important events in the life of David and, again, comparatively little has been written about them as figures in their own right. On the basis of 2 Sam. 7, Nathan has usually been considered as a representative of amphictyonic and wilderness traditions, a genuine Israelite prophet. But when we recognise the great significance of this chapter for the Deuteronomists' presentation of Israel's history, and the doubtfulness of the existence of an authentically old, prophetic wilderness tradition (Engnell, 1970, pp. 134ff), it must be seriously asked whether the evidence used to buttress this judgement is not Deuteronomic rather than amphictyonic. If account is taken of the indications of Nathan's position at the court, and especially his leading role in the party supporting Solomon's claim to the throne, where 'he appears more as a privy councillor than as a prophet' (Herrmann, 1975, p. 166), the possibility cannot be excluded as categorically as is often done that he was in origin a Canaanite inspired man (Ahlström, 1961), although a definite adherent of Yahweh after the capture of Jerusalem, as a result of the syncretism of Yahweh with El-elyon. If this is so, it provides important evidence for the link between Israelite and Canaanite prophecy, which, as we have seen, has so often been proposed.

Lastly, Elijah and Elisha, who again appear in connection with a key crisis in the history of the Northern Kingdom, which was of particular significance for the prophetic circles with which they were associated (Bronner, 1968), have been the focus of a very considerable number of recent discussions, too extensive to be adequately reviewed here. In general, they are indicative of the same current methodology and approach as those mentioned earlier, but, especially with regard to Elijah, several studies have made a real attempt, on the basis of an analysis of the literary deposit, to discover what can be attributed to Elijah as an actual historical figure (Fohrer, 1957; Steck, 1968; Hentschel, 1977). The overall impression one gains from these and other works is that, certainly as compared with Elisha, Elijah appears as a much more idealised figure and one whose real part in historical events has been greatly exaggerated in the growth of the tradition. Thus, of what are probably two incomplete, parallel legend-cycles, that dealing with Elisha seems to be older and more trustworthy (Eissfeldt, 1967), whereas Elijah's part in the famous story of Naboth's vineyard is highly problematic (Miller, 1967; Bohlen, 1978), nor can his reputed massacre of the prophets of Baal really be historical (Jepsen, 1971). On the other hand, it must be recognised that we may be able to glimpse genuine personal prophetic experiences in his case, in a way that is not possible for any other prophet, notably in what is recorded of him on Mount Horeb (Carlson, 1969; Würthwein, 1970). By contrast, Elisha is, on the one hand, firmly rooted in the actual events of his day and in a well-defined prophetic movement, as we have noted, but, on the other, the subject of a number of stories that accurately reflect both the life of prophetic groups and their facility in creating legends, which can be seen as examples of common forms (Schmitt, 1972; Schweizer, 1974). Such legends are commonly held to embody much folk-lore; what is still needed is further examination of them in the light of contemporary concepts of folk-lore – for Old Testament scholarship has in this respect hardly progressed beyond the seminal work of Gunkel (Gunkel, 1917) – and a positive assessment of their religious and theological significance for Israelite prophecy (Lindars, 1965).

To summarise, this inevitably sketchy review emphasises once again the wide range of 'prophecy' in ancient Israel, the caution that must be exercised in making generalisations about it and the importance of relating it to the actual historical development of the society with which it was so intimately bound up.

Bibliography

G. W. Ahlström 'Der Prophet Nathan und der Tempelbau', *VT* 11 (1961), 113–27.

W. F. Albright *Samuel and the Beginnings of the Prophetic Movement* (Cincinnati, 1961).

Yahweh and the Gods of Canaan (London, 1968).

R. Bach *Die Aufforderungen zur Flucht und zum Kampf im alttestamentlichen Prophetenspruch*, WMANT 9 (1962).

K.-H. Bernhardt 'Prophetie und Geschichte', SVT 22 (1972), 20–46.

R. Bohlen *Der Fall Nabot. Form, Hintergrund, und Werdegang einer alttestamentlichen Erzählung (I Kön 21)*, TTS 35 (Trier, 1978).

L. Bronner *The Stories of Elijah and Elisha as Polemics against Baal Worship* (Leiden, 1968).

R. A. Carlson 'Elie à l'Horeb', *VT* 19 (1969), 416–39.

'Elisée – le successeur d'Elie', *VT* 20 (1970), 385–405.

R. P. Carroll 'The Elijah–Elisha Sagas: Some Remarks on Prophetic Succession in Ancient Israel', *VT* 19 (1969), 400–15.

J. A. Crenshaw *Prophetic Conflict: Its Effect upon Israelite Religion*, BZAW 124 (Berlin, 1971).

S. Daiches 'Balaam – a Babylonian bārū', *Bible Studies* (London, 1950), 110–19.

W. Eichrodt *Theology of the Old Testament*, vol. I (London, 1961) (English translation of *Theologie des Alten Testaments*, vol. I, 6th ed. (Stuttgart, 1959)).

O. Eissfeldt 'Die Komposition von I Reg 16 29 – II Reg 13 25', in F. Maass (ed.), *Das ferne und nahe Wort*, BZAW 105 (Berlin, 1967), pp. 49–58.

I. Engnell 'Prophets and Prophetism in the Old Testament', in *Critical Essays on the Old Testament* (London, 1970), pp. 123–79.

V. Eppstein 'Was Saul also among the Prophets?', *ZAW* 81 (1969), 287–304.

G. Fohrer *Elia*, AThANT 31 (Zürich, 1957).

'Die Propheten des Alten Testaments im Blickfeld neuer Forschung'; 'Bemerkungen zum neueren Verständnis der Propheten', *Studien zur alttestamentlichen Prophetie (1949–1965)*, BZAW 99 (Berlin, 1967), pp. 1–31. *History of Israelite Religion* (London, 1973) (English translation of *Geschichte der Israelitischen Religion* (Berlin, 1968)).

K. Goldammer 'Elemente des Schamanismus im alten Testament', in *Studies in the History of Religion* (Leiden, 1972), pp. 266–85.

W. Gross *Bileam* (Munich, 1974).

A. Guillaume *Prophecy and Divination* (London, 1938).

H. Gunkel *Das Märchen im Alten Testament* (Tübingen, 1917).

A. H. J. Gunneweg *Leviten und Priester. Hauptlinien der Traditionsbildung und Geschichte des israelitisch–jüdischen Kultpersonals*, FRLANT 89 (Göttingen, 1965).

A. Haldar *Associations of Cult Prophets among the Ancient Semites* (Uppsala, 1945).

R. Hallevy 'Man of God', *JNES* 17 (1958), 237–44.

G. Hentschel *Die Elijaerzählungen* (Leipzig, 1977).

S. Herrmann *A History of Israel in Old Testament Times* (London, 1975) (English translation of *Geschichte Israels in alttestamentlicher Zeit* (Munich, 1973).

A. Jepsen 'Nabi'. *Soziologische Studien zur alttestamentlichen Literatur und Religionsgeschichte* (Munich, 1934).

'Elia und das Gottesurteil', in H. Goedicke (ed.), *Near Eastern Studies in Honor of William Foxwell Albright* (Baltimore and London, 1971), pp. 291–306.

A. R. Johnson *The Cultic Prophet in Ancient Israel*, 2nd ed. (Cardiff, 1962).

A. S. Kapelrud 'Shamanistic Features in the Old Testament', in C. M. Edsman (ed.), *Studies in Shamanism* (Stockholm, 1967), pp. 90–6.

W. C. Klein *The Psychological Pattern of Old Testament Prophecy* (London, 1956).

B. Lindars 'Elijah, Elisha and the Gospel Miracles', in C. F. D. Moule (ed.), *Miracles* (London, 1965), pp. 61–79.

J. Lindblom 'Zur Frage des kanaanäischen Ursprungs des altisraelitischen Prophetismus', *Von Ugarit nach Qumran: Festschrift O. Eissfeldt*, BZAW 77 (Berlin, 1958), pp. 89–104.

Prophecy in Ancient Israel (Oxford, 1962).

'Saul inter prophetas', *ASTI* 9 (1974), 14–22.

B. O. Long 'The Effect of Divination upon Israelite Literature', *JBL* 92 (1973), 489–97.

A. D. H. Mayes *Israel in the Period of the Judges* (London, 1974).

W. McKane 'Prophecy and the Prophetic Literature', in G. W. Anderson (ed.), *Tradition and Interpretation* (Oxford, 1979), pp. 163–88.

J. L. McKenzie 'The Four Samuels', *Biblical Research* 7 (1962), 3–18.

A Theology of the Old Testament (London, 1974).

T. J. Meek *Hebrew Origins*, rev. ed. (New York, 1950).

J. M. Miller 'The Fall of the House of Ahab', *VT* 17 (1967), 307–24.

S. Mowinckel 'The Spirit and the Word in the Pre-exilic Reforming Prophets', *JBL* 53 (1934), 199–227.

M. Newman 'The Prophetic Call of Samuel', in B. W. Anderson and W. Harrelson (eds.) *Israel's Prophetic Heritage* (London, 1962), pp. 86–97.

M. Noth 'Office and Vocation in the Old Testament', in *The Laws in the Pentateuch and other Studies* (Edinburgh and London, 1966), pp. 229–49 (English translation of *Gesammelte Studien zum Alten Testament*, 2nd. ed. (Munich, 1960)).

H. M. Orlinsky 'The Tribal System of Israel and Related Groups in the Period of the Judges', in M. Ben-Horin, B. D. Weinryb and S. Zeitlin (eds.) *Studies and Essays in honour of Abraham A. Neuman* (Leiden, 1962), pp. 375–87.

'The Seer in Ancient Israel', *OrAnt* 4 (1965), 153–74.

'The Seer-Priest', in B. Mazar (ed.), *The World History of the Jewish People*, vol. III (London, 1971), pp. 268–79, 338–44.

S. B. Parker 'Possession trance and prophecy in pre-exilic Israel', *VT* 28 (1978), 271–85.

J. Pedersen *Israel III-IV* (London and Copenhagen, 1940).

'The Rôle played by Inspired Persons among the Israelites and the Arabs', in H. H. Rowley (ed.), *Studies in Old Testament Prophecy* (Edinburgh, 1950), pp. 127–42.

A. Phillips 'The Ecstatics' Father', in P. R. Ackroyd and B. Lindars (eds.), *Words and Meanings* (Cambridge, 1968), pp. 183–94.

J. R. Porter 'Old Testament Historiography', in G. W. Anderson (ed.), *Tradition and Interpretation* (Oxford, 1979), pp. 125–31.

'Bene hannebî'îm', *JTS* n.s. 32 (1981), 423–28.

G. von Rad *Old Testament Theology*, vol. II (Edinburgh and London, 1965) (English translation of *Theologie des Alten Testaments, vol. II;* 'Die Theologie der prophetischen Überlieferungen Israels' (Munich, 1960)).

R. Rendtorff 'Reflections on the Early History of Prophecy in Israel', *JTC* 4 (1967), 14–34.

'*nābî'* in the Old Testament', in *TDNT*, vol. VI (1968), pp. 797–9.

J. J. M. Roberts 'The Hand of Yahweh', *VT* 21 (1971), 244–51.

H. H. Rowley 'The Nature of Old Testament Prophecy in the Light of Recent Study', in *The Servant of the Lord and other Essays on the Old Testament* (London, 1952), pp. 91–128.

'Elijah on Mount Carmel', in *Men of God* (London, 1963), pp. 37–65.

Worship in Ancient Israel (London, 1967).

H. C. Schmitt *Elisa. Traditionsgeschichtliche Untersuchungen zur vorklassischen nordisraelitischen Prophetie* (Gütersloh, 1972).

H. Schweizer *Elischa in den Kriegen*, StANT (Munich, 1974).

R. B. Y. Scott *The Relevance of the Prophets* (New York, 1944).

R. Smend *Yahweh War and Tribal Confederation* (Nashville, 1970) (English translation of *Jahwekrieg und Stämmebund, Erwägungen zur ältesten Geschichte Israels* (Göttingen, 1963)).

O. H. Steck *Überlieferung und Zeitgeschichte in den Elia-Erzählungen*, WMANT 26 (Neukirchen-Vluyn, 1968).

J. Sturdy 'The original meaning of "Is Saul also among the prophets?"', *VT* 20 (1970), 206–13.

D. Vetter *Seherspruch und Segensschilderung. Ausdruckabsichten und sprachliche Verwirklichungen in den Bileam-Sprüchen von Numeri 23 und 24* (Stuttgart, 1975).

S. J. de Vries *Prophet Against Prophet* (Grand Rapids, 1978).

A. Weiser *Samuel. Seine geschichtliche Aufgabe und religiöse Bedeutung*, FRLANT 81 (Göttingen, 1962).

C. Westermann *Basic Forms of Prophetic Speech* (London, 1967) (English translation of *Grundformen prophetischer Rede* (Munich, 1960)).

C. F. Whitley *The Prophetic Achievement* (London, 1963).

J. G. Williams 'The Prophetic "Father"', *JBL* 85 (1966), 344–8.

R. R. Wilson 'Prophecy and Ecstasy: A Re-examination', *JBL* 98 (1979), 321–37.

E. Würthwein 'Elijah at Horeb – Reflections on 1 Kings 19.9–18', in John I. Durham and J. R. Porter (eds.), *Proclamation and Presence* (London, 1970), pp. 152–66.

Three classical prophets:
Amos, Hosea and Micah

A. S. VAN DER WOUDE

Who were these impressive men whom we call the writing prophets, and how did they understand their task? Did they proclaim a message that was substantially new, or were they steeped in old Israelite traditions, which they interpreted in a new way? What was the quintessence of their message? Modern research has not reached unanimity in answering these and similar questions, and it would be presumptuous to claim that a satisfying solution to all the intricate problems posed by classical Israelite prophecy could be given here. Nevertheless, by way of introduction to a review of recent research on the books of Amos, Hosea and Micah, a few remarks are appropriate on classical Israelite prophecy in general.

I cannot subscribe without qualification to the position of liberal and pietistic Protestantism, which looked upon the classical prophets as individualists and in particular as religious personalities who rejected the institutions of their era in favour of a spiritual and personal piety. This type of approach anachronistically projected back the personal views of the scholar into the prophetic message. On the other hand, however, the modern traditio-historical and form-critical approach stands in jeopardy of overstating the prophetic commitment to old Israelite traditions and institutions at the expense of the tremendous personal experience of God to which these men bear witness; cf. Amos 7: 15; Hos. 1: 3; Isa. 6; Mic. 2: 11a (cf. below, p. 49); 3: 8 (Henry, 1969). We should therefore constantly keep in mind von Rad's famous dictum that the problems raised at the turn of the century need to be re-examined, though with clearly different historical and theological presuppositions.

A number of scholars, among them Buber (1950) and Fohrer (1967), have stated that the classical prophets aimed at converting the people of God. However, the prophetic call to return to Yahweh is of rare occurrence in their writings and is in addition usually found in indictments. This fact is consonant with the description of the prophet's task 'to declare to Jacob his transgression and to Israel his sin' (Mic. 3: 8). Did the prophets then predict a radical destruction of the chosen people? We cannot deny that Amos was convinced that the end had come for God's people (Amos 8: 2), that Hosea predicted the fall of the Jehu dynasty (Hos. 1: 4) and the punishment of Ephraim (2: 11ff; 4: 3; 9: 15ff etc.), that Isaiah announced the chastisement of Judah and Jerusalem by the Assyrians (Isa. 7: 18ff; 8: 6ff), and that Micah prophesied the total destruction of Jerusalem and the Temple mountain (Mic. 3: 12). Does all this, however, imply that no hope of new life was left for God's people and that the oracles of salvation found in the writings of these prophets are inauthentic and post-exilic additions as was held by the Wellhausen school? Recent research has stated correctly that, by virtue of its character, the Israelite faith possessed the possibility of proclaiming the destruction of Israel as an empirical people and yet of keeping the certainty that the God of Israel could bring his people to new life, even through destruction (Vriezen, 1953, p. 221). Buss has pointed out that the fact that Hosea presents some promises should not lead one to believe that he had a perspective less harsh than that of Amos, who, in his opinion, lacks them. On the contrary, it seems that Amos still entertained a hope that doom might be averted (cf. Amos 5: 14–15). Thus, according to Buss, he did not make provision for what would happen if doom did come. Hosea, however, was convinced that Israel's downfall was definitely sealed, so that it was appropriate for him to look beyond the impending disaster to a new order fulfilling the will of God. This is a very interesting view. If it is correct, the prophetic promises serve to underline the inescapability of the threats (cf. Buss, 1969, p. 129). This idea is largely in consonance with Wolff's statement that the quintessence of the prophets' message was neither a call to return to Yahweh nor the announcement of a final destruction, but the conviction that Yahweh could not be evaded and that Israel had to prepare for meeting its God (Amos 4: 12; cf. Wolff, 1977 *b*, p. 555). The secret of the prophetic activity is the double aspect of Israel: the empirical Israel as the people of God (Vriezen, 1953, p. 220). This double aspect means on the one hand that the classical prophets were convinced that the day of judgement was unavoidable (W. H. Schmidt, 1973, pp. 15ff) because of Israel's sins. On the other hand, they knew that Israel was God's people. This implies that they were well aware of their religious traditions and in particular of God's election. But whilst the latter meant to the people that they could feel secure, the prophets knew that this unique bond was the very reason for Yahweh's judgement (cf. Amos 3: 2). Whereas the priests were convinced that the sacrificial cult could atone for the sins of the people, and the cult prophets felt confident that their intercession would uphold the *shalom*, the eighth-century and later classical prophets knew that Yahweh would no longer respond to the sacrifices of Israel and that He would not forgive the people's sins any more (cf. Amos 8: 2). God's people had to pass through the absolute zero point of their downfall in order in this way to fulfil their calling.

Amos

In 1959 Mays (p. 259) wrote that Amos 'has had more than his proportional share of scholarly attention and Amos-studies are already on the way to becoming a small library on their own'. This statement holds true for the two following decades as well. The reasons for this remarkable interest are in part the fact that recent movements critical of the state of affairs in our society were attracted to Amos' cry for social justice, in part the fact that the very name of Amos, being the first of the so-called writing prophets, evokes the whole gamut of questions about the nature of classical prophecy, and not least the fact that Wolff's commentary and other publications on Amos, with their original approach, have stimulated numerous reactions. Within the confines of this survey, it will prove impossible to do justice to all the aspects of the person and the book of the prophet with which recent studies have dealt. We will limit ourselves to a discussion of the most important subjects treated in the preceding decades: the background of Amos, his profession, the character of his message and the history of the redaction of the book attributed to him.

Seeking to ascertain the *geistige Heimat* of the prophet, many exegetes point to a determinative influence upon Amos. Kapelrud (1961, p. 18) has argued that Amos hardly said a single word that had not in some way been influenced by the cult and that he borrowed his main ideas from the Psalms (1966). In his opinion that which Amos preached was not new, but forgotten knowledge. But in renewing the latter the prophet removed certain features from their original context and thereby gave them a new meaning. So the righteous were no longer identified with the rich, healthy and prosperous but with the poor and needy, and thus he went further than the Psalms on which he drew. Another view of the cultic background of the prophet is given by Würthwein

(1949–1950), who contends that Amos changed his official function of *Heilsnabi* to that of a prophet of judgement. He finds this transition reflected in the visions of Amos 7–9. Following the line of Würthwein's thesis that Amos' accusations were essentially grounded on legal codes of the Old Testament, foremost among them the Book of the Covenant, Bach (1957) avers that Amos used sacred apodictic law for proclaiming his message of doom. Building upon Würthwein, who had maintained that the provenance of the prophetic *Gerichtsrede* should not be sought in secular jurisdiction but in the cult, and that cultic prophets directed their invectives to the people of the covenant as well as to foreign nations, Reventlow (1962) applied this line of thinking to Amos in a challenging study that characterises the prophet as a holder of an office in the cult. According to this author, all the genres and literary forms in the book of Amos are rooted in the cultic situation of the covenant festival. Thus he describes the visions of Amos as a ritual proclaiming the prophetic office, the passages Amos 3: 3–6: 8 as the demand of an office and the oracles against the nations as a ritual proclamation of judgement on the occasion of the covenant renewal ceremony. Brueggemann (1965) is among those who share Reventlow's views by claiming that Amos 4: 4–13 should be interpreted as a liturgy of covenant renewal and that the intercessory formulae of Amos 7: 2, 5 are to be understood in the context of covenant liturgy and lawsuit (1969).

As one would expect, the thesis that the preaching of Amos was rooted in the cult has not been left unchallenged. Smend (1963, p. 416) has described the attempt to elevate Amos to the status of a cultic prophet as mere ingenuity and sees in the endeavour to explain the phenomenon of classical prophecy sociologically, in its institutional structure and role, a one-sided reaction to previous generations who sought to understand the phenomenon psychologically. Farr (1966) does not deny that the cult has made a deep impression on the mind of Amos, if not on his heart, but finds in the book of the prophet a blend of liturgical and non-liturgical language. In his opinion, Amos borrowed directly from the cultic tradition by quotation, but this does not mean that he was a cultic functionary. Fohrer (1967), in a broader context, has challenged the idea that prophetic forms of speech were anchored in a definite institution, that the structure of prophetic sayings reflects a cultic event and that the prophet who uses cultic forms of speech has to be a cultic official. Form and content of prophetic speech do not necessarily coincide. In his opinion a form-critical methodology that is applied critically arrives at other conclusions than one that directs attention onesidedly to the cultic situation.

Wolff especially has registered sharp criticism against the thesis that Amos' person and preaching should be explained against the background of the cult. He upbraids Reventlow for basing his conclusions on a selection of texts from the book of Amos, for using inauthentic texts to substantiate his assertions and for putting the question concerning prophetic forms of speech on a par with the question concerning the prophetic office. In Wolff's view it is a misconception to consider such passages as Amos 1: 3–3: 6; 4: 6–11 and 9: 13–15 to be characteristic examples of the use of constitutive parts of cultic formularies. The most prominent, yet constantly varied, message of the prophet: 'The end has come upon my people Israel' (Amos 8: 2), cannot, in Wolff's opinion, be understood in connection with a function that had been carried out within the cult for a long period. Furthermore, the thesis that Amos was an official of the cult is diametrically opposed by Amos 7: 15, which states explicitly that Yahweh took Amos as he followed the flock (Wolff, 1973, pp. 2–5).

Before we pursue Wolff's thesis that Amos' *geistige Heimat* should be sought in tribal wisdom, we must devote some attention to the hotly contested words of Amos 7: 14–15. For centuries the debate has endured over whether *lō' nābī' 'ānōkī* and the two subsequent nominal clauses should be translated in the present or the past tense. Against the thesis of several scholars who want to render the clauses with the past tense, Rudolph (1971, p. 256) has demonstrated that the translation 'I *was* not a prophet nor *was* I a prophet's son: I *was* a herdsman and a dresser of sycamore-figs' implies that Amos admits that he is *at present* a prophet's son and that he has abandoned his civil occupation of farmer. The direct call of Yahweh, however, excludes the possibility of his having joined a prophetic guild, and Amaziah's suggestion that Amos is operating as a seer for material gain could only be blunted by the prophet's remark that he could provide for his costs through the profits of his farm. Therefore the last two nominal clauses must be translated with the present tense and, if this is so, the same holds true for the first one. According to Rudolph, Amos denies that he is a *nābī'*, in the sense of a member of a prophetic guild. Amos is thereby neutralising not his own prophetic activity (see verse 15 and 3 : 8; 2 : 11 and 3 : 7 are inauthentic) but the institutional dependency of prophetic guilds, who exercised their trade for pay. It is almost inevitable that one should subscribe to Rudolph's interpretation of Amos 7 : 14. In any case the translation using the past tense as proposed by Rowley (1947), Gunne-weg (1960, pp. 2–3), Reventlow (1962, pp. 14ff), Clements (1965, p. 37), Mays (1976a, p. 138) and others is not necessary and is even improbable, if one looks at 3: 8. This verse implies that no Israelite, no matter who he is, can withdraw from prophesying once he has been compelled to do it. In Amos 3: 8 and 7: 15 a distinction has been made between the office and the activity of a prophet (Wolff, 1977a, p. 313).

We must skip over other explanations of Amos 7: 14–15 that have failed to find approval in the scholarly world, in order to examine Wolff's thesis concerning Amos' *geistige Heimat*. In line with Terrien (1962), who pointed out the close stylistic and theological relations between Amos and wisdom literature, Wolff seeks the background of the prophet's preaching in tribal wisdom. In order to defend his thesis, he adduces stylistic usages such as rhetorical questions, woe oracles, numerical pairs, antithetic expressions, reiteration, *Mahnrede* and the use of words like *nekōḥā*, *sōd*, *šeʾōl*, Isaac and Beer-sheba, and Tekoa. From a theological point of view he discerns a lack of concern for idolatry, interest in astronomy, an attack on luxurious living, a moral-istic conception of salvation etc. From all this he concludes that Amos was steeped in the *Sippenweisheit* (Wolff, 1973, pp. 6ff).

Crenshaw (1967, pp. 44ff) has challenged Wolff's view, first of all by pointing out that since wisdom is based on experience, a degree of similarity of style, vocabulary and theology between wisdom and prophetic and priestly traditions is unavoidable. Furthermore, a re-appraisal of the arguments adduced by Wolff to substantiate his thesis that Amos was nurtured in wisdom circles leads to the conclusion that most of them are either false or inconclusive. Indeed, Wolff has perhaps exaggerated the sapiential influence on Amos as a reaction, understand-able in itself, to a one-sided emphasis on the cultic roots of the prophet and his preaching. Besides Crenshaw, Hermisson (1968, pp. 88ff) and especially Schmid (1969, pp. 92–102) have shown that many words and forms that Wolff has attributed to wisdom do not originate from there. Along with Rudolph (1971, p. 99) one can best say therefore that it is sufficient to conclude that we should come to see Amos as a farmer knowledgeable and wise in the ways of life.

Though Crenshaw is ready to concede that Amos employed sapiential terminology and that he owed terms and themes to the cult, he thinks that there can be no question about the centrality of the theophanic language in Amos' message, albeit that the prophet reversed the content of every phrase or ritual that he borrowed from the covenant renewal ceremony and the holy-war tradition (Crenshaw, 1968). Wisdom terminology (unless simply based on daily-life experience) was mediated to the prophet through the ancient theophanic tradition. Crenshaw, however, fails to distinguish theophany (as the advent of the deity in order to proclaim his word) from epiphany (as God's interference in nature and history). The examples from the genuine passages of Amos that he cites to substantiate his thesis cannot confirm it, in my opinion. We cannot be sure that the expression 'for I will pass through the midst of you' (Amos 5: 17) is of a cultic nature because of Exod. 12: 12 (cf. e.g. Nahum 2 : 1). Amos 5 : 14 does not necessarily allude to the theophanic tradition, nor does Amos 4: 12*c* or 9: 4, 8 ('I will set my eyes upon them'). That the theme of the Day of the Lord originated in holy-war tradition is at least questionable (van Leeuwen, 1974). The mention of punishment in terms of an earthquake, as described in Amos 8: 8, does not demand the conclusion that theophanic language is being employed (as Crenshaw himself concedes), and the allusion to the Day of the Lord in the context cannot prove that such language is used in the verse. Apart from the question whether we can trace with certainty a covenant renewal ceremony, of which the theophany formed the heart, in pre-exilic Israel, the adduced phrases cannot, in my opinion, support the contention that Amos again and again reversed cultic theophanic language when he put his prophecies into words.

In conclusion, neither the thesis that Amos drew almost exclusively upon cultic traditions or even cultic texts (Gottlieb, 1967, pp. 433ff), let alone that he was a cult official, nor the assertion that his message is steeped in tribal wisdom, nor the contention that theophanic language shaped his prophecies, can be convincingly substantiated. Form-critical and traditio-historical studies exhibit a tendency to cast a prophet almost exclusively in one mould or another. Like all other men, prophets must have been exposed to many, even opposing, influences, though nobody would deny that they could have relied more on one than on another.

'The message of doom, with which prophecy commences, was delivered in the context of the particular relationship which was understood to exist between Yahweh and Israel' (Clements, 1965, p. 45). This relationship found its expression in the traditions of election and covenant, including divine laws, and in cultic ceremonies and religious festivals as well. We are not forced, however, to presuppose written law-books, cultic texts, a covenant renewal festival or an embryonic

Pentateuch to understand the message of Amos. What we find in the book of Amos is, from a traditio-historical point of view, an amalgam of traditions and influences, which the prophet borrowed, consciously or unconsciously, from the total culture in which he lived. This fact is in accordance with the tradition that Amos was a farmer who kept sheep and cows and who also dressed sycamore fig-trees. The contention that sycamores did not grow in the area of Judean Tekoa has been correctly contested by Rudolph (1971, p. 258). Therefore it is not necessary to seek Amos' descent in a Northern Israelite Tekoa (Koch, 1978, p. 82). It is very questionable whether one should explain Amos 7: 15 a ('the Lord took me as I followed the flock') ideologically, as an example of the motif of the 'legitimation of an outsider' (on the basis of the traditional language of the call of a shepherd or a countryman while at work), as suggested by Schult (1971), rather than biographically since the prophet is explicitly designated as belonging to the *nōqedīm* (Amos 1: 1). This term refers to shepherds, not to hepatoscopists, as suggested by Bič (1951; see however Murtonen, 1952), or other cultic functionaries (cf. Segert, 1967).

It is a strange fact that, apart from the superscription of the book and Amos 7: 12, where Amaziah advises Amos to flee to Judah, none of the uncontestably authentic passages of the book attest to the southern origin of the prophet. Not only the prophecy of salvation, which deals with the fallen booth of David (Amos 9: 11–12), and the prophecy against Judah in Amos 2: 4–5, but also Amos 1: 2, which presents Yahweh as roaring from Zion and thundering from Jerusalem, and the words about those who live at ease in Zion (Amos 6: 1), are regarded by the majority of scholars as spurious. That these passages are in fact inauthentic is, however, called into question by a number of exegetes. Ever since the Wellhausen era, the authenticity of Amos 9: 11–12 has been a matter of constant dispute (cf. Kellermann, 1969, pp. 169ff). Eminent scholars like Alt (cf. Wagner, 1971, cols. 661 and 669, n. 18) and von Rad (1965, p. 138), however, ventured to consider seriously the authenticity of the passage, and Wagner (1971, cols. 661–2) and Rudolph (1971, pp. 285–6) defend the view that the verses derive from Amos. Also the authenticity of the Judah-saying in Amos 2: 4–5 can no longer be dismissed with a mere reference to the Deuteronomistic language used in these verses. If one agrees with Rudolph (1971, pp. 120–1) that the conclusion of verse 4 is secondary, or with Wagner (1971, cols. 663ff) that the phrases 'and have not kept his statutes' and 'after which their fathers walked' are an addition, then the authenticity of the Judah-saying can be effectively defended. Concerning Amos 6: 1, Wagner (1971, cols. 658–9) argues for the preservation of the transmitted text as words of Amos. In any case, the metre makes the expunging of verse 1*a*β difficult. The inauthenticity of Amos 1: 2 is far from sure, if only on the ground that it is reminiscent of the language used in 3: 8.

It is high time to turn to a number of characteristics of Amos' message. Many scholars view the visions of chs. 7–9 as revelations that are directly related to the call of the prophet. As a matter of fact, the deadly seriousness and disquietude evoked by these visions pervades the preaching of Amos. Not only the foreign nations who violate human rights but especially Israel, with whom Yahweh has forged a special relationship, await an inevitable judgement; cf. Amos 3: 2. From the latter text it is clear that Amos draws upon the election tradition, and that he apparently did subscribe to it; otherwise the conclusion in 3: 2*b* would lose its force. Vriezen (1970) asserts that Amos refers to the patriarchal tradition in Amos 3: 2*a*, in particular to the Jacob-tradition of Bethel (cf. Gen. 28: 14); in that case the tension between Amos 3: 2 (3: 1*b* is spurious) and 9: 7 would be, in part, alleviated. The authenticity of Amos 9: 7–8 is, however, far from being beyond doubt (Gese, 1979), since this passage seems to reject the idea of a natural and historical *Sonderstellung* of Israel along the lines of Deuteronomic theology. If Amos 9: 7–8 is indeed inauthentic, 3: 2*a* could easily refer to the Exodus tradition, or even to the patriarchal and the Exodus traditions at the same time. Since however Amos 3: 6 seems to refer to 3: 2, and 3: 2–6, therefore, can be considered as an instance of cyclic composition, there is much to be said in favour of the contention of Labuschagne (1965, p. 126) and Stoebe (1970, pp. 221ff) that Amos 3: 3ff does not call attention to the prophet and the necessity of the prophetic activity, but to the relationship between God and his people. In that case Amos 3: 3 seems to point at the encounter between Yahweh and *Israel*. If Amos 3: (1)2–6 indeed forms a unit, then it is quite natural to relate this pericope to the Exodus tradition.

I do not find convincing evidence for the view that Amos stood completely outside the normative theological traditions of Israel, as suggested by Mays (1976*a*, p. 57). None of the writing prophets seem to have denied these traditions as such but they have drawn different conclusions from them than their contemporaries. There is nothing in

Amos 3: 2*a* or in 5: 14 (on 9: 7 see above) that supports the view that Amos uttered an ironic, scornful response to hearers who laid claim to the dogma of a special relation to Yahweh as a defence against Amos' message of judgement. On the contrary! The words of 3: 2 would lose their compelling force if based on irony, and the call of the prophet to seek good and not evil that the people may live (5: 14) would be diabolic advice if the prophet was not convinced that in that case the divine promises on which the people relied would come true. The use of '*my* people' in Amos 7: 8, 15; 8: 2 stresses that Yahweh had a special bond with this people, and it would be absurd to suggest that Amos denied this relationship and (by implication) the traditions connected with it. The dissimilarity between Amos and the people stands out in the fact that the latter are 'at ease' and 'feel secure' (6: 1), unaware of the grave situation in which they will find themselves when Yahweh intervenes on His Day (5: 18ff; cf. 6: 3). The idea of the unconditional solidarity of Yahweh with His people, because of their election and the covenant relationship, is totally overthrown by Amos' message that Yahweh will pour His wrath on *His* people *because of their sins*. The question whether Amos' preaching of doom is to be considered as an announcement of unconditional judgement or as a last attempt to induce the people to repentance and conversion probably arises from a false alternative. The solution should be sought along the lines pointed out in the introductory section of the present paper (cf. Wolff, 1977*b*). Amos was not a systematic theologian whose words can be fitted into a logically consistent system. Life's logic outstrips abstract logic! Whereas Amos was convinced that the time was ripe for Israel, he nevertheless could summon his people to seek the good (5: 4ff, 14f) in order that they might live, and he held the possibility open that Yahweh would be gracious to the rest of Joseph (5: 15).

The question whether Amos rejected the cult in principle seems to be equally academic. In any case, he did not theorise about the cult in general but emphatically rejected the cult of his day. That the prophet, however, held the opinion that Israel had not brought sacrifices during the wandering in the wilderness is a misconception. The discussion that is still raging about the meaning of Amos 5: 25 has overlooked the fact that this verse must be combined with verse 26 for grammatical reasons. The interrogative *ha-* governs two co-ordinate clauses, the first of which is subordinated to the second, so that the interrogative word strictly affects only the second; cf. GK, 150m. We have to render the two verses as follows:

> When you brought me sacrifices and offerings those forty years in the wilderness, O house of Israel,
> did you take up Sakkuth, your king, and Kaiwan,[. . .]* the star of your god, which you made for yourselves?

> * *omitting* 'your images'

The text therefore does not deny that sacrifices were brought in the wilderness, but actually presupposes this! The words are directed against a syncretistic Yahweh cult and originate (together with verse 27) from the hand of a Deuteronomistic redactor.

Whoever compares the studies of Wolff (1977a, pp. 106–13), W. H. Schmidt (1965) and Willi-Plein (1971, pp. 15–69) about the redaction history of the book of Amos and also brings the remarks of Rudolph (1971, pp. 100–3) and Mays (1976a, pp. 12–14) on this subject into consideration is confronted with very divergent pictures of the history of the book of Amos. For our present purposes, we cannot mention the details of these pictures, but we can conclude that the *redaktions-geschichtlich* approach to the book of Amos has led to results as disputable as has been the case for other prophetic books. This is the more remarkable since the book of Amos cannot be considered one of the most difficult writings among the minor prophets, from a literary point of view. It is questionable not only whether the tools at our disposal really allow us anything like the precision in describing the *redaktionsgeschichtlich* process as shown for example in Wolff's commentary but also whether additions to prophetic books (which are more than mere glosses) always *must* and *can* be confidently linked with theological, economic or social concerns prevailing in certain periods in Israel's history. So far, the *redaktionsgeschichtlich* approach has provided us with a fixing of strata in the prophetic books that is at best probable. At the present state of our knowledge, a precise and detailed reconstruction of the course that the redaction process took cannot but be conjectural in large part. This does not mean that we should waive the method, as such, because of the often disappointing or at least debatable results. A fresh reflection on the methodological lines along which the work has to be done is, nevertheless, necessary. Should one maintain the methodological postulate that not the inauthenticity of the utterances in a prophetic book but the authenticity has to be proved, as Kaiser (1975, pp. 208–9) has suggested, then it must be feared that hardly any text can with confidence be attributed to a prophet and consequently the bulk of the content of a prophetic book can only be ascribed to the process of redaction. The *redaktionsgeschichtlich* approach must guard rigidly against becoming a conscious reaction to the search for the *ipsissima verba* of the prophets. It remains to be seen whether acceptable results will emerge from the attempt undertaken by Koch (1976, pp. 2ff) and his students to bring *inter alia* the problems of the redaction-critical method closer to a solution through a structural-*formgeschichtlich* approach.

Hosea

It is remarkable that, after a high point had been reached in Hosea studies during the sixties, very few monographs have been devoted to the prophet and his book since the tumultuous period around 1970. In the sixties numerous excellent commentaries on Hosea were published (Wolff, 1961 (2nd ed., 1965; English translation 1974); Deissler, 1961; Jacob, 1965; Rudolph, 1966*b*; Ward, 1966; van Leeuwen, 1968; Mays, 1969), as well as important monographs (Brueggemann, 1968; Buss, 1969). In contradistinction to this rich harvest, the years after 1970 saw only very few contributions to the understanding of the prophet and his book, so that we cannot point to a significant advance in Hosea studies in the last decade. One may well ask what is the reason for this. Was there a feeling that the work had been done after the publication of a large number of commentaries? Or did the order of the day stimulate interest in the prophets who spoke more clearly and more fully of social justice (Amos, Isaiah and Micah) at the expense of the prophet of love? In any case the discussion about Hosea has scarcely moved beyond the issues prevalent during the sixties.

Every study of the book of Hosea runs up against the fact that the text, especially that of chs. 4ff, is very often puzzling and apparently poorly transmitted. Although Nyberg (1935) undoubtedly overstated his case by placing too much trust on the Hebrew text, he is to be credited with calling a halt to the *Konjekturfreudigkeit* of previous generations. No commentator can escape proposing a great number of conjectures (a quick glance at the commentaries of Wolff, Rudolph, and Mays will be sufficient to prove this fact), but, more than ever before, scholars are taking into account the peculiarities of the Northern Israelite dialect that was spoken by this prophet from the north. Rudolph (1966*a*; 1966*b*, pp. 20–1) has collected a great number of examples. Whether Kuhningk's attempt (1974) to explain the text of Hosea along the lines of the Dahood school with the aid of North-west Semitic languages brings the problems closer to a solution is highly questionable.

The major issue in Hosea studies is, of course, the prophet's marital life. The problems surrounding it are such that it is improbable that agreement will ever be reached (Rowley, 1956–7, p. 200), and the discussion provoked by the first three chapters of Hosea can easily lead to despair (Craghan, 1971, p. 84). The difficulties stem partly from the nature of the sources collected in these chapters: ch. 1 is biographical, ch. 2 oracular, ch. 3 autobiographical. Some scholars suggest that Hos. 3 is a parallel account of the *Fremdbericht* of ch. 1, and that, chronologic-ally, what is described in ch. 3 precedes what is described in ch. 1. To maintain this view they are forced to argue that '*ōd* ('again') in Hos. 3 : 1 is either a later addition or a reference to something that originally preceded in the autobiographical source from which ch. 3 was culled. Others propose that '*ōd* should be joined with the words 'The LORD spoke to me' (cf. Gordis, 1954, pp. 29–30; Rudolph, 1966*b*, p. 86). It seems, however, to be very unlikely that ch. 1 and ch. 3 are parallel accounts. While in Hos. 3 : 3 a long period of sexual abstention is imposed on the prophet's wife, Hos. 1 : 3 leaves the impression that she became quickly pregnant. If Gomer was an adulteress before her mar-riage to Hosea, as is said in Hos. 3 : 1, then it is not her marriage to the prophet that symbolises Israel's faithlessness to Yahweh but her mar-riage to an unknown. Furthermore, if the period of disciplinary action following the buying of the woman by Hosea (3 : 3) represents the discipline that is supposed to terminate in Israel's return to God (cf. 3 : 3–5), how is ch. 1 to be linked with ch. 3, if ch. 1 would give an account chronologically later than that of ch. 3? For these reasons many exegetes argue that Hos. 3 refers to Hosea's marriage to a woman other than Gomer. Hos. 3 mentions neither the latter's name nor the fact that the prophet took his former wife back. Against this view other scholars object that Hos. 2 implies that Gomer had abandoned her husband, and therefore can be designated an adulteress in 3 : 1. The symbolic character of Hos. 1 and 3 would also seem to argue that the same woman is involved, since after Israel's faithlessness Yahweh did not seek *another* bride (so, recently, van Leeuwen, 1968, p. 83). But the fact that the undetermined '*iššā*, 'a woman' (3 : 1), can hardly refer to the previously mentioned Gomer contradicts this explanation. Furthermore, the symbolic character of chs. 1 and 3 does not necessarily demand that we think in terms of one and the same woman, since the historical experiences of the prophet need not correspond in every respect to what is said in ch. 2. Is it not possible that Hosea experienced, in his marriage to Gomer, the faithlessness of Israel and in his second marriage the will of Yahweh to bring his people to repentance? This appears all the more so because the ingredients of the oracles of ch. 2 do not correspond exactly to the narrative in ch. 1: in ch. 2 the 'wife' and the 'children' of ch. 1 coalesce in the one figure of Israel, cf. 2: 23 (MT 2: 25). Thus Wolff (1974, p. 59) is certainly correct when he says that ch. 3 must be understood against the background of ch. 2 (in conformity with the fact that ch. 1 is presupposed in ch. 2), but the conclusion that, therefore, the woman of ch. 3 must be the unfaithful Gomer is not compelling. Ch. 2 speaks of the faithlessness of Israel and Yahweh's search for his people, but one must not lose sight of the fact that Gomer is never mentioned and that Israel is symbolised by the 'wife' and the 'children' at the same time in ch. 2. Therefore, we should find behind ch. 3 the *idea* of Yahweh's will to bring his people to repentance, not the *woman* of ch. 2 after she has been identified with Gomer of ch. 1. If this is so, there are no cogent reasons for identifying the woman of ch. 3 with Gomer of ch. 1, as recently demonstrated again by Jacob (1965, p. 34), van Leeuwen (1968, pp. 83–4) and others.

That Hos. 3 does not speak at all about a marriage, so that the bidding to 'love' a woman in Hos. 3 should be interpreted ironically (Rudolph, 1966b, p. 89), is unlikely. Not only the conclusion of Hos. 3: 3 (however one emends this difficult section of the text) but also verse 5 (which Rudolph believes to be secondary) argue against this. Even if verse 5 should be secondary, we would have before us an old explanation of ch. 3 that contradicts Rudolph's theory.

Although chs. 1 and 3 do not offer us a 'life of Hosea', since only the provocative symbolic activities are highlighted from all the experiences of the prophet, it should not be thought that the narratives are only kerygmatic (so Mays, 1969, p. 23), not biographical. This is a false dichotomy, because word and event go together in these chapters (Jacob, 1965, p. 38). An historical explanation of both chapters must not be rejected, even though the historical serves the symbolic.

Yahweh's command to Hosea to marry an *'ēšet zenūnīm* (1: 2) has spawned different explanations because of its offensive character. Some see in chs. 1 and 3 visionary experiences of the prophet or explain the chapters allegorically. Van Leeuwen (1968, pp. 30–1), however, has once more rightly pointed out that an ethically objectionable deed remains objectionable even in an allegory or a visionary experience, that it would be strange if an allegory were transmitted in two different literary genres (chs. 1 and 3), that the concrete details of chs. 1 and 3 are incompatible with the character of an allegory, and that Hosea would have been placed in an unfavourable position by these narratives if in reality he had not married a harlot. Other scholars append a proleptic explanation: only afterwards is Hosea supposed to have realised that his wife had deceived him, and that she was inclined to prostitution (Lindblom, 1928, p. 45; Gemser, 1960–1; Waterman, 1955, etc.). This thesis may lessen the offensive character of the command to marry a harlot in ch. 1, but it does not remove the offensive character of Hos. 3: 1, where it is explicitly said that Hosea was to marry an adulteress. The divine command to marry an adulteress is ethically as offensive as wedding a harlot.

Still other scholars believe that '$\bar{e}$šet zenūnīm (Hos. 1: 2) does not refer to a harlot but to an ordinary woman who worshipped the Baalim (Gordis, 1954; Coppens, 1950). This view is improbable since the uniqueness of the symbolic act would be lost should Hosea do the same as others have done, unless one should limit the symbolic act to the naming of the children and hold Hos. 1: 2b to be a text altered by the redactor of chs. 1–3, in which there was originally only mention of 'a woman' (as suggested by Rudolph, 1966b, p. 48). Also the theory of Wolff (1974, pp. 13–14), which is shared by von Rad (1965, pp. 140–1) and Deissler (1961), that '$\bar{e}$šet zenūnīm is a designation for a young marriageable woman who lost her virginity through a relationship with a stranger at the sanctuary, runs up against the objection that the uniqueness of the symbolic act would be lost in such a case. Rudolph (1963) rightly doubts whether the sexual–sacral fertility rites presupposed by Wolff existed in Israel in the time of Hosea.

We conclude that the most probable solution to the problems of Hos. 1–3 is to be found in the thesis that Hosea received the divine command to marry a harlot, perhaps a cultic prostitute (ch. 1), and that he afterwards was bidden to love another woman (ch. 3). His sad experiences gave rise to the preaching of ch. 2, the ingredients of which, however, do not correspond exactly with the historical picture given in chs. 1 and 3. In my opinion Rudolph's objection, that Hosea, in saying that God commanded him to marry a woman of ill repute, would have appeared ridiculous in the eyes of his hearers, does not refute this thesis. No prophet of Yahweh could escape insinuation.

As to the background of Hosea, Wolff (1956) has suggested that the prophet belonged to the levitical circles of the Northern Kingdom. These circles would have acquainted him with the legends of his people and their amphictyonic traditions. Many scholars have applauded the view of Wolff, but Rudolph (1966, p. 23) and Rendtorff (1962, pp. 150ff) have given voice to serious doubts, since in their opinion levitical circles are not a *conditio sine qua non* for Hosea's acquaintance with Israel's old traditions. It seems to be safer to assert that Hosea was indebted to pre-Deuteronomic traditions. This thesis would fully account for the fact that he is steeped in the Jacob and Exodus traditions, that he condemns severely the syncretistic cult of Yahweh and foreign gods, that he influenced prophets like Jeremiah (cf. especially Jer. 1–6), and that he shows affinities with Deutero-Micah's message.

Despite his severe condemnation of the 'baalised' syncretistic Yahweh cult, it is striking that Hosea finds in its rites the very material for formulating his attacks. Jacob (1963) speaks of a homeopathic method and of demythologising. By removing the myth from the domain of nature into that of history and by introducing an element of interiorisation (in that Hosea shows that love is only true if it results in the union of two wills, which was not true of the fertility cult) the prophet succeeded in preaching a truly personal God. Jacob has, however, overstated his case by asserting that the names of the three children are borrowed from Canaanite mythology (Jezreel from the chief god El, 'Not pitied' from the Ugaritic goddess *rḥm*, and 'Not my people' from the moon god '*amm*). Koch (1978, p. 102) believes that Hosea made use of the imagery of love because of the covenant idea. In his opinion the relationship between Yahweh and His people was, in Northern Israelite circles, considered to be a covenant in terms of a marriage.

We cannot go into the problem of Hosea's hostile attitude toward the monarchy (Gelston (1974) finds evidence only for an indictment directed primarily against the monarchy of his day, not for an opposition against kingship in principle) or into the intricate problems of the hotly debated ch. 12, the Jacob traditions of which are usually held to demonstrate that contemporary Ephraim followed the sinful example set by their forefather Jacob (Ackroyd (1963), however, has contested this view). A few words on the composition and style of Hosea's oracles must, however, be added. The presence of very small sense-units within the larger oracles has puzzled scholars ever since critical study of the prophetic books commenced. Wolff (1974, pp. 75–6) has suggested that in most cases each kerygmatic unit of tradition contains several small utterances spoken at one time or on a series of related occasions, largely in back-and-forth debate with the prophet's audience. These small utterances were written down at an early stage (*Auftrittsskizzen*). In his morphological approach to the book of Hosea (by which the *Sitz im Leben* is consciously related to a conception of human existence developed in co-operation with other disciplines, like social sciences, systematic theology and philosophy) Buss (1969) has called attention to the external and internal associational repetitions found in the oracles of Hosea. He finds a stricter structure in the prophetic book than proposed hitherto. Good (1966), Krszyna (1969) and van Leeuwen (1968, p. 70) have pointed to the concentric symmetry of ch. 2. Notwithstanding these inspiring studies, the composition of the book of Hosea remains puzzling in many respects.

Hosea research of the sixties had opened many doors, but the last decade saw few people entering the rooms. It is high time for a new era of Hosea studies.

Micah

In contradistinction to Hosea studies, the last decade has shown a conspicuous revival of Micah research. Apart from a number of stimulating papers and monographs, among which the contributions made by Willis (1969 *a*, 1969 *b*, 1974), Lescow (1972 *a*, 1972 *b*), Jeremias (1971), Renaud (1977) and Willi-Plein (1971) command attention, no less than six commentaries on the book of Micah have appeared since 1971 (Vuilleumier (1971), McKeating (1971), Rudolph (1975), Mays (1976 *b*), Allen (1976), van der Woude (1976, 2nd ed., 1977)).

Recently, the subject of the prophet's position in society has been reopened. Whereas Rudolph (1975, p. 22) considers only generally the possibility that Micah originated in the resident country nobility of southern Judah, Wolff (1978 *b*), being more confident about being able to pin-point the prophet's background, has tried to define his social status more precisely. Because of the particular stress laid by Micah on justice and righteousness, and because of the fact that the prophet refers to the leaders of Jerusalem and Judah by means of expressions derived from old clan language, he avers that Micah belonged to the city elders of Judah, upon whom rested the responsibility for the upholding of social justice. In that capacity Micah advocated the rights and interests of his people on making his appearance in Jerusalem. According to Wolff a number of data tell in favour of this view. Jer. 26: 17–19 proves that the elders of Judah were thoroughly conversant with the preaching of the prophet, even a century after his appearance. By putting infidelity and other sins forcibly before his opponents, Micah seems to have been fulfilling the official duties of the city elder's profession. The *Botenformel* 'Thus says the LORD' occurs only seldom in the book of Micah, and the introductory words of 3: 8, which emphasise the 'I' of the speaker, remind one of the counsels of Wisdom; cf. Ecclus. 24: 1; Prov. 8: 12, 14ff.

In my opinion the evidence marshalled by Wolff is not enough for him to be able convincingly to characterise Micah as a city elder from Moresheth-Gath. Both the epiphanic language of the prophet (1: 2ff) and the fact that 3: 8 should be seen primarily in the framework of a polemic, not against the leaders of Jerusalem and Judah, but against the false prophets from whom Micah distances himself, argue against this theory. Furthermore, the preaching of Micah demonstrates more than once the typically prophetic style of announcing judgement; cf. 1; 2: 1–3; 3: 12; 4: 10; 5: 1 (MT 4: 14). The appeal that the elders of Judah make to Micah's preaching many decades after his death would have lost much of its cogency if they had quoted a deceased colleague who had been an elder in Moresheth-Gath. It is more likely that they were comparing the preaching of the *prophet* Jeremiah with that of an earlier prophet and not with a representative from their own circle. Micah has, to a certain degree, favoured us with a glimpse into his prophetic *Selbstverständnis* (cf. in addition to 3: 8 the passage in 2: 11, where we should translate: 'If one who walks according to the Spirit could lie and falsify, then I would rant to you of wine and strong drink'), but we grope in the dark when we try to find out what Micah's profession was when he was called to be a prophet.

Opinions as to the structure, evolution and authenticity of the seven chapters of the Book of Micah are very divergent. Some scholars still hold fast to the assertion of Stade that only the first three chapters contain material that can be traced back to Micah of Moresheth himself, e.g. Mays (1976*b*), Lescow (1972*a* and *b*), Wolff (1978*a*, p. 28), whilst Willi-Plein (1971) and Renaud (1977) assign 6: 9–15 also to the prophet. But a growing group of authors are more reserved in this respect, e.g. Weiser (1961, p. 254), Beyerlin (1959), Vuilleumier (1971), Hammershaimb (1970), Rudolph (1975), Allen (1976) and myself (1976). Apart from a number of glosses, Rudolph, for instance, regards only the pericopes 4: 1–4; 5: 7–9 (MT 6–8); 7: 8–20 as inauthentic additions to the corpus of the book. I have advanced (1976, pp. 61ff) the view that Micah 1–5 is substantially authentic and that chs. 2–5 contain a discus-

sion between Micah and his opponents. I discover the latter's words in
2:12–13; 4:1–5, 6–7, 8, 9; 4:11–13; 5:5–6 (MT 4–5); 5:8–9 (MT 7–8).
In my opinion chs. 6–7 stem from another prophet who flourished in
the Northern Kingdom shortly before the fall of Samaria and who was
therefore a contemporary of Micah of Moresheth. His name may have
been Micah as well (cf. 7: 18). If so, this would help us to explain why
his preaching was combined with that of his southern colleague. A
repercussion of the combination of the writings of both prophets can
be found in the superscription of the entire book (1: 1), in which the
period of Micah's activity has not been limited to the kingship of
Hezekiah (cf. Jer. 26: 18) but includes that of Jotham and Ahaz as well.
The period of the latter is that of the appearance of Deutero-Micah.
Further, Mic. 5: 10–15 (MT 9–14) forms a Deuteronomistic linkage
between Micah and Deutero-Micah. Thereby 'cut off' in verse 10
(MT 9) hooks into 'cut off' of verse 9 (MT 8) and 'obey' (literally 'hear')
of verse 15 (MT 14) into 'hear' of 6: 1.

It is difficult to deny that chs. 6–7 bear a completely different character from the preceding chapters: the geographic and historical information in Mic. 6–7 point, without exception, to Northern Israel (Gilgal 6:
5; Bashan and Gilead 7: 14; Carmel 7: 14; Omri and Ahab 6: 16);
neither Jerusalem nor Zion nor Judah is mentioned. The words of 6:
16 a, which should be translated: 'The images of Omri and the idols of
the house of Ahab will be destroyed' (reading weyištammēd (cf. LXX)
and taking ḥuqqōt in the sense of 'images'; cf. Jer. 10: 3), prove that the
unnamed city of 6: 9 is not Jerusalem but Samaria. Just as in Hosea,
Jeremiah and Deuteronomy, the traditions of the Exodus, the wandering in the wilderness and the conquest (cf. 6: 4–5; 7: 15) play a role,
while not a single reference to Zion theology is present. The description of the nobility in Mic. 6–7 differs from that in chs. 1–5. The
language that is used in Mic. 6–7 is completely different from that of the
preceding chapters. The view that Mic. 6–7 originated in the Northern
Kingdom is not altogether new. Burkitt defended this thesis as long
ago as 1926, and certain scholars believe that Mic. 7: 7–20 is a Northern
Israelite prophecy (cf. Willis, 1974). The predominant view that chs. 6–
7 must be dated either in the exilic or the post-exilic period seems to be
untenable. Not a single objective reason can be forwarded to support
this thesis. If this section were exilic or post-exilic, why would it be
silent about Jerusalem and Judah? Willi-Plein (1971, pp. 107–8) has
rightly refuted the theory that Mic. 7: 11 speaks of the devastated walls
of post-exilic Jerusalem (gādēr is probably never used for the walls of a

town). Furthermore, Mic. 7: 11–13 is not, as is generally assumed, an oracle of salvation but an announcement of destruction directed against the Assyrian enemy addressed in 7: 8–10 (Van der Woude, 1976, pp. 253–8). It is therefore questionable whether, in line with Gunkel (1924), 7: 7(8)–20 should be viewed as a liturgy. The numerous reminiscences of the preaching of Hosea that we encounter in chs. 6–7 provide abundant confirmation that we have to do, in this part of the book, with a prophet from Northern Israel. Any attempt to illustrate the preaching of Micah of Moresheth-Gath with material from these chapters is therefore, in my opinion, unfounded.

As far as I can see, there is no objective reason for denying that 4: 1–5: 9 (MT 8), in substance, is pre-exilic. To illustrate this we can start with Mic. 5: 5–6 (MT 4–5). The introductory words of verse 5 (MT 4), usually translated by 'And he shall be (a man of) peace', in reality do not belong to the preceding oracle and should (on the strength of 2 Sam. 17: 3) rather be rendered by: 'This one here will be all right.' The words refer to the present king of Jerusalem and refute Micah's prophecy of doom (5: 1 (MT 4: 14)) and his announcement of a new messiah (5: 2–4 (MT 1–3)). The words of verses 5–6 (MT 4–5) make no sense if not spoken at the time when Assyria was a real danger to Judah and Jerusalem. Rudolph's claim (1975, pp. 99–100) that the passage Mic. 5: 5 *b*–6 *a* (MT 4 *b*–5 *a*) must be dated in the period of the Maccabees does not carry conviction, since the Maccabees could neither have hoped that foreign allies would come to their aid nor have said: 'If Assyria (= the Seleucids!) comes into our land', because the Seleucids by then had been in Palestine already for decades. The same applies with equal force to Willi-Plein's proposal (1971, p. 94) to identify Assyria with the Persians. But if there is no reason to doubt that Mic. 5: 5–6 (MT 4–5) was spoken by the leaders of Jerusalem and Judah in Hezekiah's day, when a coalition with foreign powers against the Assyrians was quite possible, and if they express by these words the conviction that no disaster will befall the present king, so that there is no need for the expectation of another messiah, the whole section Mic. 5: 1–6 (MT 4: 14–5: 5) in all likelihood originates in the time of Micah of Moresheth-Gath. The words of Mic. 5: 1 (MT 4: 14), however, are a reply to the preceding contention of the prophet's opponents (4: 11–13), which is based on the assumption of the inviolability of Zion. These words in their turn are a reply to 4: 10 in which Micah foretells the exile of the inhabitants of Jerusalem. The latter verse answers the rhetorical question of his opponents in 4: 9, as indicated by the linguistic correspondence between the two verses. The preceding verse 4: 8, also the words of Micah's opponents, must be pre-exilic, because 'ōfel is parallel to migdāl and can only mean the acropolis of Jerusalem. Since Mic. 4: 6–7 corresponds to 2: 12–13, and since the latter verses are to be attributed to Micah's opponents, as evidenced by the introductory words of 2: 11 c ('But this people ranted') and wā'ōmar ('But I said') in 3: 1, which introduces the prophet's reply to the objection of 2: 12–13, there is no sufficient reason to deny that Mic. 4: 6–7 should be attributed to Micah's opponents. The same holds true for Mic. 4: 1–5 since, as Talmon (1971, p. 579) has correctly pointed out, verses 4 and 5 of this pericope betray a real-politisch and real-religiös tendency, caused by a fundamental reinterpretation of the Isaianic prophecy quoted in 4: 1–3. In conclusion, I do not see any convincing reason to deny that 4: 1–5: 9 (MT 8) relates a discussion between the prophet and his opponents after Micah's announcement of the devastation of Jerusalem and the Temple mountain (3: 12).

If one holds this structure and interpretation of chs. 4–5 to be correct, then the question as to the possibility of Micah's having uttered prophecies of salvation is answered; cf. Mic. 4: 10 d; 5: 2–4 (MT 1–3); 5: 7 (MT 6). But also, those scholars who do not proceed from this structure have to admit that chs. 4–5 contain numerous elements that do not conflict with the circumstances prevailing during Micah's time. The number of exegetes who ascribe the prophecy of salvation in Mic. 5: 2–4 (MT 1–3) (at least in substance; in my opinion verse 3 (MT 2) is not spurious) to Micah of Moresheth-Gath is still growing. The character-istic feature of Micah's prophecies of weal is, however, the fact that salvation will only become reality through God's total destruction of Jerusalem, his sending the population into exile, and his humiliation of her king. Therefore this prophecy of salvation is not irreconcilable with the announcement of the radical destruction of Jerusalem (3: 12).

Provided that the proposed analysis of chs. 4–5 is correct in broad lines, the redaction history of the book of Micah is much less compli-cated than Lescow (1972 a and b), Willi-Plein (1971, pp. 110–14), Renaud (1977), Mays (1976 b) and others aver. What we find in the book of Micah is (apart from a number of later glosses) a Deuteronomistic redaction that combined chs. 6–7 with chs. 1–5 by linking both by means of 5: 10–15 (MT 9–14). The same redactor changed the super-scription of the entire book into its present form and added Mic. 1: 5 c and 1: 7aß to the original text (perhaps also the last words of 6: 16a and of 6: 16 b). This Deuteronomistic redaction can be dated in the time of

King Josiah (cf. Willi-Plein on 5: 10ff (MT 9ff): 1971, p. 110), which would mean that Micah and Deutero-Micah constituted one single prophetic book from that period onward.

In his recently presented first-rate survey of new aspects of Micah research, Jeppesen (1978) has, rightly, called for a reconsideration and re-evaluation of the traditional critical understanding of the prophet, since 'it is no longer possible to defer to a comfortably concluded debate' (p. 23). But he stresses, too, that we cannot speak yet of a new debate because the various authors who have contributed to Micah research in the past decade have not come to grips with each other's points of view. It is clear, however, that recent Micah studies are likely to inaugurate a re-evaluation of the established views that have found their way into Old Testament introductions and are often reproduced quite uncritically.

Bibliography

P. R. Ackroyd 'Hosea and Jacob', *VT* 13 (1963), 245–59.

L. C. Allen *The Books of Joel, Obadiah, Jonah and Micah*, NICOT (London, 1976) (on Micah: pp. 237–404).

S. Amsler *see* E. Jacob, C. A. Keller and S. Amsler.

R. Bach 'Gottesrecht und weltliches Recht in der Verkündigung des Propheten Amos', in W. Schneemelcher (ed.), *Festschrift für Günther Dehn* (Neukirchen, 1957), pp. 23–34.

W. Beyerlin *Die Kulttraditionen in der Verkündigung des Propheten Micha*, FRLANT 54 (Göttingen, 1959).

M. Bič 'Der Prophet Amos – ein Hepatoskopos', *VT* 1 (1951), 293–6.

W. Brueggemann 'Amos iv 4–13 and Israel's Covenant Worship', *VT* 15 (1965), 1–15.

   Tradition for Crisis. A Study of Hosea (Richmond, Virginia, 1968).

   'Amos' Intercessory Formula', *VT* 19 (1969), 385–99.

M. Buber *Der Glaube der Propheten* (Zürich, 1950).

F. C. Burkitt 'Micah 6 and 7. A Northern Prophecy', *JBL* 45 (1926), 159–61.

M. J. Buss *The Prophetic Word of Hosea. A Morphological Study*, BZAW 111 (Berlin, 1969).

R. E. Clements *Prophecy and Covenant*, SBT 43 (London, 1965).

J. Coppens 'L'histoire matrimoniale d'Osée', in *Alttestamentliche Studien, Festschrift F. Nötscher*, BBB 1 (Bonn, 1950), pp. 38–45.

J. F. Craghan 'The Book of Hosea. A Survey of Recent Literature', *Biblical Theology Bulletin* 1 (1971), 81–100; 145–70.

   'Amos in Recent Literature', *Biblical Theology Bulletin* 2 (1972), 242–61.

J. L. Crenshaw 'The Influence of the Wise upon Amos', *ZAW* 79 (1967), 42–51.

'Amos and the Theophanic Tradition', *ZAW* 80 (1968), 203–15.

A. Deissler and M. Delcor La Sainte Bible, vol. VIII (Paris, 1961), Part 1: 'Osée' (Deissler), pp. 25–132.

F. Diedrich *Die Anspielungen auf die Jacob-Traditionen in Hosea 12, 1–13, 3*, Forschung zur Bibel 27 (Würzburg, 1977).

G. Farr 'The Language of Amos, Popular or Cultic?', *VT* 16 (1966), 312–24.

G. Fohrer 'Bemerkungen zum neueren Verständnis der Propheten', in *Studien zur alttestamentlichen Prophetie (1949–1965)*, BZAW 99 (Berlin, 1967), pp. 18–31.

A. Gelston 'Kingship in the Book of Hosea', OTS 19 (1974), 71–85.

B. Gemser 'Vertraagde openbaringsbewustheid', *NedThT* 15 (1960–1), 241–63.

H. Gese 'Das Problem von Amos 9,7', in *Textgemäss, Festschrift E. Würthwein* (Göttingen, 1979), pp. 33–8.

E. M. Good 'The Composition of Hosea', *SEA* 31 (1966), 21–63.

R. Gordis 'Hosea's Marriage and Message', *HUCA* 25 (1954), 9–35.

H. Gottlieb 'Amos und Jerusalem', *VT* 17 (1967), 430–63.

H. Gunkel 'Der Micha-Schluss', *ZS* 2 (1924), 145–78.

A. Gunneweg 'Erwägungen zu Amos', *ZThK* 57 (1960), 1–5.

E. Hammershaimb *The Book of Amos. A Commentary* (Oxford, 1970).

M.-L. Henry *Prophet und Tradition*, BZAW 116 (Berlin, 1969).

H. J. Hermisson *Studien zur israelitischen Spruchweisheit* (Neukirchen, 1968).

S. Herrmann *Ursprung und Funktion der Prophetie im alten Israel* (Opladen, 1976).

E. Jacob 'L'héritage cananéen dans le livre d'Osée', *RHPhR* 43 (1963), 250–9.

E. Jacob, C. A. Keller and S. Amsler *Osée, Joël, Abdias, Jonas, Amos*, Commentaire de l'AT, 11a (Neuchâtel, 1965).

K. Jeppesen 'New Aspects of Micah Research', *JSOT* 8 (1978), 3–32.

J. Jeremias 'Die Deutung der Gerichtsworte Michas in der Exilzeit', *ZAW* 83 (1971), 330–54.

O. Kaiser *Introduction to the Old Testament* (Oxford, 1975) (English translation of *Einleitung in das Alte Testament*, 2nd ed. (Gütersloh, 1970)).

A. Kapelrud *Central Ideas in Amos* (Oslo, 1956, 2nd ed. 1961).

'New Ideas in Amos', in *Volume du Congrès, Genève, 1965*, SVT 15 (Leiden, 1966), pp. 193–206.

U. Kellermann 'Der Amosschluss als Stimme deuteronomistischer Heilshoffnung', *EvTh* 29 (1969), 169–83.

D. Kinet *Ba'al und Jahwe. Ein Beitrag zur Theologie des Hoseabuches* (Frankfurt am Main, 1977).

K. Koch (and others) *Amos untersucht mit den Methoden einer strukturalen Formgeschichte*, AOAT 30 (Kevelaer and Neukirchen, 1976).

Die Propheten, vol. I: 'Assyrische Zeit', Uni-Taschenbücher 280 (Stuttgart, 1978).

H. Krszyna 'Literarische Struktur von Os. 2: 4–17', *BZ* 13 (1969), 41–59.

W. Kuhningk *Nordwestsemitische Studien zum Hoseabuche* (Rome, 1974).

C. J. Labuschagne 'Amos' Conception of God and the Popular Theology of his Time', in *Studies in the Books of Hosea and Amos, Papers read at the 7th and 8th meeting of Die O.T. Werkgemeenskap in Suid-Afrika 1964–1965* (Potchefstroom, no date), pp. 122–33.

Th. Lescow 'Redaktionsgeschichtliche Analyse von Micha 1–5', *ZAW* 84 (1972), 46–85 (= 1972*a*).

'Redaktionsgeschichtliche Analyse von Micha 6–7', *ZAW* 84 (1972), 182–212 (= 1972*b*).

G. van Leeuwen *Hosea*, De prediking van het Oude Testament (Nijkerk, 1968).

'The Prophecy of Yōm YHWH in Amos v 18–20', *OTS* 19 (1974), 113–34.

J. Lindblom *Hosea, literarkritisch untersucht* (Åbo, 1928).

L. Markert *Struktur und Bezeichnung des Scheltworts: Eine gattungskritische Studie anhand des Amosbuches*, BZAW 140 (Berlin, 1977).

J. L. Mays 'Words about the Words of Amos', *Interpretation* 13 (1959), 259–72.

Hosea, Old Testament Library (London, 1969).

Amos, Old Testament Library (London, 1969, 3rd ed. 1976) (= 1976*a*).

Micah, Old Testament Library (London, 1976) (= 1976*b*).

H. McKeating *The Books of Amos, Hosea, and Micah*, The Cambridge Bible Commentary on the New English Bible (Cambridge, 1971).

A. Murtonen 'The Prophet Amos – A Hepatoscoper?', *VT* 2 (1952), 170–1.

H. S. Nyberg *Studien zum Hoseabuche*, Uppsala Universitets Årsskrift (Uppsala, 1935).

G. von Rad *Old Testament Theology*, vol. II: 'The Theology of Israel's Prophetic Traditions' (Edinburgh and London, 1965) (English translation of *Theologie des Alten Testaments*, vol. II: 'Die Theologie der prophetischen Überlieferungen Israels' (Munich, 1960).

B. Renaud *La formation du livre de Michée*, Etudes bibliques (Paris, 1977).

R. Rendtorff 'Erwägungen zur Frühgeschichte des Prophetentums in Israel', *ZThK* 59 (1962), 145–67 (= *Gesammelte Studien zum AT* (Munich, 1975), pp. 220–42).

H. Graf Reventlow *Das Amt des Propheten bei Amos*, FRLANT 80 (Göttingen, 1962).

H. H. Rowley 'Was Amos a Nabi?', in *O. Eissfeldt, Festschrift zum 60. Geburtstag* (Halle, 1947), pp. 191–8.

'The Marriage of Hosea', *BJRL* 39 (1956–7), 200–33 (= *Men of God* (London, 1963), pp. 66–97).

W. Rudolph 'Präparierte Jungfrauen?', *ZAW* 75 (1963), 65–73.

'Eigentumlichkeiten der Sprache Hoseas', in *Studia Biblica et Semitica, Festschrift Th. C. Vriezen* (Wageningen, 1966), pp. 313–17 (= 1966*a*).

Hosea, KAT 13, 1 (Gütersloh, 1966) (= 1966*b*).

Joel–Amos–Obadja–Jona, KAT 13, 2 (Gütersloh, 1971).

Micha–Nahum–Habakuk–Zephanja, KAT 13, 3 (Gütersloh, 1975).

H. H. Schmid 'Amos. Die Frage nach der "geistigen Heimat" des Propheten', *WuD* 10 (1969), 85–103.

J. M. Schmidt 'Ausgangspunkt und Ziel prophetischer Verkündigung im 8. Jahrhundert', *Verkündigung und Forschung* 22 (1977), 65–82.

W. H. Schmidt 'Die deuteronomistische Redaktion des Amosbuches', *ZAW* 77 (1965), 168–92.

Zukunftsgewissheit und Gegenwartskritik. Grundzüge prophetischer Verkündigung, BSt 64 (Neukirchen, 1973).

H. Schult 'Amos 7.15a und die Legitimation des Aussenseiters', in *Probleme biblischer Theologie, Festschrift G. von Rad* (Munich, 1971), pp. 462–78.

S. Segert 'Zur Bedeutung des Wortes *noqed*', in *Hebräische Wortforschung, Festschrift W. Baumgartner*, SVT 16 (Leiden, 1967), pp. 279–83.

R. Smend 'Das Nein des Amos', *EvTh* 23 (1963), 404–23.

H. J. Stoebe 'Überlegungen zu den geistlichen Voraussetzungen der Prophetie des Amos', in *Wort–Gebot–Glaube, Festschrift W. Eichrodt* (Zürich, 1970), pp. 209–25.

S. Talmon 'Typen der Messiaserwartung um die Zeitwende', in *Probleme biblischer Theologie, Festschrift G. von Rad* (Munich, 1971), 571–88.

S. Terrien 'Amos and Wisdom', in *Israel's Prophetic Heritage, Essays in honor of J. Muilenburg* (London, 1962), pp. 108–15.

Th. C. Vriezen 'Prophecy and Eschatology', in *Congress Volume, Copenhagen, 1953*, SVT 1 (Leiden, 1953), pp. 199–229.

'Erwägungen zu Amos 3,2', in *Archäologie und Altes Testament, Festschrift K. Galling* (Tübingen, 1970), pp. 255–8.

P. Vuilleumier and C. A. Keller *Michée, Nahoum, Habacuc, Sophonie*, Commentaire de l'AT, 11b (Neuchâtel, 1971).

S. Wagner 'Überlegungen zur Frage nach den Beziehungen des Propheten Amos zum Südreich', *ThLZ* 96 (1971), cols. 653–70.

J. M. Ward *Hosea. A Theological Commentary* (New York, 1966).

L. Waterman 'Hosea Chapters 1–3 in Retrospect and Prospect', *JNES* 14 (1955), 100–9.

A. Weiser *Introduction to the Old Testament* (London, 1961) (English translation of *Einleitung in das Alte Testament*, 4th ed. (Göttingen, 1957)).

I. Willi-Plein *Vorformen der Schriftexegese innerhalb des A.T. Untersuchungen zum literarischen Werden der auf Amos, Hosea und Micha zurückgehenden Bücher*, BZAW 123 (Berlin, 1971).

J. T. Willis 'The Structure of the Book of Micah', *SEA* 34 (1969), 5–42 (= 1969a).

'The Structure of Micah 3–5', *ZAW* 81 (1969), 191–214 (= 1969b).

'A Reapplied Prophetic Hope Oracle', in *Studies on Prophecy*, SVT 26 (Leiden, 1974), pp. 64–76.

H. W. Wolff '"Wissen um Gott" bei Hosea als Urform von Theologie',

EvTh 12 (1952–3), 533–54 (= *Gesammelte Studien zum AT* (Munich, 1964), pp. 180–205).

'Hosea's Geistige Heimat', *ThLZ* 81 (1956), cols. 83-94 (= *Gesammelte Studien zum AT* (Munich, 1964), pp. 232–50).

Die Stunde des Amos. Prophetie und Protest (Munich, 1969).

Amos the Prophet. The Man and His Background (Philadelphia, 1973) (English translation of *Amos' geistige Heimat*, WMANT 18 (Neukirchen, 1964)).

Hosea. A Commentary on the Book of the Prophet Hosea, Hermeneia (Philadelphia, 1974) English translation of *Dodekapropheton*, vol. I: 'Hosea', BKAT 14, 1 (Neukirchen, 1961, 2nd ed. 1965).

Joel and Amos. A Commentary on the Books of the Prophets Joel and Amos, Hermeneia (Philadelphia, 1977) (English translation of *Dodekapropheton*, vol. II: 'Joel und Amos', BKAT 14, 2 (Neukirchen, 1969)). (English translation cited as Wolff, 1977 a.)

'Die eigentliche Botschaft der klassischen Propheten', *Beiträge zur alttestamentlichen Theologie, Festschrift W. Zimmerli* (Göttingen, 1977), pp. 547–57 (= 1977 b).

Mit Micha reden (Munich, 1978) (= 1978 a).

'Wie verstand Micha von Moreshet sein prophetisches Amt' in *Congress Volume, Göttingen, 1977*, SVT 29 (Leiden, 1978), pp. 403–17 (= 1978 b).

A. S. van der Woude 'Deutero-Micha: ein Prophet aus Nord-Israel?', *NedThT* 25 (1971), 365–78.

Micha, De prediking van het Oude Testament (Nijkerk, 1976, 2nd ed. 1977).

E. Würthwein 'Amos-Studien', *ZAW* 62 (1949–50), 10–52 (= *Wort und Existenz* (Göttingen, 1970), pp. 68–110).

W. Zimmerli 'Das Gottesrecht bei den Propheten Amos, Hosea und Jesaja', in *Werden und Wirken des Alten Testaments, Festschrift C. Westermann* (Göttingen and Neukirchen, 1980), pp. 216–35.

The Isaiah tradition

JOHN EATON

Our subject may be broached, happily enough, by notice of Peter Ackroyd's article 'Isaiah i–xii'. He criticises the frequent assumption that Isa. 1–39 can be treated as a separate book, and that the position of the narrative section chs. 36–9 confirms this. He suggests that such narratives have rather been added at significant points within prophetic collections. His reflections thus turn our minds once more to the question of the book as a whole.

Time was when the emphasis of scholarship had all to be on proving that Isaiah was not the author of 40–66, as well illustrated by Driver (1891). New ways of regarding the relationship of earlier and later strata of the book came into view with the growing interest in prophetic disciples as bearers of tradition. Mowinckel (1926) attempted to visualise Isaiah's community of disciples in some detail – the various classes from which the members were drawn, their common concerns and the texts (extending into other prophetic collections and Deuteronomy) that they produced, especially in the seventh century. He considered that Isa. 40–55 was added to the collection fairly certainly because the author, Deutero-Isaiah, arose from the Isaiah circle or sect. Engnell (1962) was characteristically emphatic: the book was a tradition-work consisting of three major collections (Proto-, Deutero-, Trito-Isaiah), which emanated from three tradition-circles. The living bond that connected the circles reached back also to Isaiah, and Isaianic material was present in all three collections, though especially the first.

Jones (1955) gave a valuable account of the method and motivation of Isaiah in depositing the testimony among his disciples; he showed how their consequent concern with the fulfilment of Yahweh's word is passed on to their successors, appearing in the final arrangement of chs. 1–4 and in frequent statements of the theme in chs. 40–55. My own study of the Isaianic circle (1959) envisaged a less diffuse group than that portrayed by Mowinckel; I proposed a|more definite connection of master and disciples with the centre of worship, yielding a disciplined succession into and beyond the exile. In my *Festal Drama in Deutero-Isaiah* (1979, pp. 103–14), I indicated that help may be obtained for the interpretation of chs. 40–55 if we can legitimately make comparison with dominant themes in chs. 1–39.

Meanwhile, interest in the Book of Isaiah as an entity has arisen also from other concerns, as in the comprehensive treatment of 'all the Isaiahs' by Blank (1958) and in the pioneering structuralist study of Lack (1973). J. Vermeylen (1977–8), though concentrating on chs. 1–35 and attributing redactions to schools wider than any Isaianic circle, at least finds significant correlation between chs. 56–66 and ch. 1.

In various ways, then, the threads of continuity within the book still evoke research, and I am grateful for this opportunity, in honour of a distinguished scholar, to pursue further my quest for master and disciples, for their way of work, fellowship and faith.

A tradition is carried by a group, a fellowship that, by heredity and recruitment, extends through succeeding generations. If the tradition is living and growing, it is surely the product of the work peculiar to that fellowship. It should, then, be possible to tell from the character of the tradition what is the function of the fellowship within the wider society.

To treat the Book of Isaiah as a tradition, we should need to recognise readily some dominant character that pointed to such a group and its function. To my mind that character is clear enough: repeatedly and extensively the material has the character of being the prophetic expression of God's liturgical work, the divine action as experienced and formulated in the high moments of the cult. Consequently I see the fellowship behind the book as originally one that in the wider community's worship contributed prophetic realisation and interpretation of God's action.

To illustrate this view, it will be convenient to distinguish three aspects of the deity's liturgical work: (1) His assertion of His supremacy and glory, (2) His speeches and dialogues amid the congregation, (3) His bestowal of vocation and destiny on the Davidic heir. The illustration will at first be restricted to chs. 13–14, 24–7, 33, 35, 40–66, which are the most substantial sections generally taken to be later than Isaiah's own ministry. This procedure should clarify the nature of the fellow-ship in its later generations and in the end provide a good angle of approach to Isaiah himself.

I The later strata

1 *The liturgical assertion of Yahweh's supremacy*

Most directly from the Psalms, it has become apparent that at pre-exilic Jerusalem's chief festival, forerunner of the present holy days of Tishri, there was dramatic expression of Yahweh's supreme godhead. Symbolic gestures and movements, including procession to and from stations east of the Zion Temple, represented His conquest of baneful forces and a new condition where His sovereignty shone with full brightness over His world. Numerous psalms show how the worship-pers entered into the drama of this representation, dancing and singing, falling on their faces, shouting in concert and clapping hands. We get glimpses of vivid enactments, for example in Pss. 68 and 48, and frequently we meet the prospects and hopes that belong to the new reign of God – freeing of prisoners, settling of the dispossessed, feeding of the hungry, justice for widow and fatherless, downfall of usurping gods or men, new life for all creation.

But Israel, no less than other ancient religious societies, was conscious of the personal will and changing moods of the deity and of the need to watch at all times, and especially at holy seasons, for indications of His disposition. If Biblical scholars sometimes appear to believe that until the intervention of Amos in the mid-eighth century Israelite worship-pers had always, year after year, century after century, assumed that Yahweh was invariably bland towards them, they have fallen into an absurdity. Human experience, with its ample content of deprivation and horror, will have ensured that the worshippers had much concern for signs of the divine will. One of the few stories of festal celebration, indeed, relates how the very first procession of the Ark to Jerusalem was unexpectedly halted and long suspended because of a sinister portent (2 Sam. 6 : 6f). For the great procession to be received in full assurance of its betokening salvation it was necessary that the Lord should give the word; then, and only then, could the great host of tidings-bearers bring the gospel to Zion (Ps. 68: 11 (MT 12)). We have to think, then, that at all stages of the great liturgical representation there was prophetic ministry. All was a work of the Lord, the assertion of His will in word and act, and the bearing of it into the eyes, ears and hearts of the people was above all a prophetic task. Prophets, through their visions and poetic utterances, were instrumental in the bodying forth of Yahweh's conquest and advent in the imagination of all the participants. Sometimes they would be able to focus the issues by identifying particular nations or leaders upon whom the liturgical drama would bear, as when Nahum linked Nineveh with the doomed foes of Yahweh. But a veiled and mysterious style of actualisation remained characteristic.

The exile did not bring this prophetic service to an abrupt end. In Isa. 40–55 we have a cycle of utterances given somewhere between 550 and 540 B.C. and adhering essentially to the old styles and functions in spite of limiting circumstances. While the view of several commentators that the setting was services of lament in the Babylonian exile is likely enough, the festal tradition is so prominent that one may think the assemblies were convened at the old New Year season, evoking a revival of prophetic utterance characteristic of that occasion.

Not a bald prediction of Yahweh's conquest was to be given, but a bringing of the deed into reality through ecstatic imagination and the resultant flow of poetry. Amidst the hymns that had drawn the old congregations into the drama would sound the visionary's depictions of Yahweh's appearance and demeanour, His acts and – most important of all – His weapon-like word. And this is what the cycle gives us (42: 10–15):

> Sing to Yahweh a new song...
>> Yahweh comes out like a champion,
>> like a warrior he works up his fury,
>> he chants his war-cry, he roars,
>>> he menaces his foes...
>>> 'Too long have I been quiet...
>> now like a woman giving birth I will shriek...
>> I will lay waste the mountains and hills.'

The success of Yahweh's war against rivals is followed through to accomplishment by the visionary. The city, identified as Babylon, is seen as fallen and its gods likewise captured; cutting irony makes the poetry itself a deadly weapon:

> Bel bows low, Nebo grovels...
>> Down and take your seat on the dirt.
>> Princess Babylon!

> (Isa. 46: 1; 47: 1)

The humiliation of the rival gods is the festal counterpart to the glorification of Yahweh; the dethronement of the false queen-city is the counterpart to the queenly exaltation of Zion. The visionary depiction of the images of beasts in shameful procession balances the portrayals of Yahweh's victorious advent. From Isa. 13–14 we may compare the lively realisations of Yahweh's war against oppressors, which come into focus as shattering blows against Assyria and Babylon.

The advent, as an outstanding festal event, depended on authorisation and interpretation through the prophetic ministers. Such is given abundantly in Isa. 40 and 52. The word from God is of atonement, acceptance, restoration. As saviour He will indeed make procession into Zion. The scene is already given reality by the visionary:

> See, the Lord Yahweh! He comes in as conqueror...
> his spoils with him...
> like a shepherd who herds his flock.
>
> (Isa. 40: 10f)

The reception at Zion is as in the old celebrations, when eager watch was kept:

> How beautiful on the mountains the feet of the tidings-bearer
> who tells of victory...
> who declares to Zion, 'Your God now reigns!'
>
> (Isa. 52: 7)

And again we have the hymnic call to involvement:

> Break into chants of triumph,
> waste places of Jerusalem!
>
> (Isa. 52: 9)

The prophetic announcement and exposition of the ceremonial entry is especially well represented in such later strata of the book. To speak of prophetic imitations of liturgy does not go to the heart of the matter. From consideration of Isa. 40–55, with its probable setting in the Babylonian Exile, we are led rather to think of prophetic classes, which in earlier generations functioned directly in the ceremonies, and after the end of the kingdom spoke on occasion in their traditional manner and function, as far as circumstances would allow. If they came forward at a convocation in the exile, for example, there was no actual procession of the Ark to the Temple to launch and interpret, but they could still, as of old, body forth the realities of divine work that had always lain beyond the symbols. As in the days of the full ceremonies, they could use their visions and poetic words like creative acts, dramatising in the present imagination the action of God still to come in fulness. This is not an 'imitation', then, of liturgical utterance but a continuance of traditional liturgical prophesying, albeit adapted to the reduced circumstances of the worship.

And so the entry through the gates takes place, even if the gates stand now only in the prophetic vision. The old gates were in any case but symbolic of the 'eternal doors' (Ps. 24: 7, 9), and what had always mattered most was the visionary interpretation, the knowledge that the King of Glory was ascending, triumphant over all creation. 'Now we have a mighty city', affirms the prophetic minister of Isa. 26: 1–2,

> for he has set up salvation as walls and rampart.
> Open the gates that a true-minded people may enter,
> a people keeping faith!

And the minister of Isa. 62: 10f cries:

> Pass through, pass through the gates!
> Prepare the way for the host.
> Build up, build up the highway,
> clear away the stones,
> raise a standard over the people!

The moment in the old ceremonies when 'the LORD gave the word' still lives in this ministry, as the seer continues:

> See, Yahweh has announced
> to the bounds of the world,
> 'Declare to Damsel Zion,
> See, your salvation comes in,
> see, he has his spoils with him
> and his gains before him!'

(Isa. 62: 11)

In Isa. 35: 3–4 the commission to the messengers is likewise:

> Strengthen the weak hands,
> brace the stumbling knees,
> Say to the heart of the tremulous...
> 'See, your God! He comes in with vengeance.'

– just as in Isa. 40: 1, 9–10 it is

> Comfort my people, comfort them...
> say, 'See, your God,
> see, he comes in as conqueror!'

The old use of interchanges with the gate-keepers to unfold excitingly the significance of the entry (Ps. 24) lives on in the terrible vision of Isa. 63. Let the One who would enter declare His identity and account for His appalling aspect!

> Who is this entering all smeared in red,
> his garments more crimson than at grape-harvest...
> bowed under the weight of trophies?
> – It is I who have spoken for the right,
> I who am mighty to save.
> – But why is your clothing red,
> your garments like a grape-treader's?
> – Alone I trod the wine press...
> for the day of my vengeance was in my heart
> and the year for redeeming my people had come.
>
> (Isa. 63: 1–4)

2 *God's speeches and dialogues before the congregation*

The coming and royal manifestation of God in the festivals had led naturally to his speeches as covenant-lord. Pss. 81, 95 and 50 clearly show us how, close upon his manifestation, his words would be expressed in poetic form by an inspired ministry. Through this means he reiterated the basic terms of the covenant, renewed the relationship of help and dependence and strengthened resolve with a mixture of promises and harsh admonitions. Isa. 48 represents such a situation amid the restrictions of the exile. Yahweh, of whose triumphal advent preceding passages have spoken, now addresses His people as an assembly of worshippers, echoing moments from the sacred history, mixing promise of plentiful provision with blame and threat. There are several links with the psalm speeches, especially in the yearning climax:

> O that today you would hear his voice!
>
> (Ps. 95: 7)

> O that my people would listen to me...
> I would feed them with the finest of wheat!
>
> (Ps. 81: 13, 16 (MT 14, 17))

> O that you would listen to my commandments,
> then your prosperity would be like a river!
>
> (Isa. 48: 18)

The force behind Isa. 48 seems to arise from a dispute of God and people. Earlier statements of God concerning imminent salvation and the role of Cyrus have met with disbelief and resistance. And so, as often in this cycle, God's words take on the forms of argument and dispute. In other passages, laments on behalf of the congregation are actually cited in the divine rejoinders:

> Why, Jacob, do you say...
> 'My way is hidden from Yahweh
> and my case goes unnoticed by my God?'
>
> (Isa. 40: 27)

> But Zion has said,
> 'Yahweh has forsaken me, the LORD has abandoned me.'
> (Isa. 49: 14–15)

Now such speaking by the deity in interchanges with the congregation had been characteristic of the ancient worship. His words were received with strong reaction, whether of appreciation or incredulity – impassive reception of sermons seems to be a modern eccentricity! And often the utterance of God was already occasioned by a preceding lament or intercession. In any case, there was a meeting of the parties, divine and human, and through the charismatic spokesmen there was lively dialogue. The impression is well preserved in a tiny psalm:

> Save, Yahweh, for the loyal man is no more!...
> – Because of the plundering of the poor...
> now I will arise, says Yahweh...
> – Pure words are the words of Yahweh,
> silver refined in a furnace,
> seven times purified on to the earth!
>
> (Ps. 12: 1, 5, 6)

– and the closing words reiterate the people's need. From the prophet Habakkuk we can see how the one spokesman, now facing God, now facing the congregation, could mediate the dialogue. The cultic occasion might be the summoning of a special convocation in a crisis, as Joel indicates. But from what has already been said of ancient

65

audience-participation and the liveliness of encounter in worship, we should expect that the supreme encounter, the festal epiphany, would itself sometimes develop in dialogue between God and people. The close interplay of festal majesty and lament in psalms such as 9–10, 74 and 94 strengthens this view.

There are several great dialogic sequences from a background of worship in the later strata of Isaiah. Sometimes scholars consider the sequence to have been constructed only by later redactors since the units are thought not to reflect a consistent situation. If this were so, we could still think of a tradition stemming from worship, later selected and rearranged by men still at home in this tradition. But it may be that some scholars are too exacting here in their criteria for assessing originality. In passionate and poetic conversation the speakers will not always seem to digest each other's points and they may reflect differing views of the common situation. And it is of the essence of poetic prophecy that stock expressions and lines of thought dominate the utterance to the exclusion of objective description of the current circumstances. If the sequences in question are allowed to speak as they stand, with the benefit of these considerations, they do convey impressions of genuinely tense and lively dialogue in charismatic worship and so may illustrate for us the experience of the circle behind the book.

At the outset of the sequence in Isa. 59, the speech already sounds like a rejoinder. Lament that Yahweh's reach seems too short to save, His ear too deaf to hear etc. will have preceded. The prophetic answer affirms that there is nothing amiss with Yahweh's hand or ear, but much is wrong with the people's hands and mouths. The condemnation becomes harsher in verses 5–8, aimed now at a 'they' (some particular group?) who 'hatch adder's eggs' and 'weave spider's webs'. On behalf of the people the reply is contrite, confessing a sinfulness that keeps them pitifully in darkness, bereft of God's help;

> We grope for the wall like blind men,...
> stumble at midday as if at nightfall,
>   we fall among the living like dead men,
> all groaning like bears,
> moaning with moaning of doves...
> our offences are many in your sight
> and our sins witness against us.

> (Isa. 59: 10–12)

At length the prophet perceives that God is moved to intervene. The lamentation that the long-awaited saving rule of God does not come is answered with vivid pictures of Yahweh in panoply hastening to save 'Zion and the penitents in Jacob' (verse 20).

In the great sequence of chs. 63–5 it may be that the starting-point is indeed the opening vision of the god at the gates, red with the blood of crushed oppressors. The vision of help brings reassurance but, as in Ps. 82, might be followed with prayer for speedy realisation. Such prayer here flows on at length (Isa. 63: 7–64: 12); lament and admission of sin support the central plea: 'O that you would rend the heavens and come down!' (Isa. 64: 1). The concluding appeal,

> 'Will you refrain yourself for these things, Yahweh,
> will you be silent and afflict us to the extreme?'
>
> (Isa. 64: 12)

receives a rejoinder (Isa. 65: 1 *b*), sharply contesting the interpretation that God is aloof and silent. On the contrary, He had come when not sought, and He was the first to spread out hands, imploring His people! But they had been too preoccupied with their sins to know. For some at least then, doom is in prospect, though for others promises are unfolded.

Comparison is suggested with Isa. 26. After the scene at the gates (verses 1–6), evocative of hopes of salvation, the response is a lament (verses 7–19) urging the need for speedy realisation. The larger context, Isa. 24–7, is much easier to appreciate if it is seen to arise from genuine prophecy in worship, whether from a period when the great rites symbolising Yahweh's work could be carried out or whether from more restricted times when the prophetic expression of the congregation's encounter with Yahweh depended more on tradition than on present ritual. All the elements are appropriate to the prophetic ministries in worship, whether mediating announcements of God's work or direct speech of God or – from the congregation's side – leading laments, intercessions or glad celebrations. Again and again it is obvious that one element calls forth another, as in living experience. Announcement (24: 1–3) has its response in lament, urging the need for intervention (24: 4–12); this is met by further assurance, rising to hymnic praise (24: 13–16*a*), only to be followed by a prophetic revelation, which passes through terror to declaration that Yahweh is to 'become King' on Mount Zion (24: 16*b*–23). Nor should the eschatological tendency of the material make us suppose a great gulf lies between this prophesying and that in pre-exilic ceremonies. The symbolic and sacramental character of the old rites of Yahweh's royal advent meant that beyond the festal day a greater Day was apprehended. Celebration and interpretation of the former could be the occasion for prophecy about the latter, as is discernible in Zephaniah and Amos. And so in Isa. 25 it is a psalm of thanksgiving (verses 1–5) that follows the prophecy of Yahweh's kingship. This passes easily into further prediction of Yahweh's work to swallow up death (verses 6–8), and the chapter ends with a congregational song of thanksgiving (verses 9–12). Ch. 26, as mentioned, moves from a psalm of victorious entry to lamenting prayer for realisation, then confidence of having been heard (verses 18b–19) and an exhortation to the congregation (verses 20–1). In Isa. 27 the eschatological aspect – 'in that day' – is still closely adhering to the symbolic acts in the old festivals: the chaos monster defeated, Yahweh's song of love for His 'vineyard' (bride) Israel, the blaring of the great shofar, summoning the poor and needy to worship Yahweh in His holy mountain in Jerusalem.

The liturgical dialogue was indeed a fluid interchange, bringing not only oracle in response to lament but also lament (urging realisation) in response to promise, hymns and thanksgivings in response to revelation, and doublings of the whole series in quest of corroboration. The fluidity is well represented in Isa. 33. In the characteristically veiled style, announcement is made of God's intervention against the oppressor (verse 1): 'Woe to you, destroyer...!' The congregational response is lamenting prayer for realisation (verse 2): 'Yahweh...be our salvation in the time of distress!' This in turn evokes visionary depiction of Yahweh intervening to scatter the nations and appear 'in majesty on high...filling Zion with good rule and order' (verses 5–6). But then the ground is traversed again in search of confirmation. There is fresh lament portraying the antithesis of the celebrations of God's kingship:

> ministers wail in the court,
> those that should bring the good tidings weep bitterly,
> the processional routes are in disrepair.

> (Isa. 33: 7–9)

An answering oracle is given (verses 10–12): 'Now I will arise, says Yahweh...' This is reinforced by the little dialogue of verses 13–16, so reminiscent of the processional Ps. 24; Yahweh announces his mighty work far and near, a manifestation in Zion that sets her sinners quaking, and so comes the question,

> Who among us can abide with the devouring flame...?

– and the *torah*-style answer,

> He who walks rightly and speaks justly...
> > such may dwell on the heights...
> his bread provided, his water secured.

Then comes a firm, clear promise, as though to the loyal man just described (verses 17–20): he will 'look upon Zion, city of our festival' and see peace; his eyes shall see Zion's king in splendour, while no trace remains of the foreign inspectors who pried and requisitioned. The rejoinder to all this promise is a thankful hymn in congregational form (verses 21–2):

> Yes, there Yahweh will triumph for us...
> Yahweh is our ruler, Yahweh is our governor,
> Yahweh is our king, he will save us.

In the examples considered, we have met great tracts of material that owe their dialogic character to the double role of the prophetic ministries in worship. Prophets, gifted in poetry and chant, were foremost in leading the moving appeals to God and in announcing His reply, in celebrating the victories of God and in bodying them forth in visionary depiction. Interchanges in the setting of assemblies for worship may have passed through one minister or sometimes unfolded through the contributions of several from the circle. In momentous times the whole dialogue, well remembered, might be recorded in writing as a testimony for the time of fulfilment.

3 *Liturgical declaration of royal destiny*

> A king in his beauty your eyes shall behold...
> > Behold Zion, city of our festival!
> > Your eyes shall behold Jerusalem.
> > > (Isa. 33: 17–20)

In prophecies so much concerned with the royal city, the king of course has his place. All the more so, since from early times prophets assisting in the presentation of Yahweh's festal work would have words of intercession and destiny for the chief servant of Yahweh's kingship, the Davidic ruler. Historical books and Psalms attest the importance of prophetic ministers in the rites of royal installation or renewal, and even in the post-exilic period it can be seen from Haggai, Zechariah and Deutero-Zechariah that prophets were ready as of old to assist in the royal designation, installation and declarations of destiny. Despite all the controversy about the Servant Songs and adjacent pieces, it is generally conceded that the forms of the royal oracles live on:

> See, my Servant whom I uphold,
> my Chosen in whom my soul delights!
> I put my spirit on him,
> he shall send forth good rule to the nations...
> I have summoned you as rightful heir,
> your hand I grasp...
> you will bring prisoners out from dungeons,
> dwellers in darkness from prison.
>
> (Isa. 42: 1–7)

> See, my Servant shall be triumphant,
> very high shall he be, exalted, supreme...
> I give the multitudes as his portion
> and the masses he may take as his spoil.
>
> (Isa. 52: 13–53: 12)

The connection with this kind of prophetic role in ritual is evidenced in the culminating ch. 55: 3:

> And I will conclude for you an everlasting covenant,
> the permanent promises for David.

Some speeches of royal character in the first person may also descend from liturgical scenes where the prophetic voice spoke for the king:

> The spirit of the Lord Yahweh is upon me
> because Yahweh has anointed me...
>
> (Isa. 61: 1)

> Yahweh has called me from the womb,
> in my mother's belly he cited my name
> and appointed my mouth to be a sharp sword,
> in the shadow of his hand he hid me,
> yes a polished arrow he made me,
> in his quiver he concealed me,
> and he said to me, You are my Servant,
> 'Israel' through whom I will manifest my glory.
>
> (Isa. 49: 1–3)

If the old prophetic festal role of defining the Davidic destiny within the kingship of God is not as obvious here as, for example, in Zech. 9: 9–10, its influence is nevertheless strong. In times of despair, even when the old ritual framework had been broken, the festal vision that the seers had contributed could still renew itself and be conveyed in glowing poetry: Yahweh will come to His Temple as King and the irrevocable covenant with His royal Servant will take effect.

II The prophet Isaiah and the liturgy

We have now to consider whether this decidedly liturgical character of the prophesying in the later strata is matched in the fundamental deposits of the book. As mentioned above, one must first recognise that the prophetic ministries in worship were not bound to be invariably bland. The harshly threatening character of all the relevant psalms (50, 81, 95) helps us to recognise the possibility that, on occasion, prophets would interpret Yahweh's mind towards his congregation as angry. We can then recognise a key role of the prophetic classes when Isa. 1: 10f pronounces upon the acceptability of the proffered worship. For once the verdict is negative and strongly expressed, but the way to reconciliation and to the securing of harvests is also presented.

The great ch. 1 reminds us of the speeches of the manifest covenant-god to his congregation and to some extent also of the dialogues of God and congregation. The opening ('Hear you heavens, listen earth, for it is Yahweh who speaks...': Isa. 1: 2), so reminiscent of Ps. 50's speech before 'those who have made a covenant with me over rites of sacrifice', is surely from a ministry active when Yahweh came before the great assembly of covenanters and reviewed the relationship. The variety of form-units that follows may not result entirely from a process of collecting. The flow of dialogue plays some part, and the 'catchwords' may simply show how one speech prompts another. For the people, in a style like Ps. 124 the prophet responds (Isa. 1: 9): 'If Yahweh of Hosts had not left us a remnant...' (the thought prompted by the use of the same verb (*yathar*) in his preceding speech) 'we should soon have been like Sodom, we should have resembled Gomorrah'; the pathetic 'communal thanksgiving' only stirs renewed rebuke of those who can indeed be seen as 'rulers of Sodom and people of Gomorrah' (1: 10), though the aim is repentance:

> Wash and be cleansed!
> Put away the evil of your deeds!
>
> (Isa. 1: 16)

There is indeed invitation to dialogue in the promise of expiation:

> Come now, let us argue it out together,
>> says Yahweh,
> though your sins are as scarlet
>> they shall become white as snow.

(Isa. 1: 18)

It is almost the oracle of Ps. 81 in summary:

> If you are willing and heedful,
> you shall eat the good produce of the land;
>> if you refuse and rebel,
> you shall be eaten by the sword.

(Isa. 1: 19-20)

From 1: 21 to 2: 22 there are elements similar to those which occur with striking coherence in the book of Zephaniah – especially the ideal of righteous Zion, now sadly perverted but soon to be restored by judgement, and the terrible depictions of the Day of the Lord. The ritual advent of Yahweh, with the attendant purification and glorification of Zion, is here surely the starting-point for these visions; prophetic ministry in the ceremonies has here excelled itself in interpreting the sacrament of the Lord's festal work.

Zion as festal bride is the concern of the song in ch. 5. Fundamental relations are celebrated as new in the liturgy. Yahweh who comes as new King comes also as bridegroom to His bride Zion. The prophetic spokesman who may give the decrees of Yahweh the King is for the moment the 'friend of the bridegroom', like the figure in human weddings who must lead the festivities or, if need be, speak for the groom if there is dispute with the bride and her family. With consummate art, the prophet seems to begin with a praising love-song for the bride, her husband's 'vineyard'. It turns into an accusation of infidelity, and by the skill of his parable the prophet has the hearers ponder like a judicial conclave, only to condemn themselves. A loving song would, no doubt, have been the usual message of the prophets for the occasion – such as is represented in Isa. 27: 2f – but within the same prophetic ministries the possibility of an adverse message always existed and is here used to perfection.

The festal assertion of God's kingship and the subsequent festal speech of God are both vividly present in the experience recorded in ch. 6. It is important to recall that the earthly worship was one with the heavenly. Ps. 29, for example, shows how, when Yahweh takes His seat above the heavenly ocean, homage is made by heavenly beings and man alike, and His *heykal*, above and below, resounds with the ascription 'Glory!' The manifestation symbolised in Zion's rites is cosmic, and earth and heaven together thunderously acknowledge and celebrate (Ps. 150). So it is not enough to note that in Isa. 6 the high throning of Yahweh, the responsive acclamations of the seraphim, the manifestation of kingship signified by the robes and the world-wide shining of glory, the shaking of the thresholds at the din of the acclaim, the 'house' filled with smoke – all resemble moments in the liturgy. What we have here is rather the very event that the liturgy mediated, the manifestation of Yahweh's kingship, acclaimed simultaneously in heaven and in Zion. Here was an occasion when the prophetic role of expressing the meaning of the liturgical event was fulfilled through an experience of unfathomable depth. In his visionary trance Isaiah sees the heavenly reality shining through the earthly with overwhelming clarity. It is notable too how the expiation by the altar-coal reveals the unity of ritual and ethical notions in his mind.

From the deliberations of God the King in His council the decrees of the new reign are issued. To 'this people', anxiously awaiting the characterisation of the year to come, the prophet bears the message. Has Yahweh crowned the new year to be one of 'good' (Ps. 65 : 11 (MT 12))? Does he 'pronounce for prosperity' (Ps. 85 : 8 (MT 9))? Alas, the message is of the greatest severity, and the prophet's intercessory 'How long O Lord' has brought only confirmation.

For illustration of the ministry of interpreting the rites of Davidic installation we may adduce here Isa. 9: 1–7 (MT 8: 23*b*–9: 6). Here Davidic destiny is unfolded by the prophet in a ceremony marking a happy event in the Davidic succession, though it is not agreed whether the event was the installation of a new king (thereby hailed as new-born and God's son) or the birth of a prince who is invested as heir to the throne. Through the customary dual prophetic role, speech is first for God, then for people, then again for God. First there is a concrete prophecy: three areas of Northern Israel taken by the Assyrians in 734–732 B.C. will be restored (verse 1, (MT 8 : 23)). Then the situation is interpreted by the voicing of a congregational thanksgiving to God:

> The people that walked in darkness
>   see a bright dawn...
> you have given cause for great rejoicing...
> for a boy is born for us and a son given to us,
>   and power to rule is laid on his back
>   and he has proclaimed his name

'He who plans marvellously, mighty hero,
father for ever, prosperous prince'.

(Isa. 9: 2–6 (MT 1–5))

Then the prophet can give as it were God's rejoinder, a further prediction of destiny: 'Increase of dominion and prosperity shall be without end over the throne of David' (verse 7 (MT 6)).

III Conclusion

The fundamental materials of the book that have just been sampled – mighty words in chs. 1, 2, 5, 6 and 9 – can thus be seen to match the character of the later strata as expressions of Yahweh's liturgical work. It should be clear enough that Isaiah himself shared in the prophetic role of disclosing the meaning of the rites through vision and poetic utterance. What was to be expected from Yahweh's advent to Zion and assertion of His sovereignty, what was Yahweh's message of destiny for His covenant people and His reaction to their pleas, what destiny was laid on the shoulders of the Davidic representative – to all such weighty matters, brought near by the ceremonies, Isaiah, perhaps the greatest of all the charismatic ministers, contributed. The continuity of social function through the strata of the book is, then, strongly marked, and it seems to be reflected also in the way that the oldest collections are interspersed and rounded off with cultic pieces that could be of any age – for example the psalms of ch. 12, when the worshippers would draw water with rejoicing from the wells of salvation (verse 3):

Cry out and sing, queenly Zion,
for manifest in your midst is the Holy One of Israel!

(Isa. 12: 6)

It is all the more significant then, when we pass from these broad observations of unity of role to the information about Isaiah, his tradition and his disciples afforded by ch. 8.

Having bound the testimony
and sealed the oracles in [or 'among'] my disciples,
I wait for Yahweh
who has hidden his face from the house of Jacob
and I look in hope for him.
See! I and the disciples that Yahweh has given me
are signs and portents in Israel

from the presence of Yahweh of Hosts
who abides on the mountain of Zion.
    And when they say to you
  'Consult the ghosts...',
    then to the oracles and the testimony!

(Isa. 8: 16–20)

The act of forming the group is not reported but taken for granted; it is
a customary phenomenon, and it is anticipated that the group will be
consulted for divinatory guidance, as recognised prophetic groups
were, especially at the cultic centres. What has occasioned the mention
of the disciples is the special responsibility now laid upon them – to
guard Isaiah's holy utterances through the time of darkness until the
time of fulfilment, and to reiterate them when the people ask for
guidance. The passage is rich in implications for the Isaiah tradition. In
the orbit of the cultic mountain, throne-centre of Yahweh of Hosts,
lives the fellowship of Isaiah's disciples, with special charge to preserve
and apply his teachings through years of faithful endurance. Master
and disciples are one in the vocation to be themselves signs. The conditions are surely established here for the birth of a tradition of the
greatest tenacity and devotion.

Accordingly, we may conclude that the Book of Isaiah, which has
the characteristics of being a tradition and which contains a record of the
solemn founding of a tradition, should indeed be regarded as essentially
the fixation of the tradition that flowed from Isaiah through his fellowship of prophetic disciples into the period of the exile and a little beyond.
It is characterised through all its main contents by the function that its
bearers maintained in essence through all vicissitudes: they shared in
and carried forward the ancient prophetic ministries of making real to
the congregation the divine work and will brought near in the liturgy.
That this prophetic circle should have left us a tradition, and moreover
one of such coherence and grandeur, is to be explained from the solemn
and deliberate foundation so fortunately recorded in ch. 8. Aptly does
the Te Deum lead our thoughts:

'To thee cherubim and seraphim continually do cry,
Holy, holy, holy...
the goodly fellowship of the prophets praise thee,
the noble army of martyr-witnesses praise thee!'

Bibliography

P. R. Ackroyd 'Isaiah I–XII: Presentation of a Prophet', SVT 29 (1977), 16-48.

H. Barth *Die Jesaja-Worte in der Josiazeit, Israel und Assur als Thema einer produktiven Neuinterpretation der Jesaja-überlieferung*, WMANT 48 (Neukirchen-Vluyn, 1977).

S. H. Blank *Prophetic Faith in Isaiah* (London, 1958).

K. J. Cathcart 'Kingship and the Day of Yhwh in Isaiah 2.6–22', *Hermathena* 125 (Dublin, 1978), 48–59.

H. Cazelles 'La vocation d'Isaie (ch. 6) et les rites royaux', *Homenaje a Juan Prado* (Madrid, 1975), pp. 89–108.

R. J. Coggins 'The Problem of Isaiah 24–27', *ET* 90 (1979), 328–33.

S. R. Driver *Introduction to the Literature of the Old Testament* (Edinburgh, 1891).

J. H. Eaton 'The Origin of the Book of Isaiah', *VT* 9 (1959), 138–57.
Festal Drama in Deutero-Isaiah (London, 1979).
Vision in Worship (London, 1980).

I. Engnell 'Profeter', in *Svenskt Bibliskt Uppslagswerk* (Stockholm, 1962), vol. I, cols. 1140–7.

W. L. Holladay *Isaiah: Scroll of a Prophetic Heritage* (Grand Rapids, 1978).

A. R. Johnson *The Cultic Prophet and Israel's Psalmody* (Cardiff, 1979).

D. R. Jones 'The traditio of the oracles of Isaiah of Jerusalem', *ZAW* 67 (1955), 226–46.

R. Lack *La symbolisme du livre d'Isaïe*, Analecta Biblica 59 (Rome, 1973).

S. Mowinckel *Jesaja-disiplene* (Oslo, 1926).

A. Schoors 'Isaiah, the minister of royal anointment?', *Instruction and Interpretation*, OTS 20 (Leiden 1977), pp. 85–107.

J. Vermeylen *Du prophète Isaïe à l'apocalyptique: Isaïe i–xxxv, miroir d'un demi-millenaire d'expérience religieuse en Israël*, Etudes Bibliques (2 vols., Paris, 1977–8).

E. Würthwein 'Der Ursprung der prophetischen Gerichtsrede', *ZThK* 49 (1952), 1–15.
'Kultpolemik oder Kultbescheid?', in *Tradition und Situation* (Göttingen, 1963), pp. 115–30.

An alternative prophetic tradition?

RICHARD COGGINS

In the 1976 *Book List* of the Society for Old Testament Study Peter Ackroyd wrote an appreciative review of R. E. Clements' *Prophecy and Tradition*, which ended thus:

> An excellent and stimulating survey; but there is very little concern with prophecy apart from the main figures, with little or no mention of Joel, Nahum, Habakkuk, Zephaniah, Haggai or Zechariah. It is essentially one prophetic pattern that is examined here; one has the uneasy feeling that if we knew more about other kinds of prophecy – often a field for extravagant speculation – we might see more clearly how this main 'style' has imposed itself and made us read all prophecy in one way.

The review is characteristic of its author both in its generous appreciation and in its care to warn that an accepted pattern or a scholarly consensus may need a greater degree of modification than would appear. Much study of the prophets in recent years has indeed assumed that one tradition can be invoked to account for all their characteristic concerns and emphases.

A generation ago the situation was markedly different. I. Engnell, in an article substantially dating from the 1940s, argued that '*broadly speaking*, the prophetic literature may be divided into two main types, which may be called the liturgy type and the *diwan* type' (Engnell, 1970, p. 166), and he went on to list Joel, Habakkuk, Nahum and Deutero-Isaiah as characteristic examples of the 'liturgy type'. Engnell's work aroused violent controversy in his own lifetime, and there have been few scholars outside Scandinavia who have accepted his views without drastic modification. Nevertheless, it seems to be true that a divison somewhat along the lines postulated by Engnell – who was himself dependent on earlier work by A. Haldar (1945) – has in practice governed much subsequent research into the prophetic

77

literature, even though the Arabic term *diwan*, meaning 'collected works' has rarely been used. Thus it is not only at an elementary level that a distinction is made between a 'main stream', from the great eighth-century prophets through Jeremiah and Ezekiel to Deutero-Isaiah (who has not usually been set apart in the way proposed by Engnell), and perhaps including Haggai and Zechariah, and what we can only call 'the rest'.

The purpose of this essay is to consider 'the rest', not in the sense of attempting an introduction to, or commentary upon, each of them but with the more restricted aim of considering whether there is some recognisable sense in which they, or some of them, embody a distinct alternative tradition to that which is recognisable in the main stream. As will become apparent, there is an ambiguity in the word 'tradition' itself that has contributed to the problem. The primary data that are presented to us are somewhat contradictory; on the one hand, in the process of establishing a canon of sacred writings, the twelve Minor Prophets were perceived as sharing a common identity; on the other hand, a great deal of modern scholarly effort has been at pains to emphasise the differences between the different books. At first glance the only thing that might be regarded as common to Joel, Obadiah, Jonah, Nahum, Habakkuk, Zechariah 9–14 and Malachi is the fact that we cannot date any of them. (The apparent exception is Jonah, for whom 2 Kings 14: 25 supplies a point of reference; but it is all but universally agreed that the book is of much later, probably post-exilic, date.)

Clearly, therefore, no single alternative tradition holds these diverse collections together, and greater precision will be needed in establishing the criteria with which we are to work. We can begin by eliminating some of the collections from further consideration. Jonah stands out as unique among the Latter Prophets by virtue of its being in its entirety a story about a prophet, a prophetic legend, whereas that literary form plays a very minor role in the Latter Prophets as a whole. But if we take into account the material relating to prophets in Samuel and Kings, or even the third-person stories relating to Isaiah and Jeremiah, more appropriate analogues for the story of Jonah are found, and we have a good example of one stage in the development from the earlier prophetic legends to the type of story characteristic of that strand of later Judaism which is illustrated by such books as Esther and Judith.

Zechariah 9–14 and Malachi can also be dismissed from consideration here. There are major problems relating to these collections which have no solution in sight, but they are not of the kind with which we are at present concerned. They relate to such matters as dating, history of redaction and (particularly in the case of Zechariah 9–14) relation to Zechariah 1–8, rather than with the possibility of prophetism of a different type.

Obadiah, on the other hand, cannot be simply set aside. The very problematic relationship between Obadiah and Jeremiah 49 is not immediately relevant, but in another way Obadiah does embody certain characteristics to which we shall need to return. It consists of a single instance of the category 'oracles against foreign nations', the language of which will be seen to provide one of the connecting links between the collections we are here concerned with. Without giving detailed consideration to Obadiah, therefore, it needs to be borne in mind as a possible further example of the type of material that is our primary concern.

That material consists of the books of Joel, Nahum and Habakkuk. The order is that in which they are found in the collection of the twelve Minor Prophets, but it is widely argued – though not universally agreed, as we shall see – that Joel is post-exilic, and it may therefore be proper to consider Nahum and Habakkuk first. This is appropriate, not only on grounds of dating but because it is with these two prophets that questions have most often been raised regarding the possibility of a radically different type of prophecy from that found in the 'main stream'.

If we turn our attention first to Nahum, the idea has long been current that Nahum was a cultic prophet. Haupt (1907) categorised the book as a liturgical collection, though in his view the conventional seventh-century dating was a 'cover' for a work actually written in Maccabean times. But it was Haldar (1947) who worked out in detail the idea of Nahum as a cult-prophet in the period when the book was ostensibly dated, and the book was for him an announcement of the inevitable doom of Nineveh, using terminology borrowed from the myth-clothed language of the Jerusalem cult. Such an interpretation has not been universally followed – Rudolph, for example, in his commentary (1975) firmly rejected such an understanding – but it has continued to exercise an important influence, not least in the judgement of the prophet as an individual figure.

Partly because of the contrast with the 'main stream', partly because of a continuing suspicion of too close a cultic involvement, this view of Nahum has led to his being grouped among those prophets whose understanding of the people's situation differed so drastically from that of the great tradition that they were roundly condemned. Thus many interpreters, such as Eissfeldt (1965, pp. 415f), have seen in this book a prophecy of salvation of the type condemned by Jeremiah. Indeed the question has even been raised whether Nahum might not properly be regarded as a false prophet (de Vries, 1966, p. 476; Fohrer, 1970, p. 451), and the same point is raised in a slightly different way by the suggestion that Nahum's oracles were originally directed against his own people and only later reinterpreted by cultic prophets and put to a different use (Jeremias, 1969, pp. 20–42). If such a view seems implausible as it stands, it may nevertheless alert us to an important question, which has been given increasing prominence in recent years, and is vital to this whole issue of an alternative tradition, that is to say, the nature of the redactional process undergone by prophetic books. To concentrate exclusively on the prophetic figure and his individuality is to run the risk of supposing that the words of the book come to us directly from Nahum himself, without any significant editorial or redactional process intervening.

The importance of this issue is clear enough when we reflect on the way in which prophecy speaking of the doom of Assyria would need to be reinterpreted if it were to continue to hold the attention of succeeding generations. As the real empirical Assyria became no more than a stylised element in ancient traditions, it became necessary for the oracles of Nahum to be reinterpreted in the light of new circumstances. At one level this could be done by understanding 'Assyria' as an archetypal enemy and oppressor, as in the *Nahum Commentary* from Qumran, where the lion and its den of Nahum 2 are applied to 'Demetrius king of Greece' and subsequent rulers of that period (Vermes, 1962, pp. 231ff).

But at another and more positive level this interpretive process might concentrate less on the enemy to be overthrown than on the supremacy of Israel's god over all oppressors. At this level Nahum exemplifies an important element in both Jewish and Christian liturgical tradition, where 'enemies' of many kinds have lost their specific historical associations and have become symbols, stereotypes even, of the evil forces that ineffectually threaten God's control of the world.

The nature of the redactional process through which the oracles of Nahum have passed is clearly, therefore, an important element in our consideration. Before examining that in greater detail, however, it is appropriate to consider two other questions, both of which relate to the idea of Nahum as a cultic prophet, and the second of which will arise again in the consideration of Habakkuk and Joel. These are, first, the problems posed by the acrostic in ch. 1; and secondly, the relation between words of Nahum and other prophetic collections in the Old Testament.

It has been generally agreed for more than a century that traces of an acrostic can be detected in Nahum 1 (Rudolph, 1975, pp. 153–7 for a history of interpretation), though it is unlikely that the attempts of older commentators to trace it through the whole of the chapter or through the whole of the Hebrew alphabet should be accepted. Cathcart (1973, pp. 12–14) rightly warns against emending the text in a purely speculative way in order to restore a fuller acrostic pattern. In any case, this acrostic is unique in that it is the only clearly established example of this form in the prophetic corpus, but it remains doubtful whether it is legitimate to reach from this the further conclusion that Nahum himself differed in some discernible way from other prophets. Regrettably, much more effort has been expended in attempts to discover complete or partial acrostics than in the investigation of their significance and whether or not they had a specific purpose. Though it can be argued that the use of a complete alphabetical acrostic might signify completeness, and this has even been applied to the use of half the alphabet, which seems likely to be the extent of the acrostic here (Christensen, 1975, p. 171), we really have not advanced beyond the traditional theory that acrostics were used for pedagogical or mnemonic purposes, which might be applicable to prophecy as to other literary forms. In other words, it is probably right to discern in the use of an acrostic in Nahum one example of an inter-relation between prophetic forms and those characteristic of the Psalms. Links of this type are now recognizable over a broad spectrum of the prophetic literature, and the fact of such a link in Nahum should therefore occasion no more surprise than does, say, the occurrence in Isa. 42 of the 'new song' theme so well known from many psalms. The nature of the link is clearly complex, and some of its implications are discussed elsewhere in this volume; but it cannot be used of itself to establish the point that Nahum differs in some identifiable way from other prophetic collections.

With regard to the second point, we have already observed that Engnell linked Nahum and Deutero-Isaiah as examples of the 'liturgy-type' of prophecy. Without subscribing to the wider conclusions that he drew from this, it is revealing to observe some of the links between Nahum and Isa. 40–55 as part of our attempt to place Nahum within the larger context of Old Testament prophecy. One example, the use of a literary form particularly characteristic of the Psalms, has already been noted; various other links may now be traced.

First, it may be significant that the acrostic in Nahum is the only extended section of the book to have no reference to Assyria. It is descriptive of the LORD's power in wrath and judgement, which is applied to Nineveh only in later parts of the book. This is comparable to the way in which psalmic material is reapplied in Isa. 40–55, in the circumstances of the Babylonian exile. (It should perhaps be stated that in my view recent attempts to argue that the dependence is here wrongly stated, and that the psalms are secondary to Isa. 40–55, remain unconvincing.)

Secondly, in one passage there is a verbal identity between Nahum and Isaiah. Nahum 1: 15a (MT 2: 1a) is identical, save for the introductory *hinneh*, with Isa. 52: 7a. The Book of Isaiah has received many more commentaries than has Nahum, and to a remarkable extent commentators seem able to wax lyrical about the passage in Isa. 52 without any reference to Nahum, though some have argued that Nahum is dependent on Deutero-Isaiah, without expressing any view as to the implications for dating Nahum (North, 1964, p. 221). More immediately relevant is the view (Gray, 1961, p. 17) that the Isaiah passage depends on Nahum, which in turn owes its language to the Jerusalem cult. But it may be proper to question whether this judgement confuses two types of dependence that are better kept apart; if the language used is that of the Jerusalem cult, is the literary dependence of one prophetic collection on the other necessarily required? The immediate context in each case suggests further Jerusalemite links: in Isaiah the conclusion of the verse is strongly reminiscent of the psalms of Yahweh's kingship; in Nahum the allusion to the Jerusalem festal round seems clear. Gray, in his article, takes as his starting-point the assumption that Nahum differed from other prophets as being a Jerusalem cultic prophet, but, in so far as many of the prophets whose oracles have been preserved have used cultic language, the assumption seems to be unnecessary. Many prophets were able to draw on cultic language in a variety of ways as an integral part of their message.

The link between Nahum 1: 15a and Isa. 52: 7a is only the closest of many such between Nahum and the book of Isaiah. Nahum 1: 4

seems to betray similarities with Isa. 33: 9 and 50: 2, and Nahum 1: 15 *b* is closely related to Isa. 52: 1 *b*. More generally a comparison between Nahum and the foreign-nations oracles in Isaiah – both, incidentally, introduced by the title *massa* (RSV 'oracle') (Nahum 1: 1 and frequently in Isa. 13–23) – shows the reliance of both on the same imagery. For example, Nahum 2: 11–12 provides a whole series of images of the devastation of Nineveh and its effects for which close parallels can be found in the Isaianic oracles against the nations.

Thus far, therefore, we note that the particular linguistic usage of Nahum shows many links with the Book of Isaiah, which illustrate the Jerusalemite background and concerns of each, without any suggestion that Nahum should be seen as standing in a different tradition. Yet the impression of the strangeness of Nahum is not entirely dispelled, and at this point it may be helpful to give some consideration to the redactional process by which the book reached its present form.

Several of the essays in the present volume illustrate the way in which an interest in the redaction of different prophetic collections has been a characteristic feature of recent scholarly study of the Old Testament. Such a surge of interest often involves a risk of putting forward theories that outrun the evidence, as may be the case with the view of Jeremias (1969) that Nahum's oracles of doom were originally directed against his own fellow-countrymen and only at a later stage transformed into oracles against Nineveh; Schulz (1973, pp. 135–53) has shown the weaknesses inherent in this type of argument. More relevant may be the apparent absence from Nahum of any sign of Deuteronomistic reworking.

Recent studies have shown how important and widespread this Deuteronomistic stage seems to have been. Long accepted in the case of Jeremiah, it is now widely held as influential for all the eighth-century prophets (Vermeylen, 1977–8, pp. 693–709). But whereas all these collections have undergone such a process, in the case of Nahum no traces of this particular type of development seem to be present.

It would, however, be wrong to conclude from this that the oracles of Nahum are unaware of the mainstream of Old Testament tradition. In addition to the links of the type already discussed, there are close associations with other ancient ways of expressing Israel's traditions. Thus, for example, in Nahum 1: 2 the LORD is spoken of as a 'jealous God' in a form found elsewhere only at Joshua 24: 19, though the theme is integral to the Decalogue. Nahum 1: 3 uses expressions that are widely disseminated in the Old Testament: the LORD is 'slow to anger and of great might'. The expression 'slow to anger' has sometimes been regarded as a gloss, presumably on the ground that so to describe Yahweh is inconsistent after He has been spoken of as 'quick to anger' (so NEB; RSV 'wrathful') in the previous verse. But such a decision both implies a remarkably foolish glossator and also limits excessively the meaning of the Hebrew phrase. *ba'al hemah*, literally 'lord of wrath', means that His anger *can* be aroused; what is remarkable is the patience with which He withholds His anger. The whole phrase is a familiar one, found in identical or very similar forms at Exod. 34: 6 and Ps. 145: 8, and it is likely that it represents 'a well established liturgical form' (Beyerlin, 1965, p. 38; though for reasons already noted his dismissal of this verse as a gloss seems questionable).

In so far as the redactional process underlying Nahum can be traced, it appears primarily to be concerned with drawing out one particular aspect of the prophetic message. In this way it is comparable to a characteristic feature of the later prophetic collections, which increasingly focus on particular details rather than embodying the whole sweep of their eighth-century predecessors. In this case the concentration of interest is expressed by the words of the introduction in 1: 1: 'an oracle concerning Nineveh'. In one sense that brings out the vital point; in another sense it leaves it obscure, for in the prophetic oracles against foreign nations the real subject is *Yahweh's* power, exercised against whichever foreign country it might be, on behalf of His own people.

The primary concern of Nahum, therefore, is with the exposition of Yahweh's sovereignty over the nations, illustrated in the specific context of the Assyrian menace. In this respect there are striking similarities with Isa. 40–55. These have already been illustrated at the linguistic level, with the suggestion that their common roots might lie in the Jerusalem cult. There are also, it would seem, striking similarities between the message of the two prophets, and this may need to be emphasised in view of the propensity of commentators to reject Nahum as no more than a prophet of violent and bloody revenge, whereas Deutero-Isaiah is often regarded as the high-water mark of the prophetic movement. In fact these chapters of Isaiah also contain blood-thirsty and revenge-seeking elements (e.g. Isa. 49: 22–6), and it is as misleading to denigrate Nahum as it is to idealise Deutero-Isaiah. Both speak of the certainty of Yahweh's saving power being effective against the might of an apparently impregnable enemy; both have harsh words to say against the enemy, in the one case Assyria, in the other Babylon; both use language that stems from a cultic background and contains imagery and figures of speech that could be reapplied to a variety of situations. And basic to both is the absolute certainty of Yahweh's sovereign power.

Detailed consideration of Nahum, therefore, suggests caution in any proposal that a different tradition underlies our present book. Certain redactional features, commonly associated with the work of the Deuteronomists and characteristic of most of the prophetic collections, appear to be lacking; but the essential theological assertions can be paralleled elsewhere, notably in Isa. 40–55. Similar considerations may be found to be operative if we turn now to Habakkuk.

Habakkuk has regularly been associated with Nahum, partly because of their proximity in all forms of the canon, partly, one suspects, because they have been subconsciously regarded as a kind of remainder left over when more basic collections have been discussed. But however that may be, the link has commonly been expressed in terms of cultic prophecy. As with Nahum, the views of Engnell have been important here, even if only as providing an occasion for expressing dissent. Engnell (1970, p. 167) asserted that 'Joel, Habakkuk, Nahum and the so-called Deutero-Isaiah belong to the liturgy type' of prophetic collection but then differentiated within this group by stating that Joel and Habakkuk 'are probably actually cult poetry', whereas Nahum and Deutero-Isaiah were 'prophetic imitations of cult poetry'. Regrettably, this suggestion, like many others put forward by Engnell in a provocative essay that is still worthy of attention, was never developed, so that it is impossible to tell what criteria he had in mind for this assertion. The thesis has continued to exercise influence, however, so that Jeremias (1969) differentiated between Nahum and Habakkuk in an analagous way: as we have already noted, he regards Nahum as originally a prophet of doom whose words were later reinterpreted in a cultic context, whereas Habakkuk was himself a cultic prophet. Whether such a sharp differentiation between 'cultic prophets' and 'prophets of doom' is an appropriate one is a question that has already been raised by our study of Nahum, and it emerges again in connection with Habakkuk. It is also appropriate to note that this identification of Habakkuk as a cultic prophet is not universally accepted; as with Nahum, Rudolph in his commentary (1975, pp. 193f) states his inability to accept this view even though it is so widely affirmed.

Certain of the problems relating to Habakkuk need not here concern us, partly because of the extremely full discussion in Jöcken (1977) with its very detailed history of scholarship and partly, at least, for the very good reason that no certain grounds for an agreed solution appear to exist. The variant traditions with regard to the prophet's name; the uncertainties with regard to precise dating; the lack of knowledge of any geographical background – all these are issues about which speculation will no doubt continue, but for which no method of resolution appears to be in sight. More instructive may be the note in 1: 1, which characterises Habakkuk as a *nābī'*. No precise parallel to this is found in the introductory verses of other pre-exilic prophetic collections, and the suggestion has been made (e.g. by Jeremias, 1969, p. 5; pp. 103f) that this is itself an indication that Habakkuk was a cult prophet. But at least two considerations should lead to caution here. First, the attempt (characteristic of an earlier generation of scholars) to make a sharp distinction between the classical prophets and the *nebî'îm* has been shown to be unsatisfactory on many counts; recent discussions of Amos 7: 14 provide perhaps the most obvious example of how opinions have shifted. Secondly, though it is indeed true that the use of *nābī'* in Hab. 1: 1 has no parallel in pre-exilic collections, it is noteworthy that both Haggai and Zechariah are described as *nebî'îm* in the opening verses of their books, and it seems more likely to see the use in Hab. 1: 1 as part of an analogous redactional process rather than as a pointer to an identifiably different role.

One other preliminary point with regard to Habakkuk may be made. It is not relevant to the present essay to deal with the problems raised by Hab. 3, but it is at least clear that the presence of such a psalm-like passage within a prophetic collection is not of itself a matter for especial surprise. In addition to the close parallels with the Psalms in Isa. 40–55, which have already been noted, the poems in Jonah 2 and Isa. 38 provide ample illustration of the fact that the sharp distinction once drawn between prophetic oracle and psalmody is one that should now be seriously modified. (See on this whole area, Johnson, 1979, pp. 3–5 *et passim*.)

When the oracular and other material in Hab. 1–2 is considered in greater detail along the lines already set out for Nahum, three broad conclusions begin to emerge. First, as with Nahum, the collection appears to stand somewhat apart from other prophetic collections because of the absence of any trace of a Deuteronomistic redaction. Secondly, this impression is strengthened by the fact that there are fewer allusions to, or phrases held in common with, either other prophetic books or other parts of the Old Testament. Thirdly, however, the lack of anything equivalent to the violent anti-Assyrian polemic of Nahum has the effect of limiting this impression of strangeness; to return to the original question of the prophetic tradition, it is easier at first glance to envisage Habakkuk as standing within the great tradition than it would be for Nahum. This impression is, of course, enhanced by the way in which certain sections of Habakkuk have been taken up at a later date – most notably the Pauline use of Hab. 2: 4 – and built into our collective consciousness, even if their later use has differed sharply from the original thrust of the oracle.

We may turn, therefore, from these rather impressionistic observations to a more precise consideration of the grounds upon which they are based. The first two points are negative, and therefore cannot easily be established directly. With regard to the lack of any Deuteronomistic features, an indication of this is already given in 1: 1 by the lack of the characteristic dating structure, apparently meant to relate the activity of each prophet to the appropriate part of 2 Kings and found in each of those prophets whom we have classified as the 'mainstream'. Though links with Deuteronomy have been noted (Cothenet, 1972, col. 796), these are thematic rather than redactional. The same point is valid when comparison is made between Habakkuk and other prophetic collections: though each of the themes may be paralleled elsewhere, and there are certain links of vocabulary (e.g. the series of woes in Hab. 2 appears to have drawn upon a number of the same expressions as those used in Isa. 14, the woe upon the king of Babylon; each tradition was presumably dependent upon the characteristic usage of the Jerusalem cult), nevertheless many of Habakkuk's characteristic emphases remain unique.

Later use of Habakkuk, however, emphasises the point that his oracles were regarded as belonging within the great prophetic tradition. In the case of Paul it is clear that his use of Hab. 2: 4 was a matter of citing from an accepted body of Scripture, but the use of Habakkuk traditions both in the Apocryphal book Bel and the Dragon and in the Qumran community may be taken as pointing to the fact that the issues raised by Habakkuk were felt to be of central importance for different groups within later Judaism. This is particularly the case in regard to 1: 1 – 2: 5, a section that in effect consists of an extended consideration of divine justice and of the uncertainty of man's standing before God (Emerton, 1977). These issues are not explored in Habakkuk in a manner comparable with what is found in Jeremiah, still less with the intensity underlying the book of Job. Nevertheless, they serve to underline the impression already elicited from the study of Nahum – that despite certain surface differences, which are related particularly to the redactional process through which the material has passed, there is a profound similarity in basic concern with other parts of the Old Testament prophetic tradition.

By way of epilogue to our consideration of Habakkuk it is proper to pay some attention to the polemic, which, as with Nahum (and indeed other prophets), plays an important part in his message. Jöcken's survey of scholarship over the last 150 years shows how greatly this issue has dominated discussion and how subjective many of the conclusions have been. Two points may, however, properly be made, which serve to show both the similarities to Nahum and the differences therefrom. First, in Habakkuk it appears very probable that there has been a deliberate reapplication of the material in the light of changing circumstances and differing understandings of Yahweh's will. Jeremias' theory of such a remodelling, which seemed unconvincing in the case of Nahum, would fit the evidence of Habakkuk much more satis-factorily, for it is clear from even a cursory reading that more than one enemy is condemned and that oracles are likely to have been reapplied. Secondly, Habakkuk differs from Nahum in that he stands in the tradition represented earlier by Isaiah (10: 5–15) and later by Jeremiah (27: 6) that foreign oppressors must be seen as being under God's control, not only as a means of asserting the total sovereignty of Yahweh (thus far Nahum is in agreement) but also as a means of punishing His own people for their failures in obedience: Hab. 1: 6 should not be taken out of its context, as has often been done in the past, but seen as part of the total picture of judgement portrayed in the opening section of the book.

It has already been recognised that Joel stands somewhat apart from the other two prophets here considered; indeed it has proved notorious-ly difficult to 'place' Joel with any confidence in relation to any of the major questions raised by the book. Here only brief consideration can be given to those aspects of Joel which relate to the questions already posed for Nahum and Habakkuk. The variety of dates proposed for Joel (Allen, 1976, pp. 19–25) may provide a starting-point; not only does this variety illustrate the uncertainty as to the proper understanding of the book, so that Kaiser (1975, p. 280) can speak of a 'a loosening of positions rather than a general agreement' as to date and unity, but it also gives a clue to the 'liturgical' as against the 'historical' emphasis that is characteristic of Joel. If what we have in the book of Joel is a composition closely related to the Jerusalem cult (Ahlström, 1971), then questions concerning unity may come to be expressed in a somewhat different way from that which would be appropriate in the case of an oracular collection. Again, the wide variety of proposed dates suggests the renewed applicability of cultic patterns rather than the once-for-all element more characteristic of the prophet who delivers God's word to a specific historical situation. But as we have already seen, care should be taken not to exaggerate this difference; Joel 1: 1 emphasises that what is to follow is 'the word of the LORD', that is to say, the characteristic medium of communication will be that which is above all associated with the prophet as God's messenger.

Uncertainty as to the date of Joel raises further problems for the proper handling of another distinctive feature of the book: the widespread use of what appear to be allusions to, or in some cases direct quotations of, expressions found in other prophetic collections. In the case of Nahum and Habakkuk we have seen that the distinctive use of language often alleged in respect of those books is somewhat exaggerated, and that there are links with other Old Testament traditions. Nevertheless it is undeniable that they stand somewhat apart in this respect. With Joel the position is strikingly different, for, as has regularly been pointed out by commentators, expressions are found in Joel that show links with, or allusions to, a whole variety of other Old Testament traditions. To some extent, the same type of issue arises as has already confronted us with Nahum and Habakkuk, that is to say, what is the nature of the redactional process underlying these allusions? In some cases it would be possible to envisage Joel as specifically modifying the words of earlier prophets. Thus Joel 3: 10 (MT 4: 10) surely bears some relationship to the similarly expressed picture in Isa. 2: 4 and Micah 4: 3. But is that relationship properly understood as a quotation or allusion, suggesting that the earlier prophets' words can only be fulfilled by a drastic reversal of the role of ploughshares and swords, pruning hooks and spears? Or are both the use in Joel and that in Isaiah/Micah dependent upon an established metaphor from the Jerusalem cult, which would be readily enough recognised by those who heard such words? The problems related to the common use of the form in both the Isaiah and the Micah traditions might lead one to suppose that the latter is the more appropriate solution.

This possibility is reinforced by the specifically Zion language of Joel 3: 16 (MT 4: 16), in which once again we hear echoes of an earlier prophetic collection: Amos 1: 2 is verbally almost identical, while Jer. 25: 30 makes use of substantially similar language and ideas. Much the same point might be made with regard to the use of 'Day of the LORD' language. Though there is still no general agreement as to the origin of this concept, it is widely held that this should be sought in a cultic context (cf. Ahlström 1971, pp. 62–72). Several familiar passages in the pre-exilic prophets warn the community against an easy expectation that the 'Day of the LORD' will automatically lead to their vindication (Amos 5: 18ff; Isa. 2: 12ff; Zeph. 1: 14ff), and Joel also uses this tradition in language closely related to these passages (Joel 1: 15; 2: 22). But even here caution is necessary, for the prophetic passages to which these verses in Joel are most closely related are those in which the 'Day of the LORD' is pictured as the occasion for Yahweh's vengeance upon his foreign enemies (Isa. 13: 6; Ezek. 30: 2f). It does not seem necessary to postulate any complicated theory of literary dependence; it may rather be that each of these passages is ultimately dependent upon the usage of the cult, taking up a theme that could be applied either positively against the enemies of the community or negatively against the community itself. In every case except Amos the natural assumption is that the reference is to the Jerusalem cult, and even in Amos this is also likely as the background of his language, which contains many Jerusalemite features – it is impossible on the evidence available to decide against whom the oracle in Amos 5: 18 was directed. Finally in this connection, Obad. verses 8–15 provide an elaboration of the same theme in a slightly different direction; again there must be uncertainty whether it is proper to speak of literary dependence between the two prophetic books (and if so, in which direction), and it may seem more likely that the usage of the cult provides the background of the motif.

The book of Joel in particular raises many more questions than can be considered here, but it may now be possible to revert to our original question and ask again how far it is possible to detect within the Old Testament traces of a prophetic tradition separate from that which we have described as the 'main stream'. At one limited level the answer is clearly negative: there is nothing that would suggest that the books we have considered formed part of some coherent tradition, which both bound them together and served also to differentiate them, whether in form or thematic structure, from the main prophetic collections.

If, however, the question is put in more general terms, it becomes much more difficult to answer. This is partly due to the inevitable difficulty of attempting to prove a negative; how could we ever finally satisfy ourselves as to the *non*-existence of a distinct prophetic tradition? More helpfully, however, it seems possible to isolate three areas, all of them issues of contemporary scholarly debate, in which greater clarity is needed before judgements can legitimately be made concerning distinctive prophetic traditions. These concern the nature of the redactional process, the relation of the prophets to the cult and our knowledge of the prophets as individuals. Some brief reflection on these points may appropriately conclude this essay.

First, it is important to keep constantly in mind the extent to which our perception of the characteristic emphases of the main stream of prophetic tradition has been shaped by the particular concerns of the Deuteronomists. The precise significance of the promise that the community would be given a prophet 'like Moses' (Deut. 18: 15) remains in dispute, but it is clear that for the Deuteronomists the prophets were *the* characteristic intermediary figures, conveying God's message to his people and representing the people before God. It was in such a conviction that the various earlier prophetic collections were handed down and given their distinctive shape. To such a process Nahum and Habakkuk were apparently not subjected; nor indeed was Joel, but doubts as to dating make it at least possible that that was due to the simple fact that Joel lived after the period of Deuteronomic redaction. This lack of a Deuteronomic stage in the process by which Nahum and Habakkuk were handed down may account for some of the distinctiveness of those books; it should not be pushed too far and made into an assertion of a totally distinct tradition-process. Whatever the milieu in which they were handed down, it was certainly one that regarded it as entirely appropriate to include these 'books'within the one book, that is, the 'Book of the Twelve' as it has come down to us.

Secondly, a constantly recurring theme in much recent study of the prophets has been that of their relation to the cult. It seems clear that the older view, that the true prophet was in consistent opposition to cultic practice, has now been generally and rightly abandoned. Instead, there has been an increasing emphasis on the positive links between at least some prophets and the cult. The work of Johnson (1962, 1979), in particular, has made the idea of the 'cultic prophet' a familiar one. But this valuable gain in understanding often seems to be in danger of being lost through failure to indicate just what such a term would mean. For some, the fact that Jeremiah and Ezekiel are described as being members of priestly families would suffice *eo ipso* to make them cultic prophets; for others again, the use of particular literary forms, especially those characteristic of the Psalms, is the vital touchstone; others again attempt to delineate precisely the role of the prophet as an inspired individual in terms relating to cultic function. It is instructive to consider the various discussions of, say, Nahum, and whether or not he was a 'cultic prophet', with these differing definitions in mind; only too often it is impossible to tell whether the differing conclusions reached by scholars are due to different initial definitions or to differences in assessing the evidence. Until a greater measure of clarification has been achieved in this area, it will be very difficult to decide what criteria are to be employed to assess the different Old Testament prophetic collections in their mutual inter-relationships.

In one respect, however, it does appear as if a more positive judgement may legitimately be formed. We have already noted how each of the collections here considered shows links with the 'foreign nations' oracles, particularly those in Isa. 13–14; but similar links exist with the remainder of Isa. 13–23 and with Jer. 46–51. It is generally agreed that this material is less 'personal' to the prophets concerned than are other parts of the Books of Isaiah or Jeremiah; and it may be proper to see here a particularly close example of the links between prophecy and cult that have been considered in more general terms. There is no ground for doubting that one aspect of the Jerusalem cult would have been prayer for victory over foreign enemies, and every reason to suppose that the prophets would have been enlisted in such a campaign. Nahum, Habakkuk and Joel, and possibly also Obadiah, provide access to the terminology and the characteristic concerns of the Jerusalem cult, without thereby implying that they stand apart from the other prophetic figures of the period.

Finally, a word must be said about the prophets as individuals. In the English-speaking world, in particular, the characteristic introduction to the study of the prophets has been by way of their personality rather than through their message. Since we know nothing of the personalities of those who have been considered in this essay, we may have one reason for the tendency either to neglect them or to regard them as representing a tradition other than the main prophetic stream.

But along with the increasing emphasis on the importance of the redactional process, so that secondary material is no longer dismissed as inferior, and with the recognition of a cultic role, however ill-defined, for many prophets, has come a natural tendency to diminish the individuality of each prophet. Some will find this regrettable, but it may be hoped that it will have at least one desirable result: that the characteristic *themes* of each prophetic collection may be enabled to speak more clearly to us. If that were to be the case, then the collections here studied, though they would remain minor by comparison with the Books of Isaiah and Jeremiah, might be more readily seen as playing their distinctive part in the overall complex of Israel's prophetic traditions.

Bibliography

G. W. Ahlström *Joel and the Temple Cult at Jerusalem*, SVT 21 (Leiden, 1971).

L. C. Allen *The Books of Joel, Obadiah, Jonah and Micah*, NICOT (London, 1976).

W. Beyerlin *Origins and History of the Oldest Sinaitic Traditions* (Oxford, 1965) (English translation of *Herkunft und Geschichte der ältesten Sinaitraditionen* (Tübingen, 1961)).

K. W. Cathcart *Nahum in the Light of North-west Semitic*, Biblica et Orientalia 26 (Rome, 1973).

D. L. Christensen *Transformations of the War Oracle in Old Testament Prophecy*, Harvard Dissertations in Religion 3 (Missoula, 1975).

R. E. Clements *Prophecy and Tradition* (Oxford, 1975).

E. Cothenet 'Prophètes: Habacuc' in *Supplément au Dictionnaire de la Bible*, vol. VIII (Paris, 1972).

O. Eissfeldt *The Old Testament: an Introduction* (Oxford, 1965) (English translation of *Einleitung in das Alte Testament*, 3rd ed. (Tübingen, 1964)).

J. A. Emerton 'The textual and linguistic problems of Habakkuk II, 4–5', *JTS* n.s. 28 (1977), 1–18.

I. Engnell 'Prophets and Prophetism in the Old Testament' in *Critical Essays on the Old Testament* (London, 1970) (English translation of 'Profeter, profetism', *Svensk Bibliskt Uppslagsverk*, 2nd ed. (Stockholm, 1962)).

G. Fohrer *Introduction to the Old Testament* (London, 1970) (English translation of *Einleitung in das Alte Testament*, 10th ed. (Heidelberg, 1965)).

J. Gray 'The Kingship of God in the Prophets and Psalms', *VT* 11 (1961), 1–29.

A. Haldar *Associations of Cult Prophets among the Ancient Semites* (Uppsala, 1945).

  Studies in the Book of Nahum (Uppsala, 1947).

P. Haupt 'The Book of Nahum', *JBL* 26 (1907), 1–53.

Jorg Jeremias   *Kultprophetie und Gerichtsverkündigung in der später Königszeit Israels*, WMANT 35 (Neukirchen-Vluyn, 1969).

P. Jöcken   *Das Buch Habakuk*, BBB 48 (Köln-Bonn, 1977).

A. R. Johnson   *The Cultic Prophet in Ancient Israel*, 2nd ed. (Cardiff, 1962). *The Cultic Prophet and Israel's Psalmody* (Cardiff, 1979).

O. Kaiser   *Introduction to the Old Testament* (Oxford, 1975) (English translation of *Einleitung in das Alte Testament*, 2nd ed. (Gütersloh, 1970)).

C. R. North   *The Second Isaiah* (Oxford, 1964).

W. Rudolph   *Joel, Amos, Obadja, Jona*, KAT 13, 2 (Gütersloh, 1971). *Micah, Nahum, Habakuk, Zephanja*, KAT 13, 3 (Gütersloh, 1975).

H. Schulz   *Das Buch Nahum: eine redaktionskritische Untersuchung*, BZAW 129 (Berlin, 1973).

G. Vermes   *The Dead Sea Scrolls in English* (Harmondsworth, 1962).

J. Vermeylen   *Du Prophète Isaïe à l'Apocalyptique*, Études Bibliques (2 vols., Paris, 1977–8).

S. J. de Vries   'The Acrostic of Nahum in the Jerusalem Liturgy', *VT* 16 (1966), 476–81.

Visionary experience in Jeremiah

WALTHER ZIMMERLI

I

To appreciate Jeremiah's prophetic experience it is essential to keep in mind the auditory element that is a particularly important feature of his prophecies. This is to be found not only in the introductory formulae of the passages shaped according to a Deuteronomistic understanding (Mowinckel's Source C, differently presented by Thiel, 1973; cf. also Wildberger, 1942): 7: 1; 11: 1; 18: 1; etc. In addition, the account of Jeremiah's call and the collection of Jeremiah's own early oracles (chs. 2–6) stand under the rubric of a personally shaped formula for the coming of God's word (*Wortereignisformel*) (1 : 4; 2 : 1). (On this formula cf. Zimmerli, 1979*a*, pp. 144–5; on its occurrence in Jeremiah cf. Neumann, 1973; Seidl, 1979.)

In a similar way, the coming of God's word is also significant in the narrative sections of the book (Mowinckel's Source B, differently presented by Wanke, 1971). Here it is stressed that the word of Yahweh to Jeremiah did not always come immediately. Chs. 28 and 42 tell how the prophet was in acutely oppressive situations in which he had to speak directly and yet wait in obedience for the word of God. According to ch. 28 his message that Judah would have to bear the yoke of the king of Babylon appeared to be negated by the contrary preaching by Hananiah of an apparently certain message supported by an impressive act of symbolism. He left the scene in silence (28: 11*b*), but later as a result of the reception of a new word, he announced to Hananiah God's message that his death was imminent as divine judgement for his disobedient preaching. In the 'Passion narrative' (Kremers, 1953; Wanke, 1971) ch. 42 sketches the situation after the murder of Gedaliah. In fear of Babylonian revenge the survivors wanted to flee to Egypt, but were unwilling to do this without a divine decree. Jeremiah waited ten days in a situation full of anxiety until the word came to him anew, which he then announced (42: 7).

This impression persists even for the most distinctively personal words, which were probably recorded by the prophet himself (Mowinckel's Source A; cf. Thiel, 1973). In his 'Confessions' (Baumgartner, 1917; von Rad, 1936; differently Gunneweg, 1970; Welten, 1977) he describes his experience of the reception of the word in the midst of his bitter complaint and its importance for him:

> Thy words were found, and I ate them,
>> and thy word [*emended text*] became to me a joy,
>> and the delight of my heart,
> for I am called by thy name.

$$(15: 16)$$

Corresponding to this is his polemic against frivolous prophetic proclamation according to which human dreams can be equated with the word of God: 'Let the prophet who has a dream tell the dream, but let him who has my word speak my word faithfully. What has straw in common with wheat? says the LORD. Is not my word like fire, says the LORD, and like a hammer which breaks the rock in pieces?' (23: 28–9).

Already in those passages from the early period (against Rietzschel, 1966, pp. 131ff) that are structured in a form comparable to that of the 'Confessions' and speak of the coming of a 'foe from the North', it is possible to trace how the prophet is overwhelmed by the divine proclamation. Even physical convulsions are implied. He knows that the divine word repeated by him has itself the power to kindle a fire: 'Behold, I am making (*nōtēn*) my words in your mouth a fire, and this people wood, and fire shall devour them' (5: 14).

In the light of this passage the possibility cannot be excluded that the one feature of the call narrative that goes beyond mere audition – 'Then the LORD put forth his hand and touched my mouth; and the LORD said to me, "Behold, I have put (*nātattî*) my words in your mouth"' (1 : 9) – was from the first a constituent element in the narrative. In his analysis of Jer. 1 : 4–10 Thiel (1973, pp. 62–72) has rightly drawn attention to the related statement of Deut. 18 : 18. Here Yahweh promises Moses: 'I will raise up for them a prophet like you from among their brethren; and I will put (*wenātattî*) my words in his mouth.' But Thiel's conclusion is not convincing. He argues that there is a 'somewhat abrupt transition from a mere audition to a previously unimplied account of a vision' (p. 64) because the specific words of introduction to the vision itself are here lacking (contrast Ezek. 2: 9). On the other hand it is inadequate to refer only to an 'impression of feeling' (*Gefühlseindruck*), as Seierstad does (1965, p. 67). Jeremiah is aware of the way in which his lips have actually been touched. References to the 'hand of Yahweh' in the prophetic experience are found not only in Jeremiah (15: 17, in the context of a 'Confession'), but also in Isaiah (8: 11), and especially in Ezekiel; in this Ezekiel took over speech forms characteristic of the pre-classical prophets (cf. Zimmerli, 1979*a*, pp. 117–18, on Ezek. 1: 3; and p. 42).

II

Considerations of this kind make it probable that Jeremiah's bewilderment when confronted by the word of Yahweh is not adequately described as an 'auditory experience'. The hammer that breaks the rock in pieces, the fire that is kindled through the prophet against the people, the touching of his mouth by Yahweh at the time of the commissioning with the prophetic message, imply an experience that seized the prophet totally in all his different senses.

> My heart is broken within me,
>   all my bones shake;
> I am like a drunken man,
>   like a man overcome by wine,
> because of the LORD
>   and because of his holy words.
>
>   (23: 9)

When Jeremiah in his 'Confessions' describes how he has attempted to resist the necessity of proclaiming words that bore oppressively upon him, 'If I say, "I will not mention him, or speak any more in his name"', he has to admit, 'there is in my heart as it were a burning fire shut up in my bones, and I am weary with holding it in, and I cannot' (20: 9). The coming of God's word completely shatters him and its effects go far beyond auditory experience.

It is therefore not surprising that, in one of the most impassioned of the prophet's oracles from his early preaching relating to the announcement of the foe from the North, reference is also made to the bewilderment of the prophet at the vision he experiences. To the auditory affliction of the prophet, to which the words 'Violence and destruction'

(20: 8) must refer, there is added a visual distress, which has the effect of seeming to shatter the whole of his bodily sensation:

> My anguish, my anguish! I writhe in pain!
>> Oh, the walls of my heart!
> My heart is beating wildly;
>> I cannot keep silent;
> for I hear [*emended text*] the sound of the trumpet,
>> the alarm of war.
> Disaster upon disaster is summoned,
>> [*or*, Disaster follows hard on disaster?]
>> the whole land is laid waste.
> Suddenly my tents are destroyed,
>> my curtains in a moment.
> How long must I see the standard,
>> and hear the sound of the trumpet?

(Jer. 4: 19–21)

Here it is not simply words that the prophet articulates; the reality of war breaks in upon all his senses. His ears actually hear the trumpet-blast and the battle-cries; his eyes actually see the war-standards raised. In the liturgy for a time of drought (14: 1ff) there is an extract going back to Jeremiah himself, which incorporates in verses 17*aß*–18*a* a comparable terrifying vision:

> Let my eyes run down with tears night and day,
>> and let them not cease,
> for the virgin(?) daughter of my people is smitten with a great wound,
>> with a very grievous blow.
> If I go out into the field,
>> behold those slain by the sword!
> And if I enter the city,
>> behold, the diseases of famine!

In vision the prophet perceives the impending disaster[1] which he must proclaim to the people. In the most profound personal bewilderment he announces it and writhes with pain on account of what he sees. Thus the prophet who is characterised particularly as one who receives God's word is appropriately also called a 'seer'. (On the phenomenon of prophetic visions cf. Hölscher, 1914, s.v. 'vision' in the index; Lindblom, 1935 and 1962, s.v. 'vision' in the general index; Horst, 1960.)

III

It is naturally to be expected from this that there should also be found among the words in the Jeremiah tradition specific accounts of the visions he experienced, as is also the case with his slightly younger contemporary Ezekiel. In Ezekiel it is even more clearly the case than in Jeremiah that the great majority of the utterances of the prophet employ the formula for the coming of God's word in the first person. The theology of the coming of God's word is more obvious in Ezekiel than in any other prophetic book. There are fifty passages with the formula *debar Yahweh* ('the word of the LORD') in Ezekiel as against thirty in Jeremiah (cf. Grether, 1934, pp. 67f, for the statistics). But interspersed between these *debar Yahweh* passages there is also to be found material of a visionary kind, arranged in four or perhaps five major units (Ezek. 1: 1 – 3: 15; 8 – 11; 37: 1 – 14; 40 – 8; less certainly 3: 16, 22ff). These visions are structured on a grand scale in a manner comparable to the purely verbal proclamations of Ezekiel (ch. 7: the Day of Yahweh; ch. 16: the faithless woman; ch. 23: the two faithless women; ch. 27: Tyre's ship of state; ch. 34: the shepherds of Israel; etc.). In these visions the formula for the coming of God's word is missing.[2] The specific structure of the visionary description is to be found in the introductory formula, which is literally: 'I looked, and lo!' In each case it is introduced by a more precise description of the character of the visionary act by the use of the prophetic theologumena of the 'hand' or 'spirit' of Yahweh. For the most part the visions are dated, but in 37: 1 the date appears to have been lost.

In the Book of Jeremiah there are, in fact, three reports of visions. These constitute, first, the two visions of 1: 11–15(16), secondly, the unit 4: 23–6 and, finally, ch. 24, which in its present form is unmistakably Deuteronomistic. It is on these three passages that we shall concentrate in what follows.

IV

So far as redaction is concerned, Jer. 4: 23–6 is attached, without any transition or distinctive introduction, to words that enable us to perceive the whole drama of the invasion of the 'foe from the North' (4: 11–14, 15–18), which lead into the anguished cry of distress that reveals the personal bewilderment of the prophet (4: 19–21, discussed above, pp. 98f). As justification for the judgement that is about to occur, an oracle is added in 4: 22, which, in terms reminiscent of Isa. 1: 3, depicts the folly of the people in their lack of knowledge as the cause of the strange judgement. The visionary oracle, 4: 23–6, is then followed by a sequence with a new introduction by means of the messenger formula (4: 27–8). Verse 28 is a variant on the pronouncement in Amos 1: 2 concerning the mourning of the land, combined here also with the threat that the skies will be made black. The preceding statement in verse 27*b* that Yahweh will not bring about a complete annihilation corresponds to the similar passages in 5: 10 and 5: 18 and is to be understood as a mitigating gloss from the hand of a later editor; alternatively, the negative might be deleted as not original (Thiel, 1973, p. 98, n. 66), or understood as a nominal form (W. Herrmann, 1977). Verse 28*a*, however, should be accepted as original. The section 4: 29–31 reverts to the drama of the picture of the enemy breaking in, and verse 31 reveals the deep feeling of vulnerability on the part of the prophet as he describes what he has heard:

> For I heard a cry as of a woman in travail,
>> (a cry of) anguish as of one bringing forth her first child,
> the cry of the daughter of Zion gasping for breath,
>> stretching out her hands,
> 'Woe is me! I am fainting before murderers.'

Between these passages there now stands 4: 23–6, the unity of which is achieved by the repetition of the stereotyped sequence, 'I looked... and lo!', as a means of presenting the visionary experience:

> I looked on the earth, and lo, it was waste and void;
>> and (I looked) to the heavens, and they had no light.
> I looked on the mountains, and lo, they were quaking,
>> and all the hills moved to and fro.
> I looked, and lo, there was no man,
>> and all the birds of the air had fled.
> I looked, and lo, the fruitful land was a desert,
>> and all its cities were laid in ruins
>> before the LORD, before his fierce anger.

In this description there are no specific elements associated with the description of the enemy invasion of the land of Judah. The direct drama of the words of 4: 11–14, 15–18, 19–21 and 29–31 is not to be traced here. There is no cry of distress to betray the personal bewilderment of the prophet. In its place comes a deathly silence. Instead of the limited horizons of Judah and Jerusalem, which can be recognised as underlying the surrounding passages, the scene is here a universal one: earth/heavens, mountains/hills, birds of the air, (fruitful lands with) orchards, lands containing cities. It is a more than human emptying, darkening, laying waste – it is complete and universal.

In his discussion of this passage Fishbane (1971) has drawn attention to its similarities with the depiction of creation in Gen. 1. With minor variations in the sequence he finds in this passage the use of the same elements as in Genesis: Pre-creation: 'waste and void' (*tōhû wābōhû*); first day: light; second day: the heavens; third day: the earth, mountains and hills/the earth, dry land; (the fourth day, the heavenly bodies, has no equivalent in Jer. 4); fifth day: birds; sixth day: mankind. In the equivalent of the passage relating to the Sabbath day Jeremiah speaks of God's 'fierce anger', in which Fishbane sees a distant allusion to the regular return in the Babylonian hemerologies of an *ūm ibbu* (or *ūmu limnu*), a day of ill omen. It is advisable to remain cautious about the acceptance of a 'pattern', especially where we have to do with a concluding statement about Yahweh's anger, but it is not to be denied that Jer. 4: 23–6 does indeed speak of the anger of Yahweh in the context of allusions to creation. This perception led Giesebrecht (1907, p. 28), following older scholars, to state that he could not suppress his doubts about the genuineness of 4: 23–6. Similarly Volz (1922, p. 50) rejected these verses, which he regarded as speaking the language of apocalyptic and characterised with the key-word 'world catastrophe', from the range of the genuine words of Jeremiah, since, he maintained, Jeremiah nowhere speaks of a great dramatic catastrophe, of the Day of Yahweh, or of the break-up of the established world. In contrast to this Duhm (1901, p. 54) had already stated:

> The vision has a symbolic character; chaos signifies the devastation brought about by the Scythians. So-called second sight often shows a tendency of this kind. As to the interpretation of one recent scholar, who translates the perfect tenses with present tenses and regards the poem as not genuine, one can only say that he has not understood it, and that further words are unnecessary.

In view of these diverse assessments of the authenticity of the vision what judgement can be offered?

In redaction-critical terms 4: 23–6 stands at the conclusion of a collection of oracles. The new introduction by means of the messenger formula marks 4: 27 as the beginning of a new sequence. At the beginning of this sequence – whatever decision is taken about verse 27*b* – there occurs in verse 28 a statement that once again concentrates on the mourning of the earth and the darkening of the heavens; this is followed in 4: 29ff by a fresh series of threats relating to the 'foe from the North'. The conclusion (4: 23-6) of the preceding redactional unit, which was introduced at 4: 5, had the function of a final climax of the words of threat that were based on the anger of Yahweh.

In form-critical terms the passage consists of a four-times repeated and monotonous 'I looked...and lo!' Such repetitions are not in any way unusual in Jeremiah. Not only is there the mocking threefold repetition of 'I have dreamed' in the polemical quotation of the prophets' words (23: 25-6, emended text), but also the equally polemical threefold repetition of 'the temple of the LORD' in the Temple-speech (7: 4). Another threefold repetition of words from the prophet's own mouth is contained in 23: 30-2: 'Behold, I am against the prophets.' If 15 : 2 stems from a genuinely Jeremianic setting (so Rudolph, 1968, pp. 102-3; to the contrary, Thiel, 1973, pp. 190-1), this would be a fourfold enumeration of the plagues of judgement, a form that is particularly characteristic of Ezekiel as a means of expressing completeness (cf. Zimmerli, 1979*a*, p. 120). The present passage could then also be grouped with the preceding list.

Nevertheless it is clear that the four 'I looked...and lo!' passages are not in all respects parallel to one another. In verses 23-4 the verb 'I looked' is followed by an accusative (preceded by *'et* in verse 23 only) denoting the area encompassed by the prophet's vision; this accusative is lacking in verses 25-6 and the content of the vision is introduced directly by *hinnēh* ('lo!'): in verse 25, no men and no birds of the air; in verse 26, the desolation of the fruitful land and the ruin of cities. The description of destruction is much more direct in verses 25-6 than in verses 23-4. In verses 25-6 there is no longer any mention of a specific place towards which the seer looks, but instead the great void of heaven and earth is set before him directly, with the destruction of the fruitful land and of all human habitation before his very eyes.

It is particularly important to bear in mind that the two pairs of sentences with their broadly parallel form reach their climax in the closing phrase, which is not part of the formal structure, verse 26*b*αβ: 'before the LORD, before his fierce anger'. Just as the four *rā'ītî*-sentences (the sentences beginning 'I looked') have been juxtaposed in an asyndetic construction, so this final announcement consists formally of two elements joined asyndetically, in which the second element functions as an explanation of the significance of the first. This interpretive closing phrase unmistakably recalls the close of the first unit within the redactional section 4: 5–26, that is 4: 8. The theme of the dramatic and vivid oracle in that passage was the summons to flight before the invading enemy, a retreat into the fortified cities, into Zion itself. Yahweh Himself (at this point the threatening words of the Yahweh speech are presented in first-person forms) is bringing destruction from the north, destruction through a lion that has broken out of its thicket, made the land a waste place and emptied the cities of their inhabitants. So the speech demands that the people should break into laments and wailing as a result of what is taking place. To this is added a motif that is reminiscent of the repeated refrain of the poem found in Isa. 9: 8ff (MT 9: 7ff): 'For all this his anger is not turned away', found here in the form 'for the fierce anger of the LORD has not turned back from us'. What is found here in 4: 8, expressed by means of a double use of the construct state, emerges in 4: 26 as the asyndetically expressed 'before the LORD, before his fierce anger', and so supplies the justification for the vision. The whole formula, with minor variants, is characteristic of Jeremiah: cf. 12: 13, as well as secondary passages such as 25: 37–8; 30: 24; 51: 45; cf. also 49: 37. Its prototype may be Hosea 11: 9, and in other pre-exilic prophetic collections it is found in Nahum 1: 6; Zeph. 2: 2; 3: 8.

These redaction- and form-critical observations, as well as the word-links in the final phrase of the vision, make it not improbable that we are dealing in 4: 23–6 with a genuine vision of Jeremiah himself. Its distinctiveness lies in the fact that it envisages the irruption of the fierce anger of Yahweh first of all in cosmic dimensions: the laying-waste of the earth reducing it to chaos, the darkening of the skies, the shaking of mountains and hills, the disappearance of all living creatures from earth and heaven; only after this does it mention the orchards laid out by men and the cities built by them. It is a terrifying vision, which brings the terror of the prophet into view in a quite different way from the visions normally seen by him of the destruction of the land in war. However, in the final statement this visionary oracle is linked with the oracle in 4: 5–8, which proclaims an actual emergency brought about by war.

Jeremiah, unlike Amos, Isaiah, Zephaniah and Ezekiel, does not speak explicitly of the 'Day of Yahweh' (contrast the view of Reventlow, 1963, pp. 107ff; Berridge, 1979, pp. 333ff), and is thereby once again linked particularly closely with Hosea. But links with Amos and Isaiah are also not wholly lacking in Jeremiah, as we have already noted in our treatment of 4: 8, 22 (so also Berridge). It is therefore possible that themes that elsewhere have their setting in passages dealing with the 'Day of Yahweh' (darkness – Amos 5: 20; perhaps also 8: 9; the confusion of the mountains and of all that is lifted up in nature – Isa. 2: 11ff) are here also influenced from that source.

It remains open to question whether it is appropriate, with Duhm (1901), to speak simply of the 'symbolic character' of the vision. When Horst (1960, pp. 203–4) lists this in his series of 'event-visions', he correctly emphasises that for the prophet the anger of God is an actual event, which confronts him as a ghostly, paralysing sight with world-wide implications. In contrast to the other passages of Jeremiah referred to earlier, the personal emotions of the prophet under the impact of his vision are not expressed.

V

Of quite a different character is the pair of visions in Jer. 1: 11–15(16). Dependence on the series of visions in Amos is obvious enough, particularly in their formal structure. If specifically Jeremianic features are more clearly characteristic of this passage than of the vision in 4: 23–6, it is also striking that we have here the phenomenon, by no means fully explained, of an inner-prophetic tradition-link specifically involving the report of a visionary experience, in which one might have expected that the most personal and distinctive characteristics of the prophet would be revealed (cf. Clements, 1975; Zimmerli, 1977).

In redaction-critical terms the first chapter of the Book of Jeremiah reveals a structure deliberately shaped by a secondary editor. S. Herrmann (1977) has worked out the most probable pattern of composition that can be discerned as underlying the present form. The formula for the coming of God's word (verse 4) leads into the closely integrated words of commission, which make clear to Jeremiah the fact that he had been set apart for the prophetic vocation even before his birth, with no possibility of refusal (verses 5–7); these words are followed by God's promise of help and the actual event of ordaining by Yahweh (verses 8–9), with a repeated underlining of the magnitude of the prophetic task (verse 10). A carefully balanced pair of visions (so with Seidl, 1979, pp. 27–8; against Neumann, 1973, pp. 183–4) reveals the validity and the contents of the prophetic commission (verses 11–16). The conclusion (verses 17–19) recalls once more the circumstances of the commissioning and, with words similar to those used in the first section, reminds the prophet once again of the extent of his task and of Yahweh's help in it. Our own particular subject of interest within this total composition has to be confined to the two visions, verses 11–12 and 13–15. The latter is followed in verse 16 by a further amplification.

In their linguistic structure the two visions represent a twin entity, the two parts of which possess a common form, however much their contents may be different. This form is foreshadowed in the four visions, also arranged in two pairs, of Amos 7: 1–8; 8: 1–2, which may represent, along with 9: 1–4, a cycle of visions originally put together by Amos. Whether this in its present form can legitimately be seen as referring to an older 'seer-tradition', as supposed by Reventlow (1963) in his proposed reconstruction of the prophetic role in Israel's covenant liturgy, does not need to be considered further here.

It is peculiar to Jeremiah that the two visions should each be preceded by the formula for the coming of God's word (verses 11, 13), which from the outset brings the vision that has been seen into relation with the encountered word. In Amos this association with a theology of the word is lacking, however much the visions that he had seen are related directly to his proclamation to Israel. The purely visionary presentation is maintained there to the extent that all four visions are introduced by *kōh her'anî 'adonāi yhwh wehinnēh* ('Thus the LORD GOD showed me: behold'). Yahweh Himself stands unequivocally as the author of the real vision that underlies what is actually seen. The 'presence-vision' (Horst, 1960) of 9: 1ff betrays a form that is different in its presentation of subject and object. It lacks the reference to Yahweh as the revealer of the vision. As in Isa. 6 Yahweh is the object of the verb of perceiving, and the vision itself is described in the first person singular as in Jer. 4: 23–6. The second pair of visions, Amos 7: 7–8 and 8: 1–2, differs from the first in that after the vision itself a question is directed to the prophet: 'Amos, what do you see?'; the prophet's answer, which describes in an explicit way the vision he has seen, is followed by God's explanation of the meaning and a statement of His intentions. The pattern of the second pair of visions in Amos is extended in the early post-exilic period in Zechariah. There the question concerning the content and significance of what has been seen comes no longer from God's side, but from the prophet himself, who learns its significance by means of an interpreting angel. The visions in Jer. 1, by contrast, are closer to those in Amos. The linking together of the two visions is very explicitly stated: 'The word of the LORD came to me a second time.' As against the Amos passages, however, it is only in the first of the two questions that the prophet is directly addressed by his own name. Moreover the answer of the prophet in the first of the Jeremiah visions is specifically endorsed by Yahweh Himself: 'You have seen well.' The lack of this endorsement in the second Jeremiah vision, which like the third and fourth of Amos' visions leads directly into the divine announcement of the implications of the vision, creates a formal imbalance between the two Jeremiah visions that distinguishes them from the pairs of visions in Amos with their more uniform structure. These small variations, however, ought not to diminish the impression of the very great similarity of the form of the Jeremiah visions to that of the Amos visions, particularly the second pair (cf. Berridge, 1979).

The similarities between the first Jeremiah vision and the first of the second group of Amos visions can be taken one stage further. Jeremiah sees a branch or wand of almond. After the divine summons to state what he has seen and the word of endorsement from Yahweh Himself there follows a further elaboration of the divine speech in which the word šāqēd('almond') is surprisingly changed into the similar-sounding participial form of the verb šqd ('to watch'). This verb is used in Jer. 5:6 to describe the cunning lying-in-wait of the leopard for its prey. (Allusions to 1:12 are found in 44:27, where Yahweh is watching with a view to destruction, and in 31:28, where the watching will bring salvation.) In the language of the Psalms šqd is used in parallelism with šmr (Ps. 127:1, RSV 'watches' (šmr) / 'stays awake' (šqd)), and it is also found in Prov. 8:34, again in parallelism with šmr (RSV 'watching' (šqd)/'waiting' (šmr)), and in a negative sense in Isa. 29:20 (RSV 'watch to do evil'). A similar type of vision, which, by the deliberate requirement of having to give a name to what has been seen, is transformed on the basis of assonance into a word of judgement, is to be found in Amos 8:1–2. Horst (1960, p. 205) lists these as the only two examples of what he describes as 'word-play visions', part of the more extensive group of 'word-symbol visions'. In this sub-group what is seen in the vision is not significant in its customary sense as an eloquent symbol, but the proclamation derives from what is seen only after its transformation by means of an aural association of words. But any idea of a mere game must be dismissed. The word has its own 'bodily existence' even in the shift from the visual to the aural means of recognition. It proclaims itself in the vision.

Yahweh is 'watching over (His) word to perform it'. This manner of expressing the message that arises from the vision leaves many questions unanswered. Which 'word of Yahweh' is here implied? Is it the word of earlier prophets – of Amos, for example, with whose prophecy the vision we are considering has so many similarities? Is it the word of Hosea, whose influence on Jeremiah's own message has been convincingly demonstrated by Gross (1930; 1931)? But Amos and Hosea had preached against the Northern Kingdom, which in Jeremiah's day was no longer in existence. Is it then the word of the Jerusalemite Isaiah, who had combined a message of salvation and of disaster in a distinctive way? A link with Isaiah seems to be indicated by Jer. 4:22. Or is it the word that, according to the call narrative, Jeremiah himself received when the hand of Yahweh touched his lips (1:9)? In any case there is no doubt that the reference must be to a word that is pressing towards its realisation in event. Once again there is a striking similarity between Jeremiah and Ezekiel, where the verbal expression in the mouth of Yahweh, 'I the LORD have spoken, and I will do it', is frequently repeated (17:24; 22:14; 36:36; cf. also 5:13) and where the theme of the fulfilment of God's word is presented in a polemical fashion in the speech passages 12:21–5, 26–8. Deutero-Isaiah, at the end of the exilic period, should also be borne in mind; in the account of his commissioning he makes a distinction between the transitoriness of 'all flesh' and 'the word of our God (which) will stand for ever' (40:6, 8; cf. also 55:10–11). In any case it is clear that the first vision of Jeremiah leads him directly into his basic knowledge of the effective word – to the experience that, according to the evidence of the 'Confessions' of Jeremiah, is both his deepest joy and his deepest distress (15:16; 20:8).

The question is thereby immediately raised whether Jeremiah understood this 'word' to be a word of salvation or of judgement. An unambiguous answer to this question is provided by Jer. 1:13–15, verses that were apparently linked by the prophet himself with verses 11–12 to form a twin pair of visions. This second vision presents greater difficulties than the first to an immediate understanding. The almond branch is a clearly discernible objective reality. But what can be meant by 'a blown pot (that is, presumably, one under which a fire has been kindled), and whose face (front?) is from the north' (RSV 'a boiling pot, facing away from the north')? Is it implied that it has been tilted or poured out from this direction, as suggested by Bright's translation: 'It is tipped from the north'? What is clear is the message that this vision, which is to be included among the 'symbol-visions' in the more general sense, contains within itself: 'Out of the north evil shall break forth upon (or, more probably, 'shall be kindled against', reading *tuppaḥ* or *tenuppaḥ*) all the inhabitants of the land.' This is then developed in an announcement in which Yahweh Himself is the subject: 'For, lo, I am calling all the tribes/kingdoms of the north, says the LORD; and they shall come and every one shall set his throne at the entrance of the gates of Jerusalem, against all its walls round about, and against all the cities of Judah.'

It would be wise to refrain from any over-imaginative description of a specific situation in which Jeremiah might have seen the cooking-pot (or indeed, the almond branch or wand; cf. e.g. Schmidt, 1923; pp. 206–7). In the same way it is meaningless to ask whether Jeremiah knew clearly in which direction the pot that he saw before him faced. As with Hosea's marriage or many of the symbolic actions of Ezekiel, we find ourselves in a position where the significance of the vision or symbolic action has made what the prophet actually saw or did complicated and unrecognisable, so that while the announcement of the meaning of the vision or symbolic action is completely clear, the biographical details that would be of especial interest to modern ways of thought are obscured and remain out of reach. So it must be left as an open question whether the pot boiling over (or indeed, the almond branch) would also have been a visible reality to an external observer or whether it was a 'vision' that had no actual counterpart in the clear light of day. The question is also not susceptible of an answer in the case of the visions of Amos. For the symbolic actions it is, of course, true that the carrying out of the action, in whatever way this was done, was an essential part of them. With regard to the vision of the boiling pot, it may be asked whether the underlying text of Ezek. 24:1–14 ('the pot on the fire'; cf. Zimmerli, 1979a, pp. 493–501) was not inspired by it.

The two visions, which in their formal structure seem identical, do not appear to have any discernible association of content. At the same time, it is possible to see the basic point of reference in the way in which the second vision makes it clear what 'act' of Yahweh the word put in the mouth of the prophet (1:9) must announce. The second vision is obviously in a close relation with the early preaching of Jeremiah concerning an invasion by a 'foe from the North'. This foe remains unnamed, both in the vision and the words from God that explain it, and in the oracles concerning the invasion, which are found expecially in Jer. 4–6. The victory of Nebuchadnezzar at Carchemish in 605 provided this proclamation with a clear historical realisation. According to Jer. 36, the events of which took place at the same period, Jehoiakim condemned the early preaching of the prophet, which had been written on the scroll that was burned with the words: 'Why have you written in it that the king of Babylon will certainly come and destroy this land?' (verse 29). Whether or not one accepts the authenticity of these words as actually spoken by Jehoiakim (a critical assessment in Wanke, 1971, pp. 59ff), the 'foe from the North' is here named by virtue of the historical fulfilment. From then on, as far as we can make out, Jeremiah also spoke openly of the Babylonians. In Ezekiel, who stands in the succession of this proclamation of Jeremiah, this open manner of speaking of the Babylonians and their king, Nebuchadnezzar, is merely continued. The time for veiled speech is done with. Even so, its secret character subsequently inspired the prophecy concerning Gog (Ezek. 38–9), with its development towards apocalyptic.

There is no reason from the content of the two visions in Jer. 1 to deny them to the prophet himself. How far the visions belonged from the outset to the events connected with the call of the prophet is not clear. In any case the redactor who brought Jer. 1 together into its present form did not entirely miss the mark when he inserted into the total picture, which in its present form anticipates both the prophet's oracles against the nations and the expectation of reconstruction after the period of judgement and destruction, the two visions with the genuinely Jeremianic themes of the unshakable effectiveness of the word of Yahweh and the threat of the invasion of the 'foe from the North'.

VI

The vision in Jer. 24 presents even greater problems. It is reminiscent of Ezekiel in that here, by contrast to Jer. 1:11ff and 4:23–6, the vision is given a date.

It differs, however, from Ezekiel in that there is lacking here the precise dating of the event by means of year, month and day. The statement is more general, that the prophet's vision took place 'after Nebuchadnezzar king of Babylon had taken into exile from Jerusalem

Jeconiah the son of Jehoiakim, king of Judah, together with the princes of Judah, the craftsmen, and the smiths, and had brought them to Babylon'. Because this dating (which does in fact fit the following vision) destroys the connection between verses 1a and 2 and makes use of information from 2 Kings 24:14, it should be regarded from a literary point of view as a supplementary insertion (against Pohlmann, 1978, p. 21).

The prophet sees 'two baskets of figs placed before the Temple of the LORD' (perhaps better to emend the text to: 'standing before...'). Once again we cannot decide whether the two baskets, with their different kinds of figs, would have been visible to any profane eyes, or whether it was a disclosure to be seen only by the eyes of the visionary. The introduction, 'the LORD showed me, and behold', which is the same introductory formula for a vision that we have noted in Amos, leaves both possibilities open. The specific naming of the location, 'before the temple', implies that the figs will have been a gift presented before God (Deut. 26:10bα); in the normal procedure for bringing an offering there will then have followed the priestly decision, whether the offering was lerāṣôn ('acceptable') or lo' lerāṣôn 'not acceptable'; see Lev. 22 : 20–1 and cf. also Gen. 4 : 4–5, the šᵉʿh of Yahweh (RSV 'the LORD had (no) regard')). As in the second pair of visions in Amos and in Jer. 1:11, 13, the vision is here followed by the question of Yahweh to the prophet, 'What do you see?', a question the pointedness of which is emphasised by the calling of the prophet by his own name, 'What do you see, Jeremiah?', just as in Amos 7:8; 8:2; Jer. 1:11.

The immediate context does not provide any further clue as to the nature and origin of this vision. It is preceded by two blocks of material, the extent of which can be recognised by the titles: 'Concerning (RSV 'To') the house of the king of Judah' (21:11 – 23:8) and 'Concerning the prophets' (23:9–40). In 25:1ff there follows a complex unit consisting of oracles against the nations. Its date ascribes it to the time of Jehoiakim. Jer. 25 appears to be the conclusion of an originally independent collection of oracles, to which the narrative material in chs. 26ff has been appended.

Form-critically considered, Jer. 24 consists of an elaborately constructed account of a vision, containing within itself elements of the Deuteronomistic preaching of alternatives (Thiel, 1973). It differs from Jer. 1 in that the appended explanation is introduced by a new formula for the coming of God's word (verse 4). The messenger formula of verse 5 is superfluous in that the personal address to the prophet has already been given in the formula for the coming of God's word, and should perhaps be regarded as a clumsy later insertion. The explanation that then follows is introduced by the comparative particle *ke* ('like'). In two roughly equal sections it sets out, on the one hand, the judgement of Yahweh concerning those who have been deported to Babylon and, on the other, that concerning Zedekiah, his ministers and those who remained in the land, as well as those who were living in Egypt. It contrasts the unconditional condemnation of the second group with the promise of salvation, which is conditional upon their conversion (verse 7*b*), for those living in Babylon. The reference to those who had escaped to Egypt presupposes already the events after the fall of Jerusalem that are referred to in chs. 42ff. Consequently this exposition cannot be thought to have a Jeremianic origin (Pohlmann, 1978, pp. 20–31). Indeed S. Herrmann (1965, pp. 165–6) and Thiel (1973, pp. 253–61) have shown in detail how both the vocabulary and the theological outlook here are the work of Deuteronomistic redaction.

The introduction to Jer. 24 explicitly names Yahweh as the author of the vision, and in this respect it is closer to the four visions in Amos 7:1–8; 8:1–2 than Jer. 1:11–15 is. On the other hand the arrangement of paired visions employed both in Amos 7–8 and in Jer. 1 is not present here. The fact that Jeremiah sees two baskets of figs functions here to characterise the two different conditions in which Judah found herself after the partial deportation of 597. The preaching of alternatives, which, according to the closing phrase (verse 7*b*), makes the salvation alternative of verses 4–7 dependent on the conversion of those deported in 597, is formulated with only the first of the two groups in mind upon whom Yahweh's judgement is pronounced through the visionary experience. For the second group no possibility of salvation seems to exist any more.

The whole passage gives, therefore, a disunited impression. The vision of the two baskets of figs seems at first to lead to an unconditional verdict in the situation of 597: for those in exile future salvation, for those remaining in the land and for those who escaped to Egypt (in the situation of 597 envisaged proleptically) future condemnation. But then through the preaching of alternatives a conditional element is introduced into the promise of salvation, which is envisaged by the whole structure of the vision, in that the announcement of salvation to the exiles is linked to the condition of their conversion.

This double emphasis leads to a recognition that the same feature can also be traced in the Book of Ezekiel. There the polemic against those who remained in the land is very bitter in the passages dating between 597 and 587. They had concluded from the fact that they had not been carried off into exile that 'to us this land is given for a possession', whereas the exiles 'have gone far from the LORD' (Ezek. 11:15). Ezek. 33:24 shows the claim to the land being further developed after 587, since here it is even founded upon an allusion to the saving history of Abraham: 'Abraham was only one man, yet he got possession of the land; but we are many; the land is surely given us to possess.' In Ezekiel also, therefore, it is to those far away from the land that the divine promise is made that Yahweh would once again lead them back into the land. No reference is made in Ezekiel to the Jewish community in Egypt. The promise of return for those exiled in Babylon is set out quite unconditionally in some passages (Ezek. 36:24ff; 37:1–14). But at the same time it is noteworthy that Ezekiel, in his words to the exiles amongst whom he found himself, can call for repentance and conversion (14:1ff; 18; on this theme cf. Pareira, 1975). Ezek. 14:1ff is particularly reminiscent of Jer. 24, in that in both instances the covenant formula (Smend, 1963) is associated with the call to repentance. On the other hand, Jer. 24 recalls terminology to be found in Ezekiel inasmuch as Jer. 24:7aα – literally, 'I will give them a heart to know me that I am Yahweh' – links together in a striking way the assertion of recognition followed by the accusative ('know me') with the typically Ezekielian combination of the assertion of recognition ('you will know that...') and the formula of self-introduction ('I am Yahweh.' See Zimmerli, 1954: index, s.v. Jer. 24:7; cf. Zimmerli, 1979a, pp. 36–8). In the Book of Jeremiah the same linking is to be found in the wisdom saying, 9:23–4 (MT 22–3); cf. also 16:21.

Is it possible, therefore, to find a point of attachment in Jeremiah's own preaching for the vision of ch. 24? To investigate this question it is essential to engage in a more basic examination of the chapter.

As against the vision passages considered previously, which may be attributed to Jeremiah himself, the main characteristic here is not an announcement of Yahweh's intentions for the future, but an evaluation of the disastrous events for Judah that had already taken place. What would seem to be the obvious assessment of them is to be turned upside down. Yahweh's future belonged not to those who appeared in these events to have been preferentially treated by Yahweh's judgement but to those who had already been judged – provided that they returned to Yahweh, as the condition attached to verse 7 states. By means of the vision, according to the present text, Yahweh's judgement upon the two groups of people is represented; and inasmuch as it makes use of the picture of two baskets of figs it recalls, as far as the basket is concerned, Amos' vision of a basket of summer fruit (*kelûb qayiṣ*) from which Amos had made a link with the word meaning 'end' (*qēṣ*). Since in Jer. 24 the word *dûd* is used for the basket, it is not possible to postulate a direct dependence of Jer. 24 on Amos 8:1. In a similar way comparison of the two visions brings out the structural differences between them. Whereas Amos 8:1–2 reveals the coming end of Israel in an ominous way, the basis of Jer. 24 is the statement of a comparison: 'like these good figs' (verse 4) and 'like these bad figs which are so bad they cannot be eaten' (verse 8). It is at the same time true that a reference to the work of Yahweh is also added: 'so will I regard...the exiles' (verse 4) – 'so will I treat Zedekiah' (verse 8).

It is proper to raise at this point the question whether there may not lie behind the vision, as its real point of origin, a simple word picture that Jeremiah could well have used. In Jer. 2–6 we find words of Jeremiah in an elevated style, which are generally agreed to be those words of the prophet himself that can be identified as such with the greatest confidence. These make vivid and abundant use of word pictures. Thus 2:20 uses the metaphor of an animal breaking its yoke; 2:21 of a choice vine; 2:22 of washing oneself with lye; 2:23 of a restive young camel; 2:26 of a thief. We must ask whether the vision of Jer. 24, with its setting out of alternatives, which has been shaped by the rich use of polished language, does not have as its nucleus a simple pictorial comparison, expressed in Jeremiah's own words, which Jeremiah had used with reference to those who had been exiled in 597? The oracles referring to Jehoiachin (Coniah) in 22:24–30, which have been much elaborated, and especially verse 28, which by its use of the characteristically Jeremianic formal device of the triple question is shown to be an original formulation of Jeremiah himself, betray a remarkable sympathy on the part of Jeremiah for the deported king, and appear to provide evidence of a high estimation of the deported leaders of society (to whom Ezekiel also belonged). In any case, as Ackroyd (1968, pp. 55–6) has rightly emphasised, we must assume for Jer. 24 an entirely *ad hoc* comparison, directed to a particular situation, which is not to be amplified into a fixed assessment of the value of those who remained in Palestine and those who had been deported to Babylon in the way that the present form of the vision has done. The sense of security of those who had not been deported in 597, to which Ezekiel's words bear witness, would then have been challenged by the prophet with his picture of the inedible figs, just as he had characterised his people in 2:21 by the picture, even more firmly rooted in Israel's sacral language, of a choice vine that had degenerated into a wild vine (cf. also Zimmerli, 1979a, on Ezek. 15).

We are here, naturally, in the realm of the consideration of possibilities. But in any case we may discount the rather unlikely assumption that the Deuteronomistic redaction of Jeremiah could have arrived at the by no means common picture of good and bad figs without there being any support for such a picture in the transmitted words of Jeremiah himself.

This raises the question whether a further step may legitimately be taken. Did the original words of Jeremiah already contain a report of a visionary experience, in which the prophet saw baskets of figs that had been brought to the sanctuary, of which one was *lerāṣôn* ('acceptable'), and the other *lo' lerāṣôn* ('not acceptable'; cf. on the same point Mal. 1:7–9), which then was changed into Yahweh's word for him concerning the two groups of people?

Whether this is so or not, it can scarcely be doubted that the present form of the text of Jer. 24 is the responsibility of a more recent hand. A polemic of Jeremiah that was originally directed at a particular wrong attitude in a concrete situation has, at a later stage, in which it was a question not only of the two groups, those who remained in the land and those who were deported to Babylon in 597 and 587, but also of a third group, those who formed an Egyptian Diaspora, become an absolute judgement: salvation will come through the Babylonian *golah*. Such a verdict would have been anachronistic in the situation of 597. What is reported elsewhere of Jeremiah's words in the period between 597 and 587 (especially chs. 27–9) shows the prophet concerned in other ways with the survival of those who remained in Jerusalem, without forgetting those who had already been deported in 597.

Thus the assumption of an original Jeremianic background for the vision of Jer. 24 remains surrounded by many uncertainties.

VII

In summary, it can clearly be established that the preaching of Jeremiah certainly did not lack a visionary element. The utter bewilderment of the prophet at the way in which he has been seized by Yahweh cannot be mistaken in the oracles of the early period, to which belong both the twin visions that are linked with the narrative of his call (1:11ff) and the vision of 4:23-6.

The main emphasis has, however, shifted in Jeremiah entirely to the transmission of preaching – at least so far as we can see from the text that has been handed down. Indeed one can pose the question, to which a certain answer is impossible, whether the visionary element does not diminish in importance in the course of the prophetic proclamation of Jeremiah. The reason for this could well have been the conflict of Jeremiah with the prophets of salvation, who recounted their dreams and emphasised in them the visual element in order to boast of the mysterious character of their prophetic experience. Jeremiah reproaches them with preaching 'visions of their own minds' (23:16).[3] (On this cf. Quell, 1952, pp. 161ff; Ehrlich, 1953.)

But what do we know of the actual character of the prophetic experience of Jeremiah's later years? Where a third person reports of his career in the times of Jehoiakim, Zedekiah and finally the hopeless closing stage of the history of Judah, there the oracular judgement decides everything. But also the passages that are traditionally classified as 'Confessions' (11:18 – 12:6; 15:10-21; 17:14-18; 18:18-23; 20:7-18) do not contain any clear allusions to visual experience. (On this Baumgartner, 1917; von Rad, 1936; in a different sense Gunneweg, 1970; Welten, 1977.)

Jeremiah, therefore, represents a transitional stage in the direction of the preaching of Deutero-Isaiah, in which no visionary elements are to be found. There the word of Yahweh that 'will stand for ever' (Isa. 40:8) is in control of everything. The divine confirmation in history establishes 'the word of his servants'[4], that is, the prophets (Isa. 44:26). Here is the effective cause of what happens (Isa. 55:10-11). But this complete lack of a visual element is already characteristic of Hosea, with whose message Jeremiah shows close links. On the other hand Jeremiah is different in this regard from his younger contemporary Ezekiel, with whom in other respects connections can be traced (Miller, 1955). Despite the emphasis on the power of Yahweh's word, the great significance of the visionary element in Ezekiel cannot be mistaken. This aspect is developed in Zechariah after the exile and in this way is a preparation for the apocalyptic technique (Gese, 1973; Jeremias, 1977) when that reached its full maturity in Daniel after the long period of the silence of prophecy. The validity of such a development is not a matter for judgement here. With Jeremiah the validity of the experience as reflecting his own distinctive knowledge is not to be doubted.

Notes

1 The formulae 'I saw' or 'Yahweh showed me', which are characteristic of the fully developed vision, are lacking here; only the 'call to attention' *hinnēh* (KBL, 1953, p. 238) is used.

2 The formula 1: 3*a* is a heading that has been added at a secondary stage. In 11: 14–21 an independent oracle has been secondarily inserted into the vision cycle.

3 The root *ḥzh* occurs in the Book of Jeremiah only here and in 14: 14; in both passages the noun form *ḥāzôn* is used in a polemical way.

4 Emended text: cf. *BHS*.

Bibliography

P. R. Ackroyd *Exile and Restoration* (London, 1968).

W. Baumgartner *Die Klagegedichte des Jeremia*, BZAW 32 (Giessen, 1917).

J. M. Berridge 'Jeremia und die Prophetie des Amos', *ThZ* 35 (1979), 321–41.

J. Bright *Jeremiah*, Anchor Bible 21 (Garden City, New York, 1965).

R. E. Clements *Prophecy and Tradition* (Oxford, 1975).

B. Duhm *Das Buch Jeremia*, KHC 11 (Tübingen and Leipzig, 1901).

E. L. Ehrlich *Der Traum im Alten Testament*, BZAW 73 (Berlin, 1953).

M. Fishbane 'Jeremiah 4: 23–26 and Job 3: 3–13: A recovered Use of the Creation Pattern,' *VT* 21 (1971), 151–67.

H. Gese 'Anfang und Ende der Apokalyptik, dargestellt am Sacharjabuch', *ZThK* 70 (1973), 20–49 (= *Vom Sinai zum Zion. Alttestamentliche Beiträge zur biblischen Theologie* (Munich, 1974), pp. 202–30).

F. Giesebrecht *Das Buch Jeremia*, HK, 3, 2 (Göttingen, 1907).

O. Grether *Name und Wort Gottes im Alten Testament*, BZAW 64 (Giessen, 1934).

K. Gross *Die literarische Verwandschaft Jeremias mit Hosea*, Diss. (Borna, Leipzig, 1930).

'Hoseas Einfluss auf Jeremias Anschauungen', *NKZ* 43 (1931), 241–56, 327–43.

A. H. J. Gunneweg 'Konfession oder Interpretation im Jeremiabuch', *ZThK* 67 (1970), 395–416.

P. D. Hanson *The Dawn of Apocalyptic* (Philadelphia, 1975).

S. Herrmann *Die prophetischen Heilserwartungen im Alten Testament. Ursprung und Gestaltwandel*, BWA(N)T 85 (Stuttgart, 1965).

'Die Bewältigung der Krise Israels, Bemerkungen zur Interpretation des Buches Jeremia', in *Beiträge zur Alttestamentlichen Theologie, Festschrift W. Zimmerli* (Göttingen, 1977), pp. 164–78.

W. Herrmann 'Philologica Hebraica', *Theologische Versuche*, vol. VIII (Berlin, 1977), pp. 35–44.

G. Hölscher *Die Profeten, Untersuchungen zur Religionsgeschichte Israels* (Leipzig, 1914).

F. Horst 'Die Visionsschilderungen der alttestamentlichen Propheten', *EvTh* 20 (1960), 193–205.

C. Jeremias *Die Nachtgesichte des Sacharja. Untersuchungen zu ihrer Stellung im Zusammenhang der Visionsberichte in Alten Testament und zu ihrem Bildmaterial*, FRLANT 117 (Göttingen, 1977).

H. Kremers 'Leidensgemeinschaft mit Gott. Eine Untersuchung der "biographischen" Berichte im Jeremiabuch', *EvTh* 13 (1953), 122–40.

J. Lindblom 'Die Gesichte der Propheten', *Studia Theologica* ,vol. I: 'Festschrift I. Benzinger' (Riga, 1935), pp. 7–28.

Prophecy in Ancient Israel (Oxford and Philadelphia, 1962).

J. W. Miller *Das Verhältnis Jeremias und Hesekiels sprachlich und theologisch untersucht* (Assen, 1955).

S. Mowinckel *Zur Komposition des Buches Jeremia* (Oslo, 1914).

P. K. D. Neumann 'Das Wort, das geschehen ist...Zum Problem der Wortempfangstheologie in Jer. 1–25', *VT* 23 (1973), 171–217.

B. A. Pareira *The Call to Conversion in Ezekiel*, Diss. Pontificia Universitas Gregoriana (Rome, 1975).

K.-F. Pohlmann *Studien zum Jeremiabuch*, FRLANT 118 (Göttingen, 1978).

G. Quell *Wahre und falsche Propheten*, BFchrTh 46, 1 (Gütersloh, 1952).

G. von Rad 'Die Konfessionen Jeremias', *EvTh* 3 (1936), 265–76 (= *Gesammelte Studien zum Alten Testament*, vol. II, ThB 48 (Munich, 1973), pp. 224–35).

T. M. Raitt 'The Prophetic Summons to Repentance', *ZAW* 83 (1971), 30–49.

A Theology of Exile. Judgement/Deliverance in Jeremiah and Ezekiel (Philadelphia, 1977).

H. G. Reventlow *Liturgie und prophetisches Ich bei Jeremia* (Gütersloh, 1963).

C. Rietzschel *Das Problem der Urrolle. Ein Beitrag zur Redaktionsgeschichte des Jeremiabuches* (Gütersloh, 1966).

W. Rudolph *Jeremia*, HAT 1, 12, 3rd ed. (Tübingen, 1968).

T. Seidl 'Die Wortereignisformel in Jeremia', *BZ* 23 (1979), 20–47.

I. P. Seierstad *Die Offenbarungserlebnisse der Propheten Amos, Jesaja und Jeremia*, 2nd ed. (Oslo, 1965).

H. Schmidt *Die grossen Propheten*, SAT 2, 2, 2nd ed. (Göttingen, 1923).

R. Smend *Die Bundesformel*, ThSt(B) 68 (Zürich, 1963).

W. Thiel *Die deuteronomistische Redaktion von Jeremia 1–25*, WMANT 41 (Neukirchen, 1973).

P. Volz *Der Prophet Jeremia*, KAT 10 (Leipzig and Erlangen, 1922).

G. Wanke *Untersuchungen zur sogenannten Baruchschrift*, BZAW 122 (Berlin, 1971).

A. Weiser *Das Buch Jeremia*, ATD 20, 21, 5th ed. (Göttingen, 1966).

P. Welten 'Leiden und Leidenserfahrung in Buch Jeremia', *ZThK* 74 (1977), 123–50.

H. Wildberger *Jahwewort und prophetische Rede bei Jeremia* (Zürich, 1942).

W. Zimmerli *Erkenntnis Gottes nach dem Buche Ezechiel. Eine theologische Studie*, AThANT 27 (Zürich, 1954) (= *Gottes Offenbarung. Gesammelte Aufsätze zum Alten Testament*, ThB 19, 2nd ed. (Munich, 1969), pp. 41–119).

'Prophetic Proclamation and Reinterpretation', in D. F. Knight (ed.), *Tradition and Theology in the Old Testament* (Philadelphia, 1977), pp. 69–100 (English translation of 'Die kritische Infragestellung der Tradition durch die Prophetie', in O. H. Steck (ed.), *Zu Tradition und Theologie im Alten Testament*, Biblisch-theologische Studien vol. II (Neukirchen, 1978), pp. 57–86).

Ezekiel 1. A Commentary on the Book of the Prophet Ezekiel, Chapters 1–24, Hermeneia (Philadelphia, 1979) (English translation of *Ezechiel 1*, BKAT 13, 1 (Neukirchen, 1969)). (The English translation is cited as Zimmerli, 1979a.)

Ezechiel, BKAT 13, 1 and 2, 2nd ed. (Neukirchen, 1979).

The Ezekiel tradition:
prophecy in a time of crisis

R. E. CLEMENTS

There exists an inevitable measure of ambivalence in any prophecy, since it requires a certain matching up of what was actually said by a prophet with particular events in which these words could be regarded as fulfilled for a satisfactory interpretation to be achieved. Peter Ackroyd (1962) has drawn attention to the way in which a specific prophetic saying could be developed and reapplied to new situations over a period of time, since it was regarded as a 'living'word of God. This essay drew my attention to a facet of Biblical prophecy that has increasingly commanded attention as a key to understanding the peculiar structure of the major prophetic books of the Old Testament. It is clear that in no case are we here presented with a series of prophecies preserved simply as the original prophet received or preached them. Instead, they have passed through a substantial process of editing during which additional material has been introduced to amplify and expand upon the original sayings and records. There is, therefore, a kind of commentary, which is often very complex and difficult to identify because it has become woven into the text of the book itself. In some cases this expansion of an original prophetic collection has continued over a very long period and can be seen to have passed through several stages of quite major reorganisation of the material, besides the incorporation of additions to it. This is most marked in the case of the Book of Isaiah, where different stages in the redactional expansion can still be detected. Hence scholars have noted the importance of an edition made during Josiah's reign, and a further important stage added in the wake of the destruction of much of Jerusalem in 587 B.C., with the removal of the Davidic monarchy from the throne of Judah (Barth, 1977). The later stages in the growth of the Book of Isaiah show all the main characteristics of the transition from prophecy, as it was originally understood, to apocalyptic (Vermeylen, 1977; cf. Plöger, 1968; Hanson, 1975). This is most marked in regard to Isa. 24–7 and

119

56–66, but is also to be found in some other smaller sections of the book.

However, when we turn to consider the Books of Jeremiah and Ezekiel, we find that the situation is not nearly so complicated and that a far greater degree of homogeneity and planned application can be seen to have existed in the way in which this redactional shaping has taken place. More particularly we can see that a far greater homogeneity of theological outlook and institutional affinity exists in the work. I am not here concerned about individual glosses or minor textual developments, which undoubtedly continued after this major work of literary shaping took place. My concern is rather with what I might term the literary and theological shape of the major prophetic collections. Although it lies outside my immediate concern here, we might also note that a similar redactional shape has also been imparted to the book of the Twelve Prophets, although, for obvious reasons, the degree of diversity within the unified structure is more obtrusively apparent (cf. Sawyer, 1977, pp. 103ff).

In the twentieth century, once critical scholarship had firmly established the case for recognising that our prophetic books are not simply collections of the original sayings of the prophets but contain a great deal of secondary material, two theories have tended to hide the proper appreciation and evaluation of this theological redaction of these literary collections. The first has been the belief that the formation of the books has been the result of a process of continuous, and more or less unrelated, agglomeration of material. For example it was taken for granted that the contents of Deutero- and Trito-Isaiah had essentially nothing at all to do with the prophecies of the original Isaiah of Jerusalem. An almost limitless number of stages during which individual glosses and additions were made could then be posited. The second hypothesis has been that each of the great prophets, but most especially Isaiah and Ezekiel, gave rise to the organisation of a body of 'disciples', who would then have been responsible for the preservation of the original prophet-master's sayings and for the addition of further prophecies to these. A most extreme example of the pressing of this hypothesis has been offered by Engnell (1970, pp. 163ff), who uses it virtually to set aside any possibility of distinguishing between what the original prophet said and what his disciples added to this. In effect a theory of collective composition of the great prophetic books has been posited, with the assumption that something of the stamp and theological outlook of the original prophet would have remained impressed on the material that only arose later. Attractive as such a theory has been, because of its apparent ability to account for the retention of an ascription of authorship to the original prophet, it results in a great deal of vagueness and uncertainty in our evaluation of the secondary material in the particular books concerned. So long as a vague umbrella of identity as the work of a 'disciple' was maintained, quite markedly varied and disparate material could be assumed to belong to a book. Even more, such a hypothesis strains our credulity to an impossible extent, if we are required to believe that a body of Isaiah's disciples could have existed, as an identifiable and functioning entity, through a period of almost four centuries, without leaving any proper record of their existence, save for the book in which they manage to preserve their cover of anonymity.

Even more than these objections, however, the theories either of a random agglomeration of material or of a progressive process of addition by disciples fail to account satisfactorily for the extant shape of the major prophetic collections. This concerns the issue of respect for the original integrity and significance of the sayings of the great prophets. Both a process of random agglomeration and that of additions by disciples assume that the progressive building-up of the collections of sayings shared the same level of inspiration and consequent authority between prophet-master and disciple or scribe. All is assumed to partake of the same authority as the declared word of God, irrespective of the precise agency of its origin. Yet this conflicts with one of the most important points that is noted in the article by Ackroyd already referred to (1962, p. 15). This pointed to the fact that it is precisely the special nature, and consequent special authority, of the original prophetic saying that was believed to make it applicable to a whole series of situations. It was because it was regarded as uniquely meaningful that a prophetic saying given by one of the great figures of Israel's prophetic movement could be applied and reapplied in a whole sequence of situations, many of which were entirely unrelated to that of the original prophet. We have only to consider the way in which the themes of 'thorns and briers' (Isa. 5:6; 7:23–5; 10:17; 27:4) or the names Shear-jashub and Immanuel are used in the development of Isaiah's prophecies (Isa. 7:3; 10:20–3; 11:11, 16; 7:14; 8:8, 10) to see that a very considerable authority was felt to pertain to the actual words of the master's prophecy. In this respect it is precisely their possession of a unique authority that has led to their reapplication to new situations far beyond those which could have been envisaged by

Isaiah himself. If we are to think of the editors and expanders of the prophetic material as disciples of the original prophet, it can therefore only be with a marked awareness of the difference between the role of the prophet and the role of his disciples. They become merely his interpreters. This is a very different situation from that envisaged by Engnell, in which he implies that no essential difference existed between the authority of the prophet and that of his disciples.

In reality, however, it seems that little real gain is achieved by positing a band of prophetic 'disciples', who may be presumed to have remained in a separately identifiable existence after the original prophet had died. Obviously there were tradents of the prophetic sayings, and all the indications are that these tradents kept the contents of the three major collections of Isaiah, Jeremiah and Ezekiel, as self-contained literary wholes. The evident degree of cross-connection and over-lapping between the contents of the books is quite minimal. Another reason for doubting whether the definition of 'disciples', or of a 'prophetic school', adequately describes the character and work of the tradents and interpreters of the prophets who have contributed towards the formation of their books is found in the affinities between their work and that revealed in other parts of the Old Testament literature. Once we find that the work of collecting, shaping and interpreting the sayings of a great prophet has been undertaken in the language, thought-forms and situation that are related to other literary works of the Old Testament, then it seems clear that the aim of such men was more than simply to preserve a prophet's sayings. Rather it was more evidently intended to relate what the prophet had said to a particular situation and to the needs and concerns of a central religious group within the life of the nation. Nowhere is this more openly to be seen than in the case of the Book of Jeremiah. Here the preserved literary work shows an extraordinary degree of connection, in certain of its parts, with the work of what we have come to know as the Deuterono-mic school.[1] This was evidently extensively active in Judah, at least from the middle period of Josiah's reign (640–609 B.C.) until the middle of the sixth century B.C. So close are the literary and theological affinities between these parts of the Book of Jeremiah and the Book of Deuteronomy, as well as with the Deuteronomistic History (Joshua–2 Kings), that a fundamental connection between the authors of the respective works must be posited. This applies especially to the nar-ratives contained in the Book of Jeremiah (Mowinckel's source B) and to the prose sermons (Mowinckel's source C) (Mowinckel, 1914).

Clearly we have in both groups of material a direct link with the preaching and activity of Jeremiah himself. At the same time, so close are the connections of thought and theological vocabulary with those of the Deuteronomic school that we must conclude that what we are presented with here is a view of Jeremiah's work seen through the eyes of Deuteronomistic interpreters. A point of particular importance is that this presentation of Jeremiah's preaching has been particularly coloured by the fact that the Jerusalem Temple had been destroyed in 587 B.C. and that, after the murder of Gedaliah, all hope of the renewal of Israel had switched to the exiles in Babylon.

The question of the date and provenance of this Deuteronomistic edition of Jeremiah's preaching falls into several separate issues. The fact that, within the preserved book, this Deuteronomistic material is spread across the primary collection of prophecies in Jer. 1–25 and the narrative accounts of 26–8; 34–45, as well as the prophecies of hope collected together in 31–3, shows that this Deuteronomistic affiliation was influential at several stages. It is not our purpose here to reopen the discussion concerning this important feature of the study of the Book of Jeremiah, except in so far as it reflects upon the character of the prophetic literature as a whole. I have argued elsewhere that a most important connection exists between an early stage of the collection of Isaiah's prophecies and the formative period of the Deuteronomic movement during Josiah's reign (Clements, 1980). What is important, therefore, is not simply the theological character imparted to the respective literary collections by the tradents of the prophetic sayings but the time and the situation to which they have addressed them. What is most striking as far as the Jeremiah sayings are concerned, is the fact that they are viewed by the Deuteronomistic editors from a post-587 B.C. standpoint. This is most evident in the instances of the Temple prophecies of Jer. 7:1–15; 26:1–19, where it is beyond question that the destruction of the Temple in 587 B.C. has been allowed to influence the tradition of Jeremiah's authentic prophecy warning against a false trust in the Temple. It provides an excellent illustration of the way in which the sense of how a prophecy was fulfilled has been allowed to affect the formulation of what it actually pronounced. This cannot be regarded as a process of 'falsifying' a prophecy *post eventum*, but must be seen rather as an attempt to show how the fulfilment took effect. In this case it was evidently of unique importance to have been able to cite Jeremiah's prophecy, since, as we know from elsewhere (e.g. Lam. 2:6f; 4:13), the physical destruction of the

Jerusalem Temple appeared to contradict all notions of Yahweh's power and sovereignty.

That the Deuteronomistic editing of the Jeremiah material was a post-587 B.C. undertaking appears to be beyond any question, as soon as we look in detail at what it contains. Not only in detailed matters of content, but more broadly in its whole theological direction, it shows this colouring. In broad outline it uses Jeremiah's prophecies to provide a kind of theodicy for the tragic events that took place at the hands of the Babylonians in that momentous year. This is further borne out when we examine this Deuteronomistic material in relation to the two earlier major compositions from this movement: the Book of Deuteronomy and the Deuteronomistic History (Josh.–2 Kings). As Diepold (1972) has shown in respect of its theology of the land as Israel's inheritance, there can be little cause for doubting that the Deuteronomistic material in Jeremiah represents the latest stage of Deuteronomistic theological development of this major theme (cf. Perlitt, 1969, pp. 15ff). All in all, therefore, we can see that it is a matter of considerable importance that we should view the way in which Jeremiah's prophecies have been edited and addressed to a particular situation as of great concern to understanding the final stage of Deuteronomistic theological development. The issues are not simply relevant to determining the authenticity, or otherwise, of the contents of the Book of Jeremiah but are related to formative theological developments during the exilic age. Not least is this so in respect of the way in which an Israelite theology of covenant (Heb. *berit*) was built up (cf. Perlitt, 1969, pp. 7ff).

If these observations are established, then it greatly strengthens the conclusion that this Deuteronomic theological movement, or school, undertook its work in Judah during the late seventh century and the first half of the sixth century B.C. Since the law-book of Deuteronomy and the Deuteronomistic History were two works that must have been composed in Judah, where alone the literary source material for such an enterprise was available, this is obviously also the most probable setting for the editing of Jeremiah's prophecies. All the more does this appear to have been the case, since Jeremiah himself remained in Judah after 587 B.C., until his compulsory removal to Egypt (Jer. 43:6). Before leaving this question of the literary affinities of the Book of Jeremiah, we may consider a further fact. If the Deuteronomistic material was added to the collection after 587 B.C., which must be regarded as certain, then the latest date for these additions and the accompanying editorial shaping cannot have been much later than 550 B.C. This is borne out by the fact that there is no hint of the political possibilities of a return engendered by the rise of Cyrus, which became prominent after 546 B.C. Similarly the expectations of an eventual return of the Babylonian exiles appear vague and ill-defined. Their certainty is based upon theological conviction, not imminent political expectations related to the situation of either Judah or Babylon. We are led therefore to locate this editorial shaping and development of Jeremiah's prophecies in the period between 580 and 550 B.C., as the most probable time of its origin. In the face of the lack of any strong evidence to the contrary, we should also place it in Judah, where the other Deuteronomic-Deuteronomistic compositions originated. We are not therefore faced with indications of a period of progressive and protracted building-up of material in the Book of Jeremiah over an extended period but rather with an important attempt to relate Jeremiah's prophecies to a specific historical situation. As long as the analysis and consequent literary evaluation of the different types of material in the Book of Jeremiah were regarded solely as an aspect of understanding the transmission of this particular prophet's sayings, then the critical questions appeared baffling and difficult to resolve. Yet as soon as we relate the literary and theological phenomena of the book to the wider questions concerning the Deuteronomic movement in Israel and Judah, a much clearer picture emerges. The key to this understanding has been available to scholars since the commentary of Duhm (1901), but only in recent years has the value of his observations been satisfactorily explored. To think of the tradents of the prophecies as disciples of the original prophet reveals only one very partial side of their work and identity. Much more meaningful is their close association with the Deuteronomic movement and its theology. Furthermore, the particular situation to which they addressed their interpretation of the prophecies is especially important for understanding the way in which they have gone about their task.

So far my considerations regarding the formation of the prophetic books have dealt mainly with the Book of Jeremiah, rather than with Ezekiel. Yet this may be defended as a necessary way of proceeding for two reasons. The first of these is that the Book of Jeremiah provides a particularly clear instance of the title 'disciples' offering a very misleading characterisation of the aims and intentions of those who have shaped a major prophetic book. Their affiliations were clearly wider than this, so that their work must be understood in connection with the

125

history of Judah during the sixth century B.C. and the special concern that these tradents felt for the major religious institutions of Israel, especially the Jerusalem Temple, but also including the Davidic monarchy. Secondly, the problems concerning the literary and theological structure of the Book of Ezekiel are greatly illuminated by a comparison with what is to be seen in the Book of Jeremiah. If Jeremiah, both as a prophet himself and as the originating figure of the book that derives from him, is to be regarded as the prophet of Judah during the sixth century B.C., then Ezekiel is certainly to be seen as the prophet of the Babylonian exiles. Moreover, whereas all the theological connections of the book of Jeremiah are with the Deuteronomic movement, those of Ezekiel are to be found in the work of the emergent Priestly school. This may be used as a broad, and admittedly loosely-defined, title for the authors of the Holiness Code (Lev. 17–26) and the Priestly Document. There are, in any case, other grounds for asserting that the major theological and historical affinities of these literary works are with the world of the Babylonian exiles, and with their successors who returned to Judah after 538 B.C.

In recent years the Book of Ezekiel has been the subject of a very marked change of outlook on the part of critical scholars. Beginning with the work of Hölscher (1924), there was a growing inclination to recognise that the coherence and homogeneity that was at one time thought to have characterised the book could not be sustained under critical examination. There are marked variations in the formal and stylistic features between different parts of the book, and some significant changes of theological emphasis. A further turning-point was then reached with the attempt of Herntrich (1933) to show that the original prophet Ezekiel had lived and worked in Judah throughout the period of his ministry and that the Babylonian background of the book was a later overlay imposed on this. From this there emerged, almost as an inevitable critical after-thought, the claim that Ezekiel had experienced a dual ministry, as argued by Bertholet (1936), H. W. Robinson (1948) and others. For a period this belief that Ezekiel had initially worked in Judah between the years 593 and 587 B.C. and had then been taken to Babylon, where he entered upon a second phase of his prophetic activity between the years 587 and 571, assumed the proportions of something approaching a critical consensus. Yet, beginning with the publication in 1955 of Fohrer's examination of Ezekiel (cf. Fohrer, 1952), this critical assessment has been compelled to give way in favour of the position that recognises that all of Ezekiel's ministry was conducted in Babylon. There are no over-riding objections, therefore, to accepting the dates and setting that the book itself presents, which suggest that Ezekiel was a member of a Jerusalem priestly family who was taken to Babylon in 597 B.C. He then received his call to prophesy in the year 593 (Ezek. 1:2) and continued his prophetic ministry until the time of the latest of the prophecies, which are dated in 571 B.C. (Ezek. 29:17).

However, this return on the part of Biblical scholarship to a recognition of the reliability of the evidence of the setting of Ezekiel's ministry that the book itself provides has not meant a complete return to the *status quo ante* Hölscher of critical investigation. It is clear that the book does show an impressive degree of theological homogeneity and a remarkable element of planned literary structure. The major divisions of the book between ch. 1–24; 25–32; 33–9 and 40–8 are all undoubtedly the consequence of an attempt to give some literary and theological 'form' to the book as a whole. Yet this shape is also quite clearly not something that the original prophet could have imposed; nor are the broad theological features of the book all to be ascribed to the particular theological outlook of Ezekiel himself. The way in which even the most devastating invective against Judah has been rounded off with words of hope and assurance (e.g. in 16:53ff; 20:33ff) is evidence enough that a considerable amount of development and reworking of the original Ezekiel prophecies has taken place. It is for this reason that Zimmerli (1979) has posited the existence of an Ezekiel 'school', who must be looked to as the body responsible for imparting this literary and theological structure to the book. It cannot be, therefore, that the original prophet has been responsible for the extant book that bears his name; nor can we ascribe all the material within it to his authorship. In a number of instances it is clearly very difficult to ascertain whether the material that can be seen to be 'secondary', as defined by its present position, is from the original prophet or from the 'school'. Such difficulties only highlight still more emphatically the point that the question of 'authenticity' is not always the major question regarding the setting of a passage, except in so far as it bears upon the issue of time of origin. Perhaps it is not altogether surprising, therefore, that the belief in the existence of an Ezekiel 'school', and the willingness to recognise that a measure of secondary material is to be found in the book, has been capable of being carried to quite extreme lengths. Thus, for example, Garscha (1974) has renewed the demand for a more radical approach to the questions of the literary structure of the book and has argued that only a relatively small proportion of the extant prophecies come from Ezekiel, the prophet of the exile. Yet such a position appears extreme, and goes a considerable way beyond what is necessary to explain the evidence of redactional development and elaboration. Overall, the much more cautious approach shown by Zimmerli would appear to be justified, and the conclusion may be drawn that a quite remarkable part of the general homogeneity and uniformity of the book stems from the contribution of Ezekiel himself.

However, it still remains open to question whether the assumption of an Ezekiel 'school' is the best and most satisfactory way of explaining how the original prophecies of Ezekiel have been developed and edited. This is because scholarship has for long recognised that another dimension of affiliation also exists for Ezekiel's prophecies. This, as we have already noted, is to be found in the connections that exist between the theological outlook of Ezekiel and those of the Priestly Document, and more particularly the Holiness Code of Lev. 17–26. It is obviously a quite unsatisfactory assumption to suppose that it was the 'school' of Ezekiel that was responsible for the composition and theological outlook exemplified in these works. In fact the measure of theological and literary connection that can be shown to exist between them is not such as to suggest any immediate community of authorship. With the widespread application of a traditio-historical method of study to the literature of the Old Testament, especially to the Old Testament prophets, as exemplified in the work of von Rad (1965), it has appeared possible to explain much of the commonality of outlook and interest between the Book of Ezekiel and the authors of the Holiness Code and the Priestly Document as due to the dependence on the Jerusalem cult tradition that all three works shared. Ezekiel was born and brought up in the priestly traditions of the Jerusalem Temple, and this must certainly be taken to imply that he was a descendant of the Zadokite family and that he had most probably already taken an active role in that cultus before his deportation to Babylon. Such at least would appear to be the most probable explanation of his being singled out for deportation in 597 B.C. If we had not been told of this priestly derivation in Ezek. 1:3 we should in any case certainly have deduced it from the character and content of the prophecies that his book preserves (Zimmerli, 1979, pp. 16f). Valuable and helpful as this traditio-historical method of analysis and criticism has been, it is open to suggest that it is capable of being pressed too far in its effort to explain the features of theological overlap between literary works that show many common features of language and thought. The reason for suggesting this is provided by what we have already noted in connection with the literary shape afforded to the Book of Jeremiah. As it is now preserved, this prophetic book reveals a most instructive example of the way in which the work and sayings of a particular prophet have been remembered and applied to a particular situation at the hands of a very distinctive theological circle. It is neither Jeremiah's 'disciples' nor the figure of Baruch that has imparted the special stamp to the Book of Jeremiah that we now have. Nor yet is it the Deuteronomic school who have simply wrested the sayings of Jeremiah from their original setting and added their own words under the guise of the preaching of Jeremiah. Rather it is the consequence of a most fruitful marriage of the *traditio* of Jeremiah's prophecies with the situation that the Deuteronomic school found itself faced with in Judah after 587 B.C. What we find is Jeremiah's preaching seen through Deuteronomic eyes and applied to a unique situation that was understandably of paramount significance to the aims and concerns of the Deuteronomic school of Judah. It may be suggested, therefore, that we have a roughly comparable situation in respect of the prophecies of Ezekiel.

The material from the Book of Ezekiel that we are especially concerned with here is to be found in chs. 40–8, in what has come to be known as the Reconstruction Programme. That this programme is based upon an authentic vision of the prophet Ezekiel, which is dated in Ezek. 40:1 to the twenty-fifth year of exile (i.e. 573 B.C.), must be held as certain. At the same time it has come to be widely recognised, by Gese (1957) and others, that this original vision has undergone substantial expansion in order to incorporate a number of provisions for the administration of the cultus, especially in respect of the role of the priests and the Levites. This Reconstruction Programme, therefore, can be seen to have developed the Ezekiel tradition in a particular way and in regard to a specific issue, that of the restoration of the Jerusalem Temple and its cultus, which had an authentic basis in the prophet's message.

When we consider the literary and theological affinities of the Ezekiel tradition from another aspect, we find that some further valuable light is brought to bear upon how it has developed. This concerns the question of the relationship of the Book of Ezekiel, and especially of its Reconstruction Programme, to the Holiness Code (H), which has now been incorporated into the Book of Leviticus to form chs. 17–26. We may leave aside here the further question whether this

Holiness Code was incorporated first, as a self-contained entity, into the Priestly Document, or was only subsequently added to the Tetrateuch (Genesis–Numbers), after the Priestly Document had already been combined with the earlier narrative materials of JE (cf. Noth, 1965, pp. 16, 128; 1972, p. 9; Elliger, 1966, pp. 16ff). What is very clear is that there is an undoubted relationship between Ezekiel and H, but this is not one that can be reduced to any one simple formula. That Ezekiel was the author of the Holiness Code must certainly be set aside as altogether too simplistic and improbable a solution to carry conviction. Yet neither can we make the deduction that the Holiness Code is later than Ezekiel at all points, as Wellhausen concluded (1957, pp. 378f, 404; cf. Klostermann, 1893, pp. 368–418). As the broad examination undertaken by Zimmerli (1979) shows, there are some points where the dependence appears to be in one direction and others where the reverse is true. What we have in the two literary works of the Book of Ezekiel and the Holiness Code are compositions that have undoubtedly exercised a mutual influence upon each other (cf. Zimmerli, 1979, p. 52; Fohrer, 1952, pp. 144f).

We may limit our attention to two particular issues concerning the priesthood. In Ezek. 44:10ff the Levites are precluded from the enjoyment of full priestly status in the renewed sanctuary and instead are reduced to the level of providing a kind of 'second rank' clergy. The full priesthood, which is regarded as enjoying levitical descent, is to be restricted to the Zadokites, who must certainly be identified with the descendants of the Jerusalem priests of the pre-exilic era. As we know, many of these had been deported into exile in Babylon in 597 B.C., among them Ezekiel himself. Neither of these administrative regulations can be regarded as originating with Ezekiel himself, but there is every reason for supposing that they represent a point of view that emerged among the body of tradents of Ezekiel's prophecies whilst they were still in Babylon. At the latest we should date these regulations in the period shortly after the fall of Babylon to the Persians in 538 B.C. Most probably it arose before then (Gese, 1957, p. 122; Cody, 1969, pp. 156ff; Haran, 1980, pp. 103ff).

As has been widely noted, this view of the role to be enjoyed by the Zadokite priesthood presented in Ezek. 44:15ff finds no echo in the Priestly Document, or its later additions, where the qualification for the priesthood is to be one of 'the sons of Aaron'. This latter rule must certainly be a later formulation than that of the Ezekiel Restoration Programme, and in any case represents that which came finally to be accepted for the Jerusalem priesthood of the post-exilic era. What particular controversies needed to be fought and resolved before such a formula could be agreed upon can only be the subject of speculation and hypotheses. Yet one thing is clear, and this is that it was the restoration of full sacrificial worship in the rebuilt Jerusalem Temple in 516 B.C. (Ezra 6:15) that necessitated a satisfactory resolution of the issue. That it marks one aspect of the many conflicts that provoked tension between the community that returned from Babylon and that which had survived in Judah at the commencement of the Persian era can reasonably be assumed. There are good grounds, therefore, for regarding the regulations governing the priesthood that are presented in Ezek. 44:15ff as having been compiled before 516 B.C. After that date it would appear that such a formulation would have become progressively obsolete.

A number of other features have also provided pointers to indicate that we can trace a most interesting triangle of development between the preaching of the prophet Ezekiel, the work of the 'school' who have given us the Reconstruction Programme of Ezek. 40–8, and the Holiness Code of Lev. 17–26. Particularly is this detectable in the way in which the concept of holiness itself is understood (cf. Bettenzoli, 1979, especially pp. 105ff). There is much, therefore, that can be adduced to justify the conclusion drawn by Zimmerli that 'the circles which have given to H its (pre-Priestly Document) form must not be sought too far from the circles which transmitted the book of Ezekiel' (1979, p. 52). Not only is this so in regard to the major theological and linguistic affiliations that the relevant literary compositions display, but it must also be regarded as true in respect of the time at which they worked. It is surely extremely unlikely that the authors of the Ezekiel Reconstruction Programme are to be placed any later in time than 516 B.C. The completion of the work of rebuilding the Jerusalem Temple must indicate the most probable *terminus ante quem* of their work.

What we have so far considered in regard to the identity of the circles who have been responsible for the preservation and literary shaping of the Ezekiel tradition is simply a fuller elaboration of the point, already established by Zimmerli, that these circles must be sought in close proximity to those who have produced the Holiness Code. This work is itself not a fully uniform composition but shows every sign of having been composed and developed over a period of time (cf. Kilian, 1963, especially pp. 180ff). Parts of it appear to be older than Ezekiel, whilst other parts are from a time after that of the prophet of the exile. In the case of the development of the Ezekiel tradition, however, the period of its literary shaping cannot have been very extended, since the great bulk of it, including the Reconstruction Programme, must have been completed by 516 B.C., and very probably before 538 B.C. What we have is a form of literary commentary and adaptation of Ezekiel's prophecies particularly directed towards the hope of restoring the Jerusalem cultus. It emerged among the Babylonian exiles, and very probably from within the circles of the exiled Zadokite priests of Jerusalem. Understandably enough it found its inspiration and divine authority in the prophecies that Ezekiel had given. Yet it did more than simply preserve these prophecies in the manner that might be posited of disciples. Rather it extended and applied them to provide a mandate for the restoration of the Jerusalem Temple cultus in anticipation of the time when it would once again become necessary. This work is probably to be dated, therefore, to the period between 571 and 538 B.C.

It is at this point that we may draw into the discussion a further issue that has a direct bearing upon the identity and aims of the bearers of the Ezekiel tradition. This concerns the relationship that must be assumed to have existed between the Holiness Code of Lev. 17–26 and the *torah*-book of Deuteronomy. This has been the subject of an independent study by Cholewinski (1976) and has given rise to a picture of a very complex interconnectedness extending to various levels of literary composition. The precise details of Cholewinski's thesis do not directly concern us, whether or not they can be sustained in every detail. What is of primary significance is the fact that the Holiness Code can be seen to offer some kind of 'corrective' and reworking of cultic rulings and practices that are dealt with in the Book of Deuteronomy. Evidently these were felt to go too far in abandoning many of the older cultic rulings and interpretations of Israel's worship in favour of a more reasoned and theological approach. It cannot escape our attention, therefore, that, of the two great prophets of the final collapse of Judah, the Jeremiah tradition has received its shape at the hands of the Deuteronomic school, whereas the Ezekiel tradition has been fashioned within the circle of the authors of the Holiness Code and the nascent Priestly school. Furthermore it seems clear that, at least until the time of Gedaliah's murder, the Deuteronomic school was located in Judah. Against this we must set the fact that the Ezekiel tradition was certainly preserved in Babylon, at least up to the time of the Persian conquest in 538 B.C. and possibly for some little time after that.

In the light of all this it must certainly appear that we continue to recognise the important role played by distinctive circles of tradents in preserving and shaping the great prophetic collections of Jeremiah and Ezekiel, and certainly of Isaiah also, although in a rather different fashion. Perhaps 'school' is the most appropriate term by which to describe the work of these editors. In the case of Ezekiel it is clear that what they have done is to elaborate and apply the original prophet's message to the time and situation in which they found themselves placed. Nor is this situation difficult to identify, since it is quite evidently that of the latter half of the sixth century B.C., at a period when the cultic life of Jerusalem lay in ruins, and when a particular hope of its restoration had begun to take shape. In some sense they were 'disciples' of the original prophet, yet such a description fails to take adequate account of other interests and loyalties that this circle of tradents so evidently shared. Their setting has for long been recognised to be that of the priestly circles who compiled the Holiness Code.

If our thesis is supportable, then it would suggest that our prophetic literature has not been the subject of a more or less continuous and indiscriminate process of elaboration, commenting and glossing. Rather a very much more restricted activity has been undertaken, which can for the most part be assigned a relatively precise chronological location. In the case of the Books of Jeremiah and Ezekiel this can be identified with relative clarity and confidence. The case of the Book of the Twelve is necessarily somewhat different, and so also is that of the Book of Isaiah. Yet even in this latter case, if the thesis of Barth (1977) is to be followed, a quite precise and relevant edition of Isaiah's prophecies was made in Josiah's reign that has left a profound mark upon the shaping of the book.

So far as the Ezekiel tradition is concerned, we find that virtually all the substantive material in the book belongs to the sixth century B.C., even though it does not all stem from the prophet Ezekiel himself. The shape that has been given to it has made it into a charter for the rebuilding of the Jerusalem Temple and for the restoration of its cultus after the disaster of 587 B.C. That Ezekiel had himself proclaimed the divine word that authorised such a charter is not to be doubted and is, in any case, evident from the way in which Ezekiel's great vision of 593 B.C. has been reported and expanded. Thus, out of a sequence of prophecies that forewarned how God would deal with his people, there has emerged a book that is far more than a conventional prophecy and is a divine sanction for the renewal and revitalising of worship in Jerusalem after the tragic events that had brought it to an almost complete end in

587 B.C. Thereby the prophetic word itself acquired a much more durable and lasting significance.[2]

Notes

1 Duhm (1901, pp. 16ff) ascribes this 'nomistic redaction' to the fourth to third centuries B.C. Cf. Mowinckel (1914, pp. 31ff). The attempt of Weippert (1974) to ascribe this Deuteronomistic redaction to Jeremiah himself, and to deny its specifically Deuteronomistic character, must be regarded as unsatisfactory.
2 cf. Ackroyd (1977, pp. 215ff), who points out that one of the functions of preserved written prophecy was to serve as authentication for particular developments within Israel's religion. In this case the specific application of the Ezekiel prophetic tradition has been to establish the divine authenticity of the renewal of the Jerusalem Temple cultus after the exile.

Bibliography

P. R. Ackroyd 'The Vitality of the Word of God in the Old Testament', *ASTI* 1 (1962), 7–23.

'Continuity and Discontinuity: Rehabilitation and Authentication', in D. A. Knight (ed.), *Tradition and Theology in the Old Testament* (London, 1977), pp. 215–34.

H. Barth *Die Jesaja-Worte in der Josiazeit. Israel und Assur als Thema einer produktiven Neuinterpretation der Jesajaüberlieferung*, WMANT 48 (Neukirchen-Vluyn, 1977).

A. Bertholet and K. Galling *Hesekiel*, HAT (Tübingen, 1936).

G. Bettenzoli *Geist der Heiligkeit. Traditionsgeschichtliche Untersuchung des QDS – Begriffes im Buch Ezechiel*, Quaderni di Semitistica 8 (Florence, 1979).

K. W. Carley *The Book of the Prophet Ezekiel*, Cambridge Bible Commentary (London, 1974).

Ezekiel among the Prophets. A Study of Ezekiel's Place in Prophetic Tradition, SBT, Second Series 31 (London, 1975).

A. Cholewinski *Heiligkeitgesetz und Deuteronomium. Eine vergleichende Studie*, Analecta Biblica 66 (Rome, 1976).

R. E. Clements *Isaiah and the Deliverance of Jerusalem*, JSOT Supplement Series 13 (Sheffield, 1980).

A. Cody *A History of Old Testament Priesthood*, Analecta Biblica 35 (Rome, 1969).

P. Diepold *Israel's Land*, BWANT 95 (Stuttgart, 1972).

B. Duhm *Das Buch Jeremia*, HK (Tübingen and Leipzig, 1901).

K. Elliger *Leviticus*, HAT (Tübingen, 1966).

I. Engnell 'Prophets and Prophetism in the Old Testament', in *Critical Essays on the Old Testament* (London, 1970).

G. Fohrer   *Die Hauptprobleme des Buches Ezechiel*, BZAW 72 (Berlin, 1952).

G. Fohrer and K. Galling   *Ezechiel*, HAT (Tübingen, 1955).

J. Garscha   *Studien zum Ezechielbuch. Eine redaktionskritische Untersuchung von Ez. 1–39*, Europäische Hochschulschriften 23, 23 (Berne and Frankfurt, 1974).

H. Gese   *Der Verfassungsentwurf des Ezechiel (Kap. 40–48) traditionsgeschichtlich untersucht*, BhTh 25 (Tübingen, 1957).

P. D. Hanson   *The Dawn of Apocalyptic* (Philadelphia, 1975).

M. Haran   *Temples and Temple-Service in Ancient Israel* (Oxford, 1980).

V. Herntrich   *Ezechielprobleme*, BZAW 61 (Giessen, 1933).

G. Hölscher   *Hesekiel, der Dichter und das Buch. Eine literarkritische Untersuchung*, BZAW 39 (Giessen, 1924).

F. Hossfeldt   *Untersuchungen zu Komposition und Theologie des Ezechielbuches*, Forschung zur Bibel 20 (Würzburg, 1977).

R. Kilian   *Literarkritische und Formegeschichtliche Untersuchung des Heiligkeitgesetzes*, BBB 19 (Bonn, 1963).

A. Klostermann   'Ezechiel und das Heiligkeitsgesetz', in *Der Pentateuch* (Leipzig, 1893).

J. W. Miller   *Das Verhältnis Jeremias und Hesekiels sprachlich und theologisch untersucht* (Neukirchen, 1955).

S. Mowinckel   *Zur Komposition des Buches Jeremia* (Kristiania, 1914).

M. Noth   *A History of Pentateuchal Traditions* (Englewood Cliffs, 1972) (English translation of *Überlieferungsgeschichte des Pentateuch* (Stuttgart, 1948)).

Leviticus. A Commentary (London, 1965) (English translation of *Das dritte Buch Mose, Leviticus*, ATD 6 (Göttingen, 1962)).

L. Perlitt   *Bundestheologie im Alten Testament*, WMANT 36 (Neukirchen-Vluyn, 1969).

O. Plöger   *Theocracy and Eschatology* (Oxford, 1968) (English translation of *Theokratie und Eschatologie*, WMANT 2, 2nd ed. (Neukirchen Kreis Moers, 1962)).

G. von Rad   *Old Testament Theology*, vol. II (Edinburgh and London, 1965) (English translation of *Theologie des Alten Testaments*: vol. II, 'Die Theologie der prophetischen Überlieferungen Israels' (Munich, 1960)).

H. W. Robinson   *Two Hebrew Prophets. Studies in Hosea and Ezekiel* (London, 1948).

J. F. A. Sawyer   *From Moses to Patmos. New Perspectives in Old Testament Study* (London, 1977).

H. Simian   *Die theologische Nachgeschichte der Prophetie Ezechiels. Form- und traditionskritische Untersuchung zu Ez. 6; 35; 36*, Forschung zur Bibel 14 (Würzburg, 1974).

J. Vermeylen   *Du prophète Isaïe à l'apocalyptique. Isaïe i–xxxv, miroir d'un demi-millénaire d'experience religieuse en Israël*, Etudes Bibliques (Paris, 1977).

H. Weippert   *Die Prosareden des Jeremiabuches*, BZAW 132 (Berlin, 1974).

J. Wellhausen *Prolegomena to the History of Ancient Israel* (New York, 1957) (English translation of *Prolegomena zur Geschichte Israels* (Berlin, 1878; 2nd ed. 1883)).

W. Zimmerli *Ezechiel. Gestalt und Botschaft*, BSt 62 (Neukirchen-Vluyn, 1972). *The Book of Ezekiel* Part I, Hermeneia (Philadelphia, 1979) (English translation of *Ezechiel* I, BKAT 13, 1 (Neukirchen-Vluyn, 1969)).

The prophets of the restoration

REX MASON

The prophets Haggai, Zechariah and Malachi have not always been very favourably regarded. They may, to some extent, have suffered from the adverse views of Wellhausen concerning the post-exilic period generally, in which he saw a sad decline from the heights of pre-exilic and exilic prophecy to the stony depths of legalistic Judaism. Such views were often echoed, either in adverse comments on prophets who, in contrast to their forerunners, seemed to set much store by Temple and cult and who, in their concern for the institutions of religion, it was felt, exalted the form and the letter over the spirit (cf. e.g. Kennett, 1919, p. 573, and the views of Marti and Reuss, cited by Mitchell, 1912, p. 36); or else the prophets were condemned by silence, the comparative neglect of the post-exilic period being, until recently, one of the more remarkable characteristics of Old Testament scholarship. The writings of Peter Ackroyd have been particularly effective in redressing this balance, both in the attention given to these prophets and in reappraisal of their worth and significance (see especially Ackroyd, 1968).

The revival of interest in the post-exilic period, however, has not meant that the prophets of the restoration have always been viewed in a much more favourable light. Perhaps they have suffered from not fitting into some of the theories advanced to account for developments in post-exilic Judaism. These have included, most notably, those which have argued for an increasingly sharp division between theocratic and eschatological circles and various views to account for the decline of prophecy.

O. Plöger's book (1968) has been of great influence. In this he argued that two main streams of thought developed in post-exilic Judaism. There was the theocratic view, to be associated with the Priestly writers and the Chronicler. They saw the emergence of the theocratic community, rightly governed by the duly ordained priest-

137

hood, centred on the Temple and its cult and shaping its life in conformity to the Torah, as the fulfilment of God's purposes through history with Israel and a valid culmination to the hopes of the prophets. As time passed, however, and the reverses of history became sharper and deeper, groups emerged with much more radical eschatological hopes of a future transformation of the present order. These resisted what they saw as the complacency and false assurance of the theocratic party. Their outlook is represented in such passages as Isa. 24–7 and Zech. 12–14, in Joel and, above all, in Daniel. It was among such groups and in such literature that Old Testament prophecy developed into apocalyptic.

More recently, P. D. Hanson (1975) has built on Plöger's foundations but sharpened the sense of conflict between the two groups, claimed to be able to identify them and set the origins of the schism at a much earlier stage in history. Indeed, the real differences can be traced back to Ezekiel and Deutero-Isaiah. Ezekiel, the representative of the official Zadokite Jerusalem priesthood, was mainly concerned with the restoration of the theocracy after the exile. He was an 'establishment' figure who rooted God's intervention on behalf of His exiled people in the historical events of a return to the land, a rebuilding of the Temple, a return to a position of privilege for the Zadokite priesthood at the expense of the Levites, and a resumption of the cult. Deutero-Isaiah, on the other hand, although he foresaw an historical return to the land, had little interest in Temple, cult or priesthood, and spoke of the return in such near-mythical terms that with him eschatology tended towards the supra-historical and other-worldly. This tendency, strengthened in Isa. 56–66 and later in Joel and Zech. 9–14, was to prove the seed-bed of apocalyptic, the creative, germinative period of which Hanson thus put much earlier than Plöger had done. Of these two categories, now much more sharply delineated and contrasted, Hanson has no doubt that Haggai and Zechariah belong to the theocratic. With their concern for the rebuilding of the Temple, for the leadership of the Davidide Zerubbabel and Joshua the priest, and the resumption of the cult, they follow Ezekiel in identifying God's action in historical events of this world-order, which resulted in the resumption of the Jerusalem 'establishment'. It is true that they evince some eschatological hope, but this Hanson regards as only a peripheral concern, occasioned by the excitement of the political upheavals associated with the accession of Darius to the Persian throne in 522 B.C. and a deliberate attempt to gain support from the prophetic party for the hierocratic programme.

Such eschatological concern was to prove transitory and incidental to the main historical interests of the theocratic circle.

Hanson's views have not gone uncriticised (e.g. Carroll, 1979a) and are, indeed, open to question at almost every point. There are clearly differences of emphasis between Ezekiel and Deutero-Isaiah but they are not as fundamental as Hanson claims. Such a view underestimates the 'mythical', 'prophetic' element in Ezekiel's hopes (e.g. 34; 36; 37:1–14; 47:1–12 etc.) and also the degree to which Deutero-Isaiah does see a restored, cleansed community that is based on the Temple and its cult (e.g. 44:24–8; 52:11f). Passages in Isa. 40–55 apostrophising Jerusalem in apparently mythical terms prove, on closer inspection, to be speaking of a purified *people* of God (e.g. 52:1f; 54:11–14). Nor is there any concrete evidence to enable us to identify the conflicting parties of Isa. 56–66 with the Levites who had remained in the land and inherited the 'prophetic' hopes of Deutero-Isaiah, resentful of dispossession at the hands of the returning Zadokites, whose official apologists were Ezekiel, Haggai and Zechariah. Again, to dismiss the eschatological elements in the preaching of Haggai and Zechariah as merely peripheral, or a device to secure support, is to portray them in terms of near caricature since, as we shall see, the eschatological element is central to their message.

Again, the portrayal of the prophets of the restoration has suffered because they have not been found to fit neatly into a number of recent theories to account for the decline of prophecy after the exile. Petersen (1977) saw both the rise and fall of prophecy as connected with the institution of the monarchy. The main oracles of the pre-exilic prophets were directed against the king and the royal sanctuary or, as in the case of Ezekiel and Jeremiah, they 'consistently align themselves respectively with Jehoiachin and Zedekiah' (p. 3). Their oracles against foreign nations show further their relation to the foreign policy of the court. It is allowed, with Holladay (1970), that in the eighth century B.C. the writing prophets also extended their address to the whole nation but 'the locus of classical Israelite prophecy was the institution of monarchy' (*ibid.*). After the fall of the monarchy prophecy became increasingly concerned to reinterpret earlier classical prophecy in order to relate it to the new context of a non-monarchical society. Future expectation replaced earlier prophetic call for change in contemporary practice. Apocalyptic thus began to take over from prophecy. A number of passages in later prophecy bitterly attacking prophecy as such are in fact rejection of the claims of the Levitical singers to a prophetic role as exemplified in the writings of the Chronicler (pp. 27ff).

Clearly, Haggai and Zechariah fit awkwardly into such a scheme. Petersen says, 'Haggai and Zechariah constitute an exception to this thesis. However, once we realise that these two prophets were working assiduously for the restoration of the Temple community under the auspices of a Davidide on the throne, we may understand them to be the last gasp of classical prophecy' (p. 97). It is open to question whether monarchy had the cause-and-effect relationship that Petersen claims. Obviously, we could hardly expect records of prophetic activity to have been preserved earlier than the formation of the state and, naturally, monarchy and national policy fell within the purview of the prophets, especially since the cult was a royal institution. Yet, equally clearly, they apply themselves to many other national, social and religious concerns, addressing a much wider audience and attacking other institutions. Just why this change of address from monarchy to the wider nation took place in the eighth century, which Petersen allows, is difficult to explain by his own thesis. Further, it is scarcely right to claim that Haggai and Zechariah's *main* interest is 'to achieve kingship for the Davidide Zerubbabel' (p. 11, n. 26). They do speak of him in messianic terms but as *one* indication of God's purposes for His community among others that, like the resumption of Temple and cult, have much more significance. Haggai speaks of Zerubbabel in more directly messianic terms (2:23) as a concomitant of the renewal of the old Zion tradition, but Zechariah from the first seems only to have envisaged a dyarchic rule shared between Zerubbabel and Joshua (4:14). Further, Malachi has no messianic concern at all and *is* concerned to effect change in contemporary practice in a way Petersen claims exclusively for pre-exilic prophecy. To assign the role of these three prophets to that of the 'last gasp' of classical prophecy in the interests of a theory is to miss the particular contribution they have to make. Where the earlier prophets could only say 'mercy and not sacrifice' these prophets had the courage and insight to say that 'mercy and sacrifice' was a proper and possible response of God's people.

Carroll (1979 b) argues that prophecy declined because it 'failed'. Although the threats of judgement uttered by the earlier prophets were fulfilled, their promises of salvation (which cannot be entirely erased from the record of their preaching by critical methods) were not, nor did they succeed in their aim of changing the life of the community. This failure set up intolerable tensions ('dissonance') within the community. After the exile, therefore, earlier prophecy had to be reinterpreted by various means and devices. A 'delay' factor was introduced into it, often said to be because of the people's sins. Or its predictions were 'adapted' to refer to different, and still future, events. Sometimes it was said to have been 'realised' in some way other than that originally envisaged by the prophet, and so on. Haggai and Zechariah represent a typical example of the post-exilic attempt to resolve the problems posed by earlier prophecy, especially the failure of the predictions of Deutero-Isaiah concerning the signs that would accompany the return from exile.

There is much truth in this analysis and, indeed, Carroll's work affords valuable insights into Old Testament prophecy and brings to the fore issues that have too often been conveniently ignored. Specifically, however, he fails to see the difference between the preaching of such a prophet as Zechariah and the tradition in which his oracles have been handed down (see below, pp. 144f). He therefore attributes to these prophets a degree of reinterpretation in the face of the failure of earlier hopes that properly belongs to the later tradition. Thus he undervalues their own distinctive contribution. On the broader issue it needs to be said that 'failure' is an emotive and multi-valent word. It raises deep questions not only as to what 'success' and 'failure' may be in such a realm as prophecy but by whom it is regarded as being either. It is strange that, if earlier prophecy were regarded as having proved such a 'failure', the post-exilic period should have been the time when the present prophetic collections were formed and invested with increasing authority. (For another estimate of the failure of earlier prophecy, see Crenshaw (1971), to which some of the same general objections apply.) This applies equally to the collection and preservation of the words and activity of the prophets of the restoration. How we view the undeniable process of reinterpretation and reapplication of earlier prophecy to later situations involves subjective value-judgements as much for Carroll as for any other commentator. It can be regarded as merely manipulating earlier prophecy with the aim of resolving the 'dissonance'. Or it can be viewed as illustrative of the power and vitality of the divine word to address not only one historical context but a continuing number of them in new ways (Ackroyd, 1962*a*). The degree of 'failure' or 'success' attributable to Haggai and Zechariah is open to discussion. Not all their hopes for the signs that would accompany the completion of the Temple were realised. Yet the renewed Temple and cult they did inspire proved of great potency in the life of post-exilic Judaism. Perhaps the prophetic word always witnessed to a particular situation and yet carried larger overtones of God's more distant purposes in the establishment of righteousness and the overthrow of evil that we do not even yet see realised. Clearly this was the belief about them that inspired the later community to preserve their words, invest them with canonical authority and, later, gather them into their present canonical form, as Childs has recently reminded us (1979). Whether such a view is right or wrong, can the activity of those whose words proved to be such a seed-bed for faith be described properly in terms of 'failure'?

In fact, it seems far more likely that prophecy began to die, or change, after the exile, not because of its failure but because of its 'success'. The judgement of the exile was seen as confirmation of the predictions of those prophets who had not cried 'peace' when there was no peace, while the prophets of the exile showed how the 'hope of salvation' element in their preaching could be seen as applying to the time beyond the exile. For this reason we may assume that the collection of their words went on apace, such collections being regarded as more and more authoritative. That prophetic books were set alongside Torah as writings of supreme authority can be seen from the appendices to the book of Malachi forming closing words to the whole Book of the Twelve and prophetic part of the canon, which link Moses and Elijah (Mal. 4:4ff (MT 3:22ff)). But as soon as the authority of religion is found in written documents the 'living' word becomes less and less regarded. That is more likely why post-exilic prophecy becomes increasingly derivative and takes on more the nature of exegesis, the reinterpretation and reapplication of the earlier 'authoritative' word. To say this, however, does not mean it shows no originality or inventiveness. The three prophets of the restoration (to say nothing of Isa. 56–66) show considerable creativity in their selection and use of earlier material and traditions.

The Book of Haggai clearly divides into two sections: the oracles of Haggai, directly addressing the community of returned exiles, and the editorial 'framework' in which the oracles have been set (Beuken, 1967). The oracles reflect a simple, consistent message. Whereas the community had blamed their failure to rebuild the Temple on the hardships they had experienced in their pioneer attempt to restore the land, the hardships are, according to the prophet, judgement from God for their failure to rebuild the Temple. It is sometimes urged that Haggai's insistence on the need for the Temple is not a betrayal of the pre-exilic prophets' rejection of reliance on the externals of the cult but is, for him, a sign that they are seeking to put God at the centre of their life (Ackroyd, 1968, pp. 156f; Baldwin, 1972, p. 33). That is, no doubt, true, but his oracles show that, for him, the significance of the Temple is *eschatological*. It will be the place where God appears again in His glory (1:8). He meets the doubts of the community concerning the scale of the building (2:3) with the same assurance (2:6–9). Rudolph is right to draw the parallel to Ezekiel at this point (Rudolph, 1976, p. 34), but Haggai and Ezekiel here both draw on the Zion tradition expressed in the Psalms (e.g. 46, 48, 50, etc.). The vision of the cosmic sweep of God's manifestation of His glory and the pilgrimage of the nations (cf. Isa. 2:2–4 = Mic. 4:1–3) shows that Haggai stood in this tradition and sees the significance of the return to Jerusalem after the exile in the revitalisation of the hopes expressed in the pre-exilic cult of the Jerusalem Temple. This seems clear whether or not we allow, with A. R. Johnson, that Haggai and Zechariah were both cult prophets in the precise meaning of the term (Johnson, 1962, p. 65; 1979, pp. 64, 198, 329). When to these oracles we add the further expression of this hope in 2:20–3 we realise what a great proportion of the small recorded tradition of Haggai's preaching is devoted to this theme. Thus to make the claim that the eschatological element in Haggai's preaching was merely a 'ruse' on the part of the theocratic elements to influence the prophetic circles, a 'welding' of 'the eschatological fervour which was the hallmark of the prophetic group' to 'the priestly tradition of the Zadokites' (Hanson, 1975, p. 245) is, at one and the same time, to miss the essence of Haggai's preaching and to mistake the nature of the Zion tradition that was its source. Even the link between the fertility of the land and well-being of the community and the rule of God in His Temple is a further instance of the Zion theology of the pre-exilic cult (e.g. Ps. 72; 2 Sam. 23:1–7; Ps. 29 etc.). The association of messianic hope with the figure of Zerubbabel (2:23; cf. Jer. 22:24) belongs to the same tradition, as the passages just referred to clearly illustrate.

Whether Haggai is to be regarded as 'merely' a cultic prophet who sits lightly to ethical demands in his zeal for Temple and ritual, depends, to some extent, on exegesis of 2:10–14. This has tended to fall into three categories. Some have seen 'this people' as referring to the returned exiles, as in 1:2, and this oracle as parallel to those of ch. 1. The people and their offerings are unclean because they have not been obedient in building the Temple (So G. A. Smith, 1928; Wellhausen,

1898; Nowack, 1903; Marti, 1904; Driver, 1906; van Hoonacker, 1908; Mitchell, 1912; Kennett, 1919; Nötscher, 1954; Jones, 1962; Horst, 1964; May, 1968, p. 192; Chary, 1969; Baldwin, 1972). Others, finding it difficult that the returned exiles should be so spoken of here after being termed 'the remnant', see 'this people' as referring to foreigners, or to the half-mixed population that stayed in Palestine during the exile. Some have even suggested that it was Haggai's instruction to refuse the offer of help recorded in Ezra 4:1–3 (so Rothstein, 1908; Sellin, 1930; Thomas, 1956; Elliger, 1964; Rudolph, 1976). Some of the too general references to 'Samaritans' in the writings of some of those who take this view need correction in the light of Coggins' work (1975). Ackroyd has argued more generally for a reminder here that Temple-building does not of itself confer holiness on the community, while insisting that the detailed parallel between the priestly *torah* and the situation of the returned exiles should not be pressed (Ackroyd, 1968, pp. 166ff). In my view it is important to see that the real climax of the oracle citing the priestly *torah* that holiness cannot be imparted by mere contagion, whereas uncleanness can, comes in verse 14: 'So it is with this people and with this nation before me, says the LORD; and so with every work of their hands; and what they offer there is unclean.' We can take the date at the head of this section (verse 10) seriously and see the phrase 'the work of their hands' as referring to their building activity. There are plenty of reminders in the Old Testament that human activity, 'the work of men's hands', is ineffective without God's sanctifying blessing (e.g. Ps. 127: 1; Ps. 90: 17 etc.). However, in the light of his teaching elsewhere we may assume that Haggai is not just enunciating a general truth. He is saying that it is the eschatological 'Coming' of God, His 'Presence' alone (1:8; 2:9) that fills this human structure with His 'Glory'. The people have no capacity for self-regeneration, certainly not by the frenzy of their activity. It is God alone who can renew them and who, by His presence in the Temple, will do so. They, by their building, 'prepare the way of the LORD' so to speak. He, when He comes, will fulfil the prophetic hopes for the divine renewal of His people (Ezek. 36:22–32; 43:1–9). Again, we see the centrality of eschatological hope to the preaching of Haggai. He has no other message.

It is a somewhat different tradition that finds expression in the editorial framework (Beuken, 1967, pp. 27–83; Mason, 1977a). Here the phrase 'the word of the LORD came by the hand of Haggai' echoes not only the Deuteronomistic formula but especially that of the Priestly Writing in its description of Moses as the transmitter of instructions concerning the building of the Tabernacle. In the framework, as in the Deuteronomistic Books of Kings, the prophet's words are always addressed to the leaders, whereas in the oracles of Haggai he addresses the people as a whole. Again, it is the framework (1:12, 14) that describes the people as the 'remnant', although not in 1:1f, as though it was their response in obedience to the word of God through the prophet that constituted them as the 'remnant' of prophetic hope, the true continuation of the pre-exilic community. Finally, we may note the emphasis on the 'presence' of God in 2:4f (rightly assigned to the framework by Beuken, 1967, pp. 51ff). This not only echoes the Priestly Writing's emphasis on the presence of God mediated through Tabernacle and cult, but closely parallels the Levitical-type preaching recorded in the work of the Chronicler (e.g. 1 Chron. 22:6–16).

This seems to indicate that, in the period following the completion of the Temple in 515 B.C., when not all Haggai's great hopes attached to this event were seen to have been fulfilled, theocratic circles (we need not limit them as closely as Beuken does to circles akin to the Chronicler) argued that already the restored theocratic community was experiencing a valid 'first instalment' of these hopes, even if they still awaited their final fulfilment. In the resumption of the Temple cult a real link with the pre-exilic community had been established; a second 'Moses' had mediated to them instructions concerning a 'Tabernacle' in which God dwelt among them. They were therefore the true 'remnant', guided by a divinely-ordained leadership. They were called to show a zeal for God and His service like that which Haggai and his contemporaries showed. The fact that Haggai could so closely relate concern for cult and Temple to eschatology, and that the theocratic tradents themselves could still preserve and transmit his eschatological hopes, should warn us against seeing too sharp a divergence between theocratic and eschatological groups in the community in the manner of Plöger and, even more, of Hanson.

Zech. 1–8 presents rather more complex problems in distinguishing between the message of the prophet and the influence of the tradition, perhaps because the book was more literary from the beginning. The form of the prophecy in 'visions of the night' may well have been influenced by a complex web of earlier traditions. The pre-exilic prophets had vision-experiences. The prophets were described as 'watchmen', stationed, as it were, at observation posts to detect the first sign of the dawn of God's redeeming activity after the long night of the people's distress (e.g. Ezek. 33:1ff; Hab. 2:1–4; Isa. 21:6–10, 11f). There was the motif in the Psalms of God's help coming 'in the morning' (e.g. Ps. 30:5 (MT 30:6); Ps. 46:5 (MT 46:6); cf. Ziegler, 1950; Mason, 1977 *b*, pp. 29f). These visions may have been set originally in various stages of a continung ministry by Zechariah, ranging from the time of the exile until after the completion of the Temple (so e.g. Galling, 1964, pp. 109–26) but this has been vigorously contested (see e.g. Jeremias, 1977, pp. 14–38; Rudolph, 1976, pp. 61ff; cf. Rothstein, 1910, p. 4). In the final form they have been set in one night (1:7f; cf. 4:1), and all related to the context of the rebuilding of the Temple.

The message of Zechariah shows many parallels to that of Haggai and clearly utilises the same Zion traditions. Yahweh has chosen the city as His own (1:14, 16f) and is about to return to dwell in it and defend it (2:4f (MT 2:8f); 2:10 (MT 2:14)). When that happens land and community will be cleansed (5: 1–11) – visions that bring together ideas of moral and cultic renewal – the land will become prosperous (1:17) and Jerusalem will be the centre of world pilgrimage (2:11f (MT 2:15f)). If these points all echo Haggai's preaching, we should note that the building of the Temple is seen more as the result of God's activity than as a consequence of the people's response (1:16; cf. Hag. 1:8), although Ackroyd is right to urge that we should not overstress the differences (Ackroyd, 1968, p. 177), and a more 'universalist' outlook is explicit (2:11 (MT 2:15)). Whereas Haggai addressed messianic hope only to Zerubbabel, Zechariah apparently saw a joint rule of Zerubbabel and Joshua the priest (4:14). Nevertheless, the parallels between the two are more striking than the differences. Both see the promises of the old Jerusalem cult as about to be realised. It is doubtful if we should see signs of 'apocalyptic' behind these visions of Zechariah. Their antecedent seems to be that of 'the Council of Heaven' to which the prophets saw themselves to be admitted in vision and of whose decrees they were messengers (e.g. Jer. 23:18; 1 Kings 22:19–23; cf. Whybray, 1971).

The visions are set between an opening section purporting to record Zechariah's preaching (1:1–6) and a concluding set of oracular material (7–8), while other oracles have been attached to the visions themselves (1:14 *b*–17; 2:6–13 (MT 2:10–17); 3:8–10; 4:6–10 *a*; 6:9–15). The most comprehensive study of these passages has been that of Petitjean (1969), although Beuken's careful analysis remains invaluable (1967).

Our search for the part played by the tradition in the teaching of Zechariah must examine both visions and oracles.

The vision that has attracted most attention in this respect is the fourth in ch. 3, the cleansing of Joshua. It has often been claimed as additional to the original series of seven visions since the usual introductory formula is missing, there is no inquiry about the meaning of the vision from an interpreting angel and the scene unfolds independently of the prophet. None of these arguments is conclusive, singly or cumulatively, and the verdict must rest on the contents. The crowning and cleansing of Joshua could represent him simply as a representative figure symbolising the community whose fortunes God intends now to reverse. But the special privileges given to Joshua in the development of the vision suggest a more precise emphasis. He is charged with executing 'judgement' (Heb. *dīn*), which is used elsewhere most often of God's judgement, occasionally of the judgement of various officials, but also of the judgement exercised by kings (e.g. Jer. 21:12; 22:16; Ps. 72:2; Prov. 31:9). He also is to have charge of the 'courts' (Heb. *hṣr*). This term is sometimes used of the royal courts of the palace (e.g. 1 Kings 7:8) but more often of the Temple courts. The distinction cannot be pressed, however, since the Temple was a royal prerogative (e.g. Amos 7:13; 1 Kings 8:4f). This could be interpreted, therefore, as a claim for the post-exilic priesthood of the royal privileges from before the exile (see Rudolph, 1976, p. 97 for a number of telling citations). If so, this corresponds to what happens in the Priestly Writing, where the Aaronic priesthood takes to itself all the rights formerly enjoyed solely by the kings. Further, Joshua is granted the rights of access to the Heavenly Council, presumably to emphasise his unique role as mediator between God and people, also a role of the king before the exile (e.g. Ps. 110:4; Jer. 30:21). This enhanced role of the priests is further emphasised by the casting of the messianic hope of the 'Branch' (cf. Isa. 11:1), no longer identified with Zerubbabel, into the future. Now, Joshua and his priestly line are guarantors of God's continuing presence among his people and the ultimate fulfilment of the prophetic hopes of the coming Messiah (3:8).

A similar process can be detected among all the uncertainties of 6:9–14. Here it is Joshua who is to be crowned. This could be proleptic or symbolic on behalf of Zerubbabel, who is yet to come (see Ackroyd, 1968, p. 197; cf. Rignell, 1950, pp. 188f). Yet verse 14 suggests that the Temple is already standing. Here again, the coming of the 'Branch', again not named, is cast into the future when a joint rule of priestly and royal messiahs is envisaged (verses 12f). Meanwhile the 'crown' (the plural form is not significant, cf. Job 31:36), now firmly on the head of Joshua the priest (verse 11), is a reminder, or an assurance, of the certainty of the future fulfilment of the promise. Again, the priestly line exercising its enhanced office is the 'guarantor' of God's continuing purpose for His people. Verse 13 might have been an original word to Zerubbabel, but it is now assigned to the role of a future messianic figure while, in the tradition also, Zerubbabel has been reduced, as he was in the Haggai framework, to the role of Temple builder alone (4:6–10). The idea of 'building' the Temple has passed from a literal to a metaphorical sense, aided no doubt by the fact that it always had such a force in the Psalms (e.g. Pss. 51:18 (MT 51:20); 147:2, 13; cf. Eaton, 1979, pp. 268f). Thus verse 15 assures those of the later Diaspora that they too would come and have a share in the service of God in the Temple in the new age. Such a close paralleling of thought in 3:8–10 and 6:9–15 suggests that, even if the fourth vision was originally one of those related by Zechariah, it has been expanded in the tradition, which shows similar patterns of thought to the tradition of the framework of the Book of Haggai.

It is very probable that the prophet, who could see moral renewal for the community as such an integral part of God's final victory and so draws on earlier traditions, himself called on his hearers for ethical response (cf. Ackroyd, 1968, pp. 200ff). Nevertheless, there are some indications that the tradition has played an active part in relating such passages to the needs of successive generations. The survey of prophetic preaching in 1:3–6 bears striking resemblance to the levitical-type sermons recorded by the Chronicler (cf. 2 Chron. 30:6–9). Verse 6b looks as though it must refer to the response of Zechariah's hearers or else it would conflict with the report of the fathers' disobedience in verse 4. This would then parallel the description of the response to the prophet's preaching in Hag. 1:12–14 and would hold out that example as a model for all successive generations.

We can detect similar tendencies in chs. 7–8. No doubt in 7:2f a genuine incident from the prophet's ministry is recorded. The sense of the question seems to be, 'Has the new age you have promised come, or not?' (Ackroyd, 1968, pp. 206–9). It is generally agreed that Zechariah's answer comes in 8:18f and assures the delegation that all mourning rites will give way to joyous festivals celebrating God's victory. The core of this incident has been much expanded. The question has offered a peg on which to hang a homily on true fasting (cf. Isa. 58:3). As in Isa. 58 the attack is followed by entreaty for the kind of ethical action that alone gives point to cultic ceremony (verses 8–14), re-emphasising the content of earlier prophetic preaching and the consequences of the hearers' response. In 8:1–8 we have actual exposition of two of Zechariah's oracles, verse 2 = 1:14, verse 3 = 2:10ff (MT 2:14ff). These are now elaborated with mythical details of the paradisal conditions that will then obtain in a future, now indefinite, reinforced with an assurance that God will bring it about and members of the scattered Diaspora will be brought back to share in it.

In 8:9–13 we have a further echo of the levitical-type sermons of the Chronicler (e.g. 2 Chron. 15:3–7) but also of the preaching of Haggai. The prophet's promises are re-emphasised, but in a context that calls on successive generations not to lose hope but to maintain a concern for the 'building-up' of the Temple and its community like that shown by those who engaged in the literal rebuilding. Further ethical teaching (verses 14–17) shows how firmly ethical and cultic concerns were held together in the preaching of the Second Temple. Zechariah's own universalism is reinforced in verses 20–2 (cf. 2:11 (MT 2:15)), while verse 23 seems to be an addition again addressed to the Jews of the Diaspora. Not only will they have a share in the future victory but there will prove to have been theological significance in their dispersion. They will be the means of enlightening those among whom they have had to live. Like a kind of 'Servant' they will be 'a light to the nations'.

Zech. 1–8 as it stands, then, like the Book of Haggai, not only declares the message of the prophet and preserves his hopes but reveals how that message became the basis of Temple-preaching to later generations. The same assurance of their future hopes, which were still valid, formed the basis of a call to a worthy kind of ethical life.

An equally moving testimony to the preaching of the Temple officials is to be found in the Book of Malachi. The book does not contain enough data for us to be able to date it (Mason, 1977*b*, pp. 137ff). Yet perhaps for few books in the Old Testament does date matter so little. In one way we know little of the author (there is still no consensus on whether 'Malachi' is a proper name or a descriptive title), yet in another we know him well, for there breaks through his writing deep faith and intense pastoral concern. Perhaps his high sense of the calling of the priests and his intense indignation at the betrayal of that calling by so many who bear its name suggests that he belonged to their ranks. The question-and-answer style here used has already been encountered with Haggai and in the Haggai and Zechariah tradition. Ackroyd has made the interesting suggestion that such a style suits well the process of expounding older scriptural material and relating it to new situations (Ackroyd, 1979, p. 327). Further, the fact that Malachi, uniquely in the Old Testament, describes the priest as 'the messenger of the LORD of hosts' (2:7), together with the role assigned to the Levites in the tradition of expounding the law (Neh. 8:7–12), also suggests that in this book we have reflected a typical example of preaching in the Second Temple.

The characteristic style marks the book as essentially a unity, perhaps only the interpolation of the oracle against mixed marriages, the elaboration of the judgement theme in 3:1b–4 and the final additions of 4:4, 5f (MT 3:22, 23f) being secondary.

The opening oracle (1:1–5) with its harsh statement of God's election and His rejection of Esau is strange at the beginning of a book that so attacks the 'chosen' people for its sins. Rudolph suggests that those attacks are first set in the context of God's electing love (1976, pp. 254ff). But, if Edom were here seen as a 'typical' enemy, a legendary example of wickedness (cf. van Seters, 1972) then the warning is against complacency of any kind. The God who chooses, can also reject wickedness, a sense that seems to be borne out by the concluding addition, 4:6 (MT 3:24).

The attack on the priests that follows (1:6 – 2:9) reveals that here is no narrow, cult-dominated outlook. Better that the sacrifices should stop altogether than that God's covenant with the priests should be betrayed and the people misdirected (2:4f, 7). The contrast between their indifferent attitude and the zeal of worship among other nations is a shame to the 'elect' people of God. The quotation from Ps. 50 with which verse 11 opens may echo the thought of the psalm that God can do without animal sacrifice. The 'sacrifice of thanksgiving' (Ps. 50:14, 23) and right living (verses 16–23) are what most honour Him. Indeed, wherever men express their gratitude to God as Creator and Preserver (1:11) their worship, even if offered in ignorance of Yahweh's name, is more acceptable to Him than the blood sacrifices of such evil priests. This may not be 'universalism' but it shows breadth of outlook and also a clear balance between cultic and ethical demands.

The picture of marriage as a 'covenant' between two people before God, and the appeal (as with Jesus, Mark 10:6f) to God's creation equally of men and women, is a fine one, especially as it leads to a call for fidelity to the vows of youth and an outright rejection of divorce as contrary to God's purpose (2:10, 13–16). Such a view was too demanding for Judaism as it has been for Christianity (Mark 10:4–12; cf. Matt. 19:3–9).

Malachi's pastoral concern is shown in that he twice addresses himself to the doubts and despair of his contemporaries (2:17 – 3:1a, 5 and 3:13 – 4:3 (MT 3:13–21). His comfort is to reassert the truth of God's ultimate coming to judge His people, whom He knows all along and bears constantly in mind. That judgement will root out all evil and its practitioners.

The call for faithfulness in the payment of tithes (3:6–12) may seem somewhat trivial in such a context. But, just as Haggai saw concern for the building of the Temple as really concern for God, so Malachi sees concern for its upkeep as indicative of a deeper turning to God (3:7).

Malachi not only thus reveals a concern for the holding together of external and internal, in the way we have already seen as characteristic of the tradition in the Books of Haggai and Zechariah, but also holds together concern for the cultic needs of the present theocratic community and lively eschatological hope for the future. The too-absolute distinction drawn by some between 'theocratic' and 'eschatological' in post-exilic Judaism is due for considerable revision.

How are we to evaluate the prophets of the restoration? We must acknowledge first the effectiveness of their ministry. They sought primarily to inspire the rebuilding of the Temple, and this was completed in 515 B.C. Purists may regret such emphasis on the institutions of religion in what they see as a contrast to earlier prophecy. Such 'purism' is misplaced. No movement of the human spirit can survive for long or remain effective without its institutions. Only the renascence of such external links with pre-exilic life could have enabled Judaism to survive and nerve it for the ordeals that awaited it. Institutions pose constant threats to the life of the spirit, however. The prophets of the return must be credited with the ability to see this in their attempt to hold ethical and spiritual response to God in a healthy balance with the means of its expression. Further, we must credit them with an openness of vision. At a time when the community desperately needed to establish its identity they yet kept an openness towards God's purposes for people of other nations. This is most marked in Zechariah, but Malachi was no blinkered nationalist or exclusivist. If they all expected more of God's action on behalf of His people, and more immediately, than proved to be the case, this places them in some excellent company in both Old and New Testaments. For, finally, we must acknowledge that their hopes and their preaching proved a seed-bed for the faith of those who followed them. There were those who kept alive the hopes they had held by preserving and transmitting them and who found meanwhile, in the exposition of their message, a word of God that could readily be related in call and exhortation to those of later generations.

Since the tensions involved in keeping the relationship between 'spirit' and 'institutions', and between the 'now' and the 'not yet' of the Biblical promises, remain lively ones for the community of faith in every generation, perhaps these prophets deserve closer attention than they have sometimes been accorded.

Bibliography

P. R. Ackroyd 'The Vitality of the Word of God in the Old Testament', *ASTI* 1 (1962), 7–23 (= 1962*a*).

'Haggai, Zechariah', *Peake's Commentary on the Bible*, rev. ed. (London, 1962) (= 1962*b*).

Exile and Restoration (London, 1968).

'The History of Israel in the Exilic and Post-Exilic Period', in G. W. Anderson (ed.), *Tradition and Interpretation* (Oxford, 1979), pp. 320–50.

J. G. Baldwin *Haggai, Zechariah, Malachi*, Tyndale Old Testament Commentaries (London, 1972).

W. A. M. Beuken *Haggai–Sacharja 1–8* (Assen, 1967).

L. H. Brockington 'Malachi', *Peake's Commentary on the Bible*, rev. ed. (London, 1962).

R. P. Carroll 'Twilight of Prophecy or Dawn of Apocalyptic?', *JSOT* 14 (1979), 3–35 (= 1979*a*).

When Prophecy Failed (London, 1979) (= 1979*b*).

T. Chary *Aggée–Zacharie–Malachie*, Sources Bibliques (Paris, 1969).

B. S. Childs *Introduction to the Old Testament as Scripture* (London, 1979).

R. J. Coggins *Samaritans and Jews* (Oxford, 1975).

J. L. Crenshaw *Prophetic Conflict: Its Effect upon Israelite Religion*, BZAW 124 (Berlin, 1971).

S. R. Driver *The Minor Prophets*, The Century Bible (Edinburgh, 1906).

J. H. Eaton 'The Psalms and Israel's Worship', in G. W. Anderson (ed.), *Tradition and Interpretation* (Oxford, 1979), pp. 238–73.

K. Elliger *Das Buch der zwölf kleinen Propheten*, vol. II, ATD 25, 5th ed. (Göttingen, 1964).

K. Galling *Studien zur Geschichte Israels im persischen Zeitalter* (Tübingen, 1964).

The prophets of the restoration

A. J. Grieve 'Malachi', *Peake's Commentary on the Bible* (London, 1919).

P. D. Hanson *The Dawn of Apocalyptic* (Philadelphia, 1975).

J. Holladay 'Assyrian Statecraft and the Prophets of Israel', *HTR* 63 (1970), 29–51.

A. van Hoonacker *Les douze Petits Prophètes*, Études Bibliques (Paris, 1908).

F. Horst *Die zwölf kleinen Propheten*, HAT, 3rd ed. (Tübingen, 1964).

C. Jeremias *Die Nachtgesichte des Sacharja* (Göttingen, 1977).

A. R. Johnson *The Cultic Prophet in Ancient Israel*, 2nd ed. (Cardiff, 1962).
The Cultic Prophet and Israel's Psalmody (Cardiff, 1979).

D. R. Jones *Haggai, Zechariah and Malachi*, The Torch Bible Commentaries (London, 1962).

R. H. Kennett 'Haggai, Zechariah', *Peake's Commentary on the Bible* (London, 1919).

K. Marti *Das Dodekapropheten*, KAT (Tübingen, 1904).

R. A. Mason 'The Purpose of the "Editorial Framework" of the Book of Haggai', *VT* 27 (1977), 413–21 (= 1977 a).
The Books of Haggai, Zechariah and Malachi, The Cambridge Bible Commentary (Cambridge, 1977) (= 1977 b).

H. G. May '"This People" and "This Nation" in Haggai', *VT* 18 (1968), 190–7.

H. G. Mitchell *A Critical and Exegetical Commentary on Haggai and Zechariah*, ICC (Edinburgh, 1912).

F. Nötscher *Zwölfprophetenbuch oder kleinen Propheten*, Echter Bibel (Würzburg, 1954).

W. Nowack *Kleine Propheten*, HK (Göttingen, 1903).

D. L. Petersen *Late Israelite Prophecy: Studies in Deutero-Prophetic Literature and in Chronicles* (Missoula, 1977).

A. Petitjean *Les Oracles du Proto-Zacharie*, Études Bibliques (Paris, 1969).

O. Plöger *Theocracy and Eschatology* (Oxford, 1968) (English translation of *Theokratie und Eschatologie*, WMANT 2, 1st ed. (Neukirchen Kreis Moers, 1959; 2nd ed. 1962)).

L. G. Rignell *Die Nachtgesichte des Sacharja* (Lund, 1950).

J. W. Rothstein *Juden und Samaritaner. Die grundlegende Scheidung von Judentum und Heidentum*, BWAT 3 (Leipzig, 1908).
Die Nachtgesichte des Sacharja, BWAT 8 (Leipzig, 1910).

W. Rudolph *Haggai, Sacharja 1–8, Sacharja 9–14, Maleachi*, KAT 13, 4 (Gütersloh, 1976).

E. Sellin *Das zwölfprophetenbuch*, KAT, 3rd ed. (Leipzig, 1930).

J. van Seters 'The Terms "Amorite" and "Hittite"', *VT* 22 (1972), 64–81.

G. A. Smith *The Book of the Twelve Prophets*, 2nd ed. (London, 1928; 1st ed. 1898).

J. M. P. Smith *A Critical and Exegetical Commentary on the Book of Malachi*, ICC (Edinburgh, 1912).

D. W. Thomas 'Haggai, Zechariah 1-8', *The Interpreter's Bible* 6 (New York, 1956).

J. Wellhausen *Die kleinen Propheten* (Berlin, 1898).

R. N. Whybray *The Heavenly Counsellor in Isaiah XL 13–14* (Cambridge, 1971).

J. Ziegler 'Die Hilfe Gottes "am Morgen"', *Nötscher Festschrift*, BBB 1 (Bonn, 1950), pp. 281–8.

Prophecy and the emergence of the Jewish apocalypses

MICHAEL A. KNIBB

In 1963 the third edition of Rowley's well-known handbook on Jewish and Christian apocalypses was published, and in this, as in previous editions, the view that apocalyptic is the 'child' of prophecy is assumed to be almost axiomatic. A similar view was taken in the following year by Russell, whose more substantial presentation of Jewish apocalyptic to a great extent follows the broad lines of Rowley's study; here the links between prophecy and apocalyptic are very fully explored (Rowley, 1963, pp. 15–43; Russell, 1964, pp. 73–103, 178–202). In retrospect it is perhaps a little surprising that neither scholar thought it necessary to refer to von Rad's *Theologie des Alten Testaments*, in the second volume of which, published in 1960, the idea that there is any connection between prophecy and apocalyptic literature is categorically denied, and the view is presented that wisdom is the matrix from which apocalyptic literature originates. Von Rad's views have, on the whole, not been accepted, but they were influential in provoking a lively debate about the character of the apocalyptic writings. This debate has also been influenced by the attention paid to apocalyptic in New Testament studies and dogmatic theology, but this aspect of the subject lies outside the scope of the present essay (see, e.g., the survey by Koch, 1972, pp. 57–111; the essays in Funk (1969) and Pannenberg (1968); Murdock, 1967; Beardslee, 1971; Braaten, 1971). As far as the Old Testament and the Jewish apocalyptic writings are concerned, three topics seem to have been of particular importance in recent discussions, and it is these that will be examined here: (1) the definition of the terms 'apocalypse' and 'apocalyptic'; (2) the relationship between the apocalyptic literature and wisdom; (3) the precise lines of the transition from prophecy to the apocalypses. The history of the study of the apocalyptic literature has been examined more than once in recent years, and we may note here the surveys by Schmidt (1969; 2nd ed., 1976), Koch (1972), Barr (1975–6), Hanson (1976 b), Delcor (1977),

Coppens (1979, pp. 17–39), and Nicholson (1979), as well as the handbooks by Schreiner (1969), Morris (1972) and Schmithals (1975); cf. Russell (1978) and the essays in Raphaël (1977). Reference may also be made here to a study that does not fall into any neat category, namely Wilder's interesting attempt (1971) to get behind the apocalyptic writings themselves and to explore 'the underlying impulse and mode of apocalyptic discourse' (p. 449).

I

A major difficulty in the study of Jewish apocalyptic writings consists in the fact that those works that are commonly so described do not seem to have been called apocalypses by their authors, and it is thus open to question whether there really is such a thing as an apocalyptic genre. A further difficulty is to be found in the fact that modern scholars have used the term 'apocalyptic' in more than one way, and this has been a constant source of confusion.

Our use of the terms 'apocalypse' and 'apocalyptic' stems from the use of the Greek *apokalupsis* in Rev. 1:1 to describe the contents of the New Testament 'Revelation of John'. Here the term serves to indicate that the work is a divine revelation of what was to happen in the future, and it is perhaps not without interest that in Rev. 1:3 this same work is also described as a prophecy. In the ancient world Christian authors began to refer to Christian writings that were similar to the Revelation of John as 'apocalypses', and it is probably to Christian translators and editors that we are likewise to attribute the occurrence of the term 'apocalypse' in the superscriptions to a few comparable Jewish writings (Vielhauer, 1965, p. 582). Vielhauer refers in this connection to the Syriac and Greek Apocalypses of Baruch (i.e. 2 and 3 Baruch), but the same considerations no doubt also apply to the Apocalypse of Abraham, the superscription of which begins with the words: 'The Book of the Revelation of Abraham'. (The misnamed Apocalypse of Moses, i.e. the Greek recension of the Life of Adam and Eve, is, as Collins (1979b, p. 2; 1979c, p. 44) points out, a work of a different character.) In any case there is no unambiguous evidence that the Jewish works we commonly designate as 'apocalypses' were so described by their authors. However, in modern times scholars have used this term to refer to a whole group of Jewish writings the literary form of which is comparable to that of the Revelation of John, not only the Syriac and Greek Apocalypses of Baruch and the Apocalypse of Abraham, which had been given this title earlier, but also Daniel, 1 and 2 Enoch, 4 Ezra (i.e. 2 Esdras 3–14) and the Testament of Abraham, to mention only those writings which most scholars would probably agree to classify as 'apocalypses'. Whether these writings really do belong together as a group, and, if so, whether other writings also belong in this group, are debatable questions, but the important point to notice here is that 'apocalypse' is a literary term used to describe writings the form of which is similar to that of the Revelation of John, and that the corresponding adjective, 'apocalyptic', is likewise in the first instance a literary term.

Confusion has arisen, however, because 'apocalyptic' has been used not only as an adjective to describe a literary genre but also as a noun or collective term (*Sammelbegriff*: Koch, 1972, p. 20; original German edition, p. 17) to refer to a pattern of thought relating to the end of this age and the future destiny of man, a pattern of thought by no means restricted to the apocalypses. 'Apocalyptic' has thus become an ambiguous term for which it is difficult to offer any very precise definition, and there is the risk, which has not altogether been avoided, that the concept of apocalyptic will be broadened to include so many different kinds of writing that it will cease to have any value (Hanson, 1976*a*, p. 29). The ambiguous way in which the term 'apocalyptic' is often used is well illustrated in Russell's treatment of 'Jewish Apocalyptic', as, for example, in the following passage:

> The character of Jewish apocalyptic throughout the intertestamental period is complex in the extreme; there are considerable differences between one book and another, not least between the Book of Daniel and those that follow it in the apocalyptic tradition. There is, however, a homogeneity about it which justifies its classification as a distinct literary *corpus*. It is not always easy to define in what this homogeneity consists for, although it reveals certain fairly well-defined characteristics, apocalyptic is recognizable even when some of its formal characteristics are absent. It may be said to consist rather in a religious mood or temper which is different from, though related to, that of prophecy... [The] various 'marks' belong to apocalyptic not in the sense that they are essential to it, or are to be found in every apocalyptic writing, but rather in the sense that in whole or in part they build up an *impression* of a distinct kind which conveys a particular *mood* of thought and belief (Russell, 1964, pp. 104–5).

In fairness to Russell it should be added that he himself draws attention to the ambiguity of the word 'apocalyptic' (p. 105) and in a number of places makes clear the distinction between the literary genre 'apocalypse' and the apocalyptic pattern of thought (pp. 39–40, 106–7).

Recognition of the ambiguity of the word 'apocalyptic' in modern usage is no new discovery (Gunkel, 1895, p. 290; Stauffer, 1955, p. 19), but it is seemingly only in recent years that this ambiguity has been taken seriously, and an attempt has been made to offer precise definitions of the relevant terms. Here reference may be made, first of all, to the work of Koch, who drew a clear distinction between the apocalypses and the collective term 'apocalyptic' and attempted to describe the characteristics of both (Koch, 1972, pp. 18–35; cf. Barr, 1975–6, pp. 14–19; Stone, 1976, p. 450, n. 64). Thus, on the one hand, he offered the beginnings of a form-critical description of the apocalypses and, on the other, he listed what he regarded as the more important groups of motifs to be found in the intellectual movement known as 'apocalyptic'. These groups of motifs are as follows:

(1) an urgent expectation of the impending overthrow of all earthly conditions in the immediate future;
(2) the end as a vast cosmic catastrophe;
(3) a close connection between the end-time and previous human and cosmic history, and the division of world-history into segments, the contents of which have been predetermined from creation;
(4) the intervention of an army of angels and demons in the affairs of this world;
(5) a new salvation beyond the catastrophe for the righteous in Israel, but not restricted to Israel;
(6) the transition from disaster to salvation as the result of an act issuing from the throne of God and bringing about the establishment of the Kingdom of God on earth; the distinction between this age and the age to come;
(7) the frequent presence of a mediator with royal functions;
(8) use of the catchword 'glory' in descriptions of the new age.

Koch noted that the occurrence of these groups of motifs was not restricted to late Israelite and early Christian apocalyptic but argued that the arrangement of them together was characteristic only of this movement. In his view we are thus justified in recognising apocalyptic not only as a literary phenomenon but also as the expression of a particular attitude of mind, and, in consequence, in continuing to use 'apocalyptic' as a collective term (1972, p. 33).

Koch's discussion, although brief, contains much that is of value, and, in principle, as more recent studies have insisted, the clear distinctions that he drew between the apocalypses and 'apocalyptic' as an intellectual movement surely provide the only satisfactory basis for further study of both. However, Koch's presentation calls for comment in a number of respects.

First, it may be observed that, as one of two dogmatic presuppositions, he maintained that in order to gain a workable concept of 'apocalyptic' – here he seems to have in mind both the literary phenomenon and the intellectual movement – we must start from the writings that were composed in Hebrew or Aramaic, or in which the Hebrew or Aramaic spirit is dominant, namely Daniel, 1 Enoch, 2 Baruch, 4 Ezra, the Apocalypse of Abraham and the Revelation of John (Koch, 1972, p. 23). While an inductive method seems to be the only possible one in the study of the apocalypses, and while the restriction of the study to writings that, it would commonly be agreed, belong to this category, serves as a welcome corrective to the tendency to lump any and every intertestamental writing in this genre, it may be asked whether the Jewish apocalypses that were apparently composed in Greek (2 Enoch, 3 Baruch and the Testament of Abraham) do not also fall to be considered here. More problematic is the position of the Testaments of the Twelve Patriarchs and the Assumption of Moses. Koch (1972, p. 34; original German edition, pp. 31-2) regarded these, as well as several Qumran writings, as apocalyptic. It is clear from the German original, but not from the English translation, that what Koch primarily had in mind is their relationship to the intellectual movement, not the literary genre; for these two writings to be regarded as apocalypses, it would be necessary to widen the genre to include the testament, or farewell discourse (cf. von Rad, 1968, p. 331, n. 28). But this question will call for further comment later.

Attention may be drawn, secondly, to Koch's list of the characteristics of 'apocalyptic', the intellectual movement. Criticism has been directed against the value of lists of this kind in providing a real understanding of the phenomenon (Betz, 1969 a, pp. 135-6; Hanson, 1975, pp. 6-7; 1976 a, p. 29), while Stone (1976, pp. 440-1) has questioned the value of Koch's list in particular on the grounds that certain apocalypses (e.g. 3 Baruch) are lacking in almost all the characteristics noted by Koch, whereas many of the characteristics are to be found in works that are not apocalypses (e.g. the Testaments of the Twelve Patriarchs). It may be accepted that Koch's list does not do justice to the wide range of the contents of the works commonly regarded as apocalypses, and thus the relationship between 'apocalyptic' and the apocalypses is called into question, but on the more general point Koch's approach seems to be right. Lists of this kind do not, of course, provide an adequate understanding of 'apocalyptic', and this is all the more so when, as has happened in the past, literary and theological features have been lumped together in an undifferentiated way (cf. Stone, 1976, p. 441), but the identification of common characteristics is the essential prerequisite of a proper understanding and definition of both the apocalypses and 'apocalyptic' (cf. Koch, 1972, p. 23).

It is appropriate at this point to refer to Stone's discussion of these matters (1976, pp. 439–43), since it is, in part, based on a critique of Koch. Stone emphasises the confusion that has arisen from the failure to distinguish clearly between 'apocalyptic' or 'apocalypticism' and the apocalypses. That the two are not identical is made clear by the fact that apocalypticism is almost entirely lacking in some apocalypses but is, on the other hand, to be found in works that do not belong to this literary genre. Stone makes a number of perceptive observations in his short discussion, but here attention may be focussed on two points. First, Stone is surely right in his insistence that if we are to explain the apocalypses we must take account not only of apocalypticism but also of the whole range of matters that concern their authors, as, for example, the speculative interest in the cosmos reflected in such lists as are to be found in 2 Baruch 59:5–11; 2 Enoch 23:1–2; and 1 Enoch 60:11ff; it is lists such as these that form the primary focus of his essay. Secondly, and this is a point to which we must return, Stone raises the question whether it would not help to avoid confusion if we abandoned the use of the terms 'apocalyptic' and 'apocalypticism' altogether; as an alternative he tentatively suggests 'apocalyptic eschatology'.

In an article that appeared in the same year as Stone's essay Hanson (1976 a, pp. 28–31) argued that we need to make not a twofold, but a threefold distinction, namely between the apocalypses (i.e. the literary genre), apocalyptic eschatology and apocalypticism. He maintains that apocalyptic eschatology 'is neither a genre, nor a socioreligious movement, nor a system of thought, but rather a religious perspective, a way of viewing divine plans in relation to mundane realities'. He regards apocalyptic eschatology as a continuation of prophetic eschatology but believes that in the former, in contrast to the latter, the vision of God's action is no longer integrated into the realities of the political and historical situation (cf. also Hanson, 1975; see below, pp. 169f). Apocalyptic eschatology is not the same thing as apocalypticism but provides the perspective from which apocalypticism can develop. Hanson does regard apocalypticism itself as a system of thought, an ideology. It is a socioreligious phenomenon that occurs in groups ('apocalyptic movements'), which have in common: (*a*) a particular type of social setting, namely a group-experience of alienation, and (*b*) a related group response, namely the recourse to apocalyptic eschatology as the perspective from which it constructs an alternative universe of meaning. Hanson traces the birth of the first apocalyptic movements to the sixth century B.C.

It will be necessary to refer in more detail below to Hanson's views about the first apocalyptic movements (see pp. 170–6); here it must be asked whether his threefold distinction is entirely helpful. It is not clear to me that Hanson has succeeded in distinguishing clearly between apocalypticism and apocalyptic eschatology, nor, indeed, whether a worthwhile distinction can be drawn between them. The reasons given by Hanson for attempting to make the distinction – the fact that prophecy is only one current (even if the major one) in the apocalyptic writings, and the presence of apocalyptic notions in works that are not apocalypses – suggests, rather, that the important distinction to be drawn is the one between the apocalypses and apocalyptic eschatology. To put the matter another way, if a real distinction does exist between apocalypticism and apocalyptic eschatology, it seems difficult to separate apocalypticism from the apocalypses. Hanson's threefold distinction may be maintained provided we keep in mind that apocalypticism can only be approached through the apocalypses (cf. Collins, 1979 *b*, p. 4) and is not separable from them. But it seems to me more helpful to work with a simple twofold distinction, namely between the apocalypses and apocalyptic eschatology. This is not meant, however, to deny the importance of the sociological study of the apocalypses.

One of the most recent studies to take up the questions dealt with in this section of this essay is the attempt by Collins and a number of collaborators to describe and define the literary genre of the apocalypses (Collins, 1979 *a*). This attempt is based on a survey not only of the Jewish apocalypses, contributed by Collins himself (1979 *c*), but also of Christian, Gnostic, Greek and Roman, and Persian apocalypses, as well as of apocalyptic material in the Rabbinic writings; Collins (1979 *b*) also provides an introductory article that summarises the methods adopted in, and the results of, the inquiry. It is the two contributions by

Collins (1979 *b* and *c*) that are of primary concern to us here. It is important to notice that the study builds upon the earlier discussions of Koch, Stone and Hanson, adopting a number of their conclusions, and that it is concerned only with the question of the literary genre. The method followed in this work is to list the prominent recurring features in all the writings (or parts of writings) that are commonly regarded as apocalypses or appear to be similar to them, in order to assess the extent of their similarity and to decide which writings can properly be classified in this genre – the method is, that is to say, inductive. Collins argues that the significant recurring elements constitute a master-paradigm, relating to both the framework and the content of the apocalypses, and that within this paradigm certain features occur so constantly that they provide the basis for a comprehensive definition of the genre:

> A few elements are constant in every work we have designated as an apocalypse. These elements pertain to both the framework and the content. There is always a narrative framework in which the manner of revelation\[visions, auditions, otherworldly journeys, writings] is described. This always involves an otherworldly mediator and a human recipient – it is never simply a direct oracular utterance by either heavenly being or human. The content always involves both an eschatological salvation which is temporally future and presents otherworldly realities. The eschatological salvation is always definitive in character and is marked by some form of personal afterlife...
>
> This common core of constant elements permits us, then, to formulate a comprehensive definition of the genre: 'Apocalypse' is a genre of revelatory literature with a narrative framework, in which a revelation is mediated by an otherworldly being to a human recipient, disclosing a transcendent reality which is both temporal, insofar as it envisages eschatological salvation, and spatial, insofar as it involves another, supernatural world (Collins, 1979*b*, p. 9).

On the basis of the paradigm and definition, Collins believes it possible to distinguish works that are apocalypses from those which, though related in form, do not belong to the genre. He further argues that the apocalyptic genre itself can be divided into a number of types, the most important distinction being between the apocalypses that do not have an account of an otherworldly journey (1) and those that do (2); these types are further subdivided according to whether the apocalypses contain a review of history (*a*), cosmic and/or political eschatology, but no review of history (*b*), or only personal eschatology (*c*). Within the framework of this classification Collins (1979 *c*) regards the following Jewish works, which, in his view, can plausibly be dated in the period 250 B.C.–A.D. 150, as apocalypses:

(1 *a*) apocalypses with a review of history and no otherworldly journey: Dan. 7–12; 1 Enoch 85–90 (the Animal Apocalypse); 1 Enoch 93 and 91 : (11) 12–17 (the Apocalypse of Weeks); Jub. 23; 4 Ezra; 2 Baruch.

(2 *a*) apocalypses with an otherworldly journey and a review of history: the Apocalypse of Abraham.

(2 *b*) otherworldly journeys with cosmic and/or political eschatology: 1 Enoch 1–36; 1 Enoch 72–82 (the Book of the Heavenly Luminaries); 1 Enoch 37–71 (the Parables of Enoch); 2 Enoch; Test. Levi 2–5.

(2 *c*) otherworldly journeys with only personal eschatology: 3 Baruch; Test. of Abraham 10–15; Apocalypse of Zephaniah.

It is impossible here to comment in detail on this list, although a number of points do call for detailed discussion and examination, e.g., whether it is right to make such a sharp division between the two halves of Daniel and regard only the last six chapters as apocalyptic (cf. Gammie, 1976, pp. 191–4), or whether Jub. 23 really is an apocalypse. It is also impossible here to comment in detail on the paradigm and definition that underlie the list. In general, however, it may be said that this attempt to provide, on the basis of common characteristics of form and content, a precise list of the works that may properly be regarded as apocalypses marks a helpful advance.

It may perhaps be agreed that, with the possible exception of Jub. 23, all the writings included in Collins' list really are apocalypses, but here it is of more interest to observe the works that, in the light of the definition, have been excluded. In the Old Testament Collins excludes from the genre, on the one hand, Zech. 1–6 – on the grounds that, although the manner of revelation anticipates the later apocalypses, it lacks a distinctively apocalyptic eschatology – and, on the other hand, Isa. 24–7; 56–66; Ezek. 38–9; Joel; Zech. 9–14 – on the grounds that, although they contain some of the major characteristics of apocalyptic eschatology, they lack the apocalyptic manner of revelation (1979*c*, p. 29). In intertestamental literature Collins excludes both testaments (1 Enoch 91–104; the Assumption (or Testament) of Moses; the Testaments of the Twelve Patriarchs; the Testament of Job) and oracles (the Sibylline Oracles), since in neither case is the revelation mediated by an otherworldly figure (1979*b*, p. 10; 1979*c*, pp. 44–7).

(Collins (1979 c, pp. 48–9) also touches on the status of a few fragmentary writings from Qumran, which may well be apocalypses, but this question cannot be pursued here. The well-known Qumran writings are not apocalypses but are important for apocalyptic eschatology.)

The position of the Old Testament writings to which reference has been made will have to be taken up later. As far as the intertestamental writings are concerned, it is impossible here to do much more than state that the exclusion of the testamentary and oracular material from the apocalyptic genre seems right. Both literary types are obviously similar to the apocalypses, and in the case of the testaments the relationship is particularly close; it may be noted that 1 Enoch 91–104 (the Epistle of Enoch) contains within it an apocalypse (1 Enoch 93 and 91:(11) 12–17), and that material that is testamentary in character forms a part of 2 Enoch (see 2 Enoch 39–66). Despite this, the testaments and oracles are sufficiently different in character for it to be more helpful to regard them as separate genres; in the same way the apocalyptic genre overlaps with that of the Qumran Biblical commentaries but is, nonetheless, quite distinct from it. Works such as the Testaments of the Twelve Patriarchs, the Sibylline Oracles and the majority of the Qumran writings, have a significant part to play in discussions of apocalyptic eschatology, but not of the literary genre of the apocalypses.

We may usefully conclude this part of the discussion by reverting to the two questions raised in the opening paragraph of this section.

(1) Although the identification was not made in the ancient world, there is adequate evidence to enable us to identify a distinct group of writings as apocalypses. Recent studies (Vielhauer, 1965, pp. 582–7; Koch, 1972, pp. 23–8; Hanson, 1976 a, pp. 27–8; Gammie, 1976, pp. 191–4; Collins, 1979 a) have made a worthwhile beginning in a literary and form-critical description of these writings, but much more clearly needs to be done. The attempt to produce a precise list of apocalypses is helpful.

(2) A good deal of confusion would be avoided if the use of 'apocalyptic' as a noun were dropped altogether (cf. Stone, 1976, p. 443, and contrast Koch, 1972, p. 35). In my opinion, the most helpful distinction is simply that between the apocalypses and apocalyptic eschatology; the latter may properly be so called because it is a dominant element in the apocalypses, although it is not the only element in them and is not restricted to them. But the presence in the apocalypses, by the side of

this eschatological element, of a speculative interest in the cosmos, reflected in particular in parts of 1 Enoch, in 2 Enoch and in 3 Baruch, must always be kept in mind.

II

The idea that wisdom is the matrix from which apocalyptic literature originates goes back to the nineteenth century, but it has been brought into prominence in recent years by the writings of von Rad. His views on this subject were first set out in vol. II of his *Theologie des Alten Testaments* (1960, pp. 314–28; English translation of this edition, 1965, pp. 301–15), but he considerably revised and expanded his treatment of the topic for the fourth edition of this volume (1965; in fact it is the fifth edition that has been used here (1968, pp. 316–38)) and dealt with it again in his *Weisheit in Israel* (1970, pp. 337–63; English translation, 1972, pp. 263–83). Comment here is based on the arguments presented in the later editions of the *Theologie*.

Von Rad began his discussion by raising the methodological issues that were considered in the previous section of this essay. He noted that apocalyptic is a vague term that has been used in two distinct ways but argued that it was unsatisfactory to restrict the concept of apocalyptic to the literary phenomenon of the apocalypses (similarly Beardslee, 1971, p. 422). In practice, however, he did not make a consistent distinction between the apocalypses and apocalyptic.

As positive arguments for deriving apocalyptic from wisdom von Rad noted, first, that Daniel, Enoch and Ezra are presented as wise men and scribes, while, in contrast, the apocalyptic books are not attached to the names of famous prophets, and, secondly, that the concern of the apocalyptic books is with knowledge, not only about universal history but also about nature, which in the ancient world formed a part of wisdom (cf. Wisd. Sol. 7:18–20). On the negative side, von Rad argued that it was impossible to regard apocalyptic as the continuation of prophecy because he believed that the prophetic understanding of history was quite incompatible with that of apocalyptic. Thus he argued that whereas in Israel of old, and particularly in the prophets, history was the area in which Israel experienced Yahweh, and from which alone it could understand its identity, presentations of this history of Israel in the apocalyptic writings are entirely lacking in any confessional character. (With reference to Dan. 7, von Rad spoke of the visionary standing outside the events he saw, of events being presented 'from a spectator's point of view'.) The apocalyptic writers, in his opinion, show no consciousness of the sense of Yahweh's involvement in the events of history; for them the essential thing is rather that everything has been determined in advance.

In a second stage in the development of his argument von Rad emphasised the importance of a traditio-historical approach to the apocalypses. Here he touched again on the theme of determinism. He argued that the concept of the divine determination of the times, which is central in apocalyptic thought, is a fundamental presupposition of wisdom and that the understanding of the times (cf. Esther 1:13), i.e. the interpretation of oracles and dreams, is the task of the wise man, a point illustrated by reference to the parallels between Daniel and Joseph. Of the further points made here I will refer only to two: the link with wisdom seen by von Rad in the apocalyptic concern with the problem of theodicy and, related to this, the use in 4 Ezra and 2 Baruch of what von Rad regards as a stylistic device of wisdom instruction, namely a question and answer method. Von Rad concludes that the apocalyptic writings, as regards their material, the questions they raise and their argumentation, are rooted in the traditions of wisdom.

Few scholars appear to have been entirely convinced by the views of von Rad. Lebram (1978) has expressed support for his approach and Betz (1969 a, p. 136; 1969 b, p. 201), referring to von Rad, has emphasised the importance of knowledge and science in apocalypticism, although his main concern is to argue that apocalypticism cannot be regarded as a purely inner-Jewish phenomenon, but must be viewed within the context of Hellenistic–oriental syncretism. A similar emphasis to that of Betz is to be found in the study of J. Z. Smith (1975); he bases his discussion on an examination of Babylonian and Egyptian materials and argues that 'wisdom and apocalyptic are related in that they are both essentially scribal phenomena' (p. 140). He also suggests that 'Apocalypticism is Wisdom lacking a royal court and patron' (p. 154). Müller (1972, cf. 1969) has sought to defend von Rad by defining the kind of wisdom that, in his view, lies behind apocalyptic; Müller argues that we have to distinguish between educational and mantic wisdom and that apocalypticism is a continuation of the latter rather than the former. As he notes, von Rad (1968, p. 331; cf. p. 323) had himself touched on this point when he observed that only certain sectors of wisdom are continued in apocalyptic, particularly the ancient science of the interpretation of dreams and the science of oracles and 'signs'. For the most part, however, comment on the views of von Rad has been critical (cf. Vielhauer, 1965, pp. 597–8; von der Osten-Sacken, 1969; Zimmerli, 1971, pp. 139–44, especially p. 140; 1978, p. 235; Koch, 1972, pp. 42–7; Nicholson, 1979, pp. 207–11). This critical comment has followed two main lines (cf. Knibb, in *JSJ*).

On the one hand, it has been observed that if wisdom is the matrix from which apocalyptic literature originates, the differences between the wisdom books and the apocalypses are quite remarkable; in particular the complete lack of concern with eschatology in the wisdom writings needs to be explained. This problem is effectively illustrated by the contrast, to which Koch drew attention, between the more or less contemporary books, Ecclesiasticus and Daniel. Von Rad himself seems to have been conscious of the problem and he certainly emphasised that the most distinctive feature of apocalyptic was its concern with the end of history (1968, pp. 329–30). But his answer to the problem – that there are no insurmountable difficulties in the assumption that wisdom, which was in any case tending towards the encyclopaedic, became concerned in a late stage with the last things and that in this the absorption of foreign, particularly Iranian, material played a part – is not supported by any evidence.

On the other hand, it has been pointed out that there is no substance in von Rad's contention that there is no way that leads from the prophetic to the apocalyptic view of history. The distinguishing characteristic of the latter, in von Rad's opinion, was that everything had been determined in advance, but it is a commonplace of prophecy that Yahweh controls the events of history, while Deutero-Isaiah, as von der Osten-Sacken (1969, pp. 18–34) has made clear, provides a specific parallel to the apocalyptic view of history with his belief that Yahweh not only determines, but also foretells, what is going to take place. The way in which the deterministic ideas are expressed in the apocalypses is, of course, quite different from that of prophecy, but this does not mean that the apocalypses do not represent a continuation of prophecy (see the discussion in the next section of this essay). A further point that needs to be made here is that although deterministic ideas are, as von Rad notes, a common feature of both the wisdom writings and the apocalypses, the determinism of wisdom is nowhere expressed in relation to history or concerned with the eschaton, whereas these are the essential characteristics of the determinism of the apocalypses.

The force of the criticisms that have been outlined above is such that it seems impossible to accept von Rad's views as to the derivation of the apocalyptic literature, and his approach must be regarded as too one-sided (cf. Hengel, 1974, vol. I, pp. 206–7). Despite this, the evidence to which he pointed in support of his case still requires explanation. In particular, proper account must be taken of the fact that four of the most significant names to which the Jewish apocalypses of the inter-testamental period are attached are those of wise men or scribes (Daniel, Enoch, Ezra, Baruch) and that, by contrast, the names of prophets were not used (the Apocalypses of Elijah and Zephaniah provide possible, but very uncertain, exceptions; the apocalypse (chs. 6–11) contained within the Ascension of Isaiah is Christian). Wisdom features certainly are to be observed in the apocalypses, and reference may be made here to some recent attempts to take positive account of them.

First, several writers have examined what they regard as specific links between the apocalyptic writings and wisdom. Thus, e.g., Collins (1977) has argued that the Wisdom of Solomon provides the closest point of contact between the Biblical wisdom tradition and the apocalyptic literature and has attempted a comparison between Wisdom and the Jewish apocalypses. The attempt to make a precise point of contact is valuable, but the discussion is weakened because of a rather over-generalised treatment of the apocalypses. A very different kind of comparison, namely between the apocalyptic attitude to time and that of wisdom, was made by de Vries (1978); he argued that one of the essential bonds tying apocalyptic to wisdom was its timelessness – 'the most pervasive manifestation of their common tendency towards reducing all of reality to a simple universal principle' (p. 270). Reference may also be made here to Gammie's analysis (1974) of the concepts of spatial and ethical dualism in wisdom and apocalyptic literature and to his suggestion that: 'wisdom literature constituted at least one of the sources from which apocalyptic writers inherited [these] concepts' (p. 384).

Secondly, there has been increasing recognition of the need to take seriously the concern with nature and with the cosmos that is apparent in a number of apocalypses, particularly those that involve a heavenly journey, e.g. 1 and 2 Enoch (Betz, 1969 a, p. 136; 1969 b, p. 201; Stone, 1976, see pp. 425–6, 431, 434–5). This concern is indicative of the fact that the apocalypses belong within a learned tradition.

Finally, a number of studies (Collins, 1975, pp. 30–1; Willi-Plein, 1977, see pp. 66–8, 76–81; Knibb, in *JSJ*) have emphasised the way in which the authors of the apocalypses use and reinterpret the Old Testament; the apocalypses are a kind of interpretative literature, and this is a further aspect of their character as learned writings. The Jewish apocalypses are properly to be regarded as a continuation of Old Testament prophecy, but they belong very firmly within a learned tradition.

III

In a survey-article published in 1979 Nicholson has sought to focus attention on the ways in which, and the extent to which, apocalyptic has been considered to be the heir of prophecy. His survey provides a helpful account of studies on this theme that appeared in the twenty-five-year period ending in 1974, and it is unnecessary to go over this ground again. The intention here is the much more limited one of drawing attention to a number of studies, published for the most part during the past ten years, in which the lines of transition from prophecy to apocalyptic eschatology and the apocalypses have been seen to lie in different elements of the Old Testament prophetic tradition.

I may conveniently begin by referring to Hanson's study of this question, *The Dawn of Apocalyptic* (1975; see the excellent summary and critique by Carroll (1979); Hanson presented his views in a preliminary form in a number of articles (particularly 1971 *a*, 1971 *b*; cf. also Cross, 1969), but the discussion here is based only on *The Dawn of Apocalyptic*). Despite its all-embracing title, Hanson's book is only concerned with apocalyptic eschatology, which the author regards as one strand running at the heart of many so-called apocalyptic works. He argues that the transition from prophetic to apocalyptic eschatology can be observed within the collection of prophecies contained in Isa. 56–66, and it is the analysis of this collection that forms the heart of his study. Basic to his approach are his definitions of prophetic and apocalyptic eschatology, and it is worth quoting the relevant passage in full:

> Prophetic eschatology we define as a religious perspective which focuses on the prophetic announcement to the nation of the divine plans for Israel and the world which the prophet has witnessed unfolding in the divine council and which he translates into the terms of plain history, real politics, and human instrumentality; that is, the prophet interprets for the king and people how the plans of the divine council will be effected within the context of their nation's history and the history of the world.

> Apocalyptic eschatology we define as a religious perspective which focuses on the disclosure (usually esoteric in nature) to the elect of the cosmic vision of Yahweh's sovereignty – especially as it relates to his acting to deliver his faithful – which disclosure the visionaries have largely ceased to translate into the terms of plain history, real politics, and human instrumentality due to a pessimistic view of reality growing out of the bleak post-exilic conditions within which those associated with the visionaries found themselves. These conditions seemed unsuitable to them as a context for the envisioned restoration of Yahweh's people (1975, pp. 11–12; see further above, pp. 160–1).

Whereas the pre-exilic prophets rejected mythological ways of thinking and insisted on translating their vision of Yahweh's purpose into the terms of politics and plain history, Deutero-Isaiah, in response to the disastrous situation of the exile, made use of the ritual pattern of the conflict myth, which he borrowed from the defunct royal cult, in order to express his vision of Israel's God as the creator and ruler of the entire universe. Despite his use of mythological material Deutero-Isaiah maintained the tension between vision and reality, myth and history. The visionaries who followed him were, however, unable to maintain this tension. They increasingly abandoned the politico-historical realm and took refuge in the realm of mythology; thus, according to Hanson, apocalyptic eschatology was born. Because of his use of mythic motifs Deutero-Isaiah's prophecy is designated by Hanson as 'proto-apocalyptic', while Isa. 56–66, in which apocalyptic eschatology can be seen developing, is described as 'early apocalyptic' (Hanson, 1975, pp. 11–31, 126–32, 299–315). It is one of Hanson's purposes, but not our concern here, to show that the mythology that was used owes nothing, as has often been maintained, to Persian dualism, but has its roots in native Israelite, and ultimately Canaanite, traditions (particularly the myth of the Divine Warrior).

Hanson is somewhat critical of Plöger's influential book, *Theokratie und Eschatologie* (1959), but to some extent his approach is similar. Plöger argued that the contrasting attitudes of the Hasidim (whose viewpoint is reflected in Daniel) and the Maccabean movement (whose viewpoint is reflected in 1 Maccabees) were not new but had a pre-history within the post-exilic community. Thus he believed an underlying tension existed within the post-exilic community between those elements that maintained a non-eschatological theocratic viewpoint and those that kept alive an eschatological expectation; the attitude of the former (which was probably that of the ruling classes and priests) is reflected in the Priestly Writing and the work of the Chronicler, the attitude of the latter in Joel 2:28 – 3:21 (MT 3–4); Zech. 12–14; and Isa. 24–7, a series of passages that, together with others, forms a link between the older restoration eschatology and the apocalyptic form of eschatology. Hanson's approach is similar to this inasmuch as he believes there was a sharp conflict, a struggle for control of the restoration cult, between two groups within the early post-exilic community, a hierocratic and a visionary group, and that apocalyptic eschatology was born within the visionary group as the outcome of its failure to gain control; there are also, however, very substantial differences between the views of Plöger and those of Hanson.

The hierocratic party, according to Hanson's reconstruction, was a group of returned exiles who were dominated by the Zadokite priests and whose programme of restoration is contained in Ezek. 40–8. The nucleus of the visionary party consisted of disciples of Deutero-Isaiah; it was, that is to say, a prophetic group, but linked with it were various dissident elements that had remained in the land of Palestine during the exile, including levitical priests who, for a brief period during the exile, had held control of the Temple site. The restoration programme of this group is to be found in Isa. 60–2. Hanson argues that the oracles within Isa. 56–66 reflect, from the viewpoint of the levitical–prophetic group, an increasingly bitter struggle for control of the restoration cult in the latter part of the sixth century. He further argues that by means of what he describes as a contextual–typological method (see below, pp. 175–6) it is possible to arrange the oracles within Isa. 56–66 in a chronological sequence in which the successive stages of the struggle can be documented. Within the sequence the tension between vision and reality can be seen to be progressively increasing as the struggle became more bitter and the levitical–prophetic group lost ground to the Zadokite group, until in Isa. 65 and 66 the basic components of the later apocalyptic eschatology can already be seen to be present:

> The essential characteristics of apocalyptic eschatology are drawn together into a coherent whole in Isaiah 65: the present era is evil; a great judgement separating the good from the evil and marking the crossroads between the present world and the world to come is imminent; a newly created world of peace and blessing ordained for the faithful lies beyond that judgement. These teachings of world epochs, universal judgement, and a modified dualism are the basic components of later apocalyptic eschatology (Hanson, 1975, p. 160; cf. p. 185).

Hanson (1975, pp. 172-3, 193–5) dates the sequence of oracles in Isa. 56–66 in the period from shortly after the height of Deutero-Isaiah's career (Isa. 60–2) down to 515–510 B.C. (Isa. 56:9 – 57:13); he believes that the oracles were gathered into a collection between 475 and 425, to which period he attributes Isa. 56:1–8 and 66:17–24, which he regards as a redactional framework (1975, pp. 162, 186, 388–9). The history of the struggle between the hierocratic and the visionary parties is, according to his reconstruction, further documented in the so-called Isaiah Apocalypse (Isa. 24–7) and in Zech. 9–14. He devotes only a brief comment to Isa. 24–7 (1975, pp. 313–14), describing it as 'middle apocalyptic' and dating it to approximately 520 B.C., the period of the Temple controversy. However, these chapters have been studied in some detail by Millar (1976; see the review-article by Coggins, 1978–9). Millar adopts basically the same viewpoint as Hanson and uses the same contextual–typological method, but his studies lead him to different conclusions. Thus he dates Isa. 24:1–16 a; 24:16 b – 25:9; and 26:1–8 close to the time of Deutero-Isaiah (nearer to 587 than 520), with Isa. 26:11 – 27:6 somewhat later and the remaining material later still. Correspondingly, he regards Isa. 24–7 as 'proto-apocalyptic' but thinks that Isa. 26:11 – 27:6 is moving in the direction of what Hanson describes as 'early apocalyptic'.

Hanson places the oracles of Zech. 9–14 in a chronological sequence on the basis of the same methodology that he used for Isa. 56–66, but the dates that he assigns to these chapters are a good deal earlier than the dates that have sometimes been assigned to them. In his reconstruction the oracles in Zech. 9–11 and 13:7–9 more or less overlap in date with those in Isa. 56–66. Zech. 12:1 – 13:6, described as 'middle apocalyptic', is placed a little later, namely in the first half of the fifth century (1975, p. 368). Zech. 14, dating from between 475 and 425, is the latest of all the oracles in Isa. 56–66 and Zech. 9–14; this chapter, which is marked by the complete abandonment of any attempt to relate the vision of the eschatological events to the realities of the politico-historical realm, has to be characterised as apocalyptic eschatology (1975, pp. 394–400).

The viewpoint of the hierocratic party in the struggle for control of the restoration cult is, according to Hanson, reflected in Ezekiel, Haggai and Zech. 1–8, but here Hanson argues that the rise of apocalyptic in Israel is not to be traced in the tradition reaching from Ezekiel to Zechariah. The prophecies of Ezekiel, unlike those of Deutero-

Isaiah, cannot be described as 'proto-apocalyptic' because, despite the use in them of forms and symbols that were important in the later apocalyptic writings, they are dominated by a pragmatic *Tendenz*. Zech. 1–8 might be regarded as apocalyptic, if apocalyptic were to be defined strictly on the basis of literary types, but this is unsatisfactory. Visionary forms and motifs are used in Zech. 1–8, as in Haggai, as a means of mustering support for the hierocratic Temple programme, but there is no genuine eschatological thrust in these prophecies; rather a pragmatic orientation is to be discerned in Zech. 1–8; his restoratio programme never loses touch with mundane realities, and this prevent us from regarding Zechariah as the father of apocalyptic (Hansor 1975, pp. 228–59). Hanson's approach in this respect stands in marke contrast to that of Gese, whose views he explicitly rejects. Gese (1973 cf. North, 1972, and Amsler, 1972) argues that the night-visions c Zechariah form the oldest apocalypse known to us. In his view th seven visions – ch. 3, which contains the fourth of the existing eigl visions, is regarded as a later insertion – are organically connected an form a complete apocalypse, a sevenfold revelation of the in-breakin of the new era. He supports this judgement by arguing that most of th characteristics of apocalyptic, both of form and of content, are to k found in the night-visions. In the context of the present discussion it is interesting to observe that Gese emphasises the importance of this conclusion in the light of Zechariah's priestly associations; apocalyptic did not, in his view, have its origins in groups opposed to those in power but in 'official' circles (these comments (similarly Jacob, 1977, pp. 55–6) are directed at Plöger, but they apply equally to Hanson). In the further development of his argument he maintains that the one apocalyptic element that is missing in the night-visions, a description of the last great battle that would inaugurate the new era, is to be found in the material that has been added to the vision-cycle, i.e. Zech. 9–14. For the theme of the last great battle Gese refers in the first instance to Zech. 9 and 10; for Zech. 9 he adopts the view that the chapter refers to the campaigns of Alexander the Great against the Persians, an event regarded in Zech. 9 as taking place at the instigation of God and marking the beginning of the end-time. Other apocalyptic elements are also, in Gese's view, to be found within Zech. 9–14: the messianic hope (cf. 9:9–10), the concept of martyrdom at the end-time (cf. 12:10–14), the idea of a suffering messiah (cf. 13:7–9). Gese dates these chapters by means of the conventional method of identifying the historical allusions contained within them; he places Zech. 9–11 in the period approximately from 330 to 300 B.C., and Zech. 12–14 in the Ptolemaic period and, more precisely, in the third century.

For the sake of completeness I note that Erling (1972; cf. Vawter, 1960, pp. 41–2) has drawn Ezek. 38–9 once more into the discussion. He argues that the nucleus of these chapters stems from Ezekiel himself and believes that they may form one of the oldest apocalyptic passages in the prophetic writings. He does, however, state that most of the characteristics of the apocalyptic genre of literature are not present in Ezek. 38–9, and it is the influence of this passage on the later development of apocalyptic tradition that he is primarily concerned with.

The passages with which we have been concerned in the preceding pages are the ones that have traditionally been brought into the debate about the prophetic origins of 'apocalyptic' (cf. Zimmerli, 1978, pp. 228–30), and there can be little question that within them the transition from the literary genre of prophecy to that of the apocalypses, and from the future expectation of the pre-exilic prophets to apocalyptic eschatology, is marked. For the former the most important passages are clearly Ezek. 40–8 – chs. 8–11 are also relevant – and Zech. 1–8; for the latter Isa. 24–7; 56–66; Ezek. 38–9; Joel 2:28 – 3:21 (MT 3–4); Zech. 9–14. To this extent there is a considerable element of truth in all the discussions to which we have just referred. It will be apparent, however, that a great deal of uncertainty and confusion still remains about a number of issues. One instance of this is whether Zech. 1–8 contains an apocalyptic eschatology and may be regarded as an apocalypse.

Hanson, whose views are accepted by Collins (1979c, pp. 29–30), believes that the visions of Zechariah do not contain a genuine apocalyptic eschatology but rather use the visionary form to promote support for the hierocratic party. This belief is based on his understanding of the nature of prophetic and apocalyptic eschatology (cf. the definitions quoted above, pp. 169–70), which is linked with his view that the proponents of apocalyptic eschatology are the powerless and disenfranchised elements in the community. Zechariah was not the spokesman for the powerless and disenfranchised but for those in control; his visions come, as it were, on the wrong side of the divide, and Gese's view that they form the oldest apocalypse known to us cannot be accepted. But Hanson's viewpoint here seems to be somewhat artificial, and this must call into question the validity of the definitions

and arguments on which his judgement is based. It is difficult to deny
that *an* eschatology is to be found within Zech. 1–8, and since this is
expressed not by means of prophetic oracles but in accounts of visions
of the type that are used in the apocalypses, it seems natural to regard
this writing as an apocalypse itself, however inchoate its form may be.[1]
In his interpretation of Zech. 1–8 (and of Haggai and Ezekiel as well)
Hanson seems to have allowed himself to be unduly influenced by his
reconstruction of events in terms of 'a single post-exilic struggle'
(1975, p. 240). His reconstruction offers a fascinating perspective from
which to read the writings of the exilic and post-exilic periods, but it
remains a hypothetical reconstruction, and the realities may well have
been rather more complex than his account suggests. It is, furthermore,
not at all clear that his definitions of prophetic and apocalyptic eschatology, or his use of such terms as myth and history, are satisfactory,
but it is impossible here to do more than refer to the comments of
Carroll (1979, pp. 18–27).

Another question about which there remains a great deal of uncertainty is that of the dating of the prophetic oracles here considered,
particularly Isa. 24–7; 56–66; Zech. 9–14. The methods that have been
traditionally used for this purpose have led to some very uncertain
results, but it is doubtful whether the contextual–typological method
adopted by Hanson and Millar is likely to lead to results that are any
more certain. The basis of this method is to interpret the individual
oracles within the context of the community-struggle discernible
behind them and to apply typological tools to their analysis – the
typologies 'of poetic structure and meter, of prophetic oracle types
(genres), and of the prophetic eschatology–apocalyptic eschatology
continuum' (Hanson, 1975, p. 29). Hanson is not so much concerned
to date the oracles to a precise point in time as to place them in a
chronological sequence, but it seems very doubtful whether we have
sufficient material available from the exilic and early post-exilic periods
to enable us to apply his methods of typological analysis with sufficient
confidence to be able to place the individual oracles in a chronological
sequence – quite apart from the fact that the only kind of development
Hanson allows for is linear (cf. Carroll, 1979, p. 27). Moreover, the
use of different typologies or different methods can lead to different
conclusions, which, at first sight, seem just as convincing. Thus, for
example, Habets (1974, see Coggins, 1978/9, p. 332), who uses a
typological method, argues that Isa. 24–7 is to be dated not earlier
than the beginning of the third century. Vermeylen's analysis of Isa.

24–7 and 56–66, to take another example, differs sharply from that of Hanson (Vermeylen, 1977, pp. 349–81, 451–517); whatever one may think of his conclusions, his study has the merit of not assuming that Isa. 24–7 and 56–66 are self-contained entities, and of attempting to relate the composition of these sections to those of the Book of Isaiah as a whole.

In conclusion it may be said that there seems to be reasonable evidence for the view that the Jewish apocalypses represent a continuation of Old Testament prophecy, just as apocalyptic eschatology represents a continuation of the future expectation of the prophets (cf. Jacob, 1977). However, other influences, as well as the prophetic, contributed to the emergence of the apocalypses, and in particular the apocalypses have to be seen as learned compositions, standing within a learned tradition. Whether the transition from prophecy to the apocalypses was a gradual process, or whether we must, as Carroll (1979, p. 30) suggests, posit as an alternative view a number of discontinuous jumps in the development from late prophecy to apocalyptic of a classical form, must remain uncertain; as Carroll indicates, the lack of firm evidence is a major difficulty for any theory of discontinuous jumps.

Note

1 That its form as an apocalypse is inchoate hardly needs to be emphasised. It is appropriate here to refer to the study of Jeremias (1977, see especially pp. 39–108, 226–33). Jeremias, although denying that the night-visions form the oldest apocalypse known to us (Gese), carefully presents the evidence for the view that they occupy a transitional position between prophecy and apocalyptic (as represented by the book of Daniel).

Bibliography

S. Amsler 'Zacharie et l'origine de l'apocalyptique', in *Congress Volume, Uppsala, 1971*, SVT 22 (Leiden, 1972), pp. 227–31.

J. Barr 'Jewish Apocalyptic in Recent Scholarly Study', *BJRL* 58 (1975–6), 9–35.

W. A. Beardslee 'New Testament Apocalyptic in Recent interpretation', *Interpretation* 25 (1971), 419–35.

H. D. Betz 'On the Problem of the Religio-Historical Understanding of Apocalypticism', in R. W. Funk (ed.), *Apocalypticism*, JTC 6 (New York, 1969), pp. 134–56 (English translation of 'Zum Problem des religionsgeschichtlichen Verständnisses der Apokalyptik', *ZThK* 63 (1966), 391–409). (English translation cited as Betz, 1969 a).

'The Concept of Apocalyptic in the Theology of the Pannenberg Group', in R. W. Funk (ed.), *Apocalypticism*, JTC 6 (New York, 1969), pp. 192–207 (= 1969 b).

C. E. Braaten 'The Significance of Apocalypticism for Systematic Theology', *Interpretation* 25 (1971), 480–99.

R. P. Carroll 'Twilight of Prophecy or Dawn of Apocalyptic?', *JSOT* 14 (1979), 3–35.

R. J. Coggins 'The Problem of Isaiah 24–27', *ET* 90 (1978–9), 328-33.

J. J. Collins 'Jewish Apocalyptic against its Hellenistic Near Eastern Environment', *BASOR* 220 (1975), 27–36.

'Cosmos and Salvation: Jewish Wisdom and Apocalyptic in the Hellenistic Age', *HistRel* 17 (1977), 121–42.

Apocalypse: the Morphology of a Genre, Semeia 14 (Missoula, Montana, 1979) (= 1979a).

'Towards the Morphology of a Genre', in *Apocalypse: The Morphology of a Genre* (see above), pp. 1–20 (= 1979b).

'The Jewish Apocalypses', in *Apocalypse: The Morphology of a Genre* (see above), pp. 21–59 (= 1979c).

J. Coppens *La relève apocalyptique du messianisme royal*, vol. I: 'La royauté, le règne, le royaume de Dieu. Cadre de la relève apocalyptique', BEThL 50 (Louvain, 1979).

F. M. Cross 'New Directions in the Study of Apocalyptic', in R. W. Funk (ed.), *Apocalypticism*, JTC 6 (New York, 1969), pp. 157–65.

M. Delcor 'Bilan des études sur l'apocalyptique', in *Apocalypses et Théologie de l'Espérance. Congrès de Toulouse (1975)*, Présentation de L. Monloubou, Lectio Divina 95 (Paris, 1977), pp. 27-42 (= *Études bibliques et orientales de religions comparées* (Leiden, 1979), pp. 177–92).

B. Erling 'Ezekiel 38–39 and the Origins of Jewish Apocalyptic', in *Ex Orbe Religionum, Studia G. Widengren Oblata*, Supplements to Numen 21, vol. I (Leiden, 1972), pp. 104–14.

R. W. Funk (ed.) *Apocalypticism*, JTC 6 (New York, 1969).

J. G. Gammie 'Spatial and Ethical Dualism in Jewish Wisdom and Apocalyptic Literature', *JBL* 93 (1974), 356–85.

'The Classification, Stages of Growth, and Changing Intentions in the Book of Daniel', *JBL* 95 (1976), 191–204.

H. Gese 'Anfang und Ende der Apokalyptik dargestellt am Sacharjabuch', *ZThK* 70 (1973), 20–49.

H. Gunkel *Schöpfung und Chaos in Urzeit und Endzeit* (Göttingen, 1895).

G. N. M. Habets *Die Grosse Jesaja-Apokalypse (Jes. 24–27). Ein Beitrag zur Theologie des Alten Testaments*, Diss. (Bonn, 1974) (not seen).

P. D. Hanson 'Old Testament Apocalyptic Reexamined', *Interpretation* 25 (1971), 454–79 (= 1971a).

'Jewish Apocalyptic against its Near Eastern Environment', *RB* 78 (1971), 31–58 (= 1971b).

The Dawn of Apocalyptic (Philadelphia, 1975).

'Apocalypse, Genre', and 'Apocalypticism', in *IDB*, Supplementary Volume (1976), pp. 27–34 (= 1976 *a*).

'Prolegomena to the Study of Jewish Apocalyptic', in F. M. Cross, W. E. Lemke and P. D. Miller, Jr (eds.), *Magnalia Dei: The Mighty Acts of God, Essays on the Bible and Archaeology, in memory of G. E. Wright* (Garden City, New York, 1976), pp. 389–413 (= 1976 *b*).

M. Hengel *Judaism and Hellenism. Studies in their Encounter in Palestine during the Early Hellenistic Period* (2 vols. London, 1974) (English translation of *Judentum und Hellenismus. Studien zu ihrer Begegnung unter besonderer Berücksichtigung Palästinas bis zur Mitte des 2 Jh.s v. Chr.*, WUNT 10, 2nd ed. (Tübingen, 1973)).

E. Jacob 'Aux sources bibliques de l'apocalyptique', in *Apocalypses et Théologie de l'Espérance. Congrès de Toulouse (1975), Présentation de L. Monloubou*, Lectio Divina 95 (Paris, 1977), pp. 43–61.

C. Jeremias *Die Nachtgesichte des Sacharja. Untersuchungen zu ihrer Stellung im Zusammenhang der Visionsberichte im Alten Testament und zu ihrer Bildmaterial*, FRLANT 117 (Göttingen, 1977).

M. A. Knibb 'Apocalyptic and Wisdom in 4 Ezra', *JSJ* (forthcoming).

K. Koch *The Rediscovery of Apocalyptic*, SBT, Second Series, 22 (London, 1972) (English translation of *Ratlos vor der Apokalyptik. Eine Streitschrift über ein vernachlässigtes Gebiet der Bibelwissenschaft und die schädlichen Auswirkungen auf Theologie und Philosophie* (Gütersloh, 1970)).

J. Lebram 'Apokalyptik/Apokalypsen. II. Altes Testament', in *TRE* 3 (1978), pp. 192–202.

W. R. Millar *Isaiah 24–27 and the Origin of Apocalyptic*, Harvard Semitic Monographs 11 (Missoula, Montana, 1976).

L. Morris *Apocalyptic* (Grand Rapids, 1972: 2nd ed., 1973).

H.-P. Müller 'Magisch-mantische Weisheit und die Gestalt Daniels', *Ugarit-Forschungen* 1 (1969), 79–94.

'Mantische Weisheit und Apokalyptik', in *Congress Volume, Uppsala, 1971*, SVT 22 (Leiden, 1972), pp. 268–93.

W. R. Murdock 'History and Revelation in Jewish Apocalypticism', *Interpretation* 21 (1967), 167–87.

E. W. Nicholson 'Apocalyptic', in G. W. Anderson (ed.), *Tradition and Interpretation, Essays by Members of the Society for Old Testament Study* (Oxford, 1979), pp. 189–213.

R. North 'Prophecy to Apocalyptic via Zechariah', in *Congress Volume, Uppsala, 1971*, SVT 22 (Leiden, 1972), pp. 47–71.

P. von der Osten-Sacken *Die Apokalyptik in ihren Verhältnis zu Prophetie und Weisheit*, TheolEx 157 (Munich, 1969).

W. Pannenberg (ed.) *Revelation as History* (New York and London, 1968) (English translation of *Offenbarung als Geschichte* (Göttingen, 1961; 3rd ed., 1965)).

O. Plöger *Theocracy and Eschatology* (Oxford, 1968) (English translation of *Theokratie und Eschatologie*, WMANT 2, 2nd ed. (Neukirchen, 1962; 1st ed., 1959)).

G. von Rad *Old Testament Theology*, vol. II: 'The Theology of Israel's Prophetic Traditions' (Edinburgh and London, 1965) (English translation of *Theologie des Alten Testaments*, vol. II: 'Die Theologie der prophetischen Überlieferungen Israels' (Munich, 1960)).

Die Theologie des Alten Testaments, vol. II: 'Die Theologie der prophetischen Überlieferungen Israels', 5th ed. (Munich, 1968).

Wisdom in Israel (London, 1972) (English translation of *Weisheit in Israel* (Neukirchen, 1970)).

F. Raphaël (and others) *L'apocalyptique*, Études d'histoire des religions 3 (Paris, 1977).

H. H. Rowley *The Relevance of Apocalyptic. A Study of Jewish Apocalypses from Daniel to the Revelation*, 3rd ed. (London, 1963).

D. S. Russell *The Method and Message of Jewish Apocalyptic, 200 B.C.–A.D. 100*, Old Testament Library (London, 1964).

Apocalyptic: Ancient and Modern (London, 1978).

J. M. Schmidt *Die jüdische Apokalyptik. Die Geschichte ihrer Erforschung von den Anfängen bis zu den Textfunden von Qumran* (Neukirchen, 1969; 2nd ed., 1976).

W. Schmithals *The Apocalyptic Movement. Introduction and Interpretation* (Nashville and New York, 1975) (English translation of *Die Apokalyptik. Einführung und Deutung* (Göttingen, 1973)).

J. Schreiner *Alttestamentlich-jüdische Apokalyptik. Eine Einführung* (Munich, 1969).

J. Z. Smith 'Wisdom and Apocalyptic', in B. A. Pearson (ed.), *Religious Syncretism in Antiquity. Essays in Conversation with G. Widengren* (Missoula, Montana, 1975), pp. 131–56 (= *Map is not Territory. Studies in the History of Religion*, SJLA 23 (Leiden, 1978), pp. 67–87).

E. Stauffer *New Testament Theology* (London, 1955) (English translation of *Die Theologie des Neuen Testaments*, 5th ed. (Stuttgart, 1948)).

M. E. Stone 'Lists of Revealed Things in the Apocalyptic Literature', in F. M. Cross, W. E. Lemke and P. D. Miller, Jr (eds.), *Magnalia Dei. The Mighty Acts of God, Essays on the Bible and Archaeology, in memory of G. E. Wright* (Garden City, New York, 1976), pp. 414–52.

B. Vawter 'Apocalyptic: Its Relation to Prophecy', *CBQ* 22 (1960), 33–46.

J. Vermeylen *Du prophète Isaïe à l'apocalyptique. Isaïe, I–XXXV, miroir d'un demi-millénaire d'expérience religieuse en Israel* (2 vols., Paris, 1977).

P. Vielhauer 'Apocalypses and Related Subjects. Introduction', in E. Hennecke and W. Schneemelcher (eds.), *New Testament Apocrypha*, vol. II (London, 1965), pp. 581–607 (English translation of 'Apokalypsen und Verwandtes. Einleitung', in *Neutestamentliche Apokryphen*, vol II, 3rd ed. (Tübingen, 1964, pp. 407–27)).

S. J. de Vries 'Observations on Quantitative and Qualititive Time in Wisdom and Apocalyptic', in *Israelite Wisdom, Theological and Literary Essays in Honor of S. Terrien* (Missoula, Montana, 1978), pp. 263–76.

A. N. Wilder 'The Rhetoric of Ancient and Modern Apocalyptic', *Interpretation* 25 (1971), 436–53.

I. Willi-Plein 'Das Geheimnis der Apokalyptik', *VT* 27 (1977), 62–81.

W. Zimmerli *Man and his Hope in the Old Testament*, SBT Second Series 20 (London, 1971) (English translation of *Der Mensch und seine Hoffnung im Alten Testament* (Göttingen, 1968)).

Old Testament Theology in Outline (Edinburgh, 1978) (English translation of *Grundriss der alttestamentlichen Theologie*, Theologische Wissenschaft 3, 2nd ed. (Stuttgart, 1975)).

Prophecy and wisdom

R. N. WHYBRAY

In discussing the relationship between any two things it is essential to have a clear idea of the nature of the two things to be compared, and if the discussion is to be a useful one it is necessary to find satisfactory working definitions for both of them. Unfortunately these conditions are not fulfilled when the relationship between prophecy and wisdom is the subject to be considered. If, as will be indicated below, scholarly treatments of this subject have produced a great variety of conclusions, some of them mutually incompatible, this is due for the most part to the fact that the meaning of the word 'wisdom', as used in Old Testament contexts, has been a matter of wide disagreement. Some attention must consequently first be paid to this problem before the relationship of 'wisdom' to the more easily definable concept 'prophecy' can be described.

I

It is well known that in the Old Testament the word 'wisdom' has a specialised as well as a general sense. The Hebrew word *ḥokmāh*, when it occurs in the Old Testament, often means no more than 'common sense', 'brains'. In some passages it is better translated by 'ability', 'skill', 'technique'. But that a more specialised meaning is to be found in some books was recognised at a very early date, as is shown by the titles given to certain Biblical or Apocryphal books: Ecclesiasticus was known as 'The Wisdom of Jesus son of Sirach', the Apocrypha contains the Wisdom of Solomon, and Proverbs is referred to in Tosephta on *Baba Bathra* 14 b as 'The Book of Wisdom', while in the Roman Missal the readings from certain books – Ecclesiasticus, Proverbs, Wisdom of Solomon and the Song of Solomon – are introduced by the heading 'Lectio Libri Sapientiae'. These titles and headings reflect an early recognition that certain Old Testament books are especially concerned to teach something called 'wisdom'. Since the nineteenth century scholars of all religious persuasions have used the phrases 'wisdom books' and 'wisdom literature' to denote the books of Job, Proverbs and Ecclesiastes, together with the Apocryphal books of Ecclesiasticus and the Wisdom of Solomon, which are in fact all, to a large extent, concerned with the nature and application of human wisdom or with wisdom as an attribute and gift of God. The authors of these books have also been generally referred to as 'the wise men' or 'the sages'.

The wisdom books remained a relatively neglected part of the Old Testament until the 1920s when the discovery of an apparently direct literary relationship between an ancient Egyptian text – the *Wisdom of Amenemope* – and a section of the Biblical book of Proverbs (22:17 – 23:11) opened a new era of study in which it was generally recognised that the Old Testament wisdom books were closely related to an international literary tradition stretching back to the third millennium B.C. (Oesterley, 1927; Fichtner, 1933; Baumgartner, 1933). Other recently discovered works of a similar character from Egypt and Mesopotamia – especially the former – were now also compared with the book of Proverbs (see, e.g., Humbert, 1929), and, as a result of these comparative studies, the possibility emerged that substantial parts of Proverbs (chs. 10–29) might well have originated at the Judean court in the period before the Babylonian exile (see, e.g., Oesterley, 1929). In the 1930s and 1940s von Rad (1966 a, p. 203; 1966 b, pp. 293–4) gave further precision to this theory, maintaining that the earliest Israelite wisdom literature in Proverbs was the work of a professional class of scribes instituted by David and Solomon, when they established Israel for the first time as a fully developed national state whose administration was based on foreign, mainly Egyptian, models and with the assistance of Egyptian scribes. For von Rad, this was for Israel a period of 'enlightenment', when Israel was thrust suddenly into the mainstream of ancient Near Eastern political, economic and cultural life, and one of the main manifestations of this 'enlightenment' was 'wisdom literature'. To this theory von Rad joined another: 'wisdom' in Israel should be seen not just as a convenient term to describe the teaching of the books of Job, Proverbs and Ecclesiastes but as something much broader: as a specific way of thinking, which not only produced these 'wisdom books' but also influenced other literature of the period, especially the so-called 'Succession Narrative' (2 Sam. 9–20; 1 Kings 1–2) and the 'Joseph Story' (Gen. 37–50).

The effect of these new theories, which met with a large measure of agreement among scholars, was to suggest for Israel's early wisdom literature a much more precise dating and a more precise *Sitz im Leben* than had previously been thought possible. The 'sages', who had been postulated by earlier scholars as the authors of the wisdom books and often dated in the post-exilic period, were now identified as members of a professional class of scribes, first instituted in Israel in the time of David and Solomon, which was closely associated, as long as the monarchy lasted, with the king and court. It was further held that their earliest literary work – the older parts of Proverbs and certain narrative works – was produced in some kind of connection with 'wisdom schools', supposed to have been established on Egyptian models for the education and professional training of future generations of scribes and administrators. The Book of Proverbs was, then, basically 'school wisdom' (von Rad's phrase), some of it going back to the tenth century B.C., and reflecting – as did the older Egyptian 'Instructions' – the interests of government officials and the ruling class generally.

These conclusions, as we shall see, opened up in a new way the possibility that wisdom literature – or 'wisdom thought' – may in some way have been historically connected, through its practitioners, with Old Testament prophecy. Some earlier scholars had given brief consideration to the theme 'prophecy and wisdom' but, on the assumption that all the Old Testament wisdom books were, at any rate in their present literary form, post-exilic, they had attempted to see the teaching of these books, including Proverbs, as presupposing that of the classical prophets. Now, as far as the Book of Proverbs was concerned, it became clear that the relationship, if it existed, might be the reverse of this. The earliest literary wisdom in Israel had preceded the classical prophets, who might, therefore, have been influenced by its themes and literary forms. Moreover, since the 'wise men' and scribes (the two were frequently held to be identical) remained active and close to the centre of power throughout the eighth and seventh centuries, which was the period of classical prophecy, it now seemed probable that the two groups would have been aware of one another and in contact with one another; and – given the supposedly international connections and pro-monarchical attitudes of the 'wise men' and the total silence of the Book of Proverbs about Israel as God's people – at times in conflict with one another. The books of the pre-exilic prophets were therefore eagerly scanned for evidence of such contacts, both positive and negative.

The understanding of the 'wise' and of the wisdom books briefly sketched above held sway generally, with certain modifications and nuances, and with occasional expressions of dissent, in Old Testament scholarship for a number of years. Even in his latest book on the subject von Rad (1972, pp. 11–12 and n. 9; original German ed., 1970, p. 24 and n. 9), while acknowledging the existence of other explanations of the origin of Israelite wisdom, dismissed these in a paragraph and a footnote: for him even the earliest parts of Proverbs were simply 'school wisdom'.

During the last twenty years, however, there has been a growing tendency among scholars to recognise a native Israelite wisdom tradition, which already existed before the establishment of the Israelite state with its foreign cultural tradition. It is not clear whether this native wisdom tradition had a major role to play in the formation of the literary movement of which Proverbs is the main extant product, but the proponents of the theory maintain that, after the establishment of the monarchy in Israel, it continued to flourish in circles not connected with the court and its scribal schools and that it may be detected in Old Testament books outside the more formal corpus of wisdom books. This idea was not entirely new when it was put forward in the 1960s. It had already been suggested by Lindblom (1955, pp. 201–3) that there were in Israel from early times wise men who gave informal oral instruction. This suggestion was further elaborated by Terrien (1962, especially pp. 109, 114–15), who argued that the 'language, style and ideas' of the prophet Amos were influenced by wisdom but that this wisdom may have been of an oral kind, perhaps having its origins in a semi-nomadic society. He also remarked that if this was so 'it...tends to prevent the overstressing of the separation of classes among the leaders of the eighth century B.C.' and that the various groups in Israel such as priests, prophets and wise men 'lived in a common and mutually interacting environment' (p. 115). These remarks anticipated much later research, signalling a more fluid, but inevitably less precise and clear-cut, approach to the subject.

Meanwhile Audet (1960) had developed thoughts about the origin of Israelite wisdom on somewhat different lines. In a discussion of the origin of legal and wisdom traditions in the ancient Near East, including Israel, he suggested that wisdom and law had a common origin in oral parental instruction in pre-literate society. A similar conclusion was reached by Gerstenberger, with reference to Israelite law and wisdom, in a Bonn dissertation of 1961, later published in 1965. Gerstenberger was the first to use the phrase 'clan wisdom' (*Sippenweisheit*) in an Israelite context. Subsequently Wolff, in a study of Amos (1973), combined the insights of both Terrien and Gerstenberger, using the latter's term *Sippenweisheit* to describe the kind of wisdom that he believed to have influenced the teaching and style of that prophet.

It will already be evident that this new understanding of the origin of Israelite wisdom put the question of the relationship between prophecy and wisdom – and equally between wisdom and other traditions – in an entirely new light; and, indeed, it inaugurated a new era in the study of that relationship. This was now understood to be something much broader than simply a relationship between the school or court literary wisdom tradition, supposedly reflected in Proverbs, on the one hand, and the teaching of the classical prophets on the other. If Israel's 'wisdom' was a broader and more varied phenomenon than had previously been supposed, it became necessary to consider whether any supposed wisdom traits in the teaching of the prophets might be due to the survival of this older tradition, rather than to a connection between the prophets and the court or the school. The pioneering work of Terrien and Wolff in this field has been followed up by other scholars.

The most recent stage in the study of wisdom in Israel is, in a sense, a logical conclusion of the work of the preceding generation: a further step in the direction of fluidity. It is well exemplified by a recent essay by Murphy (1978). Murphy, who had earlier (1967) published an excellent survey of the study of the subject, here seeks to combine the view of Proverbs as mainly the work of court scribes – a view that no scholar would wish to deny entirely – with the more recent theories that Israelite wisdom was originally at home among the ordinary people. He writes of this wisdom as 'an approach to reality which was shared by all Israelites in varying degrees'. There were expert teachers in Israel; but 'the existence of experts. . . presupposes that the average Israelite shared to some extent in this sapiential understanding of reality. . . Such an understanding was not a mode of thinking cultivated exclusively by one class; it was shared at all levels of society that interpreted daily experience' (pp. 39–40). So 'the mentality itself was much broader than the literary remains that have come down to us'.

Murphy's concern in this passage is one that is particularly relevant to the theme 'prophecy and wisdom'. He points out that this new understanding of the origin and character of Israelite wisdom requires a complete reformulation of the problem of the relationship between wisdom literature and other Old Testament literary traditions (including prophecy): it is no longer necessary – and perhaps neither appropriate nor profitable – to look for an 'influence' of the wise men or of wisdom literature on the prophets, since whatever similarities may be found between wisdom texts and prophetical texts can be explained in terms of a 'shared approach to reality' common to all Israelites, including 'wise men' and prophets, in various degrees. In an allusion to the work of Fichtner (1949) and others, he writes: 'Thus it should come as no surprise (and hence provide no basis for classifying Isaiah among the wise) that Isaiah should use a parable, any more than that the author of the Book of Job utilised a legend concerning Job the patriarch for the framework of his sapiential discussion of a wisdom problem' (p. 40).

I have referred at some length to Murphy's essay because it appears to mark a turning-point in the study of wisdom in the Old Testament. He anticipates that his hypothesis 'will open up the research of wisdom influence upon various parts of the Old Testament'. This may prove to be so; on the other hand, it may mark the cessation of the study of the question, for Murphy's concept of a 'shared approach to reality' is so broad as to run the risk of reducing the concept of Israelite wisdom, outside the 'wisdom books' proper, to no more than native common sense such as is to be found generally in human nature. All literature would then be 'wisdom literature', in so far as it had any kind of intellectual content, and to say of any author's work that it showed traces of 'wisdom thought' would be to say no more than that he was not a fool.

It is not, however, the primary purpose of this essay to discuss the question of the nature of Old Testament wisdom *per se* but to survey the history of the study of the relationship between prophecy and wisdom. This question will now be treated in somewhat more detail.

II

Fichtner (1949) was the first to perceive that the new early dating of parts of Proverbs, and the ascription of them to professional scribes or wise men of the early monarchy, opened up the possibility that the classical prophets might have been influenced, positively or negatively, by such 'wisdom'. He found little or no such influence, however, in the books of the pre-exilic prophets, with the exception of Isaiah. Here he found, on the one hand, clear traces of a conflict between

Isaiah, as one called to proclaim God's uncompromising word to king
and people, and the wise men with their practical, pragmatic, political
policies, shaped by the prudential principles of traditional international
wisdom, and, on the other hand, equally clear evidence that Isaiah was
himself so familiar with that tradition as to be completely at home
in it. He reconciled these two sets of observations by concluding that
Isaiah, before his call to be a prophet, had himself been one of the
professional wise men. As a consequence of his prophetical call he had
come to see that the wise men of his time had embraced a false, earthly
wisdom, which would lead the nation to destruction because it had
abandoned the only true wisdom, which comes from God (11:2; 31:2).

Fichtner's hypothesis that Isaiah had at one time belonged to the
ranks of the professional wise men has not been generally accepted
(though see Martin-Achard, 1960). But some of his other assertions
and assumptions have provided the basic material for the discussion of
the question of prophecy and wisdom ever since.

(1) he assumed that in Proverbs and Isaiah the term 'wise' was frequently used as a technical term, denoting a class of professional
politicians who guided the Judean state according to the principles
of statesmanship derived from Egypt. He did not consider the
possibility of the existence of any other, native, 'wisdom' tradition,
in any sense other than that of ordinary human intelligence.
(2) he assumed that the older parts of the Book of Proverbs may
legitimately be taken as representative of the outlook of this
professional class.
(3) although he recognised that some elements, which are found in
both the prophetical books and Proverbs – e.g. ethical principles,
such as the obligation of kindness to the poor, reservations about
the cult, certain stylistic usages, such as simile and wordplay – are
derived from a common Israelite, or a common Near Eastern
heritage, he held that certain items of vocabulary such as *ḥākām*,
bīnāh, *yā'aṣ*, *'ēṣāh*, *yāda'* and phrases like 'wise in one's own eyes',
do, in fact, point to a specific and direct influence of the 'wise',
when they occur in the teaching of the prophets.

Lindblom (1955) supported Fichtner's study in some ways, though
with greater caution. He placed less reliance on specific comparisons
between the prophetical books and the Book of Proverbs and he found
very few references in the former to a professional class of wise men,
although he acknowledged that passages like Jer. 18:18 and 9:23–4

(MT 22–3) proved that such a class existed in the time of Jeremiah and earlier. With regard to the question of a possible influence of the ideas of this class on the prophets, he formulated the principle that 'we are entitled to speak of such influences...when, in the sayings of the prophets, we meet with words and thoughts which are alien to the prophetic thought-world in general, but characteristic of the doctrines of wisdom' (p. 197). With this principle in mind he cited, as examples of ideas found only in these two bodies of literature, the concept of Yahweh as wise and as showing His wisdom in creation, and the 'principle of individual retribution'. As examples of stylistic traits reminiscent of wisdom in the prophetical books he cited 'parables, allegories, proverbial expressions, comparisons, similes, metaphors' (p. 201). Unfortunately, his study is too short to offer justification for his opinion that these concepts and stylistic traits are examples of wisdom influence and not simply indicative of a common intellectual heritage, which would, in some cases at least, seem a more probable explanation. At any rate, it is evident that both his and Fichtner's methods needed much more refinement than either of these scholars gave them.

Although much has been written on this subject since the pioneering work of Fichtner and Lindblom, no reliable criteria have emerged that can be confidently used to determine the existence of 'wisdom influence' on the prophets. Terrien (1962) and Wolff (1964) listed a number of supposedly significant wisdom traits in the oracles of Amos. On the level of vocabulary and style, or form, these include consecutive numerals used in pairs (e.g. 'For three transgressions of x and for four...'), rhetorical questions, antithetical pairs of words, woe oracles (i.e. oracles beginning with *hōy*: 'woe to...'), the admonition (*Mahnrede*) and certain items of vocabulary, such as *sōd* in the sense of 'secret' (Amos 3:7) and *nākōaḥ* (Amos 3:10).

The evidential value of these features has, unfortunately, in almost every case been shown by later critics to be questionable or even nil. Thus Terrien's suggestion, that Amos' unique use of the term 'Isaac' to refer to Israel, coupled with his interest in Beersheba, points to a connection with Edom and its wisdom, is much too tenuous to bear any weight (Crenshaw, 1967). His argument that *sōd* in Amos 3:7, in the sense of 'secret', is peculiar to the wisdom tradition, and the similar argument, also maintained by Wolff, about *nākōaḥ* (Amos 3:10), is also very flimsy (Whybray, 1974, pp. 131, 140–2). Rhetorical questions are by no means peculiar to the wisdom literature

(Whybray, 1971, pp. 19–26; see also Eichrodt, 1977), and antithetical pairs abound in every type of Old Testament literature. Subsequent discussion of the woe oracles (a question that was also investigated by Gerstenberger in a detailed study published in the same year – 1962 – as Terrien's article) has established that there is no reason to suppose that this form of speech, which originated in lamentation over the dead, was not derived by the prophets directly from its original source, rather than through the medium of the wisdom literature (see especially Wanke, 1966; Hermisson, 1968, pp. 89–90; Janzen, 1972; Zobel, 1978). With regard to the device of consecutive numerals used in pairs, Roth published a full study of this question in the same year (1962) that Terrien's study of Amos appeared, in which he demonstrated that this device is a very frequent one, both in the Old Testament and in other ancient Near Eastern literature, and that it is by no means confined to wisdom texts but appears in every kind of literature, in both prose and poetry. The question of the *Mahnrede*, or admonition, of which Wolff identified several examples in Amos (4:4–5; 5:4–6, 14–15), is disputed (see Hermisson, 1968 *passim* and especially p. 91 on these passages in Amos). There are numerous examples in Proverbs but also in Deuteronomy, and it may well be (Rudolph, 1971, pp. 190–4) that the form has its origin in an ancient form of popular speech, which does not qualify for the designation 'wisdom', unless all traditional forms of speech are to be so designated.

Terrien's and Wolff's attempts to demonstrate the influence of wisdom (that is, 'clan wisdom' rather than 'school wisdom') on Amos on the basis of style and vocabulary have, then, run into difficulty (see Whybray (1974) on the problems of 'wisdom vocabulary' in general), and at the very least it can be said that they have not proved their case. Their arguments on the basis of affinities between Amos and wisdom on the level of *ideas* are even less convincing, mainly because of their imprecision. This is particularly true of Terrien, who lumps together, with little elaboration, Amos' interest in 'oriental learning, especially astronomy', his supposed interest in foreign geography, history and social customs, his belief that God rules all peoples, his knowledge of universal ethical norms, his lack of concern over idolatry and lack of interest in the cult and his apprehension of a 'moralistic conception of salvation'. Of this list of supposed wisdom affinities, some, such as Amos' acquaintance with 'oriental learning', are the result of an over-interpretation of tenuous evidence, while in other cases – e.g. God's rule over the nations – the concept in question is not, in fact, exclusive to Amos and wisdom. In yet others – e.g. Amos' supposed lack of concern with idolatry – an argument from silence is invoked, which ignores other and more probable explanations. Terrien also maintains (1962, pp. 110–11) that the belief expressed by Amos (9:2), that Yahweh has power over Sheol, is exclusive to the wisdom literature. But this judgement is based on an unduly exclusive attention to the texts that refer to Sheol or the underworld by name: other non-wisdom texts imply the existence of such a belief (see Eichrodt, 1967, pp. 221–3).

Wolff's arguments on the level of ideas are developed in more detail. According to him, Amos makes little or no use of the traditions of Exodus and Sinai, views Israel's election in a purely negative way and is much more concerned with the community of nations than with Israel. His ethical terminology is also closer to that of the wisdom literature than to other Old Testament traditions. The first of these assertions is certainly overstated (see Crenshaw, 1967), and the second relies too much on the dubious criterion of 'wisdom vocabulary' (see above): the moral principles – justice, concern for the poor, etc. – enunciated by Amos are, in spite of some differences in terminology, identical with those of the laws and of other prophets.

One of the most recent exponents of the theme 'prophecy and wisdom', Whedbee (1971), was aware of the problems attending the investigation and attempted to avoid them. In the preliminary methodological remarks with which he began his study of *Isaiah and Wisdom*, he issued a warning against the indiscriminate use of stylistic arguments by themselves: 'Only when one can make connections to wisdom on the basis of distinctive content is it justifiable to embrace figurative speech as evidence of the impact of wisdom on the prophets' (p. 24). He proposed to limit investigation, as much as possible, to comparisons between specific prophetical and wisdom texts, thus avoiding imprecision: 'the strongest line of argument is when one can show that a given prophetic speech has clear-cut parallels in distinctively wisdom texts' (p. 21). This principle is a prudent one if one is looking, for example, for the influence of a group of 'wise men', such as the authors of the Book of Proverbs, on a prophet like Isaiah, though the relative paucity and therefore, one may assume, partially unrepresentative character of the extant wisdom material would make it impossible, even so, to present a full picture of the relationship. But when Whedbee then goes on to refer to the necessity of distinguishing between 'technical wisdom and its popular counterpart' (p. 22) and to his intention to compare both with the teaching of

Isaiah, he is back again in the realm of shadows: how does one recognise 'popular wisdom' in non-wisdom texts? What are its characteristics? Whedbee confines himself to 'didactic parables and proverbial speech' because these 'display a decidedly wisdom flavour' (p. 24), together with some other literary types the wisdom character of which is more questionable: the 'summary–appraisal form' identified by Childs (1967) and the woe oracles (see above, p. 189). He also discusses a quite different aspect of the relationship between Isaiah and wisdom, namely the evidence in the Book of Isaiah for a conflict between that prophet and the wise men/politicians of the Judean court, a question, originally raised by Fichtner, to which we shall return.

That part of Whedbee's study which is concerned with parables and proverbs in Isaiah is the most thorough investigation of wisdom and prophecy up to the present time. In examining what he considers to be the three parables in Isaiah – 1 : 2–3; 5 : 1–7; 28 : 23–9 – he is at fault in assuming, without attempting to substantiate the assumption, that the parable is *per se* a 'wisdom' form of speech. However, in his detailed analysis of these three passages, he rightly uses a cumulative method, showing how each passage contains vocabulary, motifs and themes, that can all be paralleled in the specifically wisdom books of the Old Testament or of other ancient Near Eastern literatures. Thus for example he points to their didactic style (including the teacher's prefatory formula (28: 23) and the use of the father–son relationship), the vocabulary of education (in 28:29), the specifically wisdom word *tūšiyyāh*, the drawing of analogies between the natural world and human life, and animal imagery, together with some broader elements, such as the theme of the deity as teaching man his basic skills (in 28:23ff), and others that are not, perhaps, as exclusively sapiential as he maintains, such as the supposedly wisdom concept of order in the universe. His treatment of Isa. 5:1–7 is less convincing than that of 1:2–3 and 28:23–9; but his methodology is sounder than that of his predecessors in the field. He does not, however, really dispose of the problem of a common heritage of speech and ideas, which might account for many of these similarities but which, if designated by the term 'popular wisdom', would tend to empty the word 'wisdom' of any specific content. Finally, Whedbee offers some useful observations concerning the ways in which Isaiah modifies and adapts his wisdom material and insights for prophetical purposes.

Wisdom influence has been held by various commentators to be present in other prophetical books, for example in Jeremiah, although no thorough study of the question seems to have been undertaken. One of the problems here is that of distinguishing between the words of the prophet himself and later material – glosses, editorial additions, etc. – of a wisdom type, which is certainly present in several prophetical books. This is particularly true of the Book of Jeremiah, on the problems of which there is no space in this survey to comment. Reference should, however, be made to Deutero-Isaiah (Isa. 40–55), where it is unlikely that there are later additions of this kind. The opinion that wisdom influence is to be found in Deutero-Isaiah is mainly based on his exposition of the doctrine of creation, and the passage most frequently cited in this connection is 40:12–14. A typical comment is that of Muilenburg (1956, p. 437), who wrote of verses 13–14: 'The wisdom vocabulary of the strophe is striking and witnesses to the presence of wisdom speculation much earlier than is generally supposed.' This statement, like similar statements about these verses in other commentaries, cannot be accepted. The words *ʿēṣāh, yādaʿ, yāʿaṣ, bīn, lāmad, daʿat, tebūnāh*, though frequently used in the wisdom books, are not confined to them, nor is the question-form in which the strophe is cast a peculiarly wisdom form (see Whybray, 1971, pp. 19–30; 1974, pp. 123ff). In other respects the creation doctrine of Deutero-Isaiah has affinities rather with the Psalter and with Gen. 1 than with wisdom.

III

In the years that followed the studies of Fichtner and Lindblom, much attention was paid, in the light of their views, to the supposed conflict during the period of the monarchy between prophets, especially Isaiah and Jeremiah, and the wise men or statesmen of the court. McKane (1965) accepted the view that 'the wisdom literature is, for the most part, a product of the men of affairs in high places of state' (p. 44), and, on the basis of the prophetical literature and the Book of Proverbs, filled out Fichtner's picture of prophetic conflict with the wise, of the opposing principles represented by the two groups and of the way in which the prophets both attacked what he called 'old wisdom' and pointed to the true wisdom of Yahweh, reinterpreting the particular vocabulary of old wisdom in the process. Two other works pursued this question with reference to the prophet Isaiah. Whedbee, in the work mentioned above (1971), recognised that a distinction must be made between court or school wisdom and popular wisdom, but in practice his methodological decision only to make statements about wisdom influence on Isaiah that could be supported by 'wisdom texts' led him to concentrate mainly on the former. Jensen (1973) attempted to add further evidence of Isaiah's conflict with a class of professional wise men by claiming that the word *torah* when used by Isaiah in connection with Yahweh is taken not from legal or cultic terminology but from that of wisdom: Yahweh is the true teacher of His people, but His instruction (*torah*) has been set aside by the contemporary class of wise men in favour of their own, human, false wisdom.

All these writers assumed, with Fichtner, not only that there was a class of 'wise men' who were virtually identical with Judah's leading statesmen of the eighth and seventh centuries B.C., but also that they were identical with those whom Isaiah condemns for boasting of their wisdom and that the principles on which they conducted affairs can be read off from the Book of Proverbs. I have suggested elsewhere (Whybray, 1974) that there is no evidence that there ever was a distinct class known as 'the wise men' in the period of the monarchy, either of statesmen or of authors of wisdom books, and that the authors of Proverbs were, rather, representatives of a more intangible, non-institutional 'intellectual tradition', not confined to one class. If this is so, the idea of a conflict between Isaiah and 'the wise' falls to the ground. Isaiah and Jeremiah were undoubtedly in conflict with the political policies of their day, but to associate these policies specifically with a particular kind of 'wisdom doctrine' is to go beyond the evidence.

If this is so, does the phrase 'prophecy and wisdom' still have any meaning? Is it possible any longer to talk meaningfully about a relationship between the two? Brueggemann (1978) has recently made a brave attempt to do so without entering into the controversy between those who assign to 'wisdom' a narrow, concrete, class-orientated meaning and those who define it more broadly, so that it becomes intangible, vague and elusive. Taking Jeremiah as a test case, he has attempted an exegesis of Jer. 9:23–4 (MT 9:22–3) – which, unlike many scholars, he regards as a genuine saying of Jeremiah – and sees the prophet as opposing a basic attitude to life that is common to all human wisdom, however it may be defined: wisdom is on any definition 'the deposit of the best observations coming from a long history of reflection on experience' (p. 86) and, as such, it forms 'the consensus by which established order sustains and legitimates itself'

(p. 100, n. 10). Human wisdom, therefore, tends to associate itself with the centres of power and to oppose change, and so poses an inescapable challenge to the prophetic conviction that men must rely on God alone, whatever changes that reliance may bring: it is 'always a question of singular reliance on Yahweh alone or a more prudent embrace of the gifts of culture which seem more secure' (p. 88). Jeremiah may use the speech-forms and methods of wisdom instruction, but his critique of the contemporary policies of disaster is drawn not from wisdom but from his prophetic insight. Brueggemann believes that this tension between two world-views ran right through Israel's history from David to apocalyptic.

Brueggemann's analysis of the ideas behind Jer. 9:23–4 (MT 22–3) is probably correct. But it is doubtful whether the sharp dichotomy that he discerns there between the world of prophecy and that of wisdom really represents the prophetic activity as a whole. Brueggemann does not seem to allow sufficient room in his thesis for the implications of the fact that such a prophet as Isaiah can use the word 'wise' of Yahweh (Isa. 31:2) and can affirm (Isa. 28:26) that such 'practical wisdom' as man possesses in the processes of agriculture is to be attributed to divine instruction.

Brueggemann's attempt to find a common denominator in the various definitions of wisdom and so to forge a basic concept of it which will then enable the theologian to make sweeping generalisations about wisdom's fundamental opposition to prophecy conceals the impasse in which the study of the subject finds itself since the confident days of Fichtner and Lindblom. If we are now forced, as it would seem that we are, to think of wisdom in Murphy's terms as a 'shared approach to reality', then Clements's discouraging conclusions about the study of prophecy and wisdom are an accurate estimate of the present situation (1975, p. 81): 'The broader the picture of the setting of wisdom is shown to be, so much the vaguer and less meaningful do the traces of wisdom in prophecy become.' Clements sees a danger that we may 'reduce wisdom simply to the level of commonplace moral insight. Unless we can clearly mark off the separate boundaries of wisdom and prophecy with some degree of confidence we can hardly expect to trace the influence of the one upon the other.'

IV

So far in this chapter the theme 'prophecy and wisdom' has been treated as if it were synonymous with the question of the influence of the latter on the former. But did not the reverse process also take place? Did not the teaching of the prophets exercise an influence on the authors of the wisdom books? To the extent that the later wisdom books presuppose and express a developed Jewish theology, which had absorbed and integrated all the main ingredients of the earlier Israelite religious tradition, this is certainly the case (see, e.g., on prophetic influence on the Book of Job, Dhorme's comments (1967, p. 153)). But it is a much more difficult matter to trace specific, exclusively prophetic influences, whether literary or theological. That wisdom ideas or theology underwent great changes during the Old Testament period, including both what von Rad called the 'theologisation' of wisdom and also an internal crises attested in Job and Ecclesiastes, is obvious (see von Rad, 1962, pp. 441ff; Schmid, 1966, pp. 144ff). There are tremendous theological differences between the older elements in Proverbs and the later ones, between Proverbs and Job, between Job and Ecclesiastes, and between these books and the later Ecclesiasticus and Wisdom of Solomon. In the last two of these works the whole Israelite historical tradition, which does not appear in the earlier books, is prominent, and in Ecclesiasticus (chs. 44–50) the classical prophets are given a leading place in the catalogue of Israel's great men. But although the author of Ecclesiasticus was clearly familiar with the prophetical books of the Old Testament, they were for him part of the canonical corpus. It would be truer to say that he was influenced by the canonical books of the prophets than that he was influenced by a living prophetical tradition.

Some attempts have, however, been made to point to specific prophetic influence on Old Testament wisdom books. McKane (1965) attempted to show how the prophets reinterpreted the vocabulary of the earlier, secular wisdom, which he called 'old wisdom', and later, in his commentary on Proverbs (1970, pp. 10–22 and *passim*), he argued that reinterpretation of this kind is to be found even within the older sections of Proverbs itself. In his commentary he does not specifically attribute this reinterpretation to prophetic influence but prefers to speak of the appearance of 'a moralism which derives from Yahwistic piety' (1970, p. 11). However, in view of his earlier work it seems likely that he associates this piety with the teaching of the prophets.

Various attempts have been made (e.g. by Dhorme (1926; English translation, 1967) and Terrien (1966)) to show how the Book of Job was influenced by the prophets.

The lack of any systematic study of this aspect of the theme 'prophecy and wisdom' is due to the paucity of the evidence available. It is doubtful whether any direct literary connections between the prophetical and wisdom books can be found earlier than Ecclesiasticus. (There are a few instances of rather striking similarity, but in such cases the possibility of the use of a common literary tradition by two authors must be borne in mind. See Westermann, 1956, p. 32, n. 1, on the supposed dependence of Job 3:2–10 on Jer. 20:14–18.) The theological developments within the corpus of the Old Testament wisdom books were no doubt manifestations of a changing theological climate, which was itself deeply influenced, among other influences, by the teaching of the prophets. Nevertheless the literary wisdom tradition in the Old Testament seems mainly to have gone its own way, parallel with, but distinct from, other traditions (see Zimmerli, 1964), before becoming integrated, in the late post-exilic period, with the law. The recent trends of scholarly opinion with regard to the nature of the wisdom tradition referred to above have made the task of charting prophetic influence on wisdom even more difficult than before, and in the present state of scholarly research little more can be said than that wisdom eventually became interwoven with the other theological strands, including that of prophecy, to form the orthodox Jewish theological tradition, a fact that is attested by the eventual acceptance of Proverbs, Job and Ecclesiastes into the Hebrew canon of Scripture.

Is the theme 'prophecy and wisdom' played out? Is there really no more to be said about it? It is too early to answer these questions definitely in the affirmative. But even if this is indeed the case, the undertaking should not be regarded as simply a dead end. In the process of discovering that we have sometimes asked the wrong questions we have learned much, especially about the ways in which the prophets used their native inheritance in the service of their prophetic mission and about the issues that sometimes brought them into conflict with the politics of their times.

Bibliography

J.-P. Audet 'Origines comparées de la double tradition de la loi et de la sagesse dans le proche-orient ancien', in *Proceedings of the International Congress of Orientalists*, vol. I (Moscow, 1960), pp. 352–7.

W. Baumgartner 'Die israelitische Weisheitsliteratur', *ThR* 5 (1933), 259–88.

W. A. Brueggemann 'The Epistemological Crisis of Israel's Two Histories', in *Israelite Wisdom, Theological and Literary Essays in Honor of S. Terrien* (Missoula, Montana, 1978), pp. 85–105.

B. S. Childs *Isaiah and the Assyrian Crisis*, SBT Second Series 3 (London, 1967).

R. E. Clements *Prophecy and Tradition* (Oxford, 1975).

J. L. Crenshaw 'The Influence of the Wise upon Amos', *ZAW* 79 (1967), 42–52.

E. Dhorme *A Commentary on the Book of Job* (London, 1967) (English translation of *Le livre de Job*, Études Bibliques (Paris, 1926)).

W. Eichrodt *Theology of the Old Testament*, vol. II (London, 1967) (English translation of *Theologie des Alten Testaments*, Part II, 3, 5th ed. (Stuttgart and Göttingen, 1964)).

'Die Vollmacht des Amos. Zu einer schwierigen Stelle im Amosbuch', in *Beiträge zur Alttestamentlichen Theologie, Festschrift W. Zimmerli* (Göttingen, 1977), pp. 124–31.

J. Fichtner *Die altorientalische Weisheit in ihrer israelitisch-jüdischen Ausprägung. Eine Studie zur Nationalisierung der Weisheit in Israel*, BZAW 62 (Giessen, 1933).

'Isaiah among the Wise', in J. L. Crenshaw (ed.), *Studies in Ancient Israelite Wisdom* (New York, 1976), pp. 429–38 (English translation of 'Jesaja unter den Weisen', *ThLZ* 74 (1949), cols. 75–80 (= *Gottes Weisheit. Gesammelte Studien zum Alten Testament*, Arbeiten zur Theologie, Second Series 3 (Stuttgart, 1965), pp. 18–26)).

E. Gerstenberger 'The Woe-Oracles of the Prophets', *JBL* 81 (1962), 249–63. *Wesen und Herkunft des 'apodiktischen Rechts'*, WMANT 20 (Neukirchen, 1965).

H.-J. Hermisson *Studien zur israelitischen Spruchweisheit*, WMANT 28 (Neukirchen, 1968).

P. Humbert *Recherches sur les sources égyptiennes de la littérature sapientiale d'Israël* (Neuchâtel, 1929).

W. Janzen *Mourning Cry and Woe Oracle*, BZAW 125 (Berlin, 1972).

J. Jensen *The Use of 'tôrâ' by Isaiah. His Debate with the Wisdom Tradition*, CBQ Monograph Series 3 (Washington, D.C., 1973).

J. Lindblom 'Wisdom in the Old Testament Prophets', in *Wisdom in Israel and in the Ancient Near East, Essays Presented to H. H. Rowley*, SVT 3 (Leiden, 1955), pp. 192–204.

W. McKane *Prophets and Wise Men*, SBT 44 (London, 1965).

Proverbs. A New Approach, Old Testament Library (London, 1970).

R. Martin-Achard 'Sagesse de Dieu et sagesse humaine chez Isaïe', in *Maqqēl shâqēdh, La branche d'amandier, Hommage à W. Vischer* (Montpellier, 1960), pp. 136–44.

J. Muilenburg 'The Book of Isaiah Chapters 40–66. Introduction and Exegesis', in *The Interpreter's Bible*, vol. v (New York and Nashville, 1956), pp. 381–773.

R. E. Murphy 'Assumptions and Problems in Old Testament Wisdom Research', *CBQ* 29 (1967), pp. 101–12.

'Wisdom – Theses and Hypotheses', in *Israelite Wisdom, Theological and Literary Essays in Honor of S. Terrien* (Missoula, Montana, 1978), pp. 35–42.

W. O. E. Oesterley *The Wisdom of Egypt and the Old Testament in the Light of the Newly Discovered 'Teaching of Amen-em-ope'* (London, 1927).

The Book of Proverbs with Introduction and Notes, Westminster Commentaries (London, 1929).

G. von Rad 'The Beginnings of Historical Writing in Ancient Israel', in *The Problem of the Hexateuch and Other Essays* (Edinburgh, 1966), pp. 166–204 (English translation of 'Der Anfang der Geschichtsschreibung in Alten Israel', *AfK* 32 (1944), 1–42 (= *Gesammelte Studien zum Alten Testament*, ThB 8 (Munich, 1958), pp. 148–88)). (English translation cited as von Rad, 1966*a*).

'The Joseph Narrative and Ancient Wisdom', in *The Problem of the Hexateuch and Other Essays* (Edinburgh, 1966), pp. 292–300 (= J. L. Crenshaw (ed.), *Studies in Ancient Israelite Wisdom* (New York, 1976), pp. 439–47. English translation of 'Josephsgeschichte und ältere Chokma', *Congress Volume, Copenhagen, 1953*, SVT 1 (Leiden, 1953), pp. 120–7 (= *Gesammelte Studien zum Alten Testament*, ThB 8 (Munich, 1958), pp. 272–80)). (English translation cited as von Rad, 1966*b*).

Old Testament Theology, vol. I (Edinburgh, 1962) (English translation of *Theologie des Alten Testaments*, vol. I: 'Die Theologie der geschichtlichen Überlieferungen Israels' (Munich, 1957)).

Wisdom in Israel (London, 1972) (English translation of *Weisheit in Israel* (Neukirchen, 1970)).

W. Richter *Recht und Ethos. Versuch einer Ortung des weisheitlichen Mahnspruches*, StANT 15 (Munich, 1966).

W. M. W. Roth 'The Numerical Sequence $x/x+1$ in the Old Testament', *VT* 12 (1962), 300–11.

W. Rudolph *Joel–Amos–Obadja–Jona*, KAT 13, 2 (Gütersloh, 1971).

H. H. Schmid *Wesen und Geschichte der Weisheit. Eine Untersuchung zur altorientalischen und israelitischen Weisheitsliteratur*, BZAW 101 (Berlin, 1966).

S. Terrien 'Amos and Wisdom', in *Israel's Prophetic Heritage, Essays in Honor of J. Muilenburg* (London, 1962), pp. 108–15 (= J. L. Crenshaw (ed.), *Studies in Ancient Israelite Wisdom* (New York, 1976), pp. 448–55).

'Quelques remarques sur les affinités de Job avec le Deutéro-Isaïe', *Volume du Congrès, Genève, 1965*, SVT 15 (Leiden, 1966), pp. 295–310.

G. Wanke "*ōy* und *hōy*', *ZAW* 78 (1966), 215–18.

C. Westermann   *Der Aufbau des Buches Hiob*, BhTh (Tübingen, 1956).

J. W. Whedbee   *Isaiah and Wisdom* (Nashville and New York, 1971).

R. N. Whybray   *The Heavenly Counsellor in Isaiah xl 13–14. A Study of the Sources of the Theology of Deutero-Isaiah*, Society for Old Testament Study Monograph Series 1 (Cambridge, 1971).

The Intellectual Tradition in the Old Testament, BZAW 135 (Berlin, 1974).

H. W. Wolff   *Amos the Prophet. The Man and His Background* (Philadelphia, 1973) (English translation of *Amos' geistige Heimat*, WMANT 18 (Neukirchen, 1964)).

W. Zimmerli   'The Place and Limit of Wisdom in the Framework of the Old Testament Theology', *SJTh* 17 (1964), 146–58 (= J. L. Crenshaw (ed.), *Studies in Ancient Israelite Wisdom* (New York, 1976), pp. 314–26. English translation of 'Ort und Grenze der Weisheit im Rahmen der alttestamentlichen Theologie', in *Les sagesses du proche-orient ancien. Colloque de Strasbourg 17–19 mai 1962*, Bibliothèque des Centres d'Études Supérieures Spécialisés (Paris, 1963), pp. 121–37 (= *Gottes Offenbarung. Gesammelte Aufsätze zum Alten Testament*, ThB 19 (Munich, 1963), pp. 300–15)).

H.-J. Zobel   'hōy', *TDOT*, vol. III (Grand Rapids, 1978), pp. 359–64 (English translation of article in *TWAT*, vol. II (Stuttgart, 1977), cols. 382–8).

Prophecy and the cult

ROBERT MURRAY

The relationship of prophecy to the cult in ancient Israel may be viewed under three headings: (1) activity within the cult, (2) activity independent and often critical of the cult, and (3) utterances and compositions that, while not necessarily belonging to cultic occasions, reflect and echo, but often transform, liturgical language and themes. Here I propose, after a brief sketch of headings (1) and (2), to concentrate on some problems under heading (3), by an examination of the language and themes that link Isa. 33 to other prophetic passages (especially elsewhere in Isaiah) and to the Psalms. This will involve a re-examination of the notion of 'prophetic liturgy' and the suggestion that some themes, which have come to be regarded as looking forward to late apocalyptic eschatology, may rather be echoes of ancient rituals. It is a pleasure to offer Peter Ackroyd a development of some ideas first ventilated in his seminar, in which I have learned so much.

1. Activity within the cult

By 'cult' I understand primarily the liturgical and ritual activities contemporary with the prophets, but with due awareness that, whatever the original *Sitz im Leben* of the prophetic utterances, the texts as they stand also reflect their after-life and the use of them in other kinds of cult and devotional activity, which may have left its marks, as well as bequeathing to us a unified context in which we read the Old Testament, as Childs (1979) has so usefully reminded us. 'Prophecy' I am inclined to understand broadly (not, therefore, restricting the basis to particular characteristic terms) as utterance arising from the belief that someone has a communication from God that must be passed on. A broad definition has the disadvantage that activities such as divination, giving *torah* and even teaching may claim to be included under the prophetic, and thereby enable the religious establishment to take it over (cf. Blenkinsopp, 1977). Nevertheless, the Old Testament presents us with examples of institutional as well as spontaneous prophecy, and the cult is an area of both collaboration and opposition. Inevitably there is an awkward number of variables affecting our understanding of the relationship; but the evidence is clear that functions that can only be described as prophetic were exercised within the cultic system. That there were special functionaries is, of course, the thesis long proposed and recently argued at length by Johnson (1979). One may feel a certain difficulty in that no ancient term can be identified as denoting precisely 'cultic prophet'. Perhaps the only category of persons involved was that of the priests and Levites at the cult centres, and especially the Jerusalem Temple, to some of whom 'the word of the LORD' came, as to Jeremiah, Ezekiel and, according to the Chronicler, various Levites (e.g. 2 Chron. 20:14–17). However, if the identification of the functionaries remains obscure, their voice seems to sound clearly enough in all those psalms (analysed by Johnson) in which God speaks in the first person singular, often interrupting the previous movement of the psalm; or in Joel, in which the prophet's role seems closely interwoven with that of other Temple personnel. Again, we see figures, apparently already recognised as prophets, showing active concern for the restoration and purification of the cult, for example Ezekiel, Haggai and Malachi. It is reasonable to locate within the cult the utterances not only of the two last-named and Joel but also of Obadiah, Nahum, Habakkuk and Zephaniah (cf. Eaton, 1961). The title of Hab. 3 relates it closely to similar psalms, the theophany themes of which point to liturgical contexts; the four last-named and Joel are all rich in mythological themes and all suggest rituals either for the control of nature (Joel; cf. Ahlström, 1971) or against enemies (cf. Christensen, 1975).

Isaiah ben Amoz may have produced set-pieces for royal occasions, such as chs. 9 and 11 (cf. von Rad, 1966, pp. 222–31), but it is hard to see him precisely as a 'cultic prophet'; if he was, he was a highly independent one. The oracles on foreign nations, which we find in Isaiah, Jeremiah and Ezekiel, may represent a genre that had its place in the Temple cult, but they seem to have a wider range than the rituals for cursing or control that are suggested by some psalms and shorter prophetic works.

Among other forms of prophetic utterance that could have belonged within the cult, the one most studied in recent years is the *ribh* or divine 'lawsuit' (Harvey, 1967; Nielsen, 1978). It may be supposed that

Ps. 50 brings us closest to an actual liturgical text, but Mic. 6 could conceivably have the same *Sitz im Leben*, perhaps in the penitential part of a covenant renewal ceremony, whether during the New Year festival or on some other appropriate occasion. Of course, several of the passages that show features of the '*ribh* pattern' contain expressions critical of trust in the efficiency of the cult. An institution may have occasions for self-criticism built into it, but the actual criticisms of the cult that we find in the prophets can hardly be imagined as fitting comfortably into any form of worship other than one radically different from what they are criticising.

After the destruction of the Temple, of course, there were such changed forms (cf. Zech. 7:3; 8:19) in both Judea and Babylon, and this gives a plausible context for some utterances of Ezekiel and for most of Deutero-Isaiah; but from the point of view of relationship to the cult, the predominant interest of these books (as also of Zech. 12–14) lies in their abundant echoes of the old liturgy, and so is more appropriate to our third heading, as is Gunkel's category of 'prophetic liturgy'.

2. Prophetic activity independent and critical of the cult

This aspect of prophecy obviously cannot be neglected, but it will be surveyed only briefly here. Evidently it could not be expected that all prophets would function within the cult. None of the major prophetic figures mentioned in Samuel and Kings find their characteristic sphere of activity there. No attempt to enlist Amos the *noqed* in the cultic clergy has seriously challenged his proud lay status. He forced his way into the royal sanctuary in Bethel, but as an unwelcome intruder. Of the liturgical notes that sound in the Book of Amos, the most distinct tend towards parody (ch. 4) or almost certainly belong, like the doxologies and the ending, to later use of the prophetic collection as a sacred text (Crenshaw, 1975). Hosea is more outspokenly critical of the cult even than Amos. Isaiah evidently stood close to the king, and his inaugural vision might somehow reflect a liturgical experience, but apart from the royal passages mentioned above, nothing imposes a view of him as other than independent of the cult, of which his variant of the *ribh* in ch. 1 is intensely critical. On the other hand, he is the most soaked in cult language and mythology of all the prophets (Müller, 1971), a quality shared by the other writers who shelter under his name. They *could* all have spoken in liturgical contexts (though this is hardly credible of the bitter voice that sounds in ch. 66), but in the absence of clear evidence, speculation achieves little. It remains to mention Jeremiah, of priestly family and therefore an arch-traitor to the Jerusalem cult within which, presumably, Hananiah functioned and provided edification for as long as his currency enjoyed credit. Even if the most critical chapter (7) be considered Deuteronomic, Jeremiah is, to say the least, entirely detached from the cult. On the other hand, his language is rich in liturgical echoes, often shared with the Isaian tradition (Reventlow, 1963).

3. Echoes of cultic themes and language

Here we enter a field that is common to all the 'writing prophets' but is one that we cannot try to identify in the same kind of way as prophetic activity within the cult or criticism of the cult. What concerns us now is not so much the action or the message as the style and the tone with its undertones and overtones. It may no longer be possible to seek the *Sitz im Leben* of the prophetic utterance; what we are listening for is echoes of language that belonged in the cult and is now being re-used for its evocative power, whether in a way continuing its original sense, or parodying it, or using old expressions in new senses and for new purposes. Perhaps the most striking examples of all these kinds of re-use are found in the later parts of the Book of Isaiah, especially Deutero-Isaiah (Eaton, 1979 a).

But how do we recognise what we are looking for, when so few texts can be identified as rituals from the first Temple? No doubt the priestly blessing in Num. 6:22–6 should be considered here, but it has no rubrics for accompanying action. Apart from all the difficulties of estimating the age of its traditions, the Priestly Code gives a very fragmentary picture: rubrics (though often tantalisingly unclear) but few spoken formulae. In contrast the Psalms give us prayers and hymns but no rubrics (unless buried obscurely in some of the titles and in 'Selah'). Still, it is the Psalms that give us the foundation on which we can try to build. Admittedly fashion has swung far this way and that in ascribing psalms to the first or second Temple periods and in arguing for priority between the similar material in Deutero-Isaiah and the Psalms. But the work of estimating the date of poetic traditions (cf. Freedman, 1977) has gained a sureness that was lacking before the exploitation of comparative material in Ugaritic and Akkadian, and we are unlikely to go back on the present view of the greater part of the Psalter as pre-exilic and belonging to a liturgy that was dominated by the king. The recognition of cultic language or allusions in the prophets begins from coincidences with passages in the Psalms and is strengthened when other Old Testament passages, often in quite different contexts, reveal sequences of similar expressions. Further interpretation, and reconstruction of the background, can be developed by use of comparative material, though here a delicacy is required that has not always been observed. For example, Babylonian texts often have rubrics and may offer impressive similarities, but we lack a clear cultural link with Israel, in that we have no contemporary Canaanite liturgical texts. The Ugaritic texts come from nearer to Israel geographically, but there is a diachronic gap between them and the Old Testament, which some enthusiasts for the unity of 'North-west Semitic' do not always seem to take seriously enough, and few good Ugaritic parallels to Hebrew psalms and prayers have been published. The interpretation of the Baal poems as sacred drama and potentially illuminating for first Temple liturgy remains speculative. Of course, imaginative hypothesising is an activity without which scholarship will dry up; but we must be realistic about our limitations. When Hopkins writes (in the sonnet 'Patience, hard thing')

> Yet the rebellious wills
> Of us we do bid God bend to Him even so,

we know that he is using an old Latin mass collect and we know its original function. It is just this kind of certainty, about the source of expressions and their original liturgical contexts, that we hardly ever have in the prophets. Even the most easily recognisable *Leitmotive*, such as Exodus themes, leave us ignorant of their liturgical settings in the first Temple. Much more are we at sea when we are struck by a cluster of similar vocabulary as in Hos. 7:13*b*–14 and Ps. 4. What were those *miškabot* ('beds') on which people wailed and gashed themselves for grain and wine, while the psalmist and the prophet alike accuse them of *kazab* ('lies') and urge them to speak to God in their hearts? The links seem too many for there to be no connection, but what is it? Is Hosea quoting the psalm as Hopkins the collect? Or do both Hosea and the psalm reflect ancient Canaanite rituals and express the same Yahwistic reaction to them? If so, what were the rituals, and what other texts may echo them?

This little nest of problems may stand for scores of other examples in the Old Testament, and not only there. Fascinating paths may be traced in early Christian literature back to Jewish and sectarian origins, despite the trauma of the breach between Christianity and its matrix, a trauma that both sides were subsequently at pains to bury as deep as possible. But someone did a much more thorough job in burying the memory of what went on in the first Temple. The Babylonians only burned it. Somebody made it impossible for ever after to know exactly what happened in the royal liturgy; who, on earth or above or beneath it, were the objects of the formalised execrations in the Psalter, and by what rituals they were believed to be vanquished and bound. Only tantalising traces remain, such as the telltale disorder frequent in both the Hebrew text and the versions wherever there is a rumour of angels, demons, 'holy ones' and the host of heaven.

4. Isaiah 33 and its connections

These reflections may serve to introduce my chosen example and also to account for a certain dissatisfaction with the expression 'prophetic liturgy' that Gunkel (1924) so confidently proposed as the key to the chapter. When one has searched for light on the problems of Isa. 33 in a score of subsequent commentaries, only to learn that Gunkel identified the chapter's genre in 1924, one begins to realise how dark can be the shadow cast by a great scholar; a subject that he deigned to touch is put into a glass case to preserve it from further fingering. In reality it does little honour to Gunkel's memory to treat him as if he struck a question dead for ever, while those who reverently repeat his formulae do not always inspire confidence that they understand what a liturgy is, let alone a prophetic one (cf. Whybray, 1978, p. 112). The paragraph in which Gunkel expounded his definition uses 'liturgy' in a sense unusual enough, surely, to have caused some comment: 'an artificial expression belonging to the study of literary genres; we understand thereby a poetic composition which is performed by alternating voices, and in which the individual parts may belong to different genres' (Gunkel, p. 182, my translation). We have to wait thirteen pages for an explanation of why Gunkel chose the word 'liturgy' at all, though now he goes back on a main part of his previous description: 'Admittedly, such prophetic liturgies are, on the whole, no longer destined for performance by alternating voices, but remain only as *imitations* of liturgical poetry (*gottesdienstlichen Gedichte*)' (p. 195). In fact, Gunkel helped to identify the genres echoed in the various sections of Isa. 33 (though without notable advance on Mowinckel's treatment of 1921), but he did not suggest a living liturgical context for the chapter, nor did he do anything else to justify calling it a 'liturgy'.

Yet the chapter cries out for liturgical analysis. If there is a psalm that makes us feel we hear and see what is going on, it is surely Ps. 24, in which a solemn procession enters the Temple after a formal dialogue about who is worthy (24:3–6). The fact that this dialogue with its concluding declaration (another example of which occupies the whole of Ps. 15) is closely paralleled in Isa. 33:14 b–16 is enough to indicate that the chapter contains liturgical material – and much more springs to the eye. These elements have not exactly been neglected since the work of Mowinckel (1921), Gunkel (1924) and Galling (1929), yet the usual treatment of this aspect of the chapter remains unsatisfying. The reason is, I think, that authors have been mainly interested in identifying the historical reference of the chapter, namely the Assyrian crisis of 701, and in showing that these events, now long ago, are still being celebrated in language that is described as 'eschatological' and therefore late. Childs' treatment (1967) can stand for many; for an exhaustive bibliography see Vermeylen (1977–8, pp. 429–38).

A number of unexamined presuppositions are involved here, and they have tended to hinder sensitive attention to the religious language. The *šoded* ('destroyer') addressed in 33:1 has been assumed to be the Assyrian invader, and the picture of desolation in verses 7–9 to be a description of Judah under occupation; therefore the mysterious *'er'ellam* (valiant ones' (?)) and the *mal'ake šalom* ('envoys of peace') are humans, Jerusalemites (of Ariel/Šalem); the broken covenant is political, the *'arim* ('cities') are probably *'edim* ('witnesses'), or another word for treaties, *'adim. Even *'enoš* ('man') might conceal a lost word for taxes, and so the problems of the passage are solved for good (Hillers, 1971a). Those who like collecting cross-references may refer to Isa. 24:4ff, where unknown persons have broken the everlasting covenant, the land is desolate, and *'enoš* crops up again, but no one does anything with the relationship. This is understandable; Isa. 24–7 is also heavily defended by unchecked assumptions.

Again, the vision of the king and of Jerusalem in 33:17–24 has been declared 'eschatological', and the assumption that this implies 'late' has turned attention away from traces of the pre-exilic Jerusalem cult. (Chs. 24–7 have commonly suffered a like fixation of focus by being declared 'apocalyptic' and therefore late.) Finally (though it arises early in ch. 33), the introduction of the category of *Volksklagelied* for verses 2ff has made it difficult ever to see the chapter as in any sense being or reflecting '*a* liturgy', i.e. a unity. Gunkel claimed to present it thus; but if it consists of a *Hoy* oracle followed by a *Volksklagelied*, then a *Tora-liturgie* and finally an eschatological hymn, the chapter is a mere concatenation of genres and no sense is made of its use of them.

I believe we can do better than this, though the argument will necessarily remain hypothetical. But first for the aspects I do not intend to discuss. On its terms, Childs' treatment of Isa. 33 is acceptable: the historical model governing the poet's intention is likely to be the 'memory', perhaps by now quite remote, of the Assyrian invasion, the deliverance from which has long since joined that of the Exodus as a paradigm of God's protection of Israel, manifested typically in the morning (33:2*b*; cf. Ziegler, 1950). As for the oracle's immediate occasion, either historical, social or liturgical, I could not presume to suggest it, beyond voicing caution about a hasty assumption of a post-exilic date.

5. Echoes of a royal ritual?

The problem of the liturgical language in Isa. 33, its connections and possible origin, first struck me in terms of the amount of vocabulary and imagery shared with Ps. 46. In both, God is invoked in time of trial (*ṣarah/ṣarot*) and His intervention is hoped for in the morning (*lab-beqarim/lipenot boqer*). In both, the nations roar (*hamon/hamu*), an image that the psalm more clearly defines as that of raging waters (*yehemu*: 46:3 (MT 4)) – as also in Isa. 17:12–14, another passage where there is salvation in the morning, *beṭerem boqer*. In both Isaiah (33:21) and the psalm (46:4 (MT 5)) there are contrasting, peaceful waters, related (in despite of geographical facts) to Jerusalem. (If anyone wishes to follow Dahood (1966, vol. I, pp. 277–82) in banishing the river from the psalm in its supposed original form, it cannot be banished from the psalm's history, nor from Isa. 33, Ezek. 47 or Zech. 14.) In both Isa. 33 (11, 14) and Ps. 46 (9 (MT 10)), God will punish by fire; in both, the language of desolation is used, but in Isa. 33:8 *našammu* ('lie waste') and *šabat* ('ceases') suggest the breakdown of order, while in the psalm it is God who creates *šammot* ('desolations': 8 (MT 9)) and makes wars cease (*mašbit:* 9 (MT 10)). In both, God says He will be exalted (*'arum*), but the name *'Elyon* is used only in the psalm. There God is called our stronghold (*miśgab*); in Isa. 33:16 He promises a *miśgab* and a dwelling on the heights (*meromim*) to the person who measures up to the pattern of 33:15. Finally, unidentified but presumably hostile persons are called on to acknowledge (de‘u) God's might (Isa. 33:13; Ps. 46:10 (MT 11)). Their collapse (harpu, Ps. 46:10 (MT 11)) is the same as is expected of the nations in Isa. 13:7, another hamon passage, where God's battle is going to be fought by His gibborim (verse 3) and other obscurely-named members of His host.

Several authors noted the number of coincidences: Mowinckel (1921), Gunkel (rather on Ps. 46 (1926), but there he was more interested in Isa. 17:12–14), Vermeylen (1977, pp. 434–5), but none offered an explanation. Yet mere coincidence or sharing of a common background does not seem satisfactory. Further examination brought ever more passages into consideration, and the similarities with Ps. 46 began to fall into a larger picture.

The image of YHWH roaring, 'uttering his voice' (Ps. 46:6 (MT 7)), causing desolation and sending fire in punishment comes also in Amos 1:2ff; still more of the vocabulary comes in Joel 3:16–17 (MT 4:16–17) where YHWH natan beqolo and 'makes heaven and earth shake' but is a mahaseh ('refuge') and ma‘oz ('stronghold') for His people (cf. Ps. 46:1 (MT 2)), dwells in Zion and will make people 'know' that He is God. Further links were suggested by the studies of themes in the Jerusalem liturgy by Stolz (1970), Ahlström (1971) and Müller (1969; see especially the useful table on pp. 88–9), which drew more psalms into the inquiry, especially 48 and 76, and other prophetic passages, e.g. Nahum 1.

These investigations did much to illuminate the parts of Isa. 33 picturing the hamon of the nations and the exaltation above them all of YHWH in Jerusalem. But what of the opening hoy šoded section and the picture of desolation in 33:7–9? Much has been written on the hoy forms (see especially Janzen, 1972, and Vermeylen, 1977–8, pp. 603–52), among which the example in Isa. 33:1 is only the last in a whole series. The jingle on the activities of the šoded, which has parallels in Isa. 21:2 and 24:16, sounds unmistakably like a cursing formula of the kind described by Scheftelowitz (1925, pp. 111–16) as Gleichklangszauber. Not only this but also the broken covenant in 33:8 and the vocabulary of desolation in 33:9 led to a careful comparison with Isa. 24, which revealed an amazing number of verbal links. The repeated emphasis on the inhabitants of the land in ch. 24 is absent from ch. 33, but the desolation of the land is described with the same range of vocabulary: 'abelah, 'umlelah (24:4; 33:9); šammah/našammu (24:12; 33:8); šabat (24:8; 33:8); wailing 'outside' (husah, bahusot: 24:7; 33:11). Some of these, or similar images, together with God's fire and the verb šdd, appear again in Joel 1:9–12, 17–20, with echoes in Amos 1:2; Nahum

1:4ff and Hos. 4:3, in a passage that has another link with Isa. 24 in the expression 'like priest, like people' (Hos. 4:9; Isa. 24:2). All this strongly suggests traditional formulae of agrarian lamentation appropriate to the summer mourning-season, from Tammuz 17 to Ab 9, rather than mere description (Hillers, 1971*b*).

In Isa. 33:3 it is the peoples who *nadedu* ('flee'), in 24:20 the earth, in a context that clearly evokes the Flood and precisely the *priestly* cosmological picture, involving the windows of the sky (24:18*c*; Gen. 7:11; Isaiah uses *marom* where Genesis has *šamayim*). In Isa. 33:5 God dwells on the *marom* (and hence He can easily demonstrate His exaltation by the related verb: 33:10); a like dwelling is promised in 33:16 to the person described in verse 15. In Isa. 24 *marom* is even more significantly differentiated. In 24:4 the desolation affects both the *marom* and the earth; in verse 18 the *marom* is where the windows are opened to release the Flood, and finally in verse 21 Yнwн is going to punish the *seba hammarom bammarom*, together with the kings of the earth on the earth. Punish for what? The chapter taken as a whole suggests the answer that it is disorder – moral, economic and cosmic – as described in 24:4ff. This brings us to the broken covenant (24:5), also referred to in 33:8, where an unidentified impersonal agent has broken a covenant, *heper berit*. In 24:5, unidentified persons in the plural have '*aberu torot* ('transgressed the law'), *halepu hoq* ('violated the statutes') (LXX ἤλλαξαν suggests rather *hillepu*, 'altered') and *heperu berit 'olam* ('broken the everlasting covenant'). I suggest that these passages belong together in their source; they did not start life as descriptions of a political situation. What is the 'everlasting covenant'? The link already noticed with the 'priestly' Flood story suggests Gen. 9:9–16, the charter of cosmic order, between heaven and earth and between man and his fellow-creatures.

To the objection that P is late and that Isa. 24:21–2 is well on the way to Enoch, I would reply that P's traditions were not the inventions of the final redactors (cf. Kaufmann, 1961, pp. 175–200) and that Enoch's angels had a prehistory before the truncated fragment in Gen. 6:1–4 (cf. Barker, 1980) and so did the cosmic covenant before the priestly *Urgeschichte* (cf. Beauchamp, 1969, esp. pp. 322–44). This is the concept of covenant in Hos. 2:20–4, and it is probably the breach of it that is mourned by the animals in Hos. 4:3. For its cosmic aspect, see Jer. 33:20, 25; for its earthly aspect, Ezek. 34:25–31; in relationship to the animals, Isa. 11:6–9 and Job 5:22–3. Rashi connected Hos. 2:20 with Isa. 11:9; Qimhi referred to Job 5:23. It is the recent preoccupation with political covenant models that has blinded scholars to this ancient and profound aspect of covenant thought. Not that this cosmic covenant is without political connections, for the king is at the heart of it; witness Jer. 33:20–6 in relation to Ps. 89:28–9, 36–7; Ps. 72:5–7, 16 and the certainly royal character of Isa. 11. Clearly we have to do with that part of the royal ritual (no doubt centring in the New Year festival) that was concerned with ensuring rain and fertility (cf. Patai, 1939; Morgenstern, 1964).

Who are the forces threatening the kingdom's stability and the harmony of nature? In Isa. 24, taken as a whole, they would seem to be the disobedient 'host on high', together with the kings of the earth: supernatural and political enemies regarded as allied against the Holy One of Israel and His son the king, as in Ps. 2 and others. The shaking of the earth in Isa. 24:20 is described by the same verb *moṭ* as in Ps. 82:5, where this effect is laid to the charge of the misbehaving gods (cf. Tsevat, 1969–70); the verb is also important in Ps. 46 (verses 3, 6, 7 (MT 4, 7, 8)). Returning to the unholy alliance, is it possible that the frequently-mentioned 'inhabitants' on earth in Isa. 24 may have a double reference, including the sense of 'rulers' for which Dahood (1966, vol. I, p. 106, etc.) and van Dijk (1968, pp. 45, 55) have argued? And is it further possible that some of the occurrences of *'ereṣ* refer to the underworld, as Dahood (1966, vol. I, p. 106) and others have proposed for many passages? In 24:10 the *qiryat tohu* ('city of chaos') presents, to say the least, an eerie picture. But above all, 24:17–18 (which the doublet in Jer. 48:3–4 suggests is another ritual formula) points our attention towards terrors of chthonic origin. Now two of the fearsome trio, *paḥ* ('terror') and *paḥad* ('the snare'), occur in Ps. 91:3, 5. This psalm suggests a sort of apotropaic ritual against a number of demons (Caquot, 1956; 1957), including *deber* ('pestilence': verses 3, 6), *qeṭeb* ('destruction': verse 6) and possibly *rešep* (as wielder of the arrows in verse 5). *Qeṭeb* is characterised as *yašud ṣohorayim* ('wasting at noonday'). The LXX presumably read *yšwd* as *šed*, the 'noonday devil', known to Jewish folk-lore as *Qeṭeb Meriri*, most dangerous during the Tammuz-Ab season.

Now we are ready to ask who or what was once the *šoded* ('destroyer') addressed in Isa. 33:1. Something nastier than even Sennacherib, I suspect. But εἰσὶν δ'ἐπῳδαὶ καὶ λόγοι θελκτήριοι: there were incantations for almost anything. In Jer. 15:8, probably, the *šoded baṣṣohorayim* ('destroyer at noonday') is of flesh and blood, but the expression has the same source, as already 15:2–3 suggests. Job

15:21–30 may bring us nearer to it. Job 5:19–23, already referred to, may also name the terms used in a protective ritual. *Šod* ('destruction') here is not personified; but it is interesting that Rashi interpreted the 'beasts of the field' as werewolves (*grwsh*, i.e. *garoux*) and on the curious *'abne haśśadeh* ('stones of the field') showed he knew of an old variant *'adone* ('lords') *haśśadeh* referring obscurely to Lev. 17:7 on satyrs (*śe'irim*). In this case the benefit envisaged would not be destruction of the supernatural forces so much as peace with them, as with the animals. Returning to Ps. 91, the immunity promised against demons, and the protection of good angels (verses 11–12), will also give control of dangerous animals (verse 13), of which at least *tannin* may carry echoes of the *Chaoskampf*; could *peten*, too, carry such connotations, if it (as also *bašan* in Ps. 68:22 (MT 23)) is connected with the Ugaritic *btn*, the conquest of which is so remarkably echoed in Isa. 27:1? Finally, the addressee of the psalm is promised notable divine favours by a direct oracle spoken in the first person. These include the promise *'aśaggebehu* ('I will set him on high'), as in a stronghold, *miśgab*, the refuge promised to the worthy person in Isa. 33:16. Who are or is referred to in these texts? Though it can hardly be proved that the addressee in Ps. 91 is the king, no one else fits so convincingly. The king in Jerusalem was the *yośeb beseter 'elyon*, the one 'who dwells in the shelter of the Most High' (verse 1), *par excellence*, and we may well imagine him here recharging his supernatural strength by incubation in the Temple (*beṣel šadday yitlonan*) ('who abides in the shadow of the Almighty'), to receive assurance of divine favour *lipenot boqer*. As for the worthy person in Isa. 33:15–16, I suggest he was also the king, and in Pss. 15 and 24 too. Treatments of all these passages usually assume a 'democratised' interpretation, though Galling (1929, p. 128) did momentarily note the similarity between Isa. 33:15 and the royal undertakings in Ps. 101.

But we have not yet done with supernatural forces. Isa. 33:7–8 contains more than a rumour of angels. It is odd how firmly-set the consensus is that everyone mentioned is human. Yet no treatment of the 'Ariel' problem has ever given so satisfactory an account as the article by Feigin (1920) with Albright's companion-piece. Feigin sketched a coherent and credible semantic development of 'Ariel' (in its various spellings), connecting it with Akkadian *arallu*, abode of the dead, so that the champions killed by Benaiah (2 Sam. 23:20; 1 Chron. 11:22) evoke mythical heroes; the Mesha' stele uses the word for a sort of *maṣṣebah*; Jerusalem's name, together with 'Zion' and

'Ariel' (Isa. 29: 1) may all mean 'necropolis', which would explain Isa. 29 : 4. Jewish tradition still understood the *'ar'elim* ('valiant ones') of Isa. 33:7 as angels of death (b. *Ketubot* 104; Soncino translation, 1936, p. 664). Albright (1920, p. 138), while dubious about 'necropolis', makes an imaginative comment on Isa. 33:7: 'The thought seems to be that the destructive spirits of the lower world have invaded the land, howling like jackals without while they spread famine and pestilence; the spirits of heaven weep bitterly over the godlessness of the land and its consequent suffering.' Can remoter echoes of the passage's mythological background still be picked up in the use of it as a pathetic counterpoint to the 'Aqedah in *Genesis Rabba* 56:5 (Soncino translation, 1939, p. 495)? This hints that the cessation of traffic on the roads (Isa. 33:8 a) also concerns angelic travellers such as once visited Abraham. Within the terms of our inquiry, however, the theme of desolate roads is better illustrated by Lam. 1 : 4 (Hillers, 1971 b).

Continuing with Isa. 33:8 b, our argument so far points to unruly spirits as those who have broken the 'covenant'. The *'arim* they have despised are neither cities nor witnesses nor treaties but (accepting, with many scholars, a connection with Ugaritic *ǵyr* and/or *nǵr*) protecting divinities (Dahood, 1966, vol. I, p. 56; Hartmann, 1967, pp. 102–5; Irwin, 1977, p. 145).

The forces of disorder are due to be punished by God (of course with fire: Miller, 1965), in contrast with the faithful servant who meets God's requirements (verse 15) and can share His exaltation (verse 16). A theophany is promised (verse 17). The enemies described in verse 19 are primarily this-worldly; yet could their unintelligible speech remotely evoke the gibbering of ghosts? (Cf. 29 : 4 and 8 : 19 – but the vocabulary does not support such an allusion.) The peaceful waters of God's protection (verse 21), which were symbolised 'sacramentally' by the libations at the autumn festival (Patai, 1939), overcome every threat, momentarily pictured in terms of an attacking fleet. Could the incredible imagery possibly be borrowed from Phoenicia, where rituals against enemies would naturally envisage attack by sea? Do the 'ships of Tarshish' in Ps. 48:7 (MT 8) reflect borrowing of such a ritual, and might Isa. 33:23 a be illustrated by some curses in the Baal and Maqlu treaties? (cf. Hillers, 1964, p. 27). The rich borrowing of Phoenician mythology in Ezek. 26–8 (cf. van Dijk, 1968) may permit the suggestion.

One more speculation and I have done. A good ritual against enemies looks forward to the spoils (Isa. 9:3 (MT 2)). The booty mentioned in 33:4 comes up for distribution in verse 23 *b*. To whom? To the lame (*poseḥim*) says the MT. But also the blind (*'ewirin*) said the targum (Stenning, 1949, p. 111), followed by many moderns, including Gunkel and Childs (presumably *'wr* got changed into *'d*). Now the targumist *must* have been thinking of 2 Sam. 5:6. Who were these blind and lame? They have certainly infected the commentators. What would the Jebusites appeal to but protecting gods? The most recent discussion gets as far as covenant curses (Brunet, 1979, pp. 65–72) but misses the relevant story in *Pirqe d-Rabbi Eliezer* 32 that the Jebusites appeal to an ancient treaty with Abraham, which they had inscribed on images (Friedlander, 1916, pp. 276–7). Of course the story is garbled, but that is what happened to the old gods. After all, the Chronicler could not bear to mention the 'blind and lame' at all (1 Chron. 11:5). '*Iwwer* could easily conceal **'yr*, 'protector', already mentioned, which may well be part-ancestor of Aramaic *'yr*, usually rendered 'watcher' and derived from *'wr*, wake. As for *poseaḥ*, *psḥ* may be due for more investigation. In Isa. 31:5 it does look as if it means 'protect' (Glasson, 1959, pp. 79–84), though Segal (1963, pp. 97–8) insists that the sense there is dependent on the Passover sense. The beings in question might still have been originally deities connected with rituals involving leaping (Kohler, 1897, p. 803). There is more to be done here, but provisionally I suggest that the kind of ritual that may under-lie Isa. 33 would appropriately end with victory not only for *'Elyon* but also for His 'sons', among whom the ancient guardians of Jerusalem would have found their place. (Incidentally, at the end of Isa. 24, after the rebels have been punished, why does the Peshitta say that the Lord will be glorified in Jerusalem before His *qaddīsin*, not His elders?) And finally, the king. The occurrences of *škn* in Isa. 33:5 (God) and 16 (the worthy person) suggest that the *šoken* in verse 24 is no ordinary 'inhabitant'. Indeed, accepting that the paradigm of the deliverance of 701 colours the chapter, the phrase could allude to Hezekiah.

It is time to conclude. Isa. 33 reflects a ritual, and more coherently than has been recognised; it was one for the control of hostile forces, both supernatural and political. The former aspect is illustrated by Ps. 82, in which the Enoch-like mythological picture is not of late origin but very ancient. Isa. 33:1 uses an old apotropaic curse-formula against destructive spirits. It was a red herring to describe 33:2ff as a *Volksklage*, at least in any sense like those in the Psalms. In fact it is here that similarities to the 'Zion psalms' begin. The covenant mentioned in 33:8 *b* and 24:5 is that of cosmic order, related to the stability of the kingdom. The description of broken order echoes rituals of mourning for the land's lost fertility (cf. Joel 1) in the summer fast-season from Tammuz 17 to Ab 9, when Qeṭeb Meriri was most dangerous. Ab 9 is the date on which, by marvellous coincidence and poetic instinct, subjects for mourning all down the ages have located themselves (cf. *Encyclopedia Judaica*, vol. III, col. 936), especially the historical destructions of the Temple. The latter theme may already have belonged to the New Year festival liturgy (Willesen, 1952), a context suitable to all the subsequent part of Isa. 33, and perhaps to the entire chapter (though we do not have to locate everything within the New Year ritual). As well as hostile forces, 'good angels' or lesser divinities associated with 'Elyon are probably mentioned in verses 7 *b*, 8 *b* and perhaps in 23 *b*.

The above exposition may have uncovered a little of the kind of traditions that religious reorganisers, inspired by Deut. 4:19, will have been anxious to bury for ever. Yet a time can come when ancient magic no longer smells of danger but lets its strange power be harnessed to new chariots. The author of Isa. 33 re-used ancient ritual for his own purposes as T. S. Eliot was to use the *Brihad-aranyaka Upanishad* in *The Waste Land*, the *Bhagavad-gita* in *The Dry Salvages* and Christian liturgical themes constantly in his poetry. In its turn the *Midrash Rabba* re-used Isa. 33 to interweave its angelic lament with the 'Aqedah by a stroke of poetic intuition that perhaps got closer to its heart than many modern commentators.

Note

I would like to express my gratitude to Prof. Raphael Loewe for help with Jewish exegesis, to Mrs Margaret Barker for stimulating discussion and to Fr Mitchell Dahood for help with inaccessible literature.

Bibliography

G. W. Ahlström *Joel and the Temple Cult of Jerusalem*, SVT 21 (Leiden, 1971).

W. F. Albright 'The Babylonian Temple-Tower and the Altar of Burnt-Offering', *JBL* 39 (1920), 137–42.

G. W. Anderson 'Isaiah XXIV–XXVII Reconsidered', *SVT* 9 (Leiden, 1963), 118–26.

M. Barker 'Some Reflections upon the Enoch Myth', *JSOT* 15 (1980), 7–29.

P. Beauchamp *Création et Séparation* (Paris, 1969).

J. Blenkinsopp *Prophecy and Canon* (Notre Dame, Indiana, 1977).

G. Brunet 'Les aveugles et boiteux jébusites', *SVT* 30 (Leiden, 1979), 65–72.

A. Caquot 'Sur quelques démons de l'Ancien Testament (Reshep, Qeteb, Deber)', *Semitica* 6 (1956), 53–68.
'Le Psaume XCI', *Semitica* 7 (1957), 21–37.

B. S. Childs *Introduction to the Old Testament as Scripture* (London, 1979).
Isaiah and the Assyrian Crisis, SBT, Second Series, 3 (London, 1967).

D. L. Christensen *Transformations of the War Oracle in Old Testament Prophecy*, Harvard Dissertations in Religion 3 (Missoula, 1975).

J. L. Crenshaw *Hymnic Affirmations of Divine Justice*, SBL Dissertation Series 24 (Missoula, 1975).

M. J. Dahood *Psalms*, Anchor Bible (3 vols., New York: vol. I, 1966; vol. II, 1966; vol. III, 1970).

J. J. A. van Dijk *Ezekiel's Prophecy on Tyre*, Biblica et Orientalia 20 (Rome, 1968).

J. H. Eaton *Festal Drama in Deutero-Isaiah* (London, 1979) (= 1979a).
Obadiah, Nahum, Habakkuk, Zephaniah, Torch Bible Commentaries (London, 1961).
'The Psalms and Israelite Worship', in G. W. Anderson, (ed.), *Tradition and Interpretation* (Oxford, 1979), pp. 238–73 (= 1979b).

S. Feigin 'The Meaning of Ariel', *JBL* 39 (1920), 131–7.

D. N. Freedman 'Pottery, Poetry and Prophecy: An Essay on Biblical Poetry', *JBL* 96 (1977), 5–26.

G. Friedlander (trans. and ed.), *Pirke de Rabbi Eliezer* (London, 1916).

K. Galling 'Der Beichtspiegel', *ZAW* 47 (1929), 125–30.

T. F. Glasson 'The "Passover", a Misnomer: The Meaning of the Verb Pasach', *JTS*, n.s. 10 (1959), 79–84.

H. Gunkel 'Jesaia 33, eine prophetische Liturgie', *ZAW* 42 (1924), 177–208.
Die Psalmen (Göttingen, 1926).

B. Hartmann 'Mögen die Götter Dich behüten und unversehrt bewahren', in *Hebräische Wortforschung*, SVT 16 (Leiden, 1967), pp. 102–5.

J. Harvey *Le Plaidoyer prophétique contre Israël après la rupture de l'Alliance* (Paris and Montreal, 1967).

D. R. Hillers 'A Hebrew Cognate of Unuššu/Unṯ in Is. 33: 8', *HTR* 64 (1971), 257–9 (= 1971a).
'"The Roads to Zion mourn" (Lam 1: 4)', *Perspective* 1–2 (1971), 121–33 (= 1971b).
Treaty-curses and the Old Testament Prophets, Biblica et Orientalia 16 (Rome, 1964).

W. H. Irwin *Isaiah 28–33, Translation and Philological Notes*, Biblica et Orientalia 20 (Rome, 1968).

W. Janzen *Mourning-cry and Woe Oracle*, BZAW 125 (Berlin, 1972).

A. R. Johnson *The Cultic Prophet and Israel's Psalmody* (Cardiff, 1979).

Y. Kaufmann *The Religion of Israel*, translated and abridged by M. Greenberg (London, 1961).

K. Kohler Review of H. C. Trumbull, *The Threshold Covenant*, in *American Journal of Theology* 1 (1897), 798–803.

L. Laberge *La Septante d'Isaïe 28–33* (Ottawa, 1978).

W. McKane 'Prophecy and the Prophetic Literature', in G. W. Anderson (ed.), *Tradition and Interpretation* (Oxford, 1979), pp. 163–88.

P. D. Miller 'Fire in the Mythology of Canaan and Early Israel', *CBQ* 27 (1965), 256-61.

J. Morgenstern 'The Cultic Setting of the Enthronement Psalms', *HUCA* 35 (1964), 1–42.

'The Mythological Background of Psalm 82', *HUCA* 14 (1939), 29–126.

S. Mowinckel *Psalmenstudien*, vol. II (Oslo, 1921), esp. pp. 235–8.

H.-P. Müller *Ursprünge und Strukturen alttestamentlicher Eschatologie*, BZAW 109 (Berlin, 1969).

'Zur Funktion des Mythischen in der Prophetie des Jesaja', *Kairos* 13 (1971), 266–81.

K. Nielsen *Yahweh as Prosecutor and Judge*, JSOT Supplement Series 9 (Sheffield, 1978).

R. R. Ottley *The Book of Isaiah According to the Septuagint* (2 vols., London, 1904, 1906).

R. Patai 'The "Control of Rain" in Ancient Palestine', *HUCA* 14 (1939), 251–86.

G. von Rad 'The Royal Ritual in Judah', in *The Problem of the Hexateuch and Other Essays* (English translation of 'Das judäische Königsritual', *ThLZ* 72 (1947), 211–16 (= *Gesammelte Studien | zum \ Alten \ Testament*, ThB 8 (Munich, 1958), pp. 205–13)) (Edinburgh, 1966), pp. 222–31.

H. Graf Reventlow *Das Amt des Propheten bei Amos*, FRLANT 80 (Göttingen, 1962).

Liturgie und Prophetisches Ich bei Jeremia (Gütersloh, 1963).

J. Scheftelowitz *Alt-palästinensischer Bauernglaube* (Hannover, 1925).

J. B. Segal *The Passover from the Earliest Times to A.D. 70* (London, 1963).

J. F. Stenning *The Targum of Isaiah* (Oxford, 1949).

F. Stolz *Strukturen und Figuren im Kult von Jerusalem*, BZAW 118 (Berlin, 1970).

M. Tsevat 'God and the Gods in Assembly: An Interpretation of Psalm 82', *HUCA* 40–1 (1969–70), 123-37.

J. Vermeylen *Du Prophète Isaïe à l'Apocalyptique*, vols. I–II (Paris, 1977–8).

R. N. Whybray *Thanksgiving for a Liberated Prophet*, JSOT Supplement Series 4 (Sheffield, 1978).

F. Willesen 'The Cultic Situation of Psalm LXXIV', *VT* 2 (1952), 289–306.

J. Ziegler 'Die Hilfe Gottes "am Morgen"', in *Alttestamentliche Studien*, Festschrift F. Nötscher, BBB 1 (Bonn, 1950), pp. 28–88.

Septuaginta, XIV, Isaias (Göttingen, 1939).

Untersuchungen zur Septuaginta des Buches Isaias, Alttestamentliche Abhandlungen, 12, 3 (Münster, 1934).

Prophecy and law

ANTHONY PHILLIPS

As late as 1965, in his monograph *Prophecy and Covenant*, Clements held that central to the preaching of the canonical prophets was the concept of the Sinai covenant. Their unique contribution was to have reactivated the idea of the covenant, which had fallen into neglect. Indeed, Clements went so far as to assert that, without the prior fact of the covenant, the prophets would be unintelligible to us (p. 126). Clements, of course, recognised that the actual term for covenant (*berīt*) was only found twice in the eighth-century prophets, in Hos. 6:7 and 8:1, but he argued that to elect someone must lead to some kind of special relationship between him who elects and him who is elected, in which the obligations of the latter are set out. The use of the term 'covenant' to describe such a relationship was 'only of secondary importance' (p. 54).

But a decade later, in the wake of Perlitt (1969), Clements, in his second monograph, *Prophecy and Tradition* (1975 a), accepted that the covenant theology only gradually emerged to reach its classical expression in the Deuteronomic literature. The attempt to see the prophet as fulfilling the office of covenant mediator based on Deut. 18:15ff must be abandoned, for it was the Deuteronomists who interpreted the prophets as preachers of *tōrāh* and spokesmen of the covenant between Yahweh and Israel. Further, reliance on Mendenhall's thesis (1954) relating the covenant to the Hittite suzerainty treaties, allegedly reflected in the prophetic curses and lawsuit oracles, must also be given up. Instead, the prophets are to be seen as drawing on the various ways in which disaster could occur in the ancient Near East and employing the legal metaphor of a court action. The attempt to explain so many concepts within the prophetic corpus as deriving from the political suzerainty treaties implied a strange lack of theological creativeness on Israel's part when confronted with radically changed circumstances, which one would expect to be reflected in new

217

theological insights. Indeed, the use of the political treaty form probably entered Israel's theology precisely in this way, following the fall of the Northern Kingdom and the threat to Judah's own existence. This, of course, is not to deny the creativity of the prophets but merely to indicate that they did not use an already existing literary model which was only assimilated into Israel's theological thought when new circumstances made it useful.

But, while Clements admitted that 'we cannot reconstruct a consistent covenant theology as a distinctive and coherent tradition underlying the preaching of the prophets', he nonetheless went on to argue that 'we can see that the traditions which the prophets inherited and used had a place in the emergence of a distinctive covenant ideology in Israel' (1975 a, p. 23). So if, in the light of Perlitt (1969) and Nicholson (1973), the redactional work of the Deuteronomists within the prophetic corpus must now be recognised, caution must be expressed against a too-ready rejection of the development of that covenant theology over a considerable period of time, in which the prophets themselves played a part. So Barr (1977) not only questions whether the covenant of Yahweh with Israel became significant so late but, in his reply to Kutsch (1973), indicates that syntactical and linguistic, rather than ideological and theological, restrictions might explain its use in one kind of linguistic context and not in another (cf. Martin-Achard, 1978, pp. 299ff). As Clements notes in his *Old Testament Theology* (1978), while *berīt* clearly acquired a new emphasis in the Deuteronomic vocabulary, it is unlikely that it was an entirely 'novel introduction' in the seventh century to describe Israel's relationship with Yahweh (p. 101).

Deuteronomic covenant theology is, then, not in itself to be understood as an innovation, but as the end of a process, which is finally assimilated into a system, as set out in the Deuteronomic History work (see Mayes, 1979, pp. 60ff), and applied to the prophetic material (e.g. Amos 2:4; Hos. 8:1). The law and the prophets are thus seen in conjunction very early, which explains the almost total absence of the canonical prophets from the Deuteronomic History. But without a clear point of contact, this redactional activity would have been inexplicable.

A different approach was adopted by Bergren (1974), who concentrated on the offences actually cited by the prophets in their indictment. His argument rested not only on Mendenhall's thesis about the covenant origins of Israel but also on Alt's distinction, formulated in 1934, between apodictic and casuistic law (1966). He contended that, whenever the prophets used law as a basis for their condemnation of Israel, their accusation was grounded solely on the breach of apodictic law. Nowhere is there any appeal to casuistic law, though the prophets clearly knew such law (Jer. 2:34; 3:1), thus showing that the old dualism between genuine Israelite law and other law continued in the prophetic preaching. The reason for this, in Bergren's view, was that the prophets understood that God had made a covenant with Israel, conceived of as a treaty, by which it was committed to a certain standard of behaviour as set out in the apodictic law, and which God Himself would enforce. Indeed for Bergren, relying on Westermann's analysis of the forms of prophetic speech (1967), it is in the Prophetic Judgement Speech that the law and the prophets come together. Thus he maintained that comparison of Alt's apodictic laws and the content of the accusation portion of the prophetic judgement speech indicates that the latter was entirely dependent on the former. But in spite of tabulating the prophetic accusations and relating them to the Pentateuchal legislation, Bergren made no real attempt to ask why appeal was made to certain laws and not to others. While he admitted that apodictic and covenant law are not coextensive, for the prophets are unconcerned with cultic requirements, even though these can be prescribed in apodictic form, he nonetheless relied on form to the exclusion of content.

But Alt's thesis must now be very severely modified (see the full discussion by Schottroff, 1977). In the first place, studies by Mendenhall (1954), Gevirtz (1961) and Kilian (1963) have shown that the apodictic form in the second person singular is by no means unique to Israelite law but is found over a wide area of the ancient Near East. And second, while scholars such as Gerstenberger (1965) and Gilmer (1975) have refined Alt's rigid division between apodictic and casuistic law, others like Wagner (1972) have abandoned it. Indeed I argued (1970, p. 13) that while the form may be able to tell us something of the legal *Sitz im Leben* in which the law evolved, it can tell us nothing about the geographical one. Apodictic law simply denotes a situation in which those in authority – the head of the family or clan, elders, king, God – can determine public policy, enforcing this by sanctions if possible, while casuistic law has to define whether, in a particular case, that policy has been infringed (cf. Liedke, 1971; Weinfeld, 1973). The

219

prophetic appeal is not to a particular form of law but rather to its breach by certain actions interpreted by the prophets as forbidden by Yahweh. When these are examined, two distinct traditions emerge.

Amos specifically sets out his charge against Israel. After a series of oracles denouncing the foreign nations for various war crimes (1:3 - 2:3), he condemns Israel for the exploitation of those who were not in a position to protect themselves (2:6–8). While scholars have disputed what precise actions were envisaged in the examples of exploitation listed by Amos, it is clear that the prophet was not introducing new ideas but formally indicting Israel for particular actions that fall under the rulings on humaneness and righteousness found in the Book of the Covenant (Exod. 22:21–7 (MT 22:20–6); 23:1–3, 6–9). His further citations of oppression by the rich and perversion of justice are only similar examples of this original indictment. Thus the women of Samaria are condemned not for their indolent and selfish lives, nor for their possession of wealth, but because they are only enabled to live as they do through the exploitation of the needy (4:1). It is this that makes their conduct so unacceptable.

For Amos, *mišpāt* is being turned into a source of bitterness, and *ṣedāqā* entirely discarded (5:7; 6:12). Indeed, those who try to uphold justice are rejected (5:10) and, as a result, there is no check on the economic and social exploitation that now characterises Israelite society and for which no legal redress can be obtained (5:11–12). Indeed, in a wistful aside, Amos indicates that the only possible hope for Israel lies in the proper administration of justice (5:15). For Amos is under no illusion that the cult can, of itself, secure Israel's future. No matter how extravagant Israel's religious practice is, it becomes worthless if that religion lacks content (4:4–5; 5:21–4). And although Israel's business community scrupulously keeps the Sabbath law, its observance is bitterly resented as an interruption to the sharp practices whereby fortunes are being made (8:4–6).

Amos does not, then, spring surprises but simply argues that Israelite society ought to reflect that *mišpāt* and *ṣedāqā* of which the precise content should have been obvious. To indicate this, he summons foreign powers as independent witnesses to observe the state of Samaria. Instead of justice and righteousness, they are confronted with oppression and exploitation (3:9–10). Even as foreigners unacquainted with Israel's law, they are expected to condemn such action.

What is striking in Amos' indictment of Israel is the total lack of reference to those wrongs against person or property for which the law provided sanctions. While Wolff (1977) interprets 3:10 as referring to murder and robbery, comparison with Ezek. 45:9 indicates rather that general exploitation which characterises Amos' charges. Had Amos been able to cite a more obvious breakdown of law and order beyond the laws of humaneness and righteousness, he would presumably have done so. Of course, it is not to be supposed that on occasion such capital crimes as murder and adultery were not committed. Rather, we must assume that where such actions occurred, they were dealt with under the law. Certainly, the picture that Amos presents is not of an outwardly lawless society but rather of a prosperous people, confident that their prosperity arose through faithfulness to Yahweh seen not only in excessive religious zeal but also, we must assume, in the maintenance of law and order. Hence we find the business community constrained by the Sabbath requirement. Amos' indictment is that beneath this outwardly prosperous and law-abiding society (4:1; 6:1, 3–6) there lies rank disorder. But the recognition of that disorder was by no means obvious to those in control of Israelite society, who could take a justifiable pride in their prosperity (McKeating, 1971, p. 23). That the nation's very election should be renounced must have seemed even more unlikely (3:2).

Micah exhibits the same concern with social justice as Amos. So he condemns the deprivation of the small country farmers of their real estate by the wealthy and powerful Jerusalem citizens (2:1–5). As a result, their victims lose their status as free Israelites and become part of the landless poor, dependent on others for their maintenance and without a place in the running of society. There is, however, no indication that illegal means were used to evict them. The same concern for the oppressed occurs in 2:8–9.

In Mic. 3:1–4, 9–11, the prophet turns to the other main theme of Amos' condemnation, the perversion of justice. His language could hardly be more graphic. What precise actions were envisaged by the bloodshed of 3:10 are not specified: it may be a merely metaphorical reference to the oppression of the helpless, but it might also involve legal processes whereby innocent people were condemned to death (cf. Isa. 1:15). Yet, in spite of their conduct, it is clear that the authorities still envisaged Yahweh's support, which again indicates that, though their condemnation was obvious enough to the prophet, it was not at all obvious to his contemporaries whom he condemns (3:11). Certainly excessive religious practice will not protect them (6:8). The oracle on the exploitation of the poor, particularly through crooked business transactions (6:9–16), and the description of a society in which no one could be trusted (7:1–6), add nothing new and may only in part be from Micah's hand. Like Amos, although Micah may give examples of particular actions he condemns, he does not cite specific laws but appeals to the general concept of humaneness and righteousness. With such ideas his hearers were expected to be familiar, which makes their apparent non-recognition of the situation all the more surprising and again raises questions as to just how lawless was contemporary society.

The same concern for humaneness and righteousness is found in Isaiah. So the prophet affirms that Israel's relationship with Yahweh rests not on the appropriate performance of cultic rites but on the proper administration of justice and the protection of the defenceless in society (1:16–17). This theme of maladministration of justice and oppression of the poor and defenceless continues in 1:21–3; 3:14–15 and the woe oracles of 5:8–25; 10:1–4. And in a masterful play on words, a general condemnation of Israel for its lack of mišpāt and ṣedāqā concludes the song of the vineyard (5:7).

Once more then we find an eighth-century prophet charging Israel with two interrelated groups of offences – the oppression of those who cannot defend themselves and the perversion of justice. What has now become quite apparent is that here lies the hub of these three prophets' indictment. It was neither cultic wrongs nor serious capital offences that dominated their preaching, for the references to idolatry in both Micah (1:7; 5:12–14 (MT 11–13)) and Isaiah (2:8, 18, 20) must be regarded as redactional, as also the comment on murderers (1:21) (Kaiser, 1972, p. 18). Nor is there any appeal to the Decalogue or to the covenant. Their indictment rests solely on those rulings on humaneness and righteousness already made part of the Book of the Covenant, to which we must now turn.

In contrast to the formal legal corpus of Exod. 21:12 – 22:17 (MT 22:16), with its specifications of precise legal offences and appropriate sanctions to be enforced through the courts, the laws of humaneness and righteousness are not, in a technical sense, laws at all, for they envisage no legal action for their breach and specify no penalties. Rather, they are addressed directly to the recipient and envisage unquestioning obedience. Their basis is an appeal to his sense of moral responsibility for those who are not in a position to protect themselves and to his sense of justice. These humanitarian and juridical provisions reflect the break-up of a clan-dominated society, in which the orphan and widow would readily have found protection, and which would have centred upon the family tent encampment. Instead, they indicate a settled agricultural community, owning its own property, readily engaging in commerce and exhibiting considerable disparity of wealth among its members. Such a thriving capitalist society marks an advanced state of development from the early days of the settlement in Canaan and would most naturally reflect the period of the united monarchy.

This is confirmed from Gilmer's analysis (1975) of the If–You form in which these humanitarian provisions appear, both in the Book of the Covenant and in Deuteronomy. Following Gerstenberger (1965) and Weinfeld (1972), he argues that this form, with its stress on persuasion, indicates a wisdom background 'which finally comes to focus in the royal court where it was employed in the instruction of officials and in the broader context of law' (p. 110). It is in such a royal court milieu that Deuteronomy was produced. But the same *Sitz im Leben* can be argued for the laws of humaneness and righteousness in the Book of the Covenant. Indeed, as I had already argued on different grounds (1970, pp. 158ff), the Book of the Covenant is best seen as a handbook of justice for the new Davidic state, whose king, as elsewhere in the ancient Near East, was to maintain law and order (Ps. 72; Isa. 11). Thus, from its inception the royal court, through its civil servants (a more neutral term than wisdom circles), would have initiated the codification of Israelite law which, because of Israel's peculiar constitution as the people of Yahweh, would always have been done on a theologised basis.

It is this tradition that Amos, Micah and Isaiah have taken over. They discern that within an apparently orderly society there are inhuman and unjust practices, which render that society subject to the judgement of God. This explains what Wolff (1977), Schmid (1968) and Barton (1979) have identified as their appeal to 'natural' law, though there would seem to be no need to polarise this with 'revealed' law when thinking of the sources for prophetic morality (Zimmerli, 1965, p. 67). Hos. 8:12 shows that there was already a clear complex of written law accredited to Yahweh, to which appeal could be made. The innovation of Amos, Micah and Isaiah was to hold that the nation's very election depended, not merely on conformity to cultic practice and the observance of the laws for which specific sanctions were provided, but also on those principles of natural law already enshrined – but of necessity very generally – in the rulings on humaneness and righteousness in the Book of the Covenant, a breach of which any rational man ought to have been able to discern for himself. No exploitation could be justified on the grounds of national prosperity or expediency. The elect community was to exhibit that same sense of responsibility for all within its ranks as characterised it from its inception. This prophetic reliance on the rulings on humaneness and righteousness indicates the unprofitability of so much recent discussion on wisdom and prophecy, whether in the attempt to identify a particular prophet with the wise, or to differentiate the prophets from a ruling class of wise (see further Whybray's essay, above pp. 181ff). Rather, these prophets offer a different assessment of Israel's situation from that of those who guided and administered the nation. Their analysis was confirmed by the subsequent widespread Deuteronomic emphasis on humanitarianism, which even included the desacralisation of the holy-war legislation (Gilmer, 1975, p. 109). But this was not the only, nor in the end the dominant, tradition inherited from the prophets.

Bergren does not mention Hosea, presumably because he recognised the totally different standpoint of that prophet. For nowhere does Hosea make any direct reference to the exploitation of the poor and needy, except perhaps in a sarcastic comment on crooked trading practices (12:7 (MT 12:8)). Instead, his emphasis falls on Israel's apostasy, summed up in the word 'harlotry'. It openly embraces other gods, and indulges in idolatry (4:17; 8:4ff; 11:2; 13:2; 14:8 (MT 14:9)). As a result, Yahweh will no longer make Himself known to it as I AM (1:9) – a direct reference to the disclosure of the divine name in Exod. 3:14. But since there is no mention of apostasy or idolatry in Amos, Israel is not to be thought of as suddenly embracing Baalism. Rather, Hosea is to be understood as attempting to purge Yahwism of those aspects of fertility religion to which it had, from the first, been attached. In Hosea's view, Yahweh was being treated as if He were a mere nature deity. Indeed, popular religion may have continued to address Yahweh as Baal (Clements, 1975 b, pp. 412ff). But it is Yahweh and not Baal who is the giver of fertility to the land (2:8 (MT 2:10)), which is to be induced neither through ritual associated with cult prostitution (4:11–14) nor through sacrifice but which follows automatically from knowledge of Him (6:6). It is this failure of knowledge that leads to Israel's condemnation, from which there will be no escape in political alliances (5:13–14; 7:11–13; 8:9–10).

Hosea's formal indictment of Israel is set out in 4:1–3. *'emet* and *ḥesed* indicate that intense loyalty that Yahweh has a right to expect from his people. *daʿat ʾelōhīm*, lack of which is the theme of Hosea (4:6; 6:6; cf. 2:20 (MT 2:22); 5:4; 6:3; 8:2 and 13:4), describes that personal, intimate relationship that Israel can have with Yahweh as a result of its election. There can be no doubt that the five absolute infinitives of 4:2 refer to those crimes covered by the third, ninth, sixth, eighth and seventh commandments, all of which affected the person of the individual Israelite and demanded the death penalty (Phillips, 1970, pp. 145ff; Wolff, 1974, pp. 67f). Although neither vocabulary nor order correspond with the Decalogue, it is difficult not to recognise an explicit reference to it, particularly as the order of crimes can be accounted for by association: two kinds of spoken crime, two kinds of murder (the man-thief, to which Alt (1953) showed the eighth commandment referred, is called 'the stealer of life' in Deut. 24:7) and adultery. The vocabulary results from the need to use single words. Such anarchy could only lead to the end of all life (4:3).

But since there seems little indication either in Amos or Hosea of the widespread chaos envisaged by 4:2, it would appear that the Decalogue is being used theologically, as a blanket expression indicating total renunciation of Yahweh in the most complete way possible. Hosea's interest is not in the crimes of the Decalogue but rather in Israel's lack of loyalty to God, consequent upon its syncretistic cult. Murders are mentioned in 6:8–9, but these probably relate to irregularities concerning the cities of refuge (Dinur, 1954, p. 142). Nor should we understand 4:13–14 to refer to sexual promiscuity in society at large. Rather, reference is being made to the adoption of Canaanite sexual cultic practices involving brides, of which there is evidence elsewhere in the ancient world (Wolff, 1974, pp. 85ff). Only in the reference to theft and robbery in 7:1 is there any indication of general lawlessness, though these were not crimes covered by the Decalogue but civil wrongs (Phillips, 1970, pp. 132ff). This lack of general anarchy, together with the fact that the prophetic judgement speech presents the indictment twice, first negatively and then positively, raises the strong presupposition that the theological use of the Decalogue is due to Deuteronomic redaction designed to define 'knowledge of God' as the Decalogue, for it was part of Deuteronomic theology that the Decalogue alone was given to Israel at Horeb (Deut. 4:13; 5:22). Wolff (1974, p. xxxi) has noted how many ideas characteristic of Deuteronomic thought occur first in Hosea. Another such idea was the interpretation of *tōrāh* as summarising the complete expression of the will of Yahweh revealed to Israel at Horeb, obedience to which determined its future (Lindars, 1968). It is this use of 'my *tōrāh*' in 8 : 1, paralleled by 'my *berīt*', which Perlitt (1969, pp. 146ff) has shown to be Deuteronomic (cf. Amos 2:4). Uniquely, then, among the eighth-century prophets we have in Hosea appeal both to the Decalogue and *berīt*. Clearly, the redactor intends Hosea's preaching to be understood against the background of an utterly rejected Decalogue, *the covenant law* of Sinai.

While the humanitarian concerns of the other eighth-century prophets were to be emphasised by the Deuteronomists, Hosea's anti-Canaanite stance was to have even greater consequences in the reforms of Hezekiah and Josiah and the legislation that accompanied them. I have already argued (Phillips, 1970, pp. 167ff) that Exod. 32–4 reflects Hezekiah's reform and, together with Exod. 19–24, forms the literary precedent for Deuteronomy. Thus Exod. 34:10ff warns against fraternising with the Canaanites, orders the destruction of their sanctuaries and cult objects, and counsels against intermarriage – a warning that may be compared with the later absolute prohibition in Deut. 7:3. Then comes the command against making a molten god (Exod. 34:17), in the context, clearly referring back to the golden calf of Exod. 32, itself to be identified with the bulls of Jeroboam I, of so much concern to Hosea. This explains why Hezekiah was not afraid to destroy the bronze serpent Nehushtan, even though its creation was attributed to no less a person than Moses. Finally there follows the revision of the festal calendar of Exod. 23:14ff, which now requires the centralisation of the celebration of the three main festivals in Jerusalem (Exod. 34:23f).

That Deuteronomy is to be seen as a new version of the Sinai narrative, deliberately intended to supersede this earlier account, can be seen by comparing Exod. 32–4 with Deut. 9–10. Whereas in Exod. 32–4 Moses himself is instructed to write a different set of laws (Exod. 34 : 11–26) on the new tablets, in Deut. 10 : 4 it is specifically asserted that the Decalogue was rewritten on the second set of tablets by God himself. Nicholson (1977) correctly recognised the importance of the Deuteronomic assertion that the Decalogue alone was given at Horeb (Deut. 4:13; 5:22) but missed the point of that assertion. It does not indicate that the Deuteronomists did not know the Sinai pericope in its present form in Exodus, but that they wished to suppress it.

Exod. 34:10, 27–8 does, of course, envisage the second set of tablets as *berīt*, as indeed in its present context Exod. 19:5; 24:7–8 understands the first. While Nicholson (1973), following McCarthy (1963), has properly stressed the centrality of theophany in the original Sinai narrative, the latter has pointed both to the similarity and to the dissimilarity of these covenant references with Deuteronomic usage (1972 *b*, p. 114). But as Patrick (1977) has indicated in reply to Perlitt (1969) and Nicholson (1973), this covenant framework is much more at home in what have come to be known as proto-Deuteronomic circles (see literature cited by Childs, 1979, p. 166), which I would identify as those responsible for Exod. 32–4, and whose activity is also to be found within Exod. 19–24, not only in *berīt* passages but also in such parenetic material as the anti-Canaanite epilogue to the Book of the Covenant (Exod. 23 : 20–33). Indeed, the present arrangement of Exod. 19–24; 32–4 is to be understood as their response to the fall of Samaria, reflected in the destruction of the tablets, which they introduce into the narrative. Here lies the beginning of the understanding of Yahweh's relationship with Israel in terms of the political treaty-form, later to find full expression in Deuteronomy. The court-authors concerned to record Hezekiah's reform would have been well aware of such treaties.

The influence of Hosea's prophecy accounts, then, for Exod. 19–24; 32–4, which leads on to Deuteronomy and itself explains the reason for the Deuteronomic redaction of the prophecy. But the influence of the other eighth-century prophets can also be detected in Exod. 22–3 in the strengthening of the legally unenforceable laws of humaneness by the addition of clauses encouraging obedience (Exod. 22:21 *b* (MT 20 *b*), 23 *b*–24 (MT 22 *b*–23); 23:9). These motive clauses indicate that, like the prophetic speeches, the law collections were addressed to the people at large and not simply to legal officials. They were not so much codes to be administered as a way of life to be followed (cf. Gemser, 1953, p. 62). That these clauses are not part of the original injunctions can be seen by their plural form of address. So while Exod. 22:21 (MT 22:20) now seeks to obtain justice for aliens by reminding Israelites that they were once aliens in Egypt, Exod. 22:23f (MT 22:22f) utters a direct threat against those who afflict the widow and the orphan. Yahweh will kill the offenders, thus ensuring that their wives and children have the same insecure status as those whom they had oppressed – another example of the principle of poetic justice to which Barton (1979, pp. 9ff) has pointed in the eighth-century prophets. The Deuteronomists were later to introduce the further inducement that obedience to apparently uneconomic laws would bring material blessing from Yahweh (Deut. 15:10, 18; 23:20 (MT 23:21)).

This idea also characterises the Deuteronomic addition to the fifth commandment, which now promises not only possession of the land (Exod. 20:12), but prosperity too (Deut. 5:16).

The two traditions that we have isolated in the eighth-century prophets come together in Jeremiah, itself heavily redacted by the Deuteronomists, not only in the prose sermons but also in the narrative material (Nicholson, 1970). Like Hosea, Jeremiah condemns Israel for its apostasy. Though some of the references to this come from what appear to be Deuteronomistic material (Jer. 3:6–11; 11:1–14; 16:10–13), there is clear evidence elsewhere to confirm that this was a dominant theme in Jeremiah's prophecy. Thus his opening indictment, now intended by the Deuteronomists as an introduction to the book, summarises his charge against Israel as apostasy (1:16), which is then fully set out (2:1 – 3:5). Israel is pictured as a harlot (2:20; 3:1–5) or adulteress (5:7–9; 9:2 (MT 9:1); 13:27; 23:9–12), peculiarly apt descriptions in view of its preoccupation with fertility rites involving sexual acts.

Something of the great variety of popular religion in the time of Jeremiah can be seen from the references to particular apostate cultic practices. Jer. 7:16–20 and 44:17–19, 25 describe the making of cakes for the queen of heaven, clearly some fertility rite. Another specific practice was the cult of Molech, centred in the valley of Ben-Hinnom outside Jerusalem. While it is not certain precisely what was involved, the fact that Jer. 7 : 31; 19 : 5 and 32 : 35 repeat that this rite was no command of Yahweh probably indicates that the participants saw Him as the object of their devotions. It is true that Baal has been inserted in Jer. 19:5 and 32:35, and this conforms with Deut. 12:31, but to say that Yahweh never commanded child sacrifice to Baal seems hardly necessary, even to the most obtuse of Israelites. References to astral cults occur in Jer. 8:2; 19:13. These are particularly associated with the last years of the Davidic monarchy (2 Kings 21:3–5; 23:4f; Zeph. 1:5), and the commandment against images was extended to cover them (Deut. 4:15ff). Though much of this material derives from Deuteronomistic editing, there can be no doubt that the religious practices of Judah in Jeremiah's time were seen by the prophet as a betrayal of Yahweh – a going after other gods. Yet it is clear from the Temple sermon (Jer. 7; cf. 26) that the people themselves saw their religion as a guarantee of their security, hence their reliance on sacrifice (Jer. 6:20–1; 7:21–3; 11:15–16) – a reliance as misplaced as that on the presence of Yahweh in His Temple.

The Temple sermon introduces the other tradition of eighth-century prophecy, the laws of humaneness and righteousness. Although Jer. 7 in its present form is a Deuteronomistic composition, that it is based on an actual incident in Jeremiah's life is confirmed from Jer. 26. Echoes of Jeremiah's original sermon may be found in the people's threefold chant about the Temple. Verses 5–7 announce that if the people amend their ways and their doings, then Yahweh will let them continue to dwell in the land that He had given them. What amending their ways and their doings consists of is defined in verses 5 *b*–6 – the proper exercise of justice and the refusal to oppress the alien, orphan and widow, to shed blood or to go after other gods.

I have identified the exercise of justice and the protection of those who could not defend themselves as the basis of the prophetic indictment of Amos, Micah and Isaiah. This tradition is also found in Jeremiah in his general condemnation of Judah (5 : 26–8; 6 : 13–14 = 8:10–11) and his summons to the king to administer justice (21:11–12), with his specific condemnation of Jehoiakim for failing to do so (22:13–19; cf. 23:5–6).

But in describing the actual breach of law for which Jeremiah indicts his people, Jer. 7:9 makes specific reference to the Decalogue, the eighth, sixth, seventh and ninth commandments being mentioned alongside the burning of incense to Baal and going after other gods. Nicholson (1970, p. 69) sees this reference to the Decalogue as a possible echo of the prophet's original oracle, but it seems to me more likely that, as in Hos. 4:2, this specific citing of the Decalogue is due to the Deuteronomists themselves again using the Decalogue theologically as a blanket statement to indicate the total renunciation of Yahweh. Once more man-theft is associated with murder. The fact that the Deuteronomists felt it necessary to set out this crime in their law shows that the commandment retained its importance (Deut. 24:7). But outside Jer. 7:9, no reliance is placed on the Decalogue for Judah's condemnation. While Jer. 9:2–9 (MT 1–8) paints a general picture of dishonesty, this is a very different matter from the general breakdown of society that would follow the total abrogation of the Decalogue. Indeed, all the evidence indicates that, once again, those in authority thought that the nation was secure (6:14; 8:11). It would therefore seem much more likely that Jeremiah's original charge concerned oppression of the defenceless and maladministration of justice, together with apostasy, thus showing that the prophet had inherited from his eighth-century predecessors the two prophetic traditions that we have isolated.

But the fact that references to the Decalogue only found their way into Hos. 4:2 and Jer. 7:9 due to Deuteronomistic redaction does not necessarily mean that the Decalogue itself originated with the Deuteronomists, any more than that the covenant idea did. A final paragraph is no place to argue the date of the Decalogue, but two points may be made. First, examination of the Book of the Covenant indicates that the compiler is consciously trying to distinguish crimes prohibited by the Decalogue, and carrying the death penalty, from civil offences, for which compensation was required. So murder (Exod. 21:12) is contrasted with assault (Exod. 21:18ff), and man-theft (Exod. 21:16) with theft of property (Exod. 22:1ff (MT 21:37ff)). But, exceptionally assault of parents (Exod. 21:15) as well as their repudiation (Exod. 21:17) carries the death penalty; seduction of a virgin (in contrast to adultery) results in damages (Exod. 22:16f (MT 22:15f)). In my view, the compiler aims to assimilate local indigenous legal practice, long administered by the elders in the gate, to the over-riding principles of Yahwism contained in the Decalogue (Phillips, 1977). And secondly, the Decalogue has been inserted before the Deuteronomic legal corpus (12–26), not as a summary of the more important Deuteronomic laws, but rather to give those laws a proper pedigree by presenting them as deduced from the Decalogue itself, the only law written on the tablets given at Horeb. As I have indicated earlier, prophetic silence about the Decalogue and its provisions can be due to other reasons than ignorance of its existence.

Bibliography

A. Alt 'The Origins of Israelite Law', in *Essays on Old Testament History and Religion* (Oxford, 1966), pp. 81–132 (English translation of 'Die Ursprünge des israelitischen Rechts' (Leipzig, 1934) = *Kleine Schriften*, vol. I (Munich, 1953), pp. 278–332)).

'Das Verbot des Diebstahls im Dekalog', *Kleine Schriften*, vol. I (Munich, 1953), pp. 333–40.

J. Barr 'Some Semantic Notes on the Covenant', *Beiträge zur Alttestamentlichen Theologie, Festschrift für W. Zimmerli* (Göttingen, 1977), pp. 23–38.

J. Barton 'Natural Law and Poetic Justice in the Old Testament', *JTS* n.s. 30 (1979), 1–4.

R. V. Bergren *The Prophets and the Law*, Monographs of the Hebrew Union College 4 (Cincinnati, 1974).

B. S. Childs *Introduction to the Old Testament as Scripture* (London, 1979).

R. E. Clements *Prophecy and Covenant*, SBT 43 (London, 1965).

Prophecy and Tradition (Oxford, 1975) (= 1975 a).

'Understanding the Book of Hosea', *RE* 72 (1975), 405–23 (= 1975 *b*).

Old Testament Theology (London, 1978).

B. Dinur 'The Religious Character of the Cities of Refuge and the Ceremony of Admission into them', *Eretz-Israel* 3 (1954), 135–46.

B. Gemser 'The Importance of the Motive Clause in Old Testament Law', *SVT* 1 (Leiden 1953), pp. 50–66.

E. Gerstenberger *Wesen und Herkunft des 'Apodiktischen Rechts'*, WMANT 20 (Neukirchen-Vluyn, 1965).

S. Gevirtz 'West Semitic Curses and the Problem of the Origins of Hebrew Law', *VT* 11 (1961), 137–58.

H. W. Gilmer *The If-You Form in Israelite Law*, SBL Dissertation Series 15 (Missoula, Montana, 1975).

O. Kaiser *Isaiah 1–12* (London, 1972) (English translation of *Der Prophet Jesaja, Kap. 1–12*, ATD 17, 2nd ed. (Göttingen, 1963)).

R. Kilian 'Apodiktisches und kasuistisches Recht im Licht ägyptischer Analogien', *BZ* 7 (1963), 185–202.

E. Kutsch *Verheissung und Gesetz. Untersuchungen zum sogenannten 'Bund' im Alten Testament*, BZAW 131 (Berlin and New York, 1973).

G. Liedke *Gestalt und Bezeichnung alttestamentlicher Rechtssätze. Eine formgeschichtlich–terminologische Studie*, WMANT 39 (Neukirchen-Vluyn, 1971).

B. Lindars 'Torah in Deuteronomy', in P. R. Ackroyd and B. Lindars (eds.), *Words and Meanings* (Cambridge, 1968).

D. J. McCarthy *Treaty and Covenant: A Study in Form of the Ancient Oriental Documents and in the Old Testament*, Analecta Biblica 21 (Rome, 1963; 2nd ed., 1978).

Old Testament Covenant. A Survey of Current Opinions (Oxford, 1972) (= 1972 *a*).

'*bᵉrît* in Old Testament History and Theology', *Biblica* 53 (1972), 110–21 (= 1972 *b*).

H. McKeating *The Books of Amos, Hosea and Micah* (Cambridge, 1971).

R. Martin-Achard 'Trois Ouvrages sur l'alliance dans l'Ancien Testament', *RThPh* 110 (1978), 299–306.

A. D. H. Mayes *Deuteronomy*, New Century Bible (London, 1979).

G. E. Mendenhall 'Ancient Oriental and Biblical Law', *BA* 17 (1954), 26–46.

'Covenant Forms in Israelite Tradition', *BA* 17 (1954), 50–76.

E. W. Nicholson *Preaching to the Exiles* (Oxford, 1970).

Exodus and Sinai in History and Tradition (Oxford, 1973).

'The Decalogue as the Direct Address of God', *VT* 27 (1977), 422–33.

Dale Patrick 'The Covenant Code Source', *VT* 27 (1977), 145–57.

L. Perlitt *Die Bundestheologie im Alten Testament*, WMANT 36 (Neukirchen-Vluyn, 1969).

A. Phillips *Ancient Israel's Criminal Law. A New Approach to the Decalogue* (Oxford, 1970).

'Another Look at Murder', *JJS* 27 (1977), 105–26.

H. H. Schmid *Gerechtigkeit als Weltordnung: Hintergrund und Geschichte des alttestamentlichen Gerechtigkeitsbegriffes*, BhTh 40 (Tübingen, 1968).

W. Schottroff 'Zum alttestamentlichen Recht', in W. H. Schmidt (ed.), *Verkündigung und Forschung: Altes Testament*, Beihefte zu Evangelische Theologie 22 (Munich, 1977), pp. 3–29.

V. Wagner *Rechtssätze in gebundener Sprache und Rechtssatzreihen im israelitischen Recht. Ein Beitrag zur Gattungsforschung*, BZAW 127 (Berlin and New York, 1972).

M. Weinfeld *Deuteronomy and the Deuteronomic School* (Oxford, 1972).
'The Origin of Apodictic Law. An Overlooked Source', *VT* 23 (1973), 63–75.

C. Westermann *Basic Forms of Prophetic Speech* (London, 1967) (English translation of *Grundformen prophetischer Rede* (Munich, 1960)).

H. H. Wolff *Joel and Amos*, Hermeneia (Philadelphia, 1977) (English translation of *Dodekapropheton*, vol. II: 'Joel und Amos', BKAT 14, 2 (Neukirchen and Vluyn, 1969; 2nd ed. 1975).
Hosea, Hermeneia (Philadelphia, 1974)|(English translation of *Dodekapropheton*, vol. I: 'Hosea', BKAT 14, 1 (Neukirchen and Vluyn, 1965).

W. Zimmerli *The Law and the Prophets. A Study of the Meaning of the Old Testament* (Oxford, 1965).

A change of emphasis in the study of the prophets

JOHN F. A. SAWYER

Despite frequent appeals by linguistic pioneers and considerable publicity given to their contributions to Biblical criticism, there still remains a wide gap between those who employ their methods and insights and those who neither use them nor understand them, between readers of *Semeia*, one might say, and readers of *Vetus Testamentum*. One reason for this is undoubtedly the linguistic jargon: an understandable voodoo, like the one that used to prevent students faced with quaint massoretic terminology from learning Hebrew, now holds up progress towards a more enlightened approach to Biblical exegesis. Yet I believe one major contribution of twentieth-century linguistics is to be found, not so much in its terminology, important though that is, as in its perspectives and attitudes. It is to the elucidation and further development of some of these within Biblical studies, along paths already trodden by, among others, the recipient of this congratulatory volume, that the present contribution is dedicated.

If the sixties saw an increasing awareness among Old Testament scholars of the need for a more scientific approach to Semitic philology and lexicography, thanks to Barr's *The Semantics of Biblical Language* (1961), then the seventies have witnessed a new interest in stylistics and structuralism. Building on earlier studies in stylistics, notably Alonso-Schökel's *Estudios de Poetica Hebrea* (1963), Muilenburg launched a new approach to the study of the Old Testament, which he called 'rhetorical criticism', intended to take his subject beyond form-criticism, and many have found it a fruitful lead to follow (Muilenburg, 1969; cf. Jackson and Kessler, 1974; Kessler, 1980. See also Richter, 1971). The seventies also saw the emergence of a more technical approach, namely structural analysis, first in New Testament, and more recently in Old Testament, research (cf., e.g., Polzin, 1977; Jobling, 1978; Culley, 1976). A comprehensive critique of all these new developments is quite beyond the scope of this essay. In any case

233

several excellent studies of Semitic philology, Biblical structuralism and stylistics have appeared in recent years (Barr, 1979; Patte, 1976; Polzin, 1977, pp. 1–53; Thiselton, 1978–9; Fokkelmann, 1975; cf. also Alonso-Schökel, 1960). But I believe it is possible to identify within these new approaches certain common aims and attitudes which, to judge from not a few recent commentaries and other works, are as yet by no means standard practice in Old Testament studies, but which can and do bring new life into the subject (cf. Buss, 1979, pp. 1–44).

A curious fact is that, although it was not until the twentieth century that these insights were identified and submitted to theoretical analysis, some of them were widely applied to Biblical traditions in the exegetical literature of Judaism, Christianity and Islam from as far back as our sources go. What has happened is that after 200 years of higher criticism, dominated by questions about the history of the text, sources, parallels, literary form and *Sitz im Leben*, we have arrived at a stage where we can recognise common ground between the methods of Rashi and the Church Fathers, for example, and modern scientific research (cf. Magonet, 1976, pp. 121–2, nn. 91, 93; Clines, 1979 (see especially p. 43)). If, as sometimes seems to be the case, it turns out that the early scholars, like *le Bourgeois Gentilhomme*, were using sound linguistic methods all their lives without knowing it, then the value of the vast amount of Hebrew, Greek, Syriac and Arabic exegetical literature, some of it now being published for the first time, will be inestimable. Not only is it of interest and importance as literature in its own right; it can also assist our understanding of the Biblical text. To put this another way, the gap between most modern critical commentaries and the pre-1700 literature, it seems to me, is now being bridged by the insights of modern stylistic and structural analysis. Thanks to the work of Alonso-Schökel, Muilenburg, Culley, Polzin and others, rather different, perhaps more subtle, questions about the text as it stands are increasingly being asked – and these are the very questions that the Midrashim, the early Fathers and the medieval commentators saw it as their task to answer. Questions of form, date and source, reconstructions of the original meaning and textual emendations are still important, but they need no longer hold pride of place in our commentaries (for a balanced expression of this view see Whybray, 1979, col. 140). It is not only the ancient scholars, pre-critical and fundamentalist, who ask questions about the meaning of the final form of the text: these are the questions that are being asked today by descriptive linguists. In what follows, examples will be taken mainly from the prophetic literature, although the principle applies to every part of the Bible, and four areas have been selected in which the effects of this change of emphasis are evident.

(1) The degree of refinement aimed for in semantic analysis is higher than it used to be (Barr, 1979, pp. 53–4). In the first place, interest in literary and stylistic matters, as we shall see, has brought scholars back from the fields of archaeology, ancient history and ancient Near Eastern studies, to the text itself. Furthermore, etymologising rarely occurs in the crude forms in which it was familiar up to a couple of decades ago (cf., e.g., *TDOT*, where etymology and meaning are usually dealt with in separate sections). Translation is no longer assumed to be the major method of definition (*hošia'* means 'to save'; *hiṣṣil* means 'to deliver'). An excellent example of the dangers of relying on translation when one is aiming for a sophisticated semantic definition is examined by Christ in his recent monograph *Blutvergiessen im Alten Testament* (1977). His main point is that Hebrew *dam* does not mean exactly the same thing as English 'blood' or French *sang*. There is a wide overlap between these terms, but not a complete overlap: in particular Hebrew *dam* is never used in the positive sense of a family bond, as in 'blood-brother' or 'blood is thicker than water'. The Hebrew for that usage would probably be *basar* 'flesh'. The implications of this for our understanding of Exod. 24, for example, and Lev. 17:11, are extremely important, and have been misunderstood, Christ argues (1977, pp. 10–11), by some of our most distinguished scholars. Similar confusion has arisen over the word *berit* translated 'covenant' in some contexts, but 'promise' in others, neither providing in any way an accurate definition (cf. Weinfeld, 1977).

A fundamental concept underlying much modern linguistics is choice: why did the author choose this word and not that? For a linguistic theorist, opposition between related words, any of which might have been chosen for a particular slot in the sentence, is a basic principle on which semantic analysis depends (Lyons, 1971, pp. 413–14; Thiselton, 1978–9, p. 330). Thus, in practical terms, the best way to define a term is by setting it in opposition to closely related terms (Sawyer, 1972, pp. 102–11). A frequent shortcoming of word-studies is that the definition they offer could equally well apply to several other terms, and the question of precisely what the distinctive meaning is of this particular term is not fully explored: why does an author choose this term and not one of the other possibilities? A recent study of the actual usage of *hitpallel* has shown that, whatever its etymology, its primary meaning cannot be 'to intercede' (Sawyer, 1980; the intercessory meaning is still primary for Stähli, 1976). It does, of course, occur with the preposition be'ad ('on behalf of'), but then so do a good many other words, including ṣa'aq ('to call for help') and he'elah 'olah ('to make a sacrifice'), which are not primarily intercessory in meaning. The choice of hitpallel and the noun tepillah is governed by the type of prayer and the nature of the occasion on which it is made: thus almost every tepillah in the Old Testament is in formal language, like the prayers of Hannah (1 Sam. 2) and Jonah (Jon. 2), as opposed to the patriarchs' prayers and those of minor characters, like the sailors in Jonah, which are not so described. The post-Biblical evidence (see below) confirms this: hitpallel is not particularly associated with intercessory prayer but is the term for liturgical prayer. Phylacteries are called tfillin and bet tepillah is a place of worship. Similar information can be collected for related terms and new light thrown on a verse like Jer. 7:16, where three of them occur together: 'And you are not to say any prayers (hitpallel) for this people, or send up loud prayers (rinnah utepillah) on their behalf, or importune (paga') me.' The three terms are arranged in order of politeness, as it were, beginning with formal prayer and ending with the most aggressive of the terms.

It was encouraging to see that TDOT contains sections on 'synonyms', 'pertinent words', 'parallel expressions' and the like (see vol. III (1978), pp. 430, 276, 336), although, it must be said, little use is made of these in the actual semantic analysis. In the article on daraš, for example, frequent cross-references to biqqeš are given, but specific distinctions between the two terms are not made the subject of inquiry (vol. III (1978), pp. 293–307). On the other hand, Riesener's substantial study of 'ebed (1979, see p. 7) is explicitly devoted to the task of distinguishing 'ebed from other terms in the same 'field'.

The anomalous form 'išim, clearly documented in three passages (Ps. 141:4; Prov. 8:4; Isa. 53:3) and productive in post-Biblical Hebrew, provides a good example of the need to search for fine distinctions in Biblical Hebrew. Most commentators simply ignore it, and the questions of whether there is some subtle distinction between 'išim and the normal form 'anašim – and such distinctions are common in the case of social designations – is not even discussed (cf., e.g., Anderson, 1972, pp. 919–20; McKane, 1970, p. 345; Whybray, 1975, pp. 174–5). Another example occurs in Isa. 42:2. The question why ṣa'aq is used, which normally suggests crying for help or appealing for justice, was raised by D. R. Jones many years ago, although his attractive solution has not been widely accepted yet. Most commentators do not even recognise that there is a problem: *ṣaʿaq* is not the normal word for 'to shout loudly', and, in a context of blustering injustice opposed to quiet, reliable efficiency, one would have expected *qaraʾ* or *heriʿa* (see Jones, 1962, p. 519; cf. Whybray (1975, pp. 72–3), who recognises the unusual interpretation of *ṣaʿaq*).

Interest in word-pairs has led to an awareness of fine distinctions between synonyms. In a recent study of words for 'way, road, path' etc., Tidwell (1980, pp. 61–2) has shown that the word *mesillah* is distinguished in several contexts (e.g. Isa. 35:8; Ps. 84:6) from the other terms by its 'sacred religious significance'. It is to be hoped that such studies will become more frequent as attention moves away from historical or etymological issues to synchronic semantics.

(2) The enormous contribution of Jewish studies to Biblical exegesis is being increasingly realised and can be illustrated in numerous ways (cf. Magonet (1976) and Clines (1979), above p. 234). First of all, traditional Jewish reluctance to emend the text has led, over the centuries, to the application of considerable ingenuity and imagination to lexical problems that have baffled modern scholars, as well as to some that modern writers have not noticed or deliberately ignored. There is an interesting example in 2 Sam. 12:31 (Sawyer, 1978): alongside more familiar tools there appears the hapax legomenon *magzerot*. In deciding which tool best fitted the context, Rashi correctly recognised the fact that the passage is about God's punishment of evil, represented by the Ammonites, rather than about what David actually did, and so suggests the French translation *lime* 'a file' (*Miqraʾot Gedolot* III (Tel Aviv, 1959), p. 1606; cf. Sawyer, 1978, p. 101), with which the roughnesses of this godless people were rubbed away. It was only in modern times that the verse was taken literally or historically and David accused of inhumane treatment of his prisoners of war (or elaborately exonerated of the crime). Rashi and other precritical exegetes sometimes hit upon a nuance or an allusion that we would otherwise miss.

Another example, this time from the Midrash, illustrates how some interesting detail of the text, which may loom large in the precritical commentaries, is simply ignored by most modern commentaries. In the book of Jonah the big fish is *dag* (masc.) three times (2:1, 11), but *dagah* (fem.) once (2:2). Most modern scholars ignore this distinction entirely, some emend the text to achieve consistency (cf., e.g., Allen, 1976, p. 214; Bewer, 1912, pp. 42–3). But for the Midrash, this was a significant part of the data and, according to one tradition, there were in fact two fishes, one male and one female (see Ginzberg, vol. IV, 1913, pp. 249–50; vol. VI, 1928, p. 350, n. 31; Rashi *ad loc.*; cf. Bewer, 1912, p. 43). It is very probable that the distinction is not one of sex, but of style: *dag* (masc.) is the neutral term applied to any fish, whatever its sex, while *dagah* (fem.), elsewhere a collective term (e.g. Gen. 1:26, 28; Exod. 7:18, 21), is a poetic variant, selected in the verse describing Jonah praying in its belly, to highlight the miraculous or legendary nature of the fish. A close parallel is the distinction between the words *šir* (masc.) 'song' and *širah* (fem.) 'poem', a distinction well-documented in post-Biblical Hebrew but already detectable in the Old Testament (Sawyer, 1976–8, p. 33; cf. BDB where the translation 'ode' is given for *širah*). There is thus good reason to suppose that the choice of *dagah* in Jonah 2:2 was deliberate, and to ignore it is to miss a subtle and not insignificant stylistic detail. For one thing, it might suggest that the author was well aware of the unhistorical nature of the legend he is retelling.

There is another illustration of the value of the precritical Midrashic material even for modern studies of Jonah. Throughout the Jewish tradition Jonah is represented as a prophet, not merely a representative type of exclusiveness. He is exceptional in some ways, notably in his gentile audience, but he nonetheless bears all the marks of the traditional prophet: according to the Midrash, Jonah Ben Amittai was a disciple of Elisha, identified with the one mentioned in 2 Kings 6:15. Elsewhere he is identified with the boy raised from the dead by Elijah in 1 Kings 17, where the name Ben Amittai is explained by reference to *'emet*, the last word in verse 24: 'the word of the LORD on your lips is truth'. This explanation, albeit far-fetched, reminds us that the author's intention is far better investigated by following up allusions to the prophetic traditions, especially in Kings, than by seeking allegorical meanings such as the explanation that Jonah (Heb. *Yonah* 'dove') refers to Israel (cf. Hos. 7:11; 11:11) and that Ben Amittai (Heb. 'son of truth') is an ironical comment on the fact that, of all Israel's prophets, Jonah was the most unreliable and disobedient. Are not these latter explanations infinitely more naive and unsubtle than the Midrashic ones? (Cf. Allen (1976, p. 181), who rejects the allegorical interpretation of older commentators as an approach that has 'generally been abandoned'.)

There is another contribution to Biblical semantics within the field of Jewish studies, which is increasingly being exploited in modern research. I mean post-Biblical Hebrew (cf. Barr, 1979, pp. 57–8; Sawyer, 1980, pp. 132–3). It is often forgotten that this vast corpus is mostly far closer, historically, to Biblical Hebrew than Arabic or Babylonian or even Ugaritic and is, for that reason, all the more relevant to the pursuit of ancient Hebrew meanings. Of course one still has to examine the texts synchronically, but subtle semantic distinctions and associations are often better documented in the later literature and provide a better starting-point than traditional comparative philology. There is a *prima facie* case for the view that Eliezer Ben-Yehuda's *Thesaurus Totius Hebraitatis* is a more appropriate and more helpful aid to the Biblical Hebraist than the *Chicago Assyrian Dictionary* or Aistleitner's *Wörterbuch der ugaritischen Sprache*. An example will make this clear.

In trying to pinpoint the distinctive nuance of the word *hošia'* in Biblical Hebrew, the post-Biblical avoidance of the word, except in religious or liturgical contexts, which is illustrated by the fact that Ben-Yehuda (1908, vol. IV, pp. 2189ff) quotes almost exclusively Biblical examples of *hošia'*, *yešu'ah* etc., was of primary significance (see Sawyer, 1975, and forthcoming article in *TDOT*). Some prehistoric association with Arabic *wasi'a*, 'to be spacious', if there ever was such an association, has left no trace in the sources. A study of passages in which the same action is described by both *hošia'* and *hiṣṣil* confirms that the peculiar characteristic of *hošia'* is that it is used almost without exception by Israelites of their God or His appointed representative and is deliberately avoided when this is not the case. In 2 Kings 19 there is a distinction, which can hardly be accidental, although ignored by NEB translators, between, on the one hand, the Assyrian's mocking use of *hiṣṣil* in reference to Jerusalem's slender chance of being rescued (verses 11, 12) and, on the other, Hezekiah's prayer, 'save us' (verse 19), and God's answer, 'I will defend this city to save it' (verse 34), where in both cases the verb *hošia'* is used. Perhaps, too, the appearance on the scene of 'Isaiah' (whose name is formed from the same Hebrew root) was an immediate answer to Hezekiah's prayer (verse 20). At all events, the distinctive overtones of *hošia'* and related terms are clear to see. Other examples of this are 1 Sam. 4, where Israel's faith in the power of their God is expressed in the words '[the Ark] will save (*hošia'*) us from our enemies' (verse 3) and contrasted with the frightened Philistines' use of the less theological term in an exactly parallel context: 'who will deliver us (*hiṣṣil*) from these mighty gods?' (verse 8). A similar point is being made in the taunt in Judg. 10: 14 and in the mocking account of the idolatrous craftsman praying to a block of wood (Isa. 44: 17). The use of *hošia'* in these and other contexts is surely the author's way of highlighting the contrast between the power of his God and the illusory appeal of foreign gods and human might. This is the kind of discovery about the meaning of Biblical Hebrew, that comes, not from comparative philology, but from within the Hebrew language, both Biblical and post-Biblical.

(3) Structuralists have reminded us that there are still questions to be asked about larger literary units, whole chapters, even whole books, which have been neglected in much modern scholarship. For various reasons Old Testament research has tended to be preoccupied with the smaller units, single words and sentences, for the most part. On the one hand, Hebrew grammar has been taught primarily at the phonological and morphological levels, syntax and stylistics being conspicuous by their absence from most elementary grammar books. Muraoka's work on emphasis (1969; cf. Schneider, 1974, pp. 222–68), for example, is an outstanding exception. On the other hand, preoccupation with the task of identifying distinct literary units, each originally belonging to a separate *Sitz im Leben* and each with a more or less clearly defined original function, has, for over a century, diverted attention away from patterns and relationships in the large units (Alonso-Schökel, 1960, see especially pp. 161–2; Fokkelmann, 1975, pp. 1ff). Some simple examples will illustrate the kind of results we can expect from the change of emphasis evident in much recent writing.

We may begin with the view expressed in various quarters recently that the Book of Isaiah, as well as being a collection of numerous originally separate units, is also a single literary unit (Sawyer, 1977, pp. 112–18; Childs, 1979, pp. 328ff; Ackroyd, 1978). Recurring themes and motifs, both theological and lexical, such as 'the Holy One of Israel' and 'Zion', which give the book a certain 'Isaianic unity', have frequently been noted, but the exegetical and semantic implications of this are only now being fully worked out. There are several good reasons why, as scientists, we have to take account of this fact about the Book of Isaiah in our commentaries on it. First of all, it is most probable that the author of later parts of the book, chs. 40–55, for instance, was familiar with some of the earlier parts of Isaianic tradition (Petersen, 1977, pp. 19ff; Carroll, 1979, pp. 155–6). Conversely, for anyone interested in the history of interpretation, the later parts of the Isaianic corpus, such as Isa. 65, which are among the earliest documented examples, must be of particular interest. But above all, the Book of Isaiah is a piece of Hebrew literature, a single work, about which questions can be asked with the same degree of sensitivity and scientific rigour as about any other piece of literature.

Questions about the overall structure of the book have been asked before but are being treated more seriously now. Thus the function of chs. 36–9 as a transition passage leading on to chs. 40–55 suggests that the traditional division of the book after ch. 39 can be misleading (Ackroyd, 1974; Childs, 1979, pp. 325ff). The relationship between passages in chs. 1–12 and 40–55 has been noted recently (Melugin, 1976, see especially pp. 177–8; Bonnard, 1972, pp. 74–5; Watters, 1976, pp. 128–30). When discussing the meaning of any word or passage in Isaiah, an obvious control on free speculation might be the usage in other parts of the Isaianic corpus: the question 'what does x mean in an Isaianic context?' is not the same as 'what does x mean?' but it is an interesting and semantically justifiable question nonetheless. I venture to suggest that it is perhaps the primary question for the Biblical scholar. For example, a very strong argument, it seems to me, for the view that *yir'eh* (*'or*) in Isa. 53: 11 means 'he will see' (intrans.) or 'he will see light', that is, 'he will experience deliverance or salvation' (cf., e.g., Whybray, 1975, p. 180; Westermann, 1969, p. 255; North, 1964, p. 244), and not 'shall be bathed in light' (NEB), is that both the former meanings occur elsewhere in the same book (66: 14 'you shall see'; 9: 2 (MT 1) 'the people who walked in darkness have seen a great light'), while the other meaning does not. Similarly, a cross-reference to the heavenly court scene in Isa. 6 is a powerful argument for the usual interpretation of ch. 40, although most modern commentators either ignore it altogether or note it in passing as if it were of no greater significance than references to 1 Kings, Jeremiah and Amos (cf., e.g., Whybray, 1975, p. 48).

The same applies to the striking relationship between the gruesome description of a diseased body in Isa. 1 and 52: 13–53: 12. Are we, as readers, not intended to see ch. 1 as an introduction to the book as a whole, presenting all the main Isaianic themes to be dealt with later? Among these is the unforgettable image of a people weighed down with sin (verse 4), its body covered with bruises and raw wounds (verse 5), its land looking like Sodom and Gomorrah (verse 9), and it is no accident that the cure for these ills is later represented both in the image of an exalted servant and in the descriptions of the new Jerusalem and of a new heaven and a new earth (ch. 65) (Sawyer, 1977, pp. 112–18). The existence of the Book of Isaiah, all sixty-six chapters of it, is part of our data and we are not only free to exploit its insights but obliged to use them as controls on our exegesis. If confirmation of a proposed inter-pretation can be found within the Isaianic corpus, then as descriptive linguists we would need strong evidence for rejecting it in favour of an alternative, unless we are primarily concerned with isolated units, such as one of 'the Servant Songs', for example, or an eighth-century B.C. passage, considered on its own.

Another example of how taking into account the larger units can be valuable, is the 'Book of the Twelve'. It has long been customary to approach the Minor Prophets in chronological order, beginning with Amos and Hosea, considered alongside Isaiah and Micah, and leaving Malachi and Jonah for treatment in a later context. Such an approach is appropriate for a study of the history of prophecy in ancient Israel but, like the tripartite division of the Book of Isaiah, it leaves out of account a good many factors, literary and semantic, which affect our under-standing of the books in question (Clements, 1977). For example, the book of Amos is most likely an exilic composition in its present form, and to approach it primarily with a view to finding out about eighth-century society is inevitably to miss important aspects of exilic thought (Childs, 1979, pp. 399ff; Ackroyd, 1968, pp. 44–5). This question has, incidentally, been thoroughly investigated in connection with the Book of Jeremiah (cf., e.g., Nicholson, 1970).

Another point about the Book of the Twelve is that it has a quite unmistakable structure of its own, which again affects our understanding of the Minor Prophets. Jonah is the most obvious example. Taken out of its context among the eighth-century prophets, Hosea, Amos and Micah, the author's intention to present Jonah as a prophet, like Elijah and Jeremiah, and as living in the eighth century B.C., is missed (cf. Keller, 1965; Clements, 1975; Payne, 1979). The date of composition has tended to dominate discussion of this book and its obvious differ-ences from the other prophetic books, but its position in the Book of the Twelve is one part of the data that, had it not been so universally neglected, would have provided us with a valuable clue to the book's meaning. The position of the Book of Daniel in the 'prophetic penta-teuch' within the Christian canon is another piece of evidence to be taken into account in the commentaries, as is the association of the book of Psalms with the wisdom literature, in both the Jewish and the Christian canon.

(4) Finally, interest in the larger units has led us into the question of the canon and the 'final form of the text'. Yet this obvious point of contact between theologians (including fundamentalists), on the one

hand, and literary critics and linguistic theorists, on the other, is often played down. Childs (1979, p. 74), for example, in advocating 'the canonical approach' to Scripture refuses to acknowledge common ground between his position and that of literary critical methods. He distinguishes between 'the theological shape of the text' and its 'original literary and aesthetic unity'. Yet neither the theologian nor the descriptive linguist is concerned with 'originals', if both are working with the final form of the text. The 'canonical approach' cannot claim exclusive rights to work on the final form of the text, and it is not clear what the distinction is between 'interpreting the Biblical text in relation to a community of faith and practice' and describing what the text means in a particular context such as the early Church, medieval Jewish scholarship or the like (cf. Sawyer, 1972, pp. 6–16).

Another recent work that neglects this point of contact is Barr's critique of fundamentalism (1977), in which very little mention is made of modern structuralism or stylistics or the widespread interest in recent times, outside the fundamentalist tradition, in the final form of the text and in 'canonical meanings'.[1] By concentrating on the final form of the text and 'canonical meanings', the linguist does not change into something else, either a theologian or a fundamentalist. He is simply selecting one particular context in which to study meaning. In fact the context selected by many writers today, namely the final form of the text as understood by one or other of the religious communities that believe it to be in some way authoritative, happens to be a particularly interesting and important one, not only because of the influence it has had on the history of Western religious thought but also because it has been neglected in mainstream Biblical scholarship for most of two centuries (cf. Sawyer, 1972, pp. 6–16). This cannot be said for other equally legitimate contexts, such as the *ipsissima verba* of the eighth-century prophets, which have dominated Biblical studies for so long. Educationalists and theologians of every hue are probably right when they accuse the Biblical experts of having got their priorities wrong (cf. Ackroyd, 1968, pp. 9–10; Sawyer, 1977, pp. 1–11). In schools, universities and colleges the Old Testament is far more frequently studied for its contribution to the history of religious ideas than as an end in itself and, in that context, in departments of Theology or Religious Studies, the refinements of Pentateuchal source criticism and the history of ancient Israel, should belong to later, more advanced stages of Old Testament study, not to beginners' courses. Again, the descriptive approach of the modern linguist shifts the emphasis from 'What happened?' and 'Is this really by Isaiah?' to 'What is this text about?' and 'Where does this way of thinking about God, the land, the covenant, fit into a history of religious ideas?'

Two examples will illustrate the value of the 'canonical', that is, descriptive, approach to the text as it stands. As a number of writers have recently been stressing, one of the most striking differences between the original utterances or writings of ancient Israelite authors and the form in which we have them now is their titles or superscriptions. A psalm with its title means something different from the original psalm, and a decision has to be taken at the outset on the question of which meaning is to be the subject of investigation (Childs, 1971; Bruce, 1972). Similarly, the final editing of the prophetic collections, much of it attributable to a Deuteronomistic hand in all probability, has a decisive effect on our understanding of the prophet's words and on their authority as Scripture (cf. Tucker, 1977). The effect of attributing a whole book of sixty-six chapters to one eighth-century prophetic figure has already been mentioned, as has the effect of the exilic editing of the book of Amos. In its present, that is canonical, form, Amos can be considered as a 'prophet of coming salvation', like the other Old Testament prophets (Clements, 1977, p. 44). In discussing the 'prophetic canon', Clements rightly by-passes questions of authenticity, which Childs (1979, e.g. pp. 408–9), in spite of his concern for canonical meanings, still feels obliged to discuss at length.

My other example concerns the contents and arrangements of the canon as a whole, a matter that, as we have seen, must be of importance to all who work synchronically on the texts, theologians, fundamentalists and descriptive linguists, and yet one that is seldom taken seriously by any of them. The fact is that the Old Testament, in the Christian canon of Scripture, is not the same as the Hebrew Bible either in terms of its contents, if we take into account the apocryphal and pseudepigraphical works canonised by some authorities, or in their arrangement. There is a curious inconsistency in modern Christian tradition in that, while it is assumed that the canonical text of the Old Testament is the Hebrew text, massoretic or emended massoretic, the order and arrangement of the Old Testament is based universally on the Greek canon. Now this shifts the direction of the Old Testament from a descending line, Law–Prophets–Writings, with the emphasis on the Torah, to a line of rising, forward-looking expectation ending with the Prophets and inseparable from the New Testament. It is odd that, in spite of the evident interest in a synchronic approach to Biblical interpretation, more is not made of this. A recent article on Jewish–Christian relations totally ignores this matter and, as a result, the difficult question of fulfilment becomes confused (Hayman, 1979). One cannot make a straight comparison between the New Testament and the Talmud and state that 'the Talmud...is the logical development of the Old Testament' in the same way as the New Testament is (Hayman, 1979, p. 89). From a historical–critical standpoint it is, of course, true that both were composed after the Old Testament and frequently refer to it. But theologically and synchronically the New Testament and the Talmud stand in quite different relationships to the Old Testament: the New Testament, both in the arrangement of the Christian canon and in its very name, is the continuation of a line beginning at Genesis and leading forward and upward through history, poetry, wisdom and prophecy towards fulfilment, while the Talmud is a parallel line going back alongside the Torah as it were to Sinai, not a fulfilment (cf. Sawyer, 1977, pp. 2–4). Christian claims about the unity of the Bible and the continuity between the two Testaments have, it is true to say, led to widespread prejudice and ignorance about Judaism, and that is to be deplored. But it is equally misleading to ignore the plain fact that the Hebrew Bible, with its own history of interpretation, and the Old Testament, with its inseparable links to the New Testament, are simply different texts.

If the exegete or the linguist or literary critic, working synchronically, does not take into account this difference, he is neglecting part of the data and his semantic analysis may be defective. The phenomenon of prophecy and fulfilment in the Bible is a good example. It is entirely normal to consider this within the 'Deuteronomistic History' (Joshua–Kings) as an artificial literary device, but as nonetheless stylistically and theologically significant, giving structure and direction to the narrative, as well as expressing a theological view about divine intervention in history (Ackroyd, 1968, pp. 62–83; Bruggemann, 1968). There is every indication, as I have just suggested, that the text of the Bible, too, is structured in such a way as to make the same kind of theological and literary connection between Old Testament prophecy and New Testament fulfilment. It is of course hard, if not impossible, to determine when this structuring took place, and whether or not the 'redactors' responsible for it can be credited with deep theological or literary insights. In other words, the intention of an ancient author or redactor may or may not be open to our investigation, but the plain fact is that the text as it stands, a single literary work, running from Genesis to

Revelation, was for centuries approached as a whole, with rich and fascinating results, and there is absolutely no scientific reason why it cannot be approached in the same way today (Thiselton, 1978, p. 329; Payne, 1979; Magonet, 1976, p. 12).

The question 'What is the meaning of Isa. 7: 14 in the context of eighth-century B.C. Jerusalem?' is a different question from 'What is the meaning of Isa. 7: 14 in the context of the Book of Isaiah as a whole?' But it is also true to say that its meaning in the context of the Hebrew Bible must be distinguished from its meaning in the context of the Christian canon. One of the points to be made in a discussion of its meaning in the Christian canon, for example, must be its relationship to the other passage where it occurs, namely Matt. 1: 23. Cross-references of this kind between different parts of the Bible are just as legitimate and valuable controls on exegetical speculation as are cross-references within a single book or a single passage and must be taken seriously by anyone interested in synchronic semantics. The fact that such cross-references were popular in a pre-critical age is irrelevant, and so are the historical questions as to whether Isaiah actually and miraculously foretold the virgin birth eight centuries before Christ. The simple fact is that one passage provides a way of understanding the other. There can be no objection to analysing meaning in smaller units, each precisely isolated and set in its own original historical context. But equally, there is no good scientific reason why that approach should always be the primary one. 'The "setting in literature" is as important as the "setting in life"' (Alonso-Schökel, 1960, p. 162; cf. Weiss, 1972). There are good reasons, as I hope I have shown, for sometimes shifting the emphasis towards a synchronic approach to larger literary units, including the complete Christian canon.

Note

1 The index to Barr's *Fundamentalism* contains two references to 'canon', none to 'canonical meaning' (or to B. S. Childs) and none to structuralism or stylistics. Anyone interested in 'canonical meanings' can actually learn from fundamentalist exegesis, whether precritical (e.g. Jerome, Rashi) or anti-critical (Harrison, Kitchen).

Bibliography

P. R. Ackroyd *Exile and Restoration. A Study of the Hebrew Thought of the Sixth Century B.C.* (London, 1968).

'An Interpretation of the Babylonian Exile: A Study of 2 Kings 20, Isaiah 38–39', *SJTh* 27 (1974), 329–52.

'Isaiah i–xii: Presentation of a Prophet', in *Congress Volume, Göttingen, 1977*, SVT 29 (Leiden, 1978), pp. 16–48.

L. C. Allen   *The Books of Joel, Obadiah, Jonah and Micah*, NICOT (London, 1976).

L. Alonso-Schökel 'Die stylistische Analyse bei den Propheten', in *Congress Volume, Oxford, 1959*, SVT 7 (Leiden, 1960), pp. 154–64.

Estudios de Poetica Hebrea (Barcelona, 1963).

A. A. Anderson   *The Book of Psalms*, ii New Century Bible (London, 1972).

J. Barr   *The Semantics of Biblical Language* (Oxford, 1961).

Fundamentalism (London, 1977).

'Semitic Philology', in G. W. Anderson (ed.), *Tradition and Interpretation* (Oxford, 1979).

E. Ben-Yehuda   *Thesaurus totius hebraitatis* (16 vols., Berlin and Jerusalem, 1908–59).

J. Bewer   *A Critical and Exegetical Commentary on Jonah*, ICC (Edinburgh, 1912).

P. E. Bonnard   *Le second Isaïe* (Paris, 1972).

G. J. Botterweck and H. Ringgren (eds.)   *Theological Dictionary of the Old Testament* (Grand Rapids, vols. i–ii, 1974–5; rev. ed. vols. iff, 1977–) (English translation of *Theologisches Wörterbuch zum Alten Testament* (Stuttgart, 1970–)).

F. F. Bruce   'The Earliest Old Testament Interpretation', *OTS* 17 (1972), 44–52.

W. Brueggemann   'The Kerygma of the Deuteronomistic Historian', *Interpretation* 22 (1968), 386–402.

M. J. Buss (ed.)   *Encounter with the Text. Form and History, in the Hebrew Bible* (Philadelphia and Missoula, 1979).

R. P. Carroll   *When Prophecy Failed* (London, 1979).

B. S. Childs   'Psalm-titles and Midrashic Exegesis', *JSS* 16 (1971), 137–50.

Introduction to the Old Testament as Scripture (London, 1979).

H. Christ   *Blutvergiessen im Alten Testament. Der gewaltsame Tod des Menschen untersucht am hebräischen Wort dam* (Basle, 1977).

R. E. Clements   'The Purpose of the Book of Jonah', in *Congress Volume, Edinburgh, 1974*, SVT 28 (Leiden, 1975), pp. 16–28.

'Patterns in the Prophetic Canon', in G. W. Coats and B. O. Long (eds.), *Canon and Authority. Essays in Old Testament Religion and Theology* (Philadelphia, 1977), pp. 42–55.

D. J. A. Clines   'The Significance of the "Sons of God" Episode (Genesis 6: 1–4) in the Context of the "Primeval History" (Genesis 1–11)', *JSOT* 13 (1979), 33–46.

R. C. Culley   *Studies in the Structure of Hebrew Narrative*, Semeia Supplements (Philadelphia and Missoula, 1976).

J. P. Fokkelmann   *Narrative Art in Genesis. Specimens of Stylistic and Structural Analysis* (Amsterdam, 1975).

L. Ginzberg   *The Legends of the Jews* (7 vols., Philadelphia, 1911–38).

A. P. Hayman   'Judaism and the Christian Predicament', *Modern Churchman* 22 (1979), 86–100.

J. J. Jackson and M. Kessler (eds.)   *Rhetorical Criticism, Essays in Honor of J. Muilenburg* (Pittsburgh, 1974).

D. Jobling   *The Sense of Biblical Narrative. Three Structural Analyses in the Old Testament*, JSOT Supplement Series 7 (Sheffield, 1978).

D. R. Jones   'Isaiah 40–66', in M. Black and H. H. Rowley (eds.), *Peake's Commentary on the Bible*, rev. ed. (London, 1962).

C. A. Keller   'Jonas, le portrait d'un prophète', *ThZ* 21 (1965), 329-40.

M. Kessler   *see* J. J. Jackson
   'An Introduction to Rhetorical Criticism of the Bible: Prolegomena', *Semitics* 7 (1980), 1–27.

J. Lyons   *Introduction to Theoretical Linguistics* (Cambridge, 1971).

W. McKane   *Proverbs. A New Approach*, Old Testament Library (London, 1970).

J. Magonet   *Form and Meaning. Studies in Literary Techniques in the Book of Jonah*, Beiträge zur Biblischen Exegese und Theologie 2 (Berne and Frankfurt, 1976).

R. F. Melugin   *The Formation of Isaiah 40–55*, BZAW 141 (Berlin, 1976).

J. Muilenburg   'Form-criticism and beyond', *JBL* 88 (1969), 1–18.

T. Muraoka   *Emphasis in Biblical Hebrew* (Oxford, 1969).

E. W. Nicholson   *Preaching to the Exiles. A Study of the Prose Tradition in the Book of Jeremiah* (Oxford, 1970).

C. R. North   *The Second Isaiah* (Oxford, 1964).

D. Patte   *What is Structural Exegesis?* (Philadelphia, 1976).

D. F. Payne   'Jonah from the Perspective of his Audience', *JSOT* 13 (1979), 3–12.

D. L. Petersen   *Late Israelite Prophecy. Studies in Deutero-Prophetic Literature and in Chronicles*, SBL Monograph Series 23 (Missoula, Montana, 1977).

R. Polzin   *Biblical Structuralism. Method and Subjectivity in the Study of Ancient Texts*, Semeia Supplements 5 (Philadelphia and Missoula, 1977).

W. Richter   *Exegese als Literaturwissenschaft. Entwurf einer alttestamentlichen Literaturtheorie und Methodologie* (Göttingen, 1971).

I. Riesener   *Der Stamm 'ebed im Alten Testament. Eine Wortuntersuchung unter Berücksichtigung neuerer sprachwissenschaftlicher Methoden*, BZAW 149 (Berlin, 1979).

H. Ringgren   *see* G. J. Botterweck

J. F. A. Sawyer   *Semantics in Biblical Research. New Methods of Defining Hebrew Words for Salvation*, SBT Second Series 24 (London, 1972).
   'A Historical Description of the Hebrew Root *yš'*', in J. and T. Bynon (eds.), *Hamito-Semitica*, Janua Linguarum, Series Practica 200 (The Hague, 1975).

'An Analysis of the Context and Meaning of the Psalm-headings', *TGUOS* 22 (1976–8), 26–38.

From Moses to Patmos. New Perspectives in Old Testament Study (London, 1977).

'David's Treatment of the Ammonites (2 Samuel 12: 31). A Study in the History of Interpretation', *TGUOS* 26 (1978), 96–107.

'Types of Prayer in the Old Testament. Some Semantic Observations on *Hitpallel, Hithannen*, etc.', *Semitics* 7 (1980), 131–43.

Article on *yš* in *TDOT* (forthcoming; English translation of article in *TWAT* vol. III, 8/9 (1982), cols. 141–64).

W. Schneider *Grammatik des biblischen Hebräisch* (Munich, 1974).

P. Stähli '*pll* hitp. beten', *THAT*, vol. II (Munich, 1976), cols. 427–32.

A. C. Thiselton 'Structuralism and Biblical Studies: Method or Ideology?', *ET* 89 (1978–9), 329–35.

N. Tidwell 'A Road and a Way. A Contribution to the Study of Word-Pairs', *Semitics* 7 (1980), 50–80.

G. M. Tucker 'Prophetic Superscriptions and the Growth of the Canon', in G. W. Coats and B. O. Long (eds.), *Canon and Authority, Essays in Old Testament Religion and Theology* (Philadelphia, 1977), pp. 56–70.

W. R. Watters *Formula Criticism and the Poetry of the Old Testament*, BZAW 138 (Berlin, 1976).

M. Weinfeld 'bᵉrith', *TDOT*, vol. II, rev. ed. (1977), pp. 253–79 (English translation of article in *TWAT*, vol. I (Stuttgart, 1973), cols. 781–808).

M. Weiss 'Die Methode der Total Interpretation', in *Congress Volume, Uppsala, 1971*, SVT 22 (Leiden, 1972), pp. 88–112.

C. Westermann *Isaiah 40–66*, Old Testament Library (London, 1969).

R. N. Whybray *Isaiah 40–66*, New Century Bible (London, 1975).

Review of J. Cazeaux, *Critique du langage chez les Prophètes d'Israel* (Paris, 1976) in *Erasmus* 31 (1979), cols. 138–40.

Martin Buber and the interpretation of the prophets

ULRICH E. SIMON

When Buber died in 1965 his life and work were hailed in the press of the Western world as worthy of the description 'prophetic'. The reluctance of many of his Jewish contemporaries to join the chorus of praise gave an authentic note to such a description, for the office of prophet has always been conceded to be unpopular. For political reasons Buber was, and still is, often 'without honour' in Israel: his federalist ideals, comprising Jews and Arabs, could hardly commend themselves to an army under siege. But a far more deep-rooted and potentially lasting opposition came, and continues to come, from the traditionalists. This is hardly surprising, since Buber never claimed to be orthodox in matters of ritual observances. Moreover, his links with Christian theologians and his dialogue with the great men of his epoch aroused suspicions, which were not allayed by his clear allegiance to Judaism as the prophetic faith, the way of '*emunah* as distinct from the *pistis* of Greek conceptualism, with which he identified Pauline Christianity. Only a few years after his death Gershom Scholem, erstwhile disciple and active correspondent of Buber, drew a balance-sheet in fifty pages of a closely-argued indictment (Scholem, 1978, pp. 126–71). Scholem traverses the ground of Buber's many contradictions to accuse him of 'the infinite slipperiness of his formulations' and ends his evaluation with the sad verse: 'Blessed are those who sow but do not reap.'

Such a verdict is quite unacceptable, and even if the author of *I and Thou*, *Two Types of Faith*, *Moses*, and several Hasidic Tales may not quite deserve the fame that he certainly enjoyed during his lifetime, there remains one outstanding work, a monument not only to his genius but to the Biblical tradition itself. The German translation of the Old Testament (*Die Schrift*) is true to the highest norms of interpretation, proclamation and confession. In this work, to which Buber devoted at least thirty years of a busy and creative life, we do not read about

250

prophecy or discuss religious subjects or theories about history or myth but listen to the Word itself. Since his letters have now appeared in a marvellously well-edited selection, we have also a running commentary to the work in progress, especially in its earliest stages (*Briefwechsel*).

As may be expected, Buber's admirers place his interpretation of the Bible in the context of his philosophical work (Schilpp and Friedman, 1967, pp. 361–402). The famous I-and-Thou thesis recapitulates his strange synthesis of a Kierkegaardian personalism and an almost Platonic idealism. This is the inevitable and typical heritage of a Jew who reaches Berlin before the First World War. But behind this philosophical facade lurks the unchanging prophetic faith, which cannot be rooted in anything but the Prophets. Hence a life-long dialectic develops, in which Buber the prophet listens to, is addressed by and answers the prophetic Word. In this encounter he cannot but struggle with the historical ties implicit in the Biblical Word. His philosophical leanings would, one imagines, induce a Gnostic indifference to the obstacle of history and a resolute determination to clear these hurdles that become so daunting in Western critical work on the Bible. But with unending courage Buber refuses the easy way, a kind of abstraction from the concrete confusion of Biblical history. Maurice Friedmann discusses the complexity of the problem at some length and with an authoritative voice, since we know from the correspondence that he and Buber were in continual contact before this book was finally published. 'The Bible as "literal truth" and the Bible as "living literature" are thus supplanted in Buber's thought by the Bible as a record of the concrete meetings in the course of history between a group of people and the divine' (Friedmann, 1955, p. 236).

Yet, having cleared the decks in an anti-Gnostic stance, Buber equally rejects historicism and its deadening impact on the material. The Marcionite onslaught in Berlin, under and after Harnack, alerted him to the danger of killing the prophetic spirit and of relegating first the Old Testament and then Judaism and the Jews to a lowly and contemptible status. Thus Buber is not to be found in the camp of those who wish to get rid of 'myth' – 'I would not go along with Bultmann if I were a Christian: I am by no means inclined to hear my Judaism de-mythed' (*Briefwechsel*, vol. III, p. 304). Buber seeks to re-establish and re-live the Biblical dialogue, in its concrete timelessness. His success can be measured by his translation, which 'has been universally acclaimed as a miracle of fidelity and beauty' (Friedmann, 1955, p. 238).

Buber's revised statements of methods and aims is a far-reaching document and can only be summarily presented here. The Old Testament is the Word to the people, the revealed and revealing secret of the people's history, set against national and group purposes. The Sacred enters the historical world with law and blessing. It also penetrates nature without abusing it, for the Spirit seeks to complete and unify the manifold creation. But modern man is precluded from entering this world, since he cannot get beyond the cultural–historical and aesthetic. He has ceased to listen to the Word, to respond to it, to believe it. But if he is confronted with the Scriptures as the unknown, without presuppositions, he becomes a receptive vessel as the Word is *heard* by him. Familiarity with the text, far from bringing illumination, hides the original character of the book, its choice of words, structure of sentences and rhythm. The great Christian translators served their communities but, as regards the prophets, they could not do justice to their symbols, parables and the eddies of ancient Hebrew sensuousness, to convey the overpowering harmonies and passions of their music. Buber had to come to a radical break with the past in order to free himself from Luther. Rosenzweig commented wittily on the draft of Genesis: 'astonishingly German; Luther by contrast is almost Yiddish. Perhaps too German?' (*Briefwechsel*, vol. II, p. 185).

The reality of the prophetic address can only be conveyed in and by sound: speech requires speech. The message is in and out of the mouth, But the text, and only the text, can govern the speech. Buber eschews archaism for its own sake but he also rejects modernisation: bold and obedient must be the diction, content with simple words and yet also willing to create new ones. There is a letter in which the young Scholem calls upon the master, who does not yet live in the Holy Land, to soak himself in Biblical speech, and Buber responds, not by adopting the superior stance of age and authority, but by submitting to the advice. Everything that has to be translated must be known by heart; the text must run in the intellectual soul as the blood circulates in the arteries (*Briefwechsel*, vol. II, p. 212).

Buber proceeds in accord with, and yet independently of, structural theories of language. Like Popper he assumes a scientific, objective stance; like Adorno he detects the dimensions of change in poetry, the transcending power of words in a certain context among many contexts. The Word's content and form are, of course, inseparable. The kerygma penetrates, nay forms, the *Gestalt*, determines and changes the form without weakening structure. Rhythm, in a wide and special sense, performs a meaningful ordering of the static with dynamic multiformity. Thus intonation, intensity, repetition of sounds, sequence of words yield a phonetic structure. Buber develops a fine sense for phonetic rhythm as a principle of structure, not so much as philosophy of language but as a necessary recognition of the given text; the Massoretic text stands fast against even the most alluring conjectures. Buber eschews what he calls the 'coloured tapestry' behind an allegedly original text, lying in the realm of possibilities. One must be content with the redactor's version, for this is the wholeness of tradition, a unity vouchsafed by the existence of the canon. This opens a vast synoptic unity in which texts respond and refer to texts, so that the proclamation runs organically from one context to another. The translator must inhibit the lazy and trivial reading of the Bible, granting exceptional expressions to the exceptional, always acting as the interpreter of two languages, mediating creatively in dialogue-fashion. The language of the Spirit articulates the simple encounter between the individual at the intersection of time and the people in the universal flow of events.

The text is the dynamic centre from which the waves of complex power strike into the space of our comprehension. The process, which Buber enters, owes much to German poets and their interpretation of inspiration. The transcendental necessity – that it could not be otherwise – is paired, as with Hölderlin and Rilke, with endless work in patient humility. Buber is *nabi'*, for who could convey the meaning of, say, *kabod*, except one who has entered the precincts of the shrine? But Buber cannot do it by obedience to ritual; rather, like Hölderlin, he appeals to the *ruah* – wind, gale, storm, as well as spirit and insight.

All these lyrical convictions and ideals cannot evade precise problems of interpretation; indeed, they derive from them and the task that they set. For Buber, the pivot rests with the divine name; if he is wrong here, it may be said, he is likely to be wrong everywhere. The Tetragrammaton presents the supreme paradox. He agrees that there may have been an archaic form, a cry JAH, perhaps extended into Jahu. This call of a dervish kind, consisting of pronoun and interjection, remained stable. In Exod. 3: 14 the name was verbalised by an additional letter: thus '*ehejeh*' becomes the key: 'I shall be there as He who shall be'. Buber controverts the traditional metaphysical *Ego sum qui sum* rendering, an ontological formula, which excludes the dynamic presence and becoming of God. The unhappy slaves need no metaphysics (as Rosenzweig also pointed out) but the assurance of the divine presence with their leader: as such He will be present with them as befits their condition. Hence Buber rejects 'Lord' and 'L'Eternel'

(Calvin) as well as the impossible proper name Yahweh. Thus he eliminates the impossible and decides for the Pronoun: the *Du–Er* is both the I and the He, always present.

The whole range of divine titles receives the most careful attention in Buber's translation and is part and parcel of prophetic interpretation. It now remains to show, with the aid of a few selected passages, how the principles of translation operate in practice. It is natural to look at some *cruces interpretum*, but it would be very misleading to do so in isolation and in the kind of abstract silence that Buber fought against throughout. The basic principle and also the criterion of success and failure must be the kerygmatic recitation, the repeated and sonorous performance of the whole passage. Otherwise all the evocative nuances are lost and we move in that one-dimensional world, sans encounter or dialogue, from which Buber tried to preserve our godless civilisation.

Isa. 6 may be taken as a marvellous example of a translation in very free verse. The page has a bold look even for the eye, for it scans lines with eight stresses down to one single word. This format ensures order and dramatic progression. The style recaptures a certain breathlessness, expressing above all the threat to the prophet and his people. The burning fire is conveyed in the reading-out of these verses which culminate in the terrible answer to the 'How long?': *Bis dahin, dass...* the apocalyptic devastation is hammering away at the emptying of houses, the voiding of habitations, the waste land. How, then, does Buber come to terms with the appalling *pen* ('lest') of verse 10? He eschews its negative finality and renders the whole phrase: 'otherwise it could see with its eyes, hear with its ears (*sonst könnte es mit seinen Augen sehn...*)'. The subjunctive mood, now lost in English, but still potent in German, brings out the dialogue, namely between moral law and free response, marrying tragic determinism and prophetic appeal.

Buber's interpretation of the Biblical 'until' is always restrained and moves within the confines of earthly history. In this respect he knows himself to be a true representative of Judaism, with its rejection of wild apocalypticism. Writing to Bultmann from Israel in 1948 he comments with a rare flash of humour: 'Hier ist es zeitweilig schon mehr "apokalyptisch" als geschichtlich zugegangen' (*Briefwechsel*, vol. III, p. 143), but his serious opinion is best elicited by Walter Kaufmann in 1960. The reference is to Job 19: 25, and Kaufmann confesses his lack of understanding both of the passage and of Buber's translation (*Briefwechsel*, vol. III, pp. 432–5). In what sense is Job being 'redeemed'? Christian and Jewish interpretations seem straightforward, for they affirm that it occurs *after* this life. Now Buber's translation of this impossibly difficult verse is quite literal:

> da ich doch weiss, mein Auslöser lebt,
> und als der Spätgekommene wird aufstehn er überm Staub, --
> und noch nachdem meine Haut, dies da, zerfetzt ist,
> noch von meinem Fleische aus werde ich Gott schauen.

(Job 19: 25)

The translation can hardly be called a success; it is too literal. Buber must have brooded over it for years, and later substituted 'vortreten' for 'aufstehen', thus removing every possible misunderstanding. There is *no* question of any kind of resurrection. Job will be vindicated, here and now, though late in life, possibly near death. Thus he repudiates, even here, an equation of the 'until' or 'at last' with an eschatological end. Though he opposes a rationalising anti-mysticism he will not jeopardise the horizontal sequence of time, i.e. historical event, even within the context of prophecy.

Nor is he alone in this somewhat cavalier dismissal of the until-eschaton. His Christian friends and correspondents must have strengthened him in his Jewish dislike of the apocalyptic view of human existence. One is tempted to speculate that all the writers of this generation might have exerted a greater influence, both religious and political, if they had been less anti-eschatological and less inclined to dilute the eschatological essence of prophecy. Then they might have hoisted the Hitlers and terrorists with their own petard. For the Jewish Buber the 'until' in Isa. 6 cannot be universalised in the apocalyptic manner, just as for the Christian von Balthasar Isaiah's vision cannot be legitimately connected with the eschatological splendour of ch. 4 (though it would be nice if it could) (Balthasar, 1967, p. 229). For this Christian interpreter the 'until when?' is met by a transcendental eschaton, i.e. the manifestation of God's splendour. But this must again be rooted in temporal history, i.e. in the incarnation of the Messiah. Thus the interpretation of prophecy gets bogged down in some sort of *Heilsgeschichte*. This Westernisation is both asset and liability in Biblical interpretation. Its weakness becomes apparent when it is measured against Marxist–Leninist materialism, on the one hand, and Gnostic utopianism on the other.

The entrenched positions are under attack for a variety of reasons. Whereas Jerusalem and the Land could, in the past, be a symbol of national longing for the Jewish people, or the ultimate hope of universal redemption for the Christians, the emergence of Israel as a state has cut right through such an ideal of the future. At the same time the constant propaganda of Socialist governments that all hopes are now fulfilled in concrete terms, that Jerusalem is here and now, has infiltrated the contemporary scene to such an extent that Biblical texts are read in the light of these claims. For others, however, alienated by the gross materialism of Marxist ideology, these prophetic texts can only be cited and understood over against all worldly contexts. The problem was already keenly felt at the dawn of the industrial revolution. Blake, for example, never ceases to battle in his exposition of Jerusalem (Albion), both as a practical challenge and moral judgement and as a Miltonic Utopia, far beyond the reaches of political action.

Modern interpreters of prophecy are curiously insensitive to the two-fronted challenge. Buber, it is true, incurred much unpopularity because he failed to support Israeli nationalism *tout court* (*Briefwechsel*, vol. III, pp. 229, 230). But, like his prophetic masters, he succeeded neither in Germany first, nor in Israel later, in converting the materialists to a spiritual vision, or the Gnostic universalists to a serious contemplation of historic prophecy. Returning to the text of Isaiah, we can watch him best in his treatment of those passages which, in the Christian tradition, had become 'proof-texts'. The Child-oracles, though lyrical and of heightened pathos, do not refer to a supernatural event: the boy Immanuel's birth, preceded by the young woman's conception ('Die Junge wird schwanger'), belongs to the political context of the Assyrian threat and no more. The victory parade in ch. 9 culminates, not in a messianic advent in the future, but in a Davidic triumph in a prince who brings to the dynasty charismatic gifts and therefore also the corresponding titles – 'his wonder-names'. Only ch. 11, with its unambiguous ring of the golden age and utopian consummation, is allowed to proclaim not only the norms of perfect rule but also the eschatological paradox of final peace – 'then the wolf pays a visit to the lamb, the leopard lies with the kid' – and the little boy completes a natural picture of total harmony.

The messianic expectation, always a combustible issue among Biblical theologians, oscillates among exegetes between a sociological–historical and an absolute–metaphysical pole. The former is the more dangerous since it may authenticate the worst aspects of contemporary fanaticism, from Hitler, thus identified as destiny's anointed, to the endless crop of religious bullies and dictators. Buber circumvents these poles and supports the ideology of Rosenzweig's *Star of Redemption*, which in its turn becomes fused with his own philosophy and ethics. Balthasar, perhaps the best Christian exponent of this synthesis, applies this messianism to One who has come. God's freedom (Barth's normative formula) lies behind the king of Israel, his laws and customs, who recapitulates for the whole earth the covenant relationship. Like Buber, Balthasar stresses the enormity of the singular I, the messianic self, who as *'Ebed Yahweh* completes the divine task (Balthasar, 1967, p. 143). The Messiah is the *Hasid* and the distinction between prophet and Messiah narrows when the prophet obeys the Word. Balthasar can use Buber's total framework without sacrificing his Christian conviction that this splendour rests in its cosmic–ethical and eschatological recapitulation in Jesus of Nazareth (Balthasar, 1967, p. 94). Christian exegetes, however, rarely, attain to such a synthesis since, at least until quite recently, their historical perspective excludes a fundamentally meta-historical understanding of the text.

Despite our modern linguistic restraint, however, the prophetic faith shows no signs of abating. The great Isaiah oracles are still referred to as 'most controversial' and open to dispute. This dispute concerns, primarily, the historical setting and the consequent meaning (Kilian, 1968). But so strong is the messianic tradition that it confronts the purely linguistic and historical adherence to the text as such (Lindblom, 1958, p. 57). Otto Kaiser, for example, not only cites Buber among others but quite unexpectedly throws a bridge across the deep waters to christology, the role of Jesus, and even ethical obligations, as if this prophecy of doom were not merely a warning for all times but also had some real connection with the claims of fulfilment made in the New Testament. Kaiser's commentary does not merely make a concession to the Christian reader but extends the *hasidic* area of expectation to the Biblical text. Thus, in a strange manner, Jews and Christians may converge by a *tertium quid*, and this extends also to the realm of the unhistorical, namely the utopian and eschatological visions of peace (Kaiser, 1972, pp. 105, 162).

The modern interpretation of the prophets tries to escape from subjective bias and religious prejudice. But it can no more deny the past than it can be silent about the present, and even if prefiguration is now hardly ever seen to be implicit in the prophetic word, no one would wish to deny that it is meant to shape the future. In this respect the prophetic word differs from great works of art, for even if identification of persons, their environment and role, is now as active as ever, the biographer may trace the impact of his hero's work on the future, without regarding the legacy as binding or in any way intended and authentic. For example, Shakespeare's Dark Lady in the Sonnets may give rise to endless identifications, and even the influence of that figure may be noted, but there the matter ends. It may well be doubted whether Biblical prophecy can ever accept an objectivity that forgets the so-called after-life of the oracles. Its overarching impact goes beyond the disputed passages (like the *'almah* of Isa. 7: 14), but it is there that we become most sharply aware of methodological differences and problems.

The question of comparative norms in non-prophetic poetry can no longer be evaded, for the cast-iron isolation of Biblical prophecy is seen to be wrong-headed. Lindblom, in his great book, was far-sighted enough to include references not only to the common origins of prophecy, but also to later mystics, such as St Brigid (Lindblom, 1962). Since then, incisive points of substance have been raised; for example, do prophets as poets evoke and articulate themes beyond their own cognition? Is the after-life of their work part of a providential order, no longer conditioned by what originally caused the flow of words? But, far more profoundly, there arises the question whether the accomplished work has not been willed to stand for revelation in the broadest term. When we consider some European poets, such as Coleridge and Hölderlin and Rilke, there can be no doubt that for them the longed-for inspiration, their preparation for the 'song' and finally, the utterance, however changed and polished in the process of final editing and even re-editing, belonged to the realm of the timeless, sacred in form and content.

Buber guards himself against such a mystical apprehension of the Word. Jeremiah, for example, 'has to *say* what God *does*', i.e. 'to show God's sway, the pulling down and building up of the world's architect, the rooting out and the planting of the world's gardener' (Buber, 1945, p. 166). Thus there is always an 'hour' in which the eternal verity is disclosed. But the Word is certainly not 'bound' by any hour (2 Tim. 2: 9).

Buber always sees the personal dialectic in and against the collective, for this underpins his I–Thou axis of interpretation. But the sufferings of Jeremiah are also 'representative' of the people, of Israel; his 'I' is deeply set in the 'I' of the people. In the same manner, Christian interpreters draw upon the *anakephalaiosis* of Ephesians to make their claim that the Christ recapitulates all humanity. If this is taken seriously, we attain to a kind of universality of the Word, simply because the human race lives and has lived 'at sundry times and in divers manners' (Hebrews 1) by the prophetic tradition.

This approach forces itself upon the interpretation of the Servant oracles in Deutero-Isaiah, for unless we are content with a simple equation (Servant = Israel, or Servant = Jeremiah, or Servant = Jesus) a subtle and multi-dimensional understanding becomes imperative. An intellectual coolness that eschews emotional involvement cannot begin to speak about these passages in Isaiah. Buber, as it happens, must always recall that his friend and mentor Rosenzweig died as he lay paralysed, translating verses in ch. 53. To this patient sufferer, who questioned the term 'messiah' in an age without a king in Israel and who longed for dialogue between Jews and Christians in the messianic consciousness, the translation remains the lasting tribute. The Servant is the miraculous transformation from humiliation to God's triumph: pierced and tormented, he mediates penance and forgiveness, like a sacrificial lamb, buried with evil-doers (LXX instead of MT). He bared his soul to death, the soul as a guilt offering, and HE prolongs his days in fulfilment of HIS will, and thus he justifies (Bewähren!) many. Of whom speaks the prophet?

Buber's discussion in *The Prophetic Faith* reaches its climax in the chapter, 'The God of the Sufferers'. After a masterly survey, he pleads for an understanding of 'three stages', the way of the one servant, passing through all the different life-cycles, not as an individual but as a representative. The anonymous prophet announces a mystery, which includes historical figures without being confined to them. The prophet is part of the concealment and the revelation, which spans the prophetic stage of futile failure and endurance, the *acting* of the affliction, until the Prophet–Servant reaches the 'success' of His 'desire'. Liberation and world-wide light, the Kingdom of God, are not external events but the nucleus of the accomplished Word. Balthasar similarly dismisses unreal metaphors in a collectivised notion, which would cause us to lose the centre of gravity, namely the unity of the internal and external suffering. But Balthasar indicts the prophet for inadequacy in utterance, as if the need to bring together passion and splendour taxed him in such a way that he could not find the 'new word': the old covenant could only recall terms of Zion and David to express glory. The final word of redemption lay in the future and now completes what remained then unspeakable.

Neither of these great expositions can be called final or even satisfactory, and it is not surprising or unwelcome that the debate continues.

The hermeneutical battle resembles an ongoing play, of which we are given an account from time to time. We cannot help becoming conscious of our own relativity in this respect. Depending on the interpreter's history, both biographical and social, the interpretation will echo experiences, fears and hopes. Just as in physics the observer cannot be excluded from his observation, so also the humblest commentator adds his *Sitz im Leben* to the life under his eyes.

This existentialist imprisonment is not new, but our generation has probably become far more conscious of its implicit limitations and shortcomings. Hence the vast literature on language, on linguistic categories, and the ding-dong battle between positivistic and myth-making soldiers. Though the interpretation of prophecy must be submitted to their fire it will never wholly be drawn into this orbit of polemics. Prophecy is, in a sense, protected by tradition and cultus. Thus Buber's Israeli heirs, for example, turn out to be more aware of their debt to the past in Mishnah and Talmud. Similarly, Christians rediscover the Patristic evidence and the Reformers' contributions, even if only to disagree with either or both. Perhaps prophecy has become overlaid with a cushion of past expositions, and one can but wait for some outstanding prophet to interpret prophecy *de novo*. The risk is enormous, for even men of the calibre of Blake produce eccentric formulations. Jung's *Answer to Job* may serve as a prototype of downright nonsense coming from the deliberate musings of a genius. But in these days of progress through dialectics even bizarre exegesis is not to be dismissed out of hand. The dismantling of subjectivism and of false ideology remains to the credit of Positivism and it frees the creative genius to transcend both. Nothing less can suffice: the inspired prophet alone can interpret prophecy.

Bibliography

H. U. v. Balthasar *Herrlichkeit*, vol. III, 2 (Einsiedeln, 1967).

Martin Buber *Die Schrift, Verdeutscht von Martin Buber Gemeinsam mit Franz Rosenzweig*, vols. I–IV (Heidelberg, 1975–9).

Zu einer Neuen Verdeutschung der Schrift (published as a supplement to the above) (ed. cited, Heidelberg, 1976).

Briefwechsel aus sieben Jahrzehnten, vols. I–III (Heidelberg, 1972–5).

The Prophetic Faith (New York, 1945).

M. Friedmann *Martin Buber* (London, 1955).

O. Kaiser *Isaiah 1–12* (London, 1972).

R. Kilian *Die Verheissung Immanuels* (Stuttgart, 1968).

J. Lindblom *Prophecy in Ancient Israel* (Oxford, 1962).
   A Study of the Immanuel Section in Isaiah (Lund, 1958).
F. Rosenzweig *Star of Redemption* (Frankfurt, 1921; 2nd ed. 1930. English translation by W. W. Hallo (Boston, Mass., 1972)).
P. A. Schilpp and M. Friedmann *The Philosophy of Martin Buber* (London 1967).
G. Scholem *On Jews and Judaism* (New York, 1978).

Index of Biblical References

272